Audio Postproduction for Film and Video, 2nd Edition

Audio Postproduction for Film and Video, 2nd Edition

Jay Rose, C.A.S.

AMSTERDAM • BOSTON • HEIDELBERG • LONDON • NEW YORK • OXFORD
PARIS • SAN DIEGO • SAN FRANCISCO • SINGAPORE • SYDNEY • TOKYO

Focal Press is an imprint of Elsevier

ELSEVIER

Focal Press is an imprint of Elsevier
30 Corporate Drive, Suite 400, Burlington, MA 01803, USA
Linacre House, Jordan Hill, Oxford OX2 8DP, UK

Library of Congress Cataloging-in-Publication Data
Application submitted

British Library Cataloguing-in-Publication Data
A catalogue record for this book is available from the British Library.

ISBN: 978-0-240-80971-7
ISBN: 978-0-240-81051-5 (CD-ROM)

For information on all Focal Press publications
visit our website at www.elsevierdirect.com

08 09 10 11   5 4 3 2 1

Typeset by Charon Tec Ltd., A Macmillan Company
(www.macmillansolutions.com)

Printed in the United States of America

Contents

Contents

Contents

Acknowledgments

While mine is the name on the cover, it took a lot of people to make this book happen. CMP Books' Dorothy Cox and Paul Temme helped develop the concept for the first edition, letting me cover every concept I considered important. Dave Moulton (a Grammy-nominated recording engineer), and Dan Rose (Assistant Chief Engineer at WBUR, and also my son), made sure it was technically accurate. Lydia Linker kept its language understandable to non-technicians.

That edition was successful. CMP subsequently sold its interest to a much larger publisher, Focal Press. After a few years, Focal's Publisher, Elinor Actipis and I decided industry changes justified a new version. Their Associate Acquisitions Editor Michele Cronin has been in charge of its creation, shepherding resources within the publishing house and in keeping me focused. She also assembled a panel of expert educators and practitioners—including Chris Anderson, Patrick de Caumette, Harry Cheney, Jaime Estrada-Torres, Fred Ginsburg C.A.S., Jane Jackson, and Paul Werner—to review my ideas and explanations. Focal's Senior Project Manager Paul Gottehrer turned the words into a book. Despite all this help, blame me for any inaccuracy. And please, send me a correction… after all, it's my name on the cover.

I'm particularly grateful to friends who've been sharing their projects with me for more than three decades. Among them, Rob Stegman of Bluestar Media, Marc Neger of Creative Media Group, Francine Achbar of High Impact Marketing and Media, Mike Kuell of Jetpak Productions, and Trev Gowdy of Gowdy Productions let me use their clips as examples on the CD. Mitchell Greenspan and the DeWolfe Music Library provided the music, John Moran of Hollywood Edge the sound effects, and busy PBS announcer Don Wescott some narration. The female narrator on the CD is my late wife Carla, a former actress (and one-time spokesperson for Howard Johnson Motels) who then became a writer. She wrote dozens of popular books about Photoshop and digital imaging; in fact, she wrote two of them while helping me through the creation of this book's first edition. I owe her for that and pretty much everything else good in my life. The drawings and photographs, however, are my own work: It's a good thing I specialize in sound and not graphics.

Introduction

There's a funny thing about the work I do. When there's good cinematography, lighting, editing, or special effects, you can see it on the screen. Good audio postproduction, on the other hand, is mostly invisible. You can't tell how we fine-tuned an actor's dialog. You can't know which noises came from on-screen action, and which were added later. Good music editing sounds like the song was played that way in the first place. Equalization, dynamics control, noise reduction, and all the other processes discussed in this book are usually used as subtle corrections, not special effects. *When we do our jobs right, you don't know we've been there at all.*

This makes it nearly impossible for filmmakers to teach themselves audio post. Even if you've got the best ears in the world, you won't spot most of the techniques. In fact, relying on your ears alone can be a mistake. If you don't know what to listen for, or how a process actually changes a sound, you might do things that temporarily seem to help. But they actually hurt the finished track.

I wrote this book for two different groups of people. Students and beginners can use the book to understand how to improve a soundtrack, even after the actors have gone home. Experienced film producers and music engineers can learn how we solve some unique technical and creative problems of sound for picture.

The book is full of tutorials, practical examples, and cookbook recipes. But you won't need a technical background. Everything is in plain English, with plenty of demonstrations and visual analogies. I believe you're an intelligent person—after all, you bought my book—but you might not have much training in science. Ordinary common sense, a little bit of grade school math, and a CD player are all you'll need to follow the explanations.

INTRODUCTION TO THE SECOND EDITION

Film and video sound have been separate disciplines for most of my career. Film used platoons of specialists, sometimes with rooms full of interlocked transports and editing machines, to turn tiny bits of acting into tracks that would work in a theater. Video had to be smaller and faster. Even big shows often had only a few audio people, working with much longer performances and mostly the same equipment as music production. Film and video both had "sound for picture" and many of the problems were similar. But the equipment, techniques, workflows, and business models were different.

Digital changed that. Over the course of about twenty years, both worlds adopted the new audio technologies: they were faster, easier to use, and higher quality. But since the infrastructures and business models were already in place, we all pretty much kept working the way we had... just with newer equipment. Part of the reason those things didn't change was that film's *picture* was still an optical and chemical medium, with many expensive stages before it could be released. Video's picture was instantaneous.

Then pictures caught up. Some small digital cameras and desktop editing systems are now good enough to tell stories that can be shown in theaters. Blockbusters costing many millions of dollars can use essentially the same tools as well-produced corporate videos. Even if the production is shot on film (and a lot of "films" are now shot on video), most of the visual editing and post-production happens electronically. So Hollywood started looking to video sound for ways to work with it efficiently. Meanwhile, independents who had been shooting smaller videos started making features, and their sound people had to deal with theatrical-style tracks.

I'm trying to bring these worlds together. Shooting a Web video? Some feature-film track techniques might make it work better. And you theatrical guys? The video side learned tricks that could knock your socks off.

Of course this edition also updates sections on equipment and software, and fixes one or two things that I wasn't happy about in the first edition. There's a lot more meat here.[1]

Software Agnostic?

New technologies adopt old words. Before personal computers, I knew *agnosticism* only from its dictionary definition: a philosophy that says you can never understand First Causes or truly know the Ultimate Being.

Well, I understand and believe in software. But this book isn't about platforms, programs, or versions. I've used some specific applications to demonstrate certain functions, but you'll find both Mac and Windows here. Actually, the techniques in this book are scalable. They'll work on any system, from a laptop to a giant 35mm mixing theater. They were developed over 75 years of radio,

---

[1]There's also more words, thanks to more pages and tighter layout in this edition. To make it all fit, I had to sacrifice a few small sections that just don't apply as much any more. I've noted those deletions in this text, and you'll find the original versions on my website: www.dplay.com/book/missing.

movies, and television. And they'll stay useful as new software and hardware is developed. Expect to keep these pages for a long time.

HOW THIS BOOK IS ORGANIZED

Chapter 19, set off in gray and starting on page 401, provides quick help for the most common audio problems. If the solution can be explained in a couple of sentences, you'll find it there; otherwise, you'll be directed to the appropriate chapter.

Chapters 1–4: Technical basics

Chapter 1 explains what sound is, and how the digital version works. It's the basis you'll need for the rest of the book. But it's not heavy reading, and I've tried to use visual analogies as much as possible. Even you think you already know this stuff, glance through these pages anyway. You could have been misled by some of the myth and marketing hype that surrounds audio.

Chapters 2 through 4 are for those who want to build an efficient and reliable audio post setup, whether it's a single desktop computer or a fully professional suite. It includes guidelines, technical tips, and time- or money-saving shortcuts. Those chapters deal separately with practical acoustics, equipment, and software.

Chapters 5–10: Elements

Here's where we start turning sounds into a soundtrack.

Chapter 5 helps you plan and budget audio post, and understand the steps necessary for it.

Chapters 6 and 7 are about getting sound into your NLE: what settings to use when transferring from a camera , video deck, or separate audio recorder; how to maintain sync; how to record studio narrations and replacement dialog; and what to do when things go wrong.

The next three chapters specialize on the three principal sound streams: voice, music, and effects. Chapter 8 will teach you a more efficient and accurate technique for editing voices than you'll find in an NLE manual. It's how the pros do it. Chapter 9 covers how to find music for a production. Then it has you practice a *different* editing technique, the one top music editors use. Chapter 10 covers the full range of sound effects: where to find them, how to record your own, and how to fit them to picture.

Chapters 11–18: Putting it together

Chapters 11 through 16 are about shaping sounds with processes like equalization, reverb, and noise reduction. This may be the most critical aspect of creating a track, as well as the one most often done wrong. Even if you've worked in a music studio, read these chapters. Sound for picture really is different.

Chapter 17 is about mixing. It's a big chapter. There's more to a mix than you might think.

Chapter 18 covers what to do after the mix, including necessary preparations for theatrical release, TV, Web, or DVD audio. Along the way, you'll learn how compression schemes like Dolby Digital and mp3 really work—and how to make them work best.

There's glossary and CD track listing at the end of this book.

About the Cookbooks

The processing chapters, 11 through 16, include recipes: step-by-step instructions for common operations. Most are also demonstrated on the CD.

While the recipes suggest specific settings for each process, it's almost certain they won't be exactly right for your track. Every recording is different, and a tiny difference in your microphone or shooting situation can make my settings inappropriate. Read the entire chapter—not just its cookbook—and you'll know how to adjust them.

If you don't find a recipe you're looking for, read through the chapter again; it'll probably give you enough insight to solve the problem. If you're still lost— or think I've missed something important—write to me. Explain what you're trying to do. I'll try to come up with specific steps, and post them on my site for others to use. Also write me if you want to share your own recipes (with appropriate credit, of course).

Just don't expect me to solve a problem on your deadline; my clients get first priority. And never send me unsolicited files. If necessary, I'll give you uploading instructions.

From time to time, in the recipes and descriptions of processors, I'll put terms in small caps. These are the names of specific knobs on a screen or control panel. When same term appears elsewhere in normal type, it's talking about what the process does rather than a particular setting.

About the CD

This book includes a CD with about an hour's worth of diagnostics, demonstrations, examples, and tutorial tracks. It's an audio CD, rather than a data disc, so you can play it through the best speakers you own. But none of it's copy protected, so you can load it into your NLE as well.

Despite the lack of copy protection, the tracks are covered by copyright. Buyers of this book may transfer them to their hard drive to practice techniques or run the diagnostics. Any other use requires written permission. Information about licensing specific music cues is in the text.

ABOUT THIS BOOK AND PRODUCING GREAT SOUND

My other Focal Press book, *Producing Great Sound for Film and Video*, 3rd edition (2008), covers production sound—the technical and creative process of getting good dialog, interviews, or event audio while shooting picture. It starts with issues you should be thinking about before you ever pick up a camera. Then there are chapters on how to choose the most appropriate mic, how to hold a boom or get the best results from a radio lav, and how to get the best sound from cameras and field recorders. It's all important, but none of it belongs in this book you're presently holding.

Some parts of the two books necessarily overlap. The basics of sound, digital recording, monitoring, and editing belong in both books. But I've written about them differently in each, to give you a better chance of understanding these important concepts.

In other words, it's entirely reasonable to purchase both *Producing Great Sound* and *Audio Postproduction*. My publisher would certainly be happy if you did. But if you want only one:

- Choose *Producing Great Sound* for an overview of the entire audio process, with a strong emphasis on sound at the shoot.
- Choose *Audio Postproduction* for an in-depth discussion of turning that sound into a polished, finished soundtrack.

ONE OTHER THING...

It should be obvious, by now, that I haven't written a formal textbook. I'm a working sound professional who just happens to love the medium, spent a long time learning about it, and wants to spread this knowledge around. (Eventually, that'll mean more good films and videos for me to enjoy.)

In that respect I'm like a lot of my industry friends. We're not territorial, we're approachable when not overwhelmed by work, and we enjoy solving problems. Who knows? Maybe you and I will even work on a soundtrack together one day.

Meanwhile, let's talk about how to make one.

Jay Rose, C.A.S.
www.dplay.com
jay@dplay.com
Boston, July 2008

xv

CHAPTER 1
Vibrations to Volts to Bits

1

A TREE FALLS IN A FOREST...

Jokes and koans aside, we'll assume it makes a sound. We'll also assume you're doing a film about logging, and the sound is part of a title sequence. You need to record the crash. You need to edit, process, and mix it for maximum impact. And you need to do this in a way that assures the viewer hears what you intended.

You probably bought this book to help accomplish goals like that. If you're impatient, you can open the Table of Contents, find the tasks you want to accomplish, and turn to those chapters. Or, if you have issues with an existing track, flip to the gray-tinted pages at the end of this book: They're a list of common problems and what to do about them.

But I honestly believe you'll get a far better track—and ultimately be a better filmmaker—if you read this chapter first. It tells how a sound gets started, how it travels through the air, and how it turns into analog and then digital signals that are linked to pictures. When you understand this process, good sound becomes intuitive and creative. Then the rest of this book can serve as guidance, inspiration, and professional tips—things to build on, rather than steps to blindly follow.

This isn't rocket science, just grade-school math and intuitive physics. But because it isn't visual, many filmmakers surround the process with myth and hype. Take a few minutes now to think about how sound works; it'll save you time and money later.

So: To the tree.

Gotcha

In this book, you'll find a bunch of *Gotchas*. They straighten out audio myths, correct misapplied principles, and fix other audio mistakes that can affect your track. They're based on real-world confusions I hear from filmmakers, read on Internet forums, or even find in software tutorials.

HOW SOUND WORKS

If our tree fell on the moon, no one would hear it. Sound requires air,[1] whose tiny molecules surround us. Anything that moves in the air reacts with those molecules.

- As our earthbound tree's leaves pass by, they scatter air molecules aside (a soft *whoosh*).
- As branches and limbs break, they vibrate. The vibration is transferred to nearby molecules (*crackle*).
- When the thick trunk gets close to the ground, it squeezes a lot of molecules in a hurry (*bang*).
- When the trunk lands, the ground vibrates and moves molecules next to it (*thud*).

These movements eventually transfer to our ears, and we hear the tree come down. Let's concentrate on just one aspect of that sound: the tree approaching the ground.

Before the tree starts to fall, air molecules surround it evenly. Their individual positions may be random, but the overall density is the same on both sides of the trunk. If we could enlarge and see these molecules, they'd look like the black specks all around Figure 1.1.

---

[1] Unless you're making a science-fiction film. It's an accepted movie convention that explosions, rocket fly-bys, and other events make noise in the vacuum of space. Sci-fi filmmakers also generally ignore another fundamental rule of physics, as you'll learn in a couple of pages.

As the tree falls, it pushes molecules directly in front of it and squeezes them together (lower right in Figure 1.2). At the same time, it forms a partial vacuum behind it—where there was tree, now there's nothing. This vacuum pulls nearby molecules into it, spreading them out (upper left).

The squeezed air molecules in front of the tree have to go somewhere, so they push against those farther out. Those newly-pushed molecules push others even farther, and so on. This creates a wave of *compression*, or higher air pressure, moving out from the tree. Meanwhile, the partial vacuum behind the tree forms a wave of low pressure, or *rarefaction*. It also moves out from the tree and draws nearby molecules toward it.

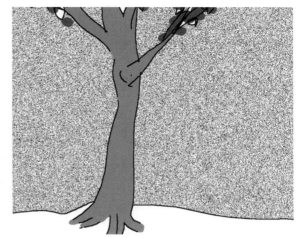

FIGURE 1.1
Air molecules distributed evenly around a standing tree.

Trees aren't two-dimensional blobs like my drawing. In the real world, molecules flow around a three-dimensional trunk and branches. So as our waves spread out, other molecules rush in to equalize the pressure behind them. The result is a growing bubble of compression and rarefaction that constantly spreads out from the tree. If you could freeze it, it would look like Figure 1.3.

The Speed of Sound

Push one end of a piece of wood, and the other end immediately moves. But molecules in air aren't connected that way. Push an air molecule, and it takes a moment for pressure to build up enough to move its neighbor. *This is a vitally important concept: The farther sound has to travel, the longer it takes.* Our pressure bubble spreads from the tree at about 1,100 feet per second.[2] It might seem pretty fast, but sound is a slowpoke compared to light.

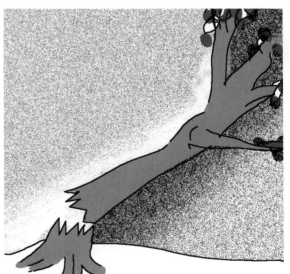

FIGURE 1.2
The falling tree squeezes molecules in front, and spreads out those behind.

When a sound is being picked up by two mics, differences in the length of time it takes to reach each can affect sound quality. We'll deal with that in Chapter 7.

---

[2] Actually, sound travels 1,087 feet per second at 32° Fahrenheit, gaining about 1.1 foot per second per degree, with minor variations based on pressure and humidity. We round it to 1,100 feet per second. That's close enough for filmmaking.

3

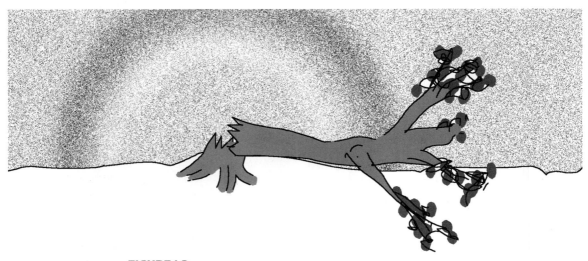

FIGURE 1.3
A growing bubble of compression and rarefaction spreads out from the tree.

 Gotcha

Twelve yards is a frame! A video frame is roughly 1/30th second, and sound travels only about 36 feet in that time.[3] If you have a shouted conversation with someone across the street, their voice arrives about one frame after you see their lips move. If you see someone shoot a gun on the other side of a football field, the bang reaches you five frames after you see the barrel flash!

In other words, the real world is frequently out of sync. It affects the film world as well: In a very large theater, people in the back rows will hear dialog a few frames after it leaves the speaker mounted behind the screen.

Frequency

A tree falls just once, so our example creates a single pressure wave—something you're as likely to feel as to hear. But most things that make sound tend to vibrate for a while. Consider the imaginary guitar string in Figure 1.4. When it's pulled back (1.4a), it stores energy. When it's let go, it snaps forward quickly and creates a pressure wave. But since it snaps past its resting position (1.4b),

---

[3]An analog video frame in the United States and other National Television System Committee (NTSC) countries is 1/29.97 second; in Phase Alternating Line (PAL) countries it's 1/25 second. A film frame is 1/24 second. There are some other variations for special purposes, including digital television. These fractions are all pretty close, and have similar effects in terms of sync.

tension draws it back, creating rarefaction. The process repeats (1.4c) until all the energy from the pull is absorbed by the air.

The result is a regular, constant series of compression and rarefaction bubbles—a *sound wave*—spreading out from the string. If we could freeze it, it would look like Figure 1.5, with those bubbles spreading out from a source on the left. When the wave hits our ears, it vibrates our eardrums, moves the tiny bones inside, and is carried to the fluid in our inner ears. There it activates a few of the specialized nerves and we hear a *ping*.

Which nerves get activated is determined by how frequently the pressure peaks hit our eardrum,[4] which is how fast the string was vibrating. We call this the string's *pitch*. Hi-fi books often say we can hear pitches between 20 and 20,000 peaks per second, though the term is *Hertz* (Hz) and it's called a *frequency range* of 20 Hz to 20 kHz. Some people say sounds as high as 30 kHz are critical for truly hearing music.

A few exceptional humans can hear 20 kHz. Many young people can hear up to 17 kHz or so. But even the best high-frequency hearing deteriorates with age and can be destroyed by prolonged exposure to high-level sound (at the workplace, in a club, or because of over-driven headphones and car stereos). Very few adults hear quiet sounds above 15 kHz, though trained ears can often sense a sort of openness when higher frequencies are present.

Fortunately, there's not much going on up there. With very few exceptions, we perceive frequency as a ratio between two pitches, not as an absolute number of Hertz. So a difference of a few Hertz on the lower end of the audible band can be as important as a few hundred at the top. You can see how this works in Figure 1.6, a piano keyboard with three major thirds (a common musical interval) highlighted. I've written the frequencies above each note:

- Middle C is at 261.6 Hz (rounded to the nearest tenth). The E above it is 329.6 Hz, a difference of 68 Hz.
- The C that's two octaves below is 65.4 Hz, and its closest E is 82.4 Hz—only 17 Hz higher.
- The C two octaves above is 1046.5 Hz, and its E is 1318.5 Hz. That's 272 Hz higher.

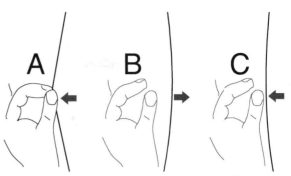

FIGURE 1.4
The guitar string vibrates back and forth after you let go.

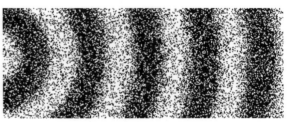

FIGURE 1.5
If you could freeze a sound wave, you'd see a regular pattern of compression and rarefaction.

5

---

[4] And by how much pressure the peaks have. This pressure component is the secret behind perceptual encoders like mp3, as you'll learn in Chapter 16.

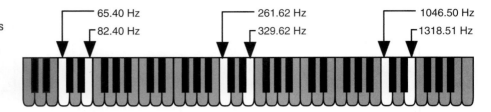

FIGURE 1.6
Musical thirds always sound like the same size jump, no matter how many Hertz are involved.

Yet the size of the jump from C to E sounds the same in each case, as you can hear on part one of Track 1 of this book's CD. It's also always the same ratio, about 1:1.25.

 Gotcha

The misplaced middle. This nonlinear way we hear means that lower frequencies contain more information per hertz than upper ones. Many filmmakers—and quite a few programmers writing software to deal with sound—get this wrong.

Since the audio range is usually quoted as reaching 20 kHz, you might think that 10 kHz should sound like it's right in the middle. But that's not the case. We hear pitch differences as ratios, so the middle of the audio band is the frequency that has about the same ratio to the bottom as it does to the top. That works out to be about 1 kHz: it's 20 times higher than 50 Hz (a very low tone indeed), and of course it's 1/20th of 20 kHz. Keep listening to Track 1—a series of pure tones with voice identification—and you'll hear for yourself. Learning to identify approximate frequency ranges is an important step in building a soundtrack. Track 1 will help you practice this.

 Hear for yourself

Track 1 of this book's CD is in two parts: First the jump from C to E in different octaves, then a series of tones with voice identification.

HARMONICS

Those pure tones on track 1 sound electronic, because real-world sounds are seldom pure. Purity has a precise meaning here: A pure tone has energy at only one frequency. Engineers call it a *sine wave*.[5]

---

[5]That's because a graph of its pressure looks like a graph of the geometric function, something important to mathematicians.

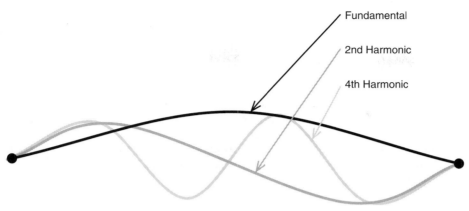

FIGURE 1.7
A fundamental and two harmonics on a vibrating string.

Remember our imaginary guitar string vibrating at one pitch? For any particu-lar string and tension, the pitch is determined by what size vibration fits exactly from one end of the string to the other. This pitch is called the *fundamental frequency*. But guitar strings are flexible: they bend in the middle, so multiple instances of shorter waves at higher pitches can also fit neatly from end to end. These are called *harmonics*, and they're in precise ratios to the fundamental. Figure 1.7 shows a fundamental, along with harmonics at twice and four times the fundamental pitch.

Because fundamental and harmonics happen simultaneously, they combine and force the vibrating string into complicated, constantly-changing wiggles. You can see this with an oscilloscope, a gadget which displays changing volt-ages over time. (Normally, you'd use a microphone to convert changing air pressure to voltage for the scope. But since we're dealing with an imaginary string, I created its wave in software.)

 Hear for yourself

Track 2 has two sounds: a pure tone at 200 Hz, and one adding just the two harmonics shown in Figure 1.7 (400 Hz and 800 Hz). Even though this is a very simple sound, you should hear a difference. The first tone will sound electronic. The other is more like a pipe organ.

Figure 1.8 is a scope photo of the combined fundamental and harmonics from Figure 1.7.

7

FIGURE 1.8
The complex wave from Figure 1.7, as shown on an oscilloscope.

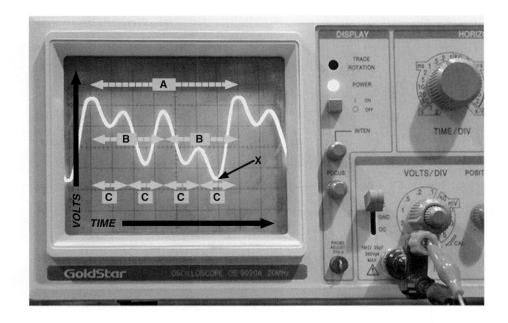

- The area A is the fundamental, measured from one compression peak to the next.
- B is the second harmonic. We see exactly two of them for each fundamental wave, meaning its frequency is exactly twice as high.
- Note how the compression phases of both A and B add together at the start of the wave.
- C is the fourth harmonic, exactly four times the frequency of the fundamental.
- Rarefaction phases of all three waves coincide at point X. They also add together, giving this point the lowest voltage of the entire wave.

There's no theoretical limit to how many harmonics can exist for any fundamental (though you might not hear the highest ones). In these examples, I've shown only even-numbered harmonics; real-world sounds can also have odd-numbered ones. Also, I've shown the fundamental and harmonics as having the same strength. But real harmonics' strengths are determined by mechanical properties of the vibrating element, resonances in the instrument body, and even where you plucked or hit it. The strength of each harmonic changes over time. It's these differences in harmonics that make a Fender Classic sound different from a classical guitar, or from a student's classroom guitar.

FREQUENCY RANGE

Without harmonics, instruments playing the same note would sound virtually the same. You wouldn't be able to tell the difference between a violin and a flute. That's why it's important for a sound system to carry frequencies above the 5 kHz fundamental of the highest orchestral instruments.

But the system doesn't have to extend much higher. Most instruments pack a lot of harmonics below 10 kHz. This is a good thing, because most real-world playback systems are useless half an octave above that limit. Despite how speaker manufacturers may brag about "20 Hz to 20 kHz ranges," most computer, multimedia, and consumer-level stereo speakers fall far short of that goal. The advertising relies on fudged numbers or unspecified qualifiers. Test your system (and your ears) with Track 3 of the CD.

Gotcha

Few sounds have just one frequency! Real-world sounds are rich, moving tapestries of harmonics that extend across the audible spectrum—far more than the two in our simple example. So don't expect to find a magic frequency in an equalizer that will emphasize only violins in the orchestra, or separate male voices from female.

Hear for yourself

Track 3 consists of a few repeating musical selections[6] that alternate between being played at full fidelity and through a filter that cuts off at specified high frequencies. If your speakers (and ears) are really hearing above those frequencies, you'll be able to hear when the filter switches in and out. But if the highs aren't making it through your system, the filter won't make any difference.

Try playing Track 3 through your best hi-fi speakers and note how high you can hear. Then try loading it into your NLE and listening to it there… and then, listen on a laptop. You may be shocked at how much you're missing. But also notice that even when I apply a fairly low cutoff filter (7.5 kHz), enough harmonics are present that the music is still recognizable—if somewhat dull.

By the way, this track was produced with very high-quality digital filters, far sharper than those provided with most NLEs or audio programs. If you try to create a similar test, be sure your filters aren't lowering sounds below the specified cutoff; otherwise, the results will be meaningless. There's more about filters in Chapter 11.

UNPITCHED SOUNDS

Some sounds don't have regular vibrations. Our falling tree trunk, a gunshot, or the clap of a film slate create a single pressure wave of no particular frequency. Many continuous sounds don't have a frequency either; the crunch of breaking branches, the hiss of the phoneme /s/, or the fizz of a glass of soda are

[6] "Swing Out Brother" (J. Trombey, DWCD219/10), "Queen of the Night" from *Magic Flute* (Mozart, DWCD142/2), "Rock Hits" (R. Hardy/B. White, DWCD293/11). All from the DeWolfe Music Library, protected by copyright and used by permission. You'll learn more about this library, as well as a lot more about working with music, in Chapter 9.

collections of essentially random movements. The best we can do is describe their predominant frequency ranges. When we talk about the low pitch of rumbling thunder, we're not talking about a specific pitch but about how this random noise centers around low frequencies.

 Gotcha

Hiss doesn't have frequency. Unpitched sounds are virtually impossible to remove with an equalizer, unless you don't mind doing serious damage to dialog. This includes a lot of the noises that plague film and video shoots: ventilation systems and computer fans, traffic, and the electronic junk from wireless mics or poor camera preamps. The best you can do is make these sounds less annoying; see Chapter 15 for some tips.

HOW HIGH IS ENOUGH?

While 20 kHz is the standard upper frequency limit for DV tape, don't assume every soundtrack must extend that high:

- The upper limit for U.S. analog television and FM stereo is 15 kHz. Frequencies higher than that cause transmission problems. Knowing this, TV manufacturers don't worry about building higher-frequency capability into their products.
- Even digital broadcasting may be limited to near 15 kHz for a while. Station hard-disk servers and satellite links often cut off at that frequency to conserve resources.
- Most Hollywood films made before the 1970s—including most popular musicals—stop around 12.5 kHz, the limit for optical soundtracks. Outside of major cities, you'll find a lot of theaters still don't go much higher.
- Acoustic and orchestral music has surprisingly little energy above 15 kHz, though a good ear can certainly hear when it's missing. (Heavily processed pop music sometimes emphasizes very high frequencies electronically, often to the point of harsh distortion.)

Loudness

Our falling tree will move a lot more molecules with more force than the guitar string; that's why we hear it as "louder." The human ear can handle an amazingly wide range of loudness; the sound of a nearby jet plane hits your eardrum with about 10,000,000,000 times stronger molecular movement than the quietest tones used for testing your ears. We cope with this range by hearing loudness as ratios instead of absolutes, just as we do with frequency. The *difference* in loudness between one tuning fork and a pair of them sounds the same as the difference between one tuba and two.

So in the technical world, we use ratios to gauge the strength of a sound: The sound is compared to a standardized loudness, and its volume is expressed as the resulting fraction. The fastest way to deal with complex fractions is a math shortcut, *logarithms*. You don't have to know how logarithms work. Just remember that they stand for fractions, but with one important twist: adding two logs actually multiplies the numbers they represent. Subtracting them divides the numbers. In other words, *log 1 + log 2 = log 3* really means *ten times a hundred equals a thousand* ... something every schoolchild knows.[7]

Decibels

The common measurement to express the level of sounds and electronic signals, the *decibel* (dB), is a logarithm. Unlike a watt or a degree Fahrenheit, which are measurable quantities, decibels are fractions of something else. They're mostly meaningless until you know what they're fractions *of*.

When we talk about the loudness of a sound in air, we're almost always referring to the fraction formed by it and a theoretical "softest sound a human can hear," the *threshold of hearing*.[8] Log 0 means a fraction of 1/1, so something at exactly that threshold would be written as 0 dB SPL (sound pressure level). Few things are that soft. The quietest recording studios are about +30 dB SPL. A good shooting stage would be around +40 dB SPL. Average dialog level at a boom mic may be around +65 dB SPL. Average playback level in a movie theater is supposed to be 85 dB SPL, but is usually much higher, particularly during coming attractions. A jackhammer, close up, would be around +125 dB SPL.

 Gotcha

A sound can't have "so many decibels." Decibels make sense only when you know their reference. We've talked about dB SPL for sounds in air because SPL is a standard reference. Sounds in a digital signal chain are almost always measured as dBFS (defined later in this chapter); those on an analog wire may be dBu, dBm, or dBV (discussed in Chapter 3). But decibels without extra initials—just plain dB—are simply fractions, useful only when talking about how much a sound should be boosted or lowered ... or when you want to impress a novice with meaningless audio jargon.

The Inverse Square Law

Remember how the falling tree created a spreading bubble of compression and rarefaction? As the bubble gets farther from the tree, its surface area grows, just like the skin of an expanding balloon. But the total energy can't change; that would require another tree. When the bubble was small, its energy was directed at only a few molecules. When the bubble is bigger and there are more molecules around it, it can't push each one as hard.

---

[7] That's if the logs have a *base* of 10, which is common in audio. Mathematicians use other log bases for other purposes.
[8] A pressure fluctuation of 0.0002 microbars, which is an energy of 0.0002 dynes per square centimeter. It may be theoretical, but it's set by international standard.

This is a long way of explaining what you already know: a falling tree sounds louder when it's nearby and softer when it's far away. But few people appreciate *how much* the volume changes based on distance. The effect is geometric, because the surface of a bubble grows much faster than its diameter.

Each time you *double* the distance from a sound source, the sound's power is one quarter as much. Each time you *halve* the distance, it's quadrupled. And these effects multiply. If you quadruple the distance, the sound's power is one-sixteenth. This is called the *inverse square law:* Sound power will change according to the square of the distance change.

Gotcha

Closer is better. A lot of filmmakers never consider how many ways the inverse square law applies to their work. A camera mic at four feet will pick up only half as much dialog as a boom at two feet. But noises and echoes can come from all around a room, so getting farther from the actor doesn't mean you're getting farther from these problems. In practical cases, doubling the distance from desired sound usually makes noises and echoes twice the volume by comparison. Unless you're dealing with ideal acoustic circumstances, there's no way a camera mic at six to eight feet can sound as good as a properly used boom or lav. This is just physics; it doesn't depend on how much you spend for that mic.

The same principle affects postproduction setups. When you listen to monitor speakers, you also hear reflections from nearby walls. Unless you're in a perfectly tuned acoustic space, the reflections subtly change what you hear, which can affect your mixing and processing decisions. Move the speakers closer to your ears, and you'll make better decisions.

Volume Changes Over Time

While the fundamentals of a violin and piano playing the same note may be identical, their *envelopes* are different.

Very few sounds, outside the test lab, are absolutely constant. Their volume can vary over times ranging from a few hundred milliseconds to many seconds. For example, a violin string starts vibrating weakly as the bow begins to move across it, builds strength, and then continues to sound while the bow keeps moving. A piano string, on the other hand, is violently struck by a hammer and starts making noise immediately. But because there's no other hammer hit, it starts to fade down almost immediately. How a sound's volume changes over time is its envelope.

Figures 1.9 and 1.10 compare envelopes of a violin and piano, shown in an audio program's waveform display.[9] Each picture represents about two seconds.

---

[9] I couldn't use an oscilloscope for this, because envelopes are too slow to display on that device.

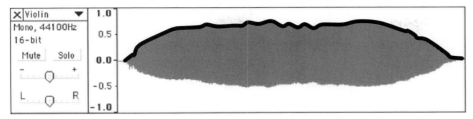

FIGURE 1.9
A violin sound grows slowly, but continues as long as the instrument is bowed.

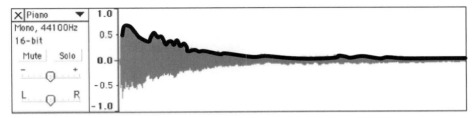

FIGURE 1.10
A piano note starts suddenly, then begins to fade almost immediately.

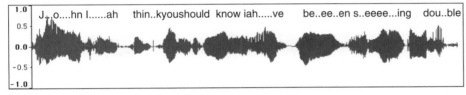

FIGURE 1.11
Spoken-word envelopes don't necessarily correspond to individual words.

I've drawn heavy black lines along the tops to trace the envelopes. The jaggy bits you see on the bottom are individual soundwaves.

The envelope of human speech depends on what's being said but doesn't necessarily follow individual words. Figure 1.11 shows an actress saying, "John, I think you should know I've been seeing…." She's speaking smoothly, but some words are jammed together and others are slowed down. I added text above each individual sound so you can see how uneven her envelope is.

 Hear for yourself

Track 4 is the sounds whose envelopes we've just looked at: violin and piano (both with and without harmonics), and the woman's dialog clip.

13

Gotcha

When envelope and frequency overlap. The *j* sound that starts "John" is about 1/20th of a second long,[10] but as we've discussed, frequencies around 20 Hz can be audible. So is the *j* sound part of the envelope or a single soundwave by itself?

In this case, it's part of the envelope, both because the woman's natural voice doesn't go down as low as 20 Hz and because it's nonrepeating. This issue becomes important when you're dealing with dynamics processing to automatically control levels. If the system isn't set properly, you'll hear a kind of muffling. Learn to avoid it in Chapter 12.

Analog Audio

So far, we've examined sound mostly as variations of air pressure. Electronic equipment deals with electrical pressures (voltage) and quantity (current), not air pressure changes. The basic way to turn sound into electricity—dating from the very first telephones—is to make a changing voltage that corresponds exactly to the sound wave. When there's compression, the voltage is positive; when there's rarefaction, it's negative. The amount of voltage at any moment reflects the strength of the wave. In other words, it's an *exact analogy* of the sound.

You may be working with digital cameras and editors, but this analog audio is still at the heart of the process. Microphones and speakers are analog devices—even if they have digital connections—and most postproduction studios have a lot of analog wiring. But analog signals are fragile. Things that change the voltage add distortion or noise. If you don't understand what's going on with analog audio, bad things can happen to your track.

PRESSURE TO VOLTAGE AND BACK

Microphones and speakers work like tiny generators and motors. The dynamo at a power plant uses a rotating turbine to spin a coil inside a magnetic field; this creates a changing voltage. The dynamic mics used for handheld interviews and voice-overs work exactly the same way, except the coil doesn't rotate. Instead, it's attached to a thin diaphragm that flexes in response to air pressure.

A speaker is a microphone in reverse (Figure 1.12). Instead of a diaphragm, it has a large paper cone attached to the coil. Changing voltage—the audio signal—is applied to the coil, making it move back and forth inside a magnetic field. This vibrates the cone, which then pushes and pulls against air molecules.

Dynamic mics and speakers are so similar that their functions can be interchangeable. Many intercoms use a speaker to both radiate and pick up sound.

---

[10] Actually, the sound *j* consists of a very fast "d"—about 1/60 of a second long—followed by a drawn out ZH "zh" (say "John" very slowly and you'll hear what I mean). This kind of analysis is important for serious dialog editing, and is covered in Chapter 6.

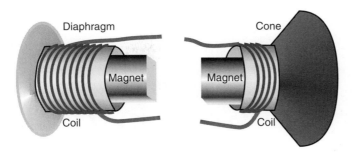

FIGURE 1.12
Dynamic mics (left) and speakers (right) have very similar construction.

Conversely, radio station engineers have been known to play tricks on air talent by temporarily sending the talkback signal into a mic. Done right, the mic itself will start to whisper at the announcer just before a broadcast.[11]

The condenser elements in most dialog mics don't have magnets and won't work as speakers. But their function is the same: turning changing air pressure into changing voltage. There's a deeper discussion of mics in Chapter 7.

Balanced Wiring

When you connect a mic to a camera, or an NLE to a mixer or audio input, the analog wiring can act like an antenna and pick up nearby electric fields. Video monitors and data cables broadcast high frequencies; power cords and the wiring in the walls radiate low-frequency noise. Since you can't avoid these fields, the trick is keeping them from mixing with your track.

As you probably remember from grade school or model trains, any electric circuit requires two conductors. Most consumer line- and mic-level wiring accomplishes this with a single conductor for each audio channel, surrounded by a foil or braid shield that serves both as the return conductor and a barrier to high-frequency noise. This scheme, *unbalanced wiring*, is cheap and moderately effective. Unfortunately, the shield isn't very good at stopping power-line hum, timecode, or crosstalk from other audio channels.

The solution is to have two separate but identical wires, twisted very close to each other, inside the shield. While one wire is carrying current in one direction, the other's current is going the opposite way. Analog audio constantly changes polarity to reflect the compression and rarefaction of the sound waves. But at any given instant, the voltage on one wire will be positive while the other is negative. That's why it's called *balanced wiring*. It's connected to an input circuit that looks just at the voltage difference between the wires. Figure 1.13 shows how this works.

15

---

[11] Done wrong, it can damage the equipment. I was a little devil of a radio engineer when I was much younger, and made sure to do this hack properly.

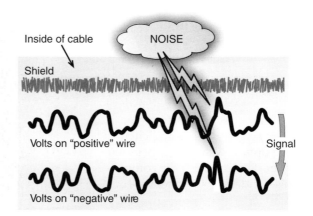

FIGURE 1.13
Balanced wiring uses symmetrical signals to reject asymmetrical noise.

Since the wires are physically identical and very close together, any noise that bursts through the shield is picked up by both. The voltage that results from the noise is the same on both wires, so subsequent equipment doesn't detect it. The math is easy:

Conductor	Original signal	Noise	Total on wire
A	+1.0 v	+0.5 v	+1.5 v
B	−1.0 v	+0.5 v	−0.5 v
Difference between A and B	2.0 v	0 v	2.0 v

Balanced wiring does not require XLR connectors, nor do these connectors guarantee a circuit is balanced. But they are often used together, particularly in microphone cables. Mic signals are so small that they're easily polluted by external noise.

 Gotcha

Balanced wiring requires balanced equipment. Balanced wires don't actually reject the noise; that magic happens in whatever the wires get plugged into. Both the signal source and the destination need special circuits for balancing. These circuits can be expensive and are usually left out of prosumer equipment.

While unbalanced wiring doesn't offer this protection, it doesn't have to be noisy if you plan it properly. Chapter 3 discusses practicalities of both wiring schemes and how to connect between the two.

16

DIGITAL AUDIO

Those bugaboos of noise and distortion in analog audio are cumulative. Each time a signal goes through a different processor or is stored on another generation of analog tape, it gets slightly noisier or more distorted. In the days before digital recording, a movie soundtrack could go through dozens of processing circuits and six magnetic or optical generations between stage and moviegoer. Finding the best compromise between noise and distortion was a constant battle.

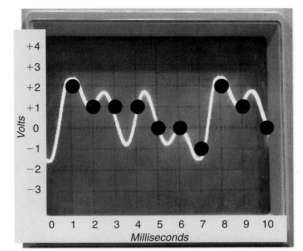

FIGURE 1.14
Sampling a
soundwave's voltage,
once per millisecond.

But computer data doesn't deteriorate that way. The words I'm typing now are captured flawlessly to RAM, written to hard disk, and e-mailed to a publisher. Editors, tech reviewers, and designers will work on successive copies before it's sent to the printer. Yet, no data errors are introduced by these multiple computer generations.[12] Digital ones and zeros are unambiguous and easy to copy, and computers include safeguards to correct many errors.

If we turn an analog audio signal into digital data, it should be just as robust. Of course the process of turning constantly changing analog voltages into data and back has its own pitfalls. Twenty-five years ago, when the technology was new, these problems gave digital a bad reputation among audio purists. Today, we've learned to deal with all of them. Digital, when done right, is the best recording medium we've got. Musicians may argue that some of analog's imperfections are part of their art, but for professional film and video, digital's advantages are so great that the older method has been virtually abandoned.

Digitizing

The process of turning analog to digital is easy to visualize with an oscilloscope. For any moment, you can measure exactly what the voltage is. Scopes have grids printed on their displays to track time and voltage; the values depend on how you set the controls. In Figure 1.14, I've assigned the grid very simple numbers: each vertical unit represents one volt, and each horizontal is one millisecond. The wave is the dual-harmonic we examined earlier.

When children first learn to count, they do it in whole numbers: *1 apple, 2 apples, 3 apples.* Their math skills don't yet include the concept of "half an apple." Neither does a computer's. One bit is the smallest possible unit, and there can be no such thing as half a bit. But we can assign that smallest bit any

---

[12] I'm not guaranteeing this text is error-free. Just that the errors are human (and probably mine).

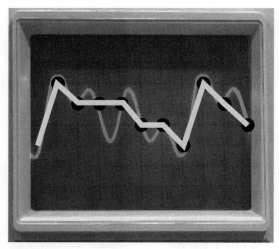

FIGURE 1.15
Our low-resolution
recording isn't very
accurate.

FIGURE 1.16
Doubling the number
of bits lets us mark
half-volts. Doubling
the speed gives
us twice as many
samples.

unit we want. It can be something whole, like a penny. Or it can be a fraction of a unit, like a hundredth of a volt.

These values may be tiny, but if you string bits together to make words, you can express much bigger numbers. A one-bit digital word has two possible values, 1 or 0. A two-bit word has four possible values: 00, 01, 10, 11. Word processors typically express characters and letters with a *byte*, or 8-bit word. Modern computers frequently string multiple bytes together into a single word. Using two bytes for a 16-bit word, you get 65,536 possible values.

Let's keep things simple. For our first digital audio, we'll use three-bit words, which have eight possible values. We'll count in volts, scaled from -3 to $+4$ on our scope screen. Digital 000 would be -3 volts, digital 001 is -2 volts, and so on. The wave fits nicely in that range.

Using the grid, let's turn our wave digital. Once per millisecond (that is, once per horizontal unit) we'll read the voltage. Since our counting unit is a volt, we round to the nearest whole one:

> At 1 ms it measures $+2$ volts
> 2 ms it measures $+1$ volt
> 3 ms it measures $+1$ volt
> … etc.

This string of analog numbers, *+2, +1, +1…* could be recorded on digital tape as the three-bit words: *101, 100, 100…* I've marked the value for each millisecond with a black dot on the screen. You can see in Figure 1.14 how the dots follow the sound wave.

To play this string of numbers back as sound, we create an analog wave that has the right voltage at the right time. Visually, this is as easy as connecting the dots (it isn't much harder in audio circuits). But the result—the light gray line in Figure 1.15—doesn't resemble the original much. What went wrong?

Actually, two things are at fault. Those rounded whole volts—the best we can do with our three-bit words—are too far apart to accurately record the wave. And a sample rate of once per millisecond isn't fast enough to accurately capture an 800 Hz harmonic. Both problems are easy to fix.

Each time you add one more bit to a digital word length, you double the number of possible values. So let's bump up to four-bit recording: instead of just eight possible values between −3 and +4, we now have 16. This lets us count in half volts. Let's also double the speed and take a fresh sample every half millisecond (you'll learn why that's sufficient in the next few pages). Figure 1.16 shows these new samples as smaller black dots: twice as many as in Figure 1.14, now rounded to the nearest half volt.

We haven't added much data—four bits would be considered a very low-resolution system. Two thousand samples per second (usually written as a *2 kHz sample rate*, or *2 kHz s/r*) is only fast enough for bass-effect channels. But the recon-structed wave is a lot more accurate. Figure 1.17 shows how well it follows the original. Even more important, CD Track 5 lets you judge the result: an actual four-bit, 2 kHz s/r recording of the multi-harmonic wave from Track 2. It was converted back to CD standard so you could play it, but that didn't restore the lost data. You're hearing what four bits at 2 kHz s/r really sounds like!

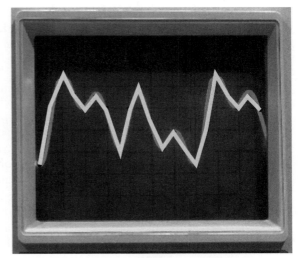

FIGURE 1.17
This "doubled" recording gives much more accurate results.

 Hear for yourself

Track 5 lets you hear the actual wave produced by Figure 1.17, along with the original wave for comparison.

Bit Depths and Full Scale

Track 5 sounds as good as it does because even low-bit systems can handle simple waves recorded at the right level. Even today's basic systems use 16-bit audio words for considerably more accuracy and volume range. When the signal has to be converted to or from analog, circuit designers choose a maximum possible voltage. This is defined as when all 16 bits are ones, or *full scale*. The smallest bit is then 1/65,536 of full scale, or about 0.00013 dB of it.

Some rounding off is still necessary because even those tiny bits aren't the same as a constantly changing wave. The worst case is when a signal is halfway between two minimum bits; it causes a maximum error of about 0.00007 dB of full scale—far less than humans can hear. But each time you manipulate the signal—say, by changing volume or adding a processor—you're doing some math on the samples. Since the result isn't likely to fall perfectly on a whole-bit value, it's rounded off again. These errors are cumulative. Do enough processing, and the result is audible distortion or noise. For that reason, audio professionals now use 24-bit words, for a possible error of 0.00000026 dB. They do as much as possible in that domain, and then reduce the final output to 16 bits when necessary for compatibility with other media.

There's another way to consider bit depth. Each bit doubles the possible number of values, increasing the ratio between media noise and full scale by 6 dB[13] (that ratio is often called *signal/noise*, or *s/n*). An eight-bit signal, common in early computers, has 48 dB s/n. Sixteen-bit DV and CDs have a theoretical 96 dB s/n, though the analog circuits are seldom that good. Twenty-four-bit signals have 144 dB s/n—beyond the range of the most golden-eared humans, as well as most electronics—but it provides significant margin for error.

Some DV cameras also support 12-bit recording at a reduced sample rate, to double the number of audio tracks on a videotape. Twelve bits means 72 dB s/n, which isn't bad compared to older analog media. But 12-bit recordings are frequently noisy. That's because there's no safety margin, and it's almost impossible to set levels accurately enough in the field to take full advantage of the range.

 Gotcha

Digital signals have no relation to voltage. The digital audio values on a CD or stored on your hard drive represent fractions of full scale. But the actual value of full scale depends on the analog circuits: it might be 0.01 volts at a camcorder's mic input, 3.5 volts on a balanced line connector, 8 volts in a hi-fi speaker, or whatever the equipment designer prefers.

This is a good thing. It means while the signal is in the digital domain, you don't have to worry about absolute values at all. The software doesn't care whether a track is destined for a thousand watt theater system, the Internet, or your own headphones.

For this reason, digital audio levels are always expressed as dBFS, a decibel ratio to full scale. Full scale is the absolute maximum, so a ratio of 1:1 (0 dBFS) is the loudest you can get. Because no voltage changes can be recorded above full scale, if the original analog voltage exceeds the design limit, the digitized result has an absolutely flat-topped waveform: total (and very ugly) distortion.

Circuit designers frequently flash the "overload" light when a signal approaches −1 dBFS to avoid this distortion. But there really isn't a digital overload. That would require a digital signal greater than 0 dBFS, which is impossible.[14]

---

[13] Actually, 6.0205999 dB. But you can round it off. What's a few hundredths dB among friends?
[14] Except in the case of one particular and ugly-sounding test signal, which never occurs in a soundtrack.

DITHER

Humans can't hear a single sample's worth of rounding error, but a bunch of them in a row produce a distortion that's annoying because of the way it follows the signal. The solution is to add analog noise—dithering—at about one-third the level of a single bit. This randomizes the error so it doesn't sound like distortion any more. The ear is good at tracking desired sounds even when they're obscured by noise, so dithering can effectively extend the dynamic range. Dithering can also be noise-shaped, making the random signal stronger at frequencies where the ear is less sensitive. Its randomness continues to hide distortion, but we don't hear the noise as much.

 Gotcha

What signal to noise? When measuring s/n in the analog world, it's customary to refer to a nominal signal level, typically 0 VU. That's because while analog circuits start distorting once you reach that level, you can still record a louder signal. Momentary peaks 6 dB higher than 0 VU can sound fine, even though longer sounds that loud would reveal the distortion.

Since digital recording has an absolute limit of 0 dBFS, that level is usually used for digital s/n measurements. But prosumer audio gear often has its nomal operating level set to −12 dBFS (−20 dBFS for pro gear) to leave room for peaks. When comparing digital s/n to analog, you must take that safety margin into effect. So while 16-bit digital has 96 dB s/n, a 16-bit miniDV isn't capable of sounding better than an 80 dB analog s/n.[15]

Audio programs may give you some choices for dithering when you need to reduce bit depth. If your program does this, use dithering and play with the noise-shaping options. The effects may be too subtle for most media production, unless you're translating a 16-bit signal to 8 bits. Most NLEs' audio capabilities aren't sophisticated enough to use dithering at all.

Sample Rates

Sound exists only when pressure *changes* over time. Eliminate the time component, and all you've got is air pressure—useful for weather forecasts, but not soundtracks. So it makes intuitive sense that how often you sample a signal's level influences how accurately it gets recorded.

This principle was known long before practical digital recording was invented. In the 1920s, a Bell Labs engineer, Harry Nyquist, proved mathematically that the highest frequency you can faithfully reproduce has to be less than half the sample rate. Sounds above the *Nyquist Limit* start to mix with the sample rate itself. The resulting data implies additional frequencies, which aren't

---

[15] That's a theoretical maximum, with ideal electronic circuits. Many mass-marketed cameras don't even come close.

harmonics of the original wave. When you play back the data, those frequencies are re-created as well as the desired one. What you get is a horrible squeaking or whistling overlaid on the original.

To avoid this, analog-to-digital conversion circuits use *antialiasing* filters to reject high frequencies before they get digitized. Digital-to-analog circuits have similar *reconstruction* or *smoothing* filters. They're often set to about 45 percent of the sample rate.

- CDs are set at 44.1 kHz s/r so they can carry a 20 kHz audio signal, generally accepted as the minimum requirement for high fidelity.
- Computer media often use a 22 kHz s/r to save data. This implies an upper audio limit of 10 kHz, about the same as AM radio.
- Analog TV and FM stereo sound are cut off at 15 kHz; the transmitter uses higher frequencies for other purposes. So broadcasters often set a 32 kHz s/r in their storage systems and satellite links. These systems might be part of an HD radio or TV chain as well, even though the transmitters use 44.1 kHz (HD radio) and 48 kHz (HDTV).
- U.S. telephones traditionally cut off at 3.5 kHz. So when switching networks and long-distance lines were converted to digital, a sample rate of 8 kHz was chosen.
- Our example in Figures 1.15 and 1.16 has a second harmonic at 800 Hz. This puts it safely below the Nyquist Limit of our 2 kHz sampling. That's why Track 5 can accurately play the harmonic.

Higher is not necessarily better. Professional video is standardized at 48 kHz sampling. But most equipment that handles 48 kHz s/r also supports 44.1 kHz s/r and uses the same filters for both. That means there's no advantage to the higher rate. Some professional equipment uses 96 kHz sampling, but very few engineers believe we can hear as high as 40 kHz, and it's certainly not necessary for dialog. The higher rate was chosen to keep filter artifacts—which increase as you reach their cutoff frequency—far from critical audio.

DIGITAL VS. ANALOG

Many music producers like the distortion created by overloaded analog tape, and will dub their digital masters through vintage studio recorders just to get it. Then they'll redigitize for CD release. But that's actually adding distortion, not compensating for any limitations of digital recording.

Arguments about the superiority of one medium over the other can be intense as Presidential elections. Some people insist that audio hit its peak with vinyl records and has gone downhill since; they point to awful mp3s on the Internet as proof. Others assert that digital is inherently "steppy" or can't reproduce certain shapes of waves. Those last two assertions are absolutely true. But they ignore how analog circuits suffer from problems that are exactly equivalent.[16]

---

[16] Want proof? See my book *Producing Great Sound,* or my Web site www.dplay.com/gotcha.

It's not worth fighting about. If you're doing any serious soundtrack production these days, digital audio will be part of your life. What's important—particularly if your background is analog—is understanding some fundamental differences between the two systems.

Analog Handles Overloads More Gracefully

When an analog mixer, processor, or recorder receives a signal that's too loud, it starts to distort. The distortion is gentle at first and increases as the input gets louder. If an unexpected signal peak causes a sudden overload, the distortion may be tolerable.

That's not true for digital. Anything louder than full scale—even for a single sample—gets badly distorted. This often shows as a crackling that obscures the signal. And it doesn't have to happen during the original recording: if a signal is boosted too much inside a digital processor or while you're mixing in an NLE, the distortion is the same. In some systems, you can't even spot the distortion until after things are rendered. The only cure is to watch all your levels carefully. If the software doesn't allow that, listen to the final product and be prepared to redo if there are problems.

Analog Deteriorates with Each Error; Digital Conceals Errors, then Fails Totally

In a digital system, an error is missing or inaccurate data. In an analog system, it's usually a burst of noise. Neither medium is particularly prone to errors, but either can have them because of malfunctioning equipment, dirty tapes, noisy environments, and other problems.

It sometimes seems like digital has more things to go wrong. Problems like unsynchronized clocks (Chapter 3) can cause clicking or hiccups that are hard to trace, and there's no equivalent error in the analog realm. But the fact is, analog has its own unique array of problems. We've simply been dealing with them longer.

Digital systems have two kinds of safeguards against problems. Small errors can be corrected perfectly, with mathematical techniques. Larger ones are detected but can't be corrected; instead, missing parts of the waveform are interpolated from the surrounding good data. Usually, this error concealment is undetectable. Very large sections of bad data cause the system to either produce noise or mute automatically. In practice, if a digital signal is getting progressively worse, you can keep hearing clean audio through much of the damage and not even know there's a problem. Then it disappears entirely.

Analog systems have no such safeguards. Once noise mixes with the signal, it's there to stay. But the signal's there, too, and you'll probably still hear it. In practice, as analog signals get progressively worse, you hear the changes and know something's wrong.

Analog Degrades with Each Process; Digital Doesn't Have To

Even the best analog equipment adds a tiny amount of noise and distortion. Knowledgeable engineers strive for as simple an analog signal chain as possible, and avoid extra tape generations except for special effects. But good digital recorders don't degrade digital input signals at all, and good digital processors do so little damage that you'd have to string together hundreds before you'd notice anything.

However, you still have to be knowledgeable if you want digital good sound. Processors can be misused. Each conversion from digital to analog and back adds some generation loss. Avoiding these problems isn't hard, once you're armed with some basic understanding and the proper techniques. This chapter's been about the understanding. The rest of this book is about the practicalities.

CHAPTER 2

The Studio: Acoustics and Monitoring

My first audio post suite was a shelf in the living room. It had three consumer tape decks, a PA system mixer, a graphic equalizer, and a homebrew patch bay. I used my stereo amp and speakers for monitoring.[1] This ragtag assembly should have sounded awful. But I'd engineered at three radio stations and spent a couple of years working in film sound, so I had a couple of tricks up my sleeve. Careful wiring and constant tweaking kept the equipment at its peak. This setup never sounded great. But it certainly sounded better than pro gear used wrong.

My current suite is considerably nicer (Figure 2.1), and is good enough for projects I do for Disney and MGM. But it was also built on a low budget, and I used ideas similar to those from that first studio (plus a few decades of additional experience). Call it guerrilla engineering—knowing when you have to follow the rules, and when it's okay to cheat.

This section of the book describes acoustic treatments, wiring, and equipment for both audio-only rooms and video or film editing rooms where sound is considered important. While sound studios are usually built to higher acoustic standards than rooms that concentrate on picture, there's absolutely no difference in the principles involved. The advice here works equally well for both, whether

---

[1]Projects from that rinky-dink setup included a couple of national radio spots, some federally funded PSAs, and audio for a major-market museum show. I had a lot more nerve than equipment.

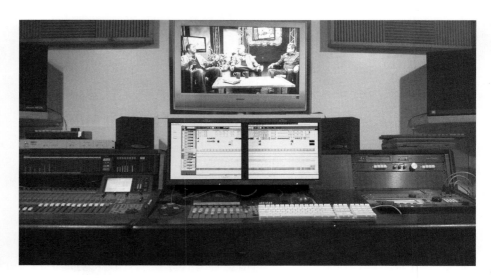

FIGURE 2.1
My current studio,
the Digital Playroom.

you're starting construction from scratch or retrofitting an existing office (or living room). It can even be applied to a garage studio where your band hangs out.

FACILITY GOALS

Before investing in construction, soundproofing, and other equipment, take a minute to figure out how you'll use them. You might be able to save some money.

- Are you planning to edit here but then take tracks somewhere else for cleanup and mix? This may be the most cost-effective strategy if you're making only a few short films. You won't need much more than a NLE and a small speaker. You can even use headphones.
- Are you planning to record as well? Obviously, you'll need a mic. But take care of the acoustics first: a hundred dollars spent in this area can help more than a thousand-dollar microphone. Treating a room for narrations is fairly easy, because the talent can work close to the mic. If you're recording replacement dialog or Foley, the mic will be farther and the acoustics are more exacting.
- Planning to mix your videos yourself? If you want to be reasonably sure of how the track will sound on viewers' sets or in a theater, good monitors and acoustics are the most important component.
- Planning to make a living in this room with clients showing up to supervise? They'll expect both good acoustics and some space to spread out. If you're going after ad agency clients, you'll need glitz as well: a lounge area, refreshments, wi-fi, and lots of pretty winking lights.[2]

---

[2]A former boss once told me, "People hear with their eyes." He'd insist I consider the knob-to-light ratio when specifying equipment (the more lights, the better). His audio suites certainly looked great, even if they didn't sound as good as I'd want. They also made money, so maybe he was right.

It's most likely your needs fall somewhere in the middle; you want a room where you can accurately edit and mix your own tracks with an occasional voiceover recording. You don't want outside noises to interfere, and you don't want to annoy other people in the building. And your budget is limited.

If you know what you're doing, none of this is a problem.

ACOUSTICS

I was visiting a friend, an Avid editor at a TV station that had recently built new, luxurious offices. The facility was beautiful: Every surface was either pastel enamel or oak, and the large square rooms had sparse furniture so people wouldn't feel cramped. His new edit room—designed to impress local advertisers—was designed to match. It even featured a giant TV on the wall opposite the client chairs. Figure 2.2 shows the approximate layout.

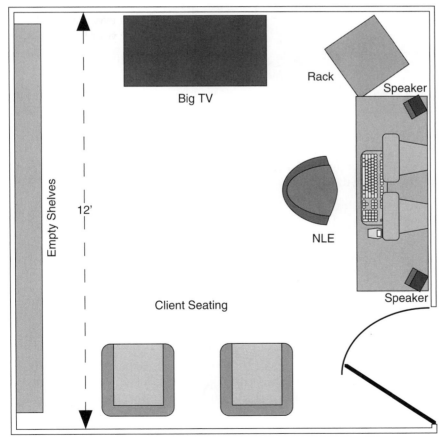

FIGURE 2.2
This edit room looked great, but it had problems.

He couldn't understand why his mixes sounded okay in the NLE but were virtually unintelligible when clients watched them on the TV. If you read the previous chapter, you can probably guess what was going on:

- The hard walls and empty bookcase reflected all the sound that hit them. The room was actually an echo chamber.
- When he was sitting at the NLE, he was much closer to his tiny monitor speakers than to the back wall. Thanks to the inverse square law, returning echoes weren't loud enough to damage what he heard.
- But when clients sat in their chairs, the direct sound from the TV's speakers traveled almost about as far as echoes from behind the clients or from the side walls. Since these various paths were all different lengths, these sounds got to the clients at slightly different times, blurring what they heard.

Vibrating air between two parallel hard walls works like the string of a guitar. It resonates at a frequency based on the distance between the walls and at harmonics of that frequency. This resonance makes echoes stronger at those frequencies than at others. In nontechnical terms, the space is *boomy*.

 Gotcha

A square room won't sound cool. Parallel walls are almost always a problem, and the more energy the wall reflects, the worse things will sound. A perfectly square room with hard walls can't sound good because resonances in both directions will be the same.

Also, his tiny personal monitors at the NLE weren't very efficient at the low frequencies affected by those boomy resonances. So he tended to turn up the bass when he was mixing. This further excited the room resonances from the TV's speakers, making the booming worse.

Since he was stuck with the basic room shape, I suggested he fill the bookcase with randomly-sized tape boxes to break up some of the reflections, and hang as many fiberglass or foam panels as possible on the walls to absorb echoes. He could also move the client chairs a lot closer to the TV set. If he got better monitor speakers for his NLE, he wouldn't overemphasize the bass. And if he planned to show off finished spots through those better monitors, he should move the speakers next to the TV before clients showed up.[3]

Fighting Resonance: Build a Crooked Room

If you do have a chance to specify the room's shape, the best way to avoid problems is to make sure the walls aren't parallel. Nonparallel walls spread the resonances out over a lot of frequencies instead of having them build up at just a few. Crooked rooms can sound better than rectangular ones.

---

[3]When sound and video don't come from the same direction, it makes lipsync problems seem a lot worse.

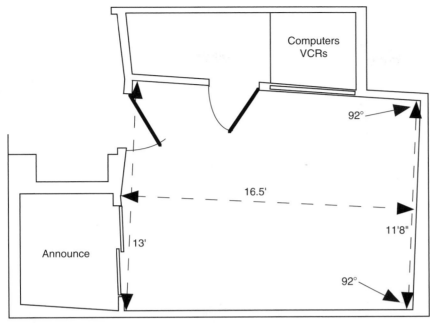

FIGURE 2.3
The contractor couldn't understand why I wanted the room this way, until he heard it.

These angles don't have to be extreme. Anyone entering my mix room for the first time will think it has normal dimensions. But in Figure 2.3—the room's plan—you can see there are no parallel walls: The corners are 92 degrees.

Even though the room is crooked, it should be symmetrical. When you're seated at the listening position, the size and shape of the room to your left should match the size and shape to your right as closely as possible. The room in Figure 2.3 is aligned to the center of the wall opposite the announce booth—where the "16.5 feet" dashed line appears. (In Figure 2.1, the picture monitor, two computer monitors, and audio workstation control surface are centered on that wall.)

If you don't have the luxury of building new walls, try to find a room where width, length, and ceiling height aren't exact multiples of each other. This keeps resonances from ganging up in a single group of frequencies. If possible, work across a corner so the sound source faces the longest diagonal dimension of the room, while maintaining that symmetry on both sides. The most important thing is to add wall treatments that absorb the reflections. But if you need soundproofing—as opposed to echo control—you should soundproof first.

Fighting Sound Transmission

Most modern construction is virtually transparent to sound; the best you can expect from a standard sheetrock wall is about a -30 dB reduction in the middle of the band—subjectively about an eighth of the original volume and still audible. Sound reduction at low frequencies is much worse.

Whether you're building from scratch or improving an existing room, there are only two practical ways to keep sound out: make the walls massive, or make them springy (also called *decoupling*). When sound hits one side of a conventional wall, it's carried through the studs and vibrates the wallboard on the other side. If you make the surfaces thicker and heavier, they won't vibrate very much when activated by sound. If you decouple the surfaces so they're not rigidly connected by a stud, vibrations won't be carried very well.

One common solution is to add a second layer of wallboard on one or both sides. This adds mass. You can use different thicknesses of board to give the sides different densities, so they resonate at different frequencies. One common arrangement is to put double 5/8-inch board on one side and a layer each of 5/8-inch and 1/2-inch on the other.

> ### ⚠ Gotcha
>
> **Soundproofing happens inside the walls.** Ask most people what soundproofing is and they'll describe foam tiles, egg crates, or other treatments on the walls. While foam tiles or other treatments can control reverberation, they don't stop sound. Egg crates are only good for storing eggs.

A different approach is to isolate one of the wall's surfaces from the studs entirely. This was traditionally done with sound-deadening board, a kind of spongy panel laid between the studs and the drywall. It's often called *Homasote*, after its original manufacturer. A newer method uses resilient steel channels (usually called *RC-1*, and shown in Figure 2.4) running horizontally along the length of the wall every two feet or so. The lower, flat surface has holes for screwing to studs or an existing wall. Another layer of drywall is laid against the channels' upper surface and is attached with special screws that aren't long enough to reach the studs or existing wall. You can get both at big lumber yards or acoustic suppliers, and they don't require any special skills to install.

Wood or Metal Stud

RC-1

Standard Screw

Wallboard

Special short screw that can't reach stud

FIGURE 2.4
Low-cost RC-1 channels isolate the wall surface from the studs.

Remember that sound travels vertically as well as horizontally; resilient channels and extra drywall work just as well on ceilings as they do on walls. Channels and drywall aren't appropriate for floors; instead, use hard rubber cubes and 5/8-inch plywood. The cubes are sold specifically for sound control and are already mounted in fiberglass batts. Some builders instead put a layer of Homasote under a standard floor; this is cheaper but not as effective.

If you've got the space, a wall can be built with double studs, staggered from each other on a wider plate. This works like the resilient channels; they disconnect one surface of the wall from the other, with the added advantage of more air space between the surfaces. Sound insulation can be woven between the studs for additional isolation. Using a combination of these techniques, you can bring a wall's attenuation up to about 60 dB—as good as the best recording studios.

To prevent sound leaks, caulk all wallboard to the floor and ceiling. Weatherproofing materials and techniques are appropriate. If you're using double wallboard, stagger the joints and tape both layers. Completely seal any penetrations, including plumbing and electrical. Use surface-mounted boxes so you don't have to cut into the wall for outlets and switches, and make sure the other side of the wall is also free from cutouts.

 Gotcha

Sound is sneaky stuff. Walls don't stop much if they have holes in them. Vibrating molecules can get through the tiniest holes. Any soundproofing technique will be useless if the wall isn't also air-proof.

I once had to soundproof an existing room because of a teletype machine next door. I decided to add mass by lining the walls with sheet lead,[4] to be covered with standard wallboard. When the lead was almost completely up, I worried it was a bad choice: the teletype was still very audible. But as we closed those last few inches, the sound went completely away. It was as if the machine had been turned off!

To keep an HVAC system quiet, use flexible ducting connected to commercial HVAC silencers mounted in the wall. The silencers are metal cylinders with baffles inside and are about 2 feet in diameter and 3 feet long. If it's not possible to mount silencers, put right angles in the duct. HVAC will also be quieter if you specify a low-velocity fan and large ducting. It's a good idea to avoid standard diffusers on the vents; when they spread air around, they also generate a lot of noise. In my studio, the 8-inch ducts go into normal 2-foot square ceiling vents from a home supply store, but I took the vents' diffusers off with a pliers. It significantly quieted the system—and gave my ceiling more of a high-tech look.

---

[4] Sheet lead is lead that's been rolled into a heavy foil, is very limp, and weighs one pound per square foot. It's still available for soundproofing, but has to be treated specially because of health concerns. Newer, non-toxic plastic alternatives are available.

Doors need significant mass, as well as a sealing mechanism to stop sound. If you can't afford expensive soundproof door systems, specify solid-core doors. Then add a layer of ½-inch plywood on each side for more mass. You might need special hardware and a steel frame to support the heavier door. Caulk the frame to the wall and use tubular weather stripping on all four sides for sealing.

 Gotcha

The missing upper wall. Modern office buildings are often built with vast interior spaces. A suspended tile ceiling is installed across the entire space, and then walls are built to break the large space into rooms. Unfortunately, these walls only stretch up to the tile ceiling. The space above is wide open for air ducts and wiring… but it's also wide open to sound.

You can get a reasonable improvement by adding fiberglass batts, made for this purpose, above the false ceiling. The batts are denser than normal thermal insulation and available at acoustics suppliers. This technique is effective at voice frequencies but not for bass.

Fighting Echoes

Small rooms have echoes, even though you probably can't hear them. If a room is less than 12 feet wide, early reflections are too fast to hear as separate sounds.

- If the echoes are frequency selective, like in my friend's edit room, they can add a boominess to everything.
- Even if you angled the walls or broke up their surfaces, echoes can still combine with existing sounds to reinforce some frequencies and cancel others. This makes mixing or equalizing difficult.
- If you're recording in a small room without echo treatment, the mic won't pick up directional and visual cues that usually help you ignore echoes. The track will sound echoey on playback, even if it didn't when you were in the room recording it.

Fortunately, echoes are the easiest sound problem to cure. Auralex, SDG, and Sonex all make wedge-surfaced 2- to 4-inch-thick foam tiles designed to absorb sound reflections. They cost between $4 and $16 per foot at broadcast suppliers. The different brands will sound the same for most purposes; make your choice based on appearance and price. But don't just tack them on the wall. With a few simple additions, you can build absorbers that look better and are more effective, and may even use fewer tiles.

Turn back to Figure 2.1 (page 27) to see the corners of a couple of these absorbers in my studio; they're the things toward the top of the photo on both sides of the video monitor. There are plenty more on the walls beyond the photo. About one-quarter of the total wall surface is covered with these things. The absorbers' surface is 2-inch grooved foam tiles. The two secret ingredients are fiberglass and air. The fiberglass isn't the pink stuff sold for attics; that's not very good for sound. Instead, use 2-inch-thick Owens-Corning 703, a semi-rigid yellow panel made specifically for its acoustic properties. It's available at acoustic suppliers or large lumber yards in bundles of 40 square feet for about a dollar a foot.

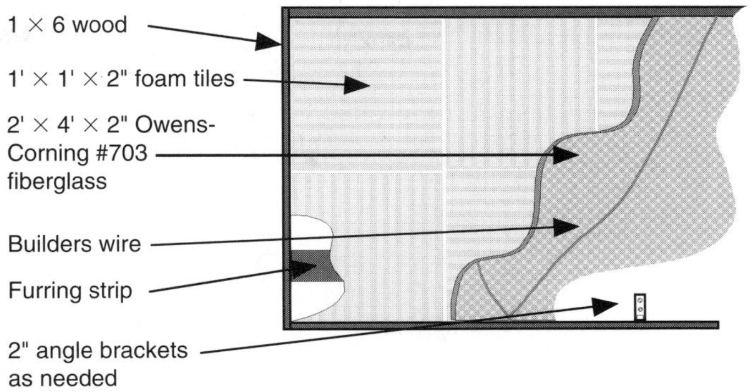

1 × 6 wood

1' × 1' × 2" foam tiles

2' × 4' × 2" Owens-Corning #703 fiberglass

Builders wire

Furring strip

2" angle brackets as needed

FIGURE 2.5
An easy-to-build, low-cost sound absorber.

Figure 2.5 shows how the absorber gets put together. Build a frame out of 1-inch by 4-inch boards (pine is fine, but oak looks better) and attach it to the wall. Press to fit the fiberglass into the frame—you can trim the fiberglass with a knife and compress it slightly to make it stay in place—and secure it with builder's wire stapled to the frame. Then cement the foam tiles onto the 703 panel with construction adhesive. Since 1-inch by 4-inch lumber is actually about 3.5 inches wide, the tiles' grooves will stick out half an inch for a nicely finished appearance. If you don't mind the grooves sticking out a little more, mount ½-inch furring strips (rough lumber, also known as *strapping*) on the wall. This puts an airspace behind the 703 panel, which makes it absorb even better.

You can make the frame any size you want, but it's most convenient to keep the inside dimensions multiples of your particular brand tile's size. How much absorber do you need? There are complex formulas to answer that precisely (check www.dplay.com/gotcha for some books on the subject). But you can get good results by covering about one-third of the wall area with fiber and tile, or you can cover one-quarter of the wall with the airspace version; that should be enough to make any hard-walled room sound good for editing and mixing. Mount the panels so their centers are about ear level. Use a little more coverage if you'll also be recording voiceovers.

If you're going to be mixing music or theatrical tracks with a lot of bass, be aware that low frequencies can be hard to control even when speech and higher frequencies are being absorbed nicely. The common solution for this is a *bass trap*, a fairly large kind of absorber usually mounted in the corners of a room. The best ones are designed for specific frequencies and are built into the space; but if you're hearing boominess, you may be able to get by with triangular foam ones costing about $60 each. If the room is a good size and you're not dealing with extreme bass, and you don't hear a problem, save the space and don't worry about trapping.

33

MONITORING

When choosing loudspeakers, many new filmmakers turn into misers. They buy the cheapest models they can get away with and figure on upgrading when their skills and budgets improve. It may make sense to buy an editing system this way, since computers keep getting faster and cheaper. But it's a bad idea for monitors.

Speaker designs don't change very quickly. Today's "improved" versions might benefit from new materials or slight tweaks in philosophy, but the differences are minor. Monitor systems that are a couple of decades old (ancient in computer years) are still in daily use at professional studios. So it makes sense to buy a little more quality than you think is appropriate now. With inflation, you'll pay more tomorrow for what you could have bought—and been using—today.

The speakers you choose have a profound effect on the quality of your soundtrack. They're the lens through which you judge everything else. No matter how good your ears are, they can't compensate for bad speakers. Unfortunately, a lot of the powered desktop speakers bundled with NLE systems are totally wrong for making mix decisions. These speakers are chosen by dealers as checklist items—a "complete package" has to have speakers, whether they're good or not—so size and wholesale cost may be more important to them than sound. Unless you're using the setup strictly for editing and will never equalize or mix on them, they're a waste of money.

Nearfield and Small Speakers

We've talked about how reflections from nearby walls can color what you hear from a monitor. Fortunately, the inverse square law can help. If you sit closer to a speaker than to reflecting surfaces, echoes will be comparatively softer. This kind of nearfield monitoring became popular about two decades ago and works when the speakers are three times closer than the nearest hard surface. The technique by itself doesn't guarantee good sound; it just means that a good speaker won't appear worse because of the room.

Today, the market is flooded with so-called nearfield speakers. The term refers to size: a speaker has to be pretty small to sit on an editing desk and be in that magic nearfield. Unfortunately, it's hard to build a very small speaker that sounds good. You have to move air molecules a lot for decent low-frequency performance, and that takes either a large cone or one that can handle extended movement. High frequencies require a specialized driver, which takes up more space.

One solution is to integrate small, individual components with an amplifier tuned to make up for their deficiencies; professional systems taking this approach can sound excellent. But good components and precisely calibrated electronics are expensive—the better nearfield systems typically cost a few thousand dollars, sometimes more than large speakers of equivalent quality.

Modestly priced small speakers, costing a few hundred dollars, are often full of compromises: cheap components and a *lot* of compensation in the electronics. This results in uneven response and plenty of distortion across the band. The speakers may boast an impressive frequency range, but none of those frequencies sound good.

The bottom line: accurate nearfield monitoring is expensive. It may be more cost-effective to treat the room so that bigger speakers can be used at a slightly greater distance. Or follow the Hollywood example: do your editing in whatever space is handy; but only do cuts, or the simplest fast crossfades, there. When it's time to tweak the sound quality and mix, walk into a properly tuned room.[5]

Be aware that where a nearfield sounds best in an average room is a fairly small area. Beyond that range, reflections start to color the sound. A producer, editor, and client might hear slightly different mixes, unless they're sitting in each others' laps.

 Gotcha

Real-world speakers aren't. Some people claim small, cheap speakers are better because they're like the ones in cheap TV sets. The reasoning is that these speakers will give a more accurate picture of what most people will hear. If a viewer does have better speakers than most people, things can only improve.

The fact is cheap speakers are bad in random ways. What improves sound on one can make it worse on another. What *is* consistent is that most cheap speakers miss an octave or more on both ends of the spectrum. This affects how you balance voice and music because music has more energy at those extremes. Their restricted range can hide serious problems with hum, boominess, and noise. And they usually add distortion across the band, making it impossible to tell when your electronics or mix technique are contributing their own distortion.

Make broadcast decisions on good speakers, so you know what's actually going to be on the track. Then feel free to check it on bad ones, to see if it's still intelligible under the worst conditions.

35

SUBWOOFERS

Another philosophy is to use small high-frequency speakers—sometimes only a few inches wide—and couple them with an extended bass speaker somewhere out of the way. The logic is that high frequencies are more directional than low ones (which is true), so you can still get an effective stereo image without large low-frequency drivers in each speaker. These systems are popular among computer gamers who surround themselves with the tiny speakers for

---

[5]There's more about this philosophy in Chapter 8.

an immersive experience. They're also sold for unobtrusive background music systems, because the small speakers are easy to hide.

Most of these systems are horrible for dialog. The thumping bass they provide can be nice for music and game environments but has nothing to do with what people will hear on TV or in a theater. Most of these systems sacrifice the lower mid-range to achieve small size at a reasonable price. Frequencies between 125 Hz and 500 Hz or so—where vowels live in dialog—are either missing or heavily distorted.

Having a speaker concentrate on just the lowest frequencies isn't necessarily a bad idea. Theatrical sound systems use subwoofers; they're the *1* in surround schemes like *5.1*.[6] But these systems also have full-size speakers for the main channels. The subs deal only with extreme bass effects, and the full normal range is carried by the mains.

CHOOSING A SPEAKER

If you want to hear what you're mixing or equalizing and can't afford a top-notch set of nearfields, you need full-size monitors. (You also need acoustic treatment, which is why we covered it first.) The best place to buy these speakers is often a broadcast, studio supplier, or high-end audio dealer. The worst may be an electronics chain or music store.

The problem is that consumer speakers are designed to be impressive with music. This often means unrealistically loud bass and very bright highs aimed at a relatively small area. They're great if you want to be entertained in a living room, but they're nowhere near accurate for dialog. Fortunately, there are ways to sort out the best speakers for production.

Read the specs. Some manufacturers brag about *frequency ranges*—alleged limits the system will reach. But frequency ranges are meaningless unless you know how much the volume can vary from one frequency to another. This variation is expressed in dB. If speaker A is rated simply as having "a 40 Hz–20 kHz range," and speaker B claims "60 Hz-18 kHz ± 4 dB," speaker B probably sounds better. The mere fact that the manufacturer took more care in expressing the specs also suggests they took more care in building the speaker. The best models include a graph showing precisely how the sensitivity varies across the band, along with distortion specifications. If the speaker has a built-in amplifier, make sure the spec applies to the whole system, not just the amp.

Check a speaker's weight. Better speakers usually are heavier. Magnets have to be bigger to generate stronger fields. Amplifiers need bigger transformers for more current. And the cases are made out of denser, more rigid materials.

---

[6]"Dot-one" isn't a marketing handle or version number. It's actually the decimal fraction "point one": the Nyquist Limit (see Chapter 1) says bass frequencies need a much lower sampling rate than the other channels, so they use only 1/10th the data.

Learn to trust your ears. Assemble a CD with some well-recorded but unprocessed dialog in various voices, some music typical of the kind you use in productions, and a few sections of good voice-music mixes from films you respect. If possible, spend a few dollars to listen to this CD in a well-equipped sound studio until you know what it really sounds like. Get very familiar with the ratio of voice to music in the premixed pieces.

Then go to a dealer who lets you audition by switching between different speakers while playing the same material. Start with two models near the top of the dealer's range, adjust them for about the same volume, and switch back and forth between them while listening to your CD. Knock the *better* speaker out of the running. (If they both sound the same, discard the more expensive one.) Pair the remaining model with the next model down in price. Keep comparing, working your way down in model and price until you notice that the CD doesn't sound like it did in the studio. Then go back up one notch: that's your speaker. If it's a little more expensive than you planned, remember that these things don't wear out or become obsolete. Think of it as an investment in your art. You'll be using it for years.

Gotcha

Louder sounds better. Most people have a hard time separating loudness from quality. A subtle boost in level gives one speaker a definite edge. Sneaky dealers sometimes do this intentionally, setting a slightly higher volume for the more profitable models. Make sure that volumes match before comparing quality. If a dealer won't let you adjust the volume, won't let you bring your own CD, or won't let you compare multiple brands in the same listening session, go somewhere else.

Hear for yourself

Track 6 is a frequency sweep to help you test individual speakers. Listen to it at a moderately loud level. The sine wave should sound smooth for the entire track. Watch out for a thickening at some frequencies or for a second note added an octave above the tone; this is a sign of distortion. Listen for rattles at any frequency; this indicates loose components, a sign of sloppy manufacturing.

Don't rely on this track to judge a speaker's frequency response, even if you're using a sound-level meter. Room acoustics will reinforce some frequencies and suppress others, making the measurement inaccurate.

Self-Powered or Separate Amplifier?

It may be more convenient to install speaker systems with a built-in amp; all you need to do is run an audio cable from your editing system, and plug the

37

speaker into the wall. Keeping the amp and speaker in the same box means you don't have to worry about heavy-gauge speaker cables, or matching the amp to the speaker. But before you choose a self-powered speaker, make sure you've considered these points:

- Some large systems use the same cheat as the cheap nearfields, by using an amp that sacrifices distortion for wide response. It may be a legitimate compromise in a consumer speaker intended for music, but the distortion it adds can hurt your perception of dialog. Make sure both voice and music are perfectly clear.
- USB or other digital speaker systems aren't anything special; they just have a circuit tacked inside that normally lives elsewhere. There's no reason for them to sound any different from a speaker with analog inputs, or be any better value for your money.

Make sure a separate amplifier is powerful enough. Professional rackmount or high-end hi-fi amps are usually conservatively rated. They can actually deliver the continuous power they promise. Look for one rated at least 50 watts per channel. (Be wary of "peak power" ratings on consumer amplifiers; these typically include a lot of distortion.) Power also requires heavy-gauge cable. Thin wires waste watts and limit the amplifier's ability to control speaker movement. For most installations, 16-gauge unshielded copper wire should be sufficient. It doesn't have to be anything special; ordinary wire from a hardware or chain electronics store will do the job.

Use cable where each wire is a different color or has other definite marking. The amp and speaker terminals will also be coded (one red and one black, or one + and one−). Make sure terminals and wires are matched the same way for all speakers; this is known as correct speaker *phasing*. Otherwise, one might be pushing molecules while the other is pulling on them. If you have any doubts, use Track 7 to check the installation.

 Hear for yourself

Track 7 helps you test phasing of stereo speakers. It has two short bursts of simultaneous low- and high-frequency narrowband noise on both channels, with voice announcements about the bursts' phase. Sit in a good position (see Figure 2.6) and listen to the entire track. If the bass seems louder in the first half, the speakers are properly wired. If it seems louder in the second half, swap the two conductors at one speaker only. Leave the other speaker and the amplifier alone.

Room Equalization

Just like self-powered speaker systems can have tailored amplifiers to make up for deficiencies in the speakers, you can add an equalizer ahead an amp to compensate for problems in the room. At least, that's the theory. When this technique is done subtly by a knowledgeable engineer with good test equipment, it can make a near-perfect room and great monitor system slightly better. But it's never a good idea to use equalization to fix a badly designed room or compensate for poor speakers: instead of fixing the problem, it just adds more distortion.

Speaker Placement

While the actual distances involved depends on your setup, most experts say you and the speakers should form an equilateral triangle (Figure 2.6). It's not supercritical, and a little variation shouldn't make much difference. But if accurate stereo monitoring is important, you should be centered between the speakers—no closer than 2/3 the distance between them, and no farther than 4/3 their distance. Get much closer, and sounds in the center won't be correct. Get much farther and you start to lose a sense of stereo. But how close or far you should be depends on the room. Good acoustics give you a lot more flexibility.

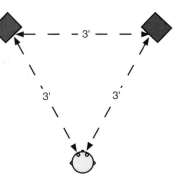

FIGURE 2.6
For best stereo, you and the speakers should form an equilateral triangle.

The high-frequency drivers (the smallest speaker element you can see) should be pointing towards you and at about ear level. There shouldn't be anything between the speakers and you—the back of a video monitor or tape deck can reflect high frequencies away. Ideally, there shouldn't be anything even *close* to the path between them and you. It could cause reflections that reinforce different frequencies unevenly.

Elevate small speakers to ear level. This usually means putting them on the same shelf as the picture monitors. If the speakers make the shelf rattle, it's more than annoying—it means you're losing sound energy at specific frequencies. A foam pad, under the speaker, may lower the annoyance by absorbing those frequencies before the shelf can. But it's far better to use a rigid shelf so it doesn't resonate.

 Gotcha

Magnetically shielded speakers aren't. Good loudspeakers have large magnets that can interfere with the sweep of conventional TV picture tubes when they get too close. If this happens, the result is an area of distorted colors on the part of the screen closest to the speaker. For this reason, many manufacturers make "shielded" speakers with reduced magnetic fields around them[7].

LCD and plasma video monitors aren't subject to magnetic interference, so this is rapidly becoming a non-issue.

---

[7]Actually, the magnets aren't shielded; that technique is too expensive. Instead, smaller magnets are strategically placed around the main one. They cancel the main magnet's field in directions where stray magnetism could cause problems.

Monitoring for Surround

If you're mixing surround productions, things get a bit more complicated. Ideally, all of the room's walls should be treated with exactly the same absorption materials. Then there's the question of where to put the speakers. The experts disagree.

The center channel, often used just for dialog in theatrical mixes, obviously should be centered in front of you. Ideally it's centered behind a screen that's transparent to sound, which is fairly easy in a theater with projectors. But that's impossible with LCD or plasma screens, so mount the speaker just above or below the screen—whichever will place it most level with the viewer's ears.

The ".1" speaker, usually called *LFE* (Low Frequency Effects) in theater systems and *subwoofer* in consumer ones, can be almost anywhere convenient: the ear can't tell what direction extreme lows are coming from. Try different locations; the results will depend on specific room acoustics. The best position is usually where walls intersect, in a corner of the room.

What happens next depends on a compromise between perfection and reality. The International Telecommunications Union (ITU) says the speakers should be at the angles in Figure 2.7, and all exactly the same distance from the listener. The Society of Motion Picture and Television Engineers (SMPTE) has a similar spec.

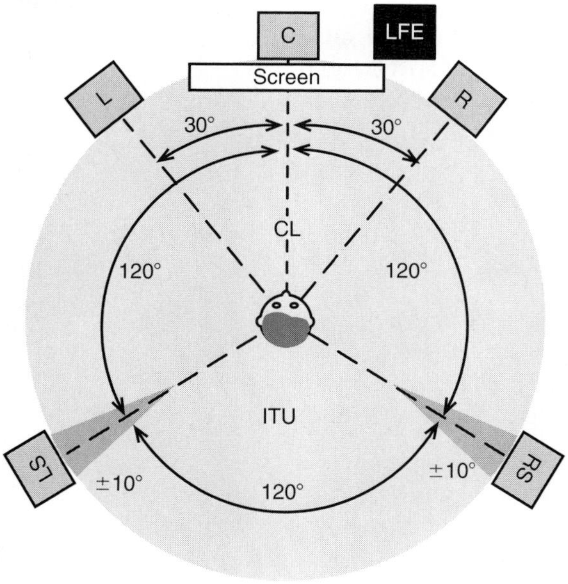

FIGURE 2.7
Standard ITU surround layout.

These specs are great as far as they go, but they don't go very far: their speaker placement will be ideal only for one viewer, in the exact center of the room, and the listening area has to be as wide as it is deep.[8] This obviously isn't practical in an audience situation.

Dolby's spec for home theaters or very small mix rooms has the front speakers in a straight line, as even with the screen as possible, as in Figure 2.8. (The room is symmetrical, so I drew only one side. The left side should be a mirror image, except without the subwoofer.) Since the front speakers are in a straight line, their relative distances to each viewer will depend on where each is sitting. This is a compromise—relative volume and timing from the Left and Right Mains will vary depending on position—but accommodates a larger audience. Since theatrical dialog is almost always mixed to the Center speaker, everybody will hear voices coming from the center of the screen. Music and large

---

[8]That doesn't necessarily imply a square room, which you already know is bad for sound. These specs assume a much bigger room, or one in which walls are treated with so much absorption that reflections aren't a problem.

sound effects will skew toward the side of the room you're sitting in, which might not be a bad thing.

A bigger compromise is in the shape of the layout. The Surround speakers should be directly to the side of, or just slightly behind, the viewers (Dolby allows a range of 90°–110°). And they can be closer than the Mains, to accommodate rectangular rooms. The volume level from those speakers can be lowered to partially compensate, but again, surround effects will skew depending on where you're sitting. THX's home theater layout is similar to Dolby's.

Home theater surround speakers are to your side, rather than behind you, because of how movies are mixed. The seating area in a movie theater is much bigger than that in a home theater or small mix room, and Dolby's theatrical spec (Figure 2.9) takes that into account. Left, Center, and Right are still spread across the screen, just as in a home theater. But instead of having a single speaker for each of the Surrounds, there are multiple speakers alongside and behind the audience, all fed with either the Left or Right Surround signal. Their sounds appear to come from large diffuse areas from the side, and only slightly behind you.

This diffusion of the surround signal affects the mixing philosophy. In an ITU room viewers can be inside the action, with dramatic activity or orchestral instruments taking place all around them. It's fun, but only for very small audiences in very large rooms.[9] In a theater, the action takes place in front. Only the biggest effects, and the reverb from the music recordings, surround you. This experience can't have as much impact for the select few in the center, but at least everybody in the room hears something that's appropriate. The large dub stages designed for film mixing have a similar layout, so the director can predict what an audience will hear. And since this is how films are being mixed, home theater speaker placement has been adjusted to match.

How about Headphones?

Headphones let you deal with bad acoustics by ignoring them; they create a private world for your ears. This can be helpful when editing because you hear things that might otherwise be missed. But they're not a good idea for the mix. They emphasize subtle details,

<hr />

[9]Or in an environment intended for music listening, where it doesn't matter that the acoustic image doesn't match a front visual image.

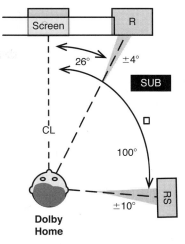

FIGURE 2.8
Dolby home theater surround layout. To save space, only one side of the room is shown.

41

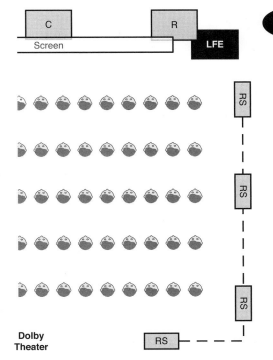

FIGURE 2.9
Dolby theatrical surround layout.

tempting you to mix music and sound effects too softly for the non-headphone wearing viewer.

Headphones are necessary to prevent feedback, of course, when you're recording narration or sound effects in the room. You have to monitor what you're getting, and using a speaker would interfere with the mic. Headphones come in three types:

- Closed-cup headphones surround the ear and create tiny, sealed air chambers. These can do a good job of blocking the outside world and are preferred for location recording. It's hard to create good bass in a small sealed area, so they seldom are very accurate in the low end. But they're great at revealing problems in voice recordings.
- Open, or vented, headphones have soft, porous foam pads that rest against the ear. Air molecules are free to flow around the pads, so the headphones can produce much more accurate sound. This also makes them fairly transparent to outside noises. Announcers generally prefer this type because a little of their natural voice can be heard from the room, along with their amplified voice from the mic. But if you're recording with them, make sure the earphone's sound isn't being picked up by the mic.
- In-ear monitors are molded to fit in the ear canal. They're unobtrusive, and can provide excellent isolation. But making them accurate requires careful engineering (and often, custom molding for the user's ear), so good ones are expensive.

Monitor Switching

Any good studio recording console has a mono test switch, which temporarily combines the stereo channels and routes them to both speakers. This is essential because phase problems can make parts of a mix sound hollow, or even disappear completely, for mono listeners. A few programs have a similar mono test feature in software. You can buy speaker controllers at music stores, starting around $100, to add this function to an NLE setup. (Or you can build your own for about $10. Instructions are at my Web site, dplay.com/gotcha.)

Surround systems used for mixing need more elaborate controllers, to allow various combinations of mono and stereo signals, solo individual channels for testing, and provide a smooth calibrated volume control for all the channels simultaneously. Many also include bass management functions, routing extreme lows to the LFE channel and providing a switchable LFE boost. The units, starting around $700 (and going *way* up), are available from high-end studio suppliers.

Metering

Good speakers will tell you a lot about spectral balance, noise, and distortion. But human beings aren't good judges of volume, and our perception of it changes from moment to moment. Metering is particularly important if you're producing for broadcast. TV stations are very strict about the volume they send to their transmitters. Networks even insist on specific volumes in their program contracts. Unfortunately, the design of a volume meter is affected by history.

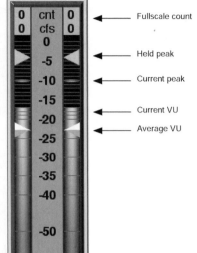

FIGURE 2.10
A good level meter combines peak and VU or average functions.

Fullscale count

Held peak

Current peak

Current VU

Average VU

Back in analog days, distortion was proportional to volume. Nominal levels didn't distort too badly. Overloads would distort more, but if they weren't too loud and were over quickly, the distortion wouldn't be noticeable. It takes a moment for us to judge volume, so fast loud sounds didn't seem too loud or distorted. *VU* (volume unit) meters were invented with both these facts in mind. They had mechanical provisions to limit how fast the needle could move: a proper VU meter would take 0.3 second to move from one side of the scale to the other. The scale was calibrated with 0 VU at the nominal level and then calibrated in decibels above and below zero.

But digital signals max out at 0 dBFS. If a signal reaches that level for even a single sample, the waveform may be distorted. If there are three or four samples above 0 dBFS (they're called *overs*) in a row, there's a good probability[10] it's unusable. The only way to deal with this is with a meter than can respond instantly. Good digital meters go from zero to full scale in a matter of microseconds and are described as *peak-reading* rather than VU. Peak-reading meters are designed to fall back more slowly, on the order of 1/10th of a second, so you can actually see the peaks. The best ones will leave the top light on for a few seconds (so you can read its level) while the rest of the column goes back to normal operation.

You need peak-reading to catch overloads and something like VU ballistics to judge perceived volume. Good audio level meters combine these functions and use multiple colors or brightness to show average, peak, and maximum levels simultaneously. Figure 2.10 shows the level meter in SpectraFoo, an audio analysis system for the Mac.

Unfortunately, NLE meters are seldom designed with this kind of sophistication, and you might not have the processing power to run a separate metering program while using mixing. A reasonable solution can be an external meter

---

[10]*May* be distorted? *Probability* there's a problem? By definition, a digital signal can't be even the teeniest slice of a decibel over 0 dBFS, so there's no way for the software to know when there's been an overload—it could be just a very loud, but undistorted, signal. However, real-world waveforms almost never have flat tops or bottoms that would keep the signal that loud for longer than a sample or two. So if there's a series of readings at 0 dBFS, we make the assumption something is wrong.

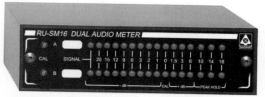

FIGURE 2.11
A relatively low cost but accurate external meter.

like the Radio Design Labs RU-SM16 (Figure 2.11). It's about $200 and can be switched between VU and peak mode. Hook it up to your computer or tape deck output and calibrate it using the manufacturer's instructions.

A more comprehensive solution, but still cheaper than devoting a separate computer to metering, is the simultaneous peak/ loudness/maximum Dorrough unit in Figure 2.12. The manufacturer developed their own algorithm for determining the relationship between loudness and time, similar to a VU meter's but more accurate. These Dorrough meters cost money (about $850 for the stereo model pictured), but are an investment that'll be usable for decades. You'll find them in good film and television mixing suites.

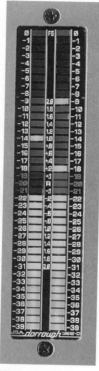

FIGURE 2.12
A comprehensive but more expensive external meter.

 Gotcha

Most VU meters aren't. Very few companies make mechanical meters with true VU ballistics any more, and they charge a lot for their product if they do. These precision instruments are usually found only on high-end studio equipment.

More often, the things that *look* like VU meters are cheap voltmeters with random time characteristics. This happens even in serious professional video gear costing thousands of dollars. These toy meters are too fast to indicate loudness but too slow to catch peaks that could overload a digital system.

CHAPTER 3

The Studio: Equipment and Wiring

REMEMBER THIS:

- There are specialized gadgets that can improve both your sound and your working life. Many of these gadgets don't appear in video catalogs.
- While audio comes in lots of different voltages and signal formats, they often use the same connector. Just because a plug fits, don't assume it'll work right. Consult this chapter whenever you're not sure.
- It's hardware. It will break. But hardware problems can often be fixed without a soldering iron or advanced engineering degree.

HARDWARE FOR AUDIO

Aside from the computer, a basic postproduction system doesn't need more than the accurate monitoring described in the last chapter. But some other gadgets can be helpful, even in simple setups, and may be essential as your work gets more sophisticated.

In Chapter 2, we discussed how monitor systems don't become obsolete the way computers do. Moore's Law—twice the capability at half the cost every 18 months—doesn't apply to a lot of audio hardware. Microphones frequently outlive the studios that originally bought them. Even relatively high-tech items like CD players and digital mixers don't depend on cutting-edge technology; they'll stay productive until their mechanical parts break down. The bottom line? This stuff is an investment. Choose accordingly.

 Gotcha

So what brand and model? This chapter describes hardware that can make your projects easier and sound better. I've tried to describe what's available and what features to ask for, with some guidelines about price. But a book like this can't predict what model will be best for you on the day you're ready to buy. Check the online forums and magazines for current information.

Audio Input/Output

You could probably create a complete movie without ever plugging an audio cable into your computer. Dialog can be imported with picture via FireWire, or copied as files from a double-system recorder; music and sound effects can be ripped from CDs or downloaded from the Web. But many filmmakers will need sound from sources that aren't computer friendly, like microphones or analog video decks. If you're mixing or making processing decisions, you also want a high-quality way to take sound *out*; otherwise, you can't trust your monitors. You could use your camera as an audio-to-FireWire device, but few cameras have good built-in sound. The analog audio that comes with most computers has noise problems because its circuits are too close to the CPU chip, and may also have distortion problems on loud signals because of limited power supplies. Track 8 of this book's CD will reveal some of these issues. (A few computers—including all current Macs—solve these problems with built-in digital audio connections.)

 Hear for yourself

Track 8 contains voice, music,[1] and test signals designed to reveal deficiencies in a system's audio output. Instructions in the track tell you what to listen for. Play it through your computer's CD-ROM drive (or use a ripped file version). It may help to also play it as a reference with a good CD player connected to the same monitors.

The traditional way to improve a computer's audio is to install a third-party sound card with driver software. Professional internal cards start around $300 at music and broadcast supply stores and can include features like XLR balanced audio, AES/EBU or s/pdif, and MIDI or SMPTE timecode support.[2] If you're editing on a laptop, you can get an analog I/O adapter in PC card format.

Unfortunately, internal interfaces for these cards keep changing; a card that works in one computer might not work in another, even from the same manufacturer. For this reason, and to avoid internal noise, the industry is moving away from cards. Instead, most manufacturers now offer small external boxes that connect via USB or FireWire, and offer excellent sound. Many have timecode or MIDI as well, and some include multiple audio channels and video or deck control interfaces.

---

[1]"Finding Your Way" (C. Glassfield, DWCD226/2), "Elizabethan Fantasy" (F. Silkstone/ N. Parker, DWCD128/38). From the DeWolfe Music Library, protected by copyright and used by permission. More about this library in Chapter 10.
[2]All these connection standards are described later in this chapter.

Gotcha

When good I/O goes bad. External audio I/O devices don't wear out, and their connection schemes are more or less universal. So you can keep using the same one when you upgrade computers.

Driver software, on the other hand, can become obsolete overnight. A CPU change or even an operating system upgrade may cause problems ranging from occasional static to complete failure. Audio hardware manufacturers try to keep on top of these issues. Check their Web sites any time you upgrade your system.

A few external I/O devices include remote mixing and editing controls for your software: physical (rather than virtual, on-screen) volume faders, jog/shuttle knobs, and transport buttons. These functions are discussed later in this chapter, in the section on Control Surfaces.

READING THE SPECS

There are serious differences in analog quality among the various audio I/O devices on the market. Check the specs, particularly for:

Frequency response. Look for three separate numbers: upper and lower frequency limits, and a volume range in dB. A spec like *20 Hz – 20 kHz ± 2 dB* is good for an audio I/O system running at 48 kHz s/r. Be sure the spec refers to the complete chain from analog to computer and back; it's useless if it just refers to one side or the other. Frequency response is dependent on sample rate; make sure you're reading it for the one you'll be using most.

Distortion. Again, the spec should include the complete chain. The analog side should be running at its rated nominal level. Distortion is usually expressed as a percentage (less than 0.01 percent is very good; as low as 0.003 percent is common in pro systems) and may be specified at a single frequency like 1 kHz.

Oversampling. This is a technique that increases high-frequency accuracy and lowers high-frequency distortion; you'll find it in the best cards.

Signal to noise ratio or dynamic range. The ratio of a system's self-noise over the loudest signal it can support is its *dynamic range*; the bigger this number, the better. A 16-bit digital signal is theoretically capable of 96 dB dynamic range.[3] This kind of calculation is easy in digital audio, because the loudest possible signal is always Full Scale, or 0 dBFS. Analog gear is trickier, since "loudest" depends on how much distortion you can tolerate. Instead, analog designers take the nominal signal level (usually 0 VU on the equipment's meters, also known as *tone level*) and measure

---

[3]6 dB range per bit (as you learned in Chapter 1), so 16 × 6 = 96. I told you it isn't rocket science…

how soft the noise is compared to it; this becomes the *signal to noise ratio* (s/n). In analog, it's acceptable to record momentary peaks that are louder than nominal. The ear forgives analog distortion in small doses. So these systems always leave a few dB extra above nominal level; these are known as *headroom*.

While analog distortion can be tolerable for short periods—things just get fuzzy—digital starts crackling as soon as signals reach Full Scale. So digital recordings are always made at a nominal level below Full Scale, leaving room for unexpected momentary peaks. Nominal recording level for miniDV is −12 dBFS. Those extra 12 dB of safety are the digital equivalent of headroom. Figure 3.1 shows how dynamic range, headroom, and s/n fit together.

In the figure, analog measurements are on the left, calibrated the way a traditional VU meter would be. Note how distortion—shown as darker grays at the top—comes in gradually as the level exceeds 0 VU. How much headroom an

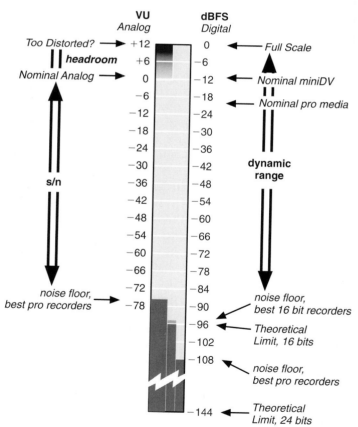

FIGURE 3.1

Analog and digital recording ranges. Note how 0 VU analog is equivalent to −12 dBFS digital in miniDV.

analog system allows depends on how much distortion you (or the manufacturers) think is tolerable.

Digital measurements are on the right. There's no distortion at the top, until you reach 0 dBFS. So the nominal recording level or digital tone level is set somewhat lower, and the area between nominal and 0 dBFS is the equivalent of headroom. Since the ratio of nominal to Full Scale is given, you can convert dynamic range to s/n by simply subtracting that headroom … but only in the digital domain.

Noise levels, at the bottom of the diagram, depend on both the equipment quality and (for digital) the number of bits. The best 16-bit recorders come very close to a theoretical maximum dynamic range of 96 dB. Twenty-four-bit recorders have a much higher theoretical range, 144 dB, but even the best are limited by analog components that convert the signal. They can achieve almost 108 dB—far better than any analog or 16-bit digital recorder—but that's the practical limit with today's technology.

 Gotcha

Dialog need not apply. In practice, the dynamic range discussion applies to steady tones only. Analog VU meters react to average levels spread over roughly 1/3 second—a standard invented by the phone company close to 60 years ago, and similar to how we hear loudness. Digital meters must react instantly, since even very fast peaks can cause digital crackling.

The ratio of peak to average depends on the sound. It's predictable only for absolutely steady signals, like lineup tones.

Bottom line #1: If you're calibrating recording levels in a system that has both analog and digital meters, use a tone instead of dialog or music.

Bottom line #2: If you want to judge average levels or subjective loudness in a digital system, use one of the averaging meters discussed at the end of Chapter 2.

49

DIGITAL I/O

In theory, there shouldn't be any difference between how two I/O systems handle a s/pdif or AES/EBU digital audio stream. That's usually true in the lab. The real challenge is how well the unit does with less-than-perfect digital signals in the real world. If your other equipment has problems—or even if you use the wrong kind of cable—the data can be compromised. Well-designed circuits can figure out the signal anyway and produce perfect audio. But some older or lower-cost systems can't; the result may be subtle damage to the stereo field, periodic clicking or high-frequency hash mixed with the signal, or total silence.

Unfortunately, you won't find any specs to compare digital I/O performance. The best you can do is judge from a piece's overall quality. If you do encounter some of the problems above, try a different cable… or routing the signal through some newer gear to condition it.

Mixer

Most DV filmmakers who do their own mixes, do it in software. But a low-cost hardware mixer can still be useful for preselecting sources, boosting mic signals to NLE levels, and adjusting digitizing volume.

You can even use it as a mixer! When you're auditioning music, put a CD player on one set of inputs and your NLE timeline or source footage on another. That way, you can hear how well the proposed music works with your video—without wasting the time to transfer or render anything.

Analog mixers with a couple of balanced mics and a few unbalanced line inputs are available at music stores, starting around $100. As the price goes up, expect more flexibility, cleaner sound, and varying degrees of field-worthiness, which might make the costlier mixers useful for production audio. Digital mixers start around $600. Many of the digital ones offer programmability—you can store libraries of configurations or equalization settings, saving setup time. Most have analog inputs and outputs as well, and some include USB or FireWire connections for your computer. Analog and digital mixers are rated with the same kind of specs as audio I/O cards, and the information in the previous section applies.

Control Surfaces

Many professional studios have hardware that looks like a mixer, with knobs and multiple sliders. It's actually a controller to work the on-screen mixers in audio software. Each knob on the hardware panel works like an individual mouse, dedicated to a particular function on the screen. The biggest advantage is you can use both hands—or all ten fingers—to manipulate multiple controls at the same time. This is important because many cross-fades require simultaneous adjustment of more than one track, while listening to the combination of them all. It's also a serious time-saver, not only because you don't need separate automation passes for complex transitions, but because no time is wasted moving a mouse around the screen looking for a particular function.

Figure 3.2 shows one of the simplest models, a Behringer BCF-2000, about $200. Each of the faders on the left controls a different track's volume in the on-screen mixer, each of the round knobs adjusts the track's panning, and the buttons on the top set the track's mute and solo status. The faders are also readouts: Tiny motors move each one up and down to reflect automation moves you've already written. When they're working, it's like watching ghost fingers fade one scene out while you fade the next one in. The faders are touch-sensitive: if you grab one in the middle of its motorized movement, you can take control and re-write the automation.

Since a production often has more than eight tracks, buttons on the right let you assign faders to different on-screen tracks. Good audio software lets you

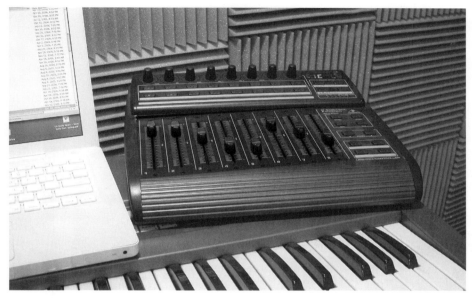

FIGURE 3.2
A small, low-cost way to control multiple track levels in an NLE or DAW.

preset groups of tracks for various functions (dialog premixes, music submixes, dialog/music/effects masters, and so on), and activate them at the touch of a button. Even if a track's fades aren't assigned to a physical fader on the controller, any automation you've written for that track still plays back properly. Many audio programs also let you assign the controls to other functions, such as equalizers or reverb, and record hands-on adjustments.

> ⚠️ **Gotcha**
>
> ***Play nicely together.*** Controllers and editing software are usually made by different companies, and not every combination will work together. Some NLEs won't work with any controllers at all, some support only specific functions, and some controllers work only with specific software. Check their Web sites before buying.

A few low-cost controllers have just one motorized fader, which can be assigned to individual tracks as desired. While they're faster and easier to use than mixing with a mouse, they require multiple passes for even the simplest transitions. These are useful tools in music production for adjusting a single instrument over the length of a song, but the multi-layer scene changes common in movies are virtually impossible with them.

Some controller configurations have dozens of faders, to be operated by more than one person at the same time, but nobody expects them to match the sixty

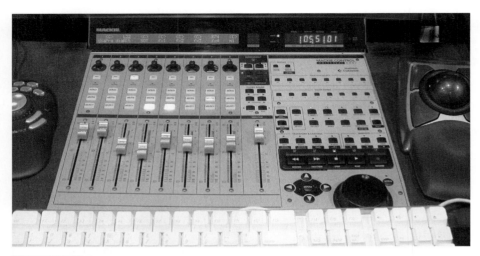

FIGURE 3.3
A full-featured controller (Mackie MCU-Pro) in my studio, with some other gadgets to speed up editing.

to a hundred tracks of a feature film. My personal preference is to use a small controller with eight or ten assignable faders, with LCDs above each to show which track they're manipulating at the moment. That leaves plenty of room nearby for additional transport and editing controls, like the ones in Figure 3.3. Besides, as one of my clients points out, I've only got ten fingers.

Many of the controllers available today connect via USB, so you can use a convenient hub to run them, your keyboard, and mouse or trackball at the same time. Some require MIDI (later in this chapter) but those are becoming less common outside the music studio, and a few use RS-232 or Ethernet. Some controllers also include multi-channel analog input and output, and connect via FireWire.

Selecting and Routing Signals

As you gather more equipment, keeping the right pieces connected can get complex. Reaching behind the gear and replugging every time you change functions is more than time-consuming; it can wear out the connectors. A mixer large enough to handle every signal combination can get expensive.

Patchbays

These panels, found in every recording and broadcast studio, simply extend the various equipment connections and keep them in one convenient place. Even low-cost ones (often around $50 at music stores) can have rugged ¼-inch jacks, which last longer and provide a better connection than the miniature or phono jacks on your equipment. Low-cost patchbays usually have jacks on

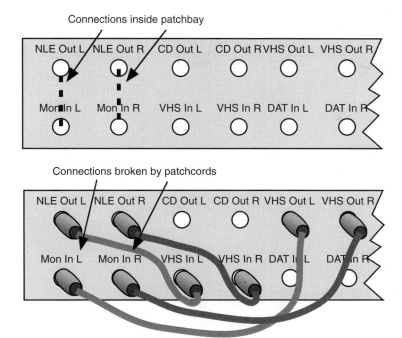

FIGURE 3.4
Internally normalled connections (*top*) disconnect when you use a patchcord (*bottom*). Often, all
the upper/lower pairs in a patchbay are internally normalled.

both front and back, so they can be installed easily with premade cables. Studio
versions may use solder or data-style punchblock connections on the back for
higher reliability. Short cords to connect the front jacks are usually only a few
dollars each; even less in multiple packs.

Most consumer patchbays *normal* their connections. When no cord is plugged
in, vertical pairs of jacks are connected internally. As soon as you plug in the
patchcord, this connection is broken. An example appears in Figure 3.4; the
NLE's output is on the top row and monitor amp's input right below it; normally, the editor's signal is directed to the speakers. If you need to make a VHS
copy, you can run a cord from NLE output to tape in—breaking the normal—
and another from tape output to monitor in.

Most patchbays include *half normals* that break the connection only when you
plug into one jack of the pair. The other jack taps the signal, sending it to both
the patchcord and the normalled device—highly useful if you're dubbing to
two analog decks simultaneously. Because modern equipment generally has
much higher impedance at the input than the output, the two devices don't
interfere with each other. You can also do the same thing with a Y-connector, or
in some cases, with a simple, molded dual-headphone adapter; engineers call
this function a *mult*. You'll get distortion or signal loss if you try to mult two
outputs to a single input, or mult older transformer-coupled audio devices.

Watch those half normals! If you plug a signal into a jack that doesn't break a connection, you could be inadvertently multing two outputs: the intended one, and the unbroken normalled one. Even if the unintentional device is silent, it'll still drag signal levels down or cause distortion. Plug a cord into the unused jack in that pair—you can let the cord's other end dangle—to break the normal.

 Gotcha

Normally howling. When you're setting up a normalled patchbay, don't put any device's input and output on the same vertical row. It may look neater that way, but the normals will cause feedback. Instead, offset them as in Figure 3.4.

DIGITAL ROUTER

Digital audio signals operate at very high frequencies and don't work reliably in a standard patchbay. They also require matched impedance, so standard multing is impossible. The usual solution to both problems is a digital audio router, which has internal buffers to feed any input to any combination of outputs. Routers start around $300 for six input and output channels.

AES/EBU and s/pdif digital audio puts both channels of a stereo signal on a single wire or fiber, so a 6 × 6 router actually handles 12 simultaneous audio streams switched in pairs. Music studios sometimes use ADAT optical, which puts 8 channels on a single optical fiber that can be switched as one, but these are rarely used in film or video.

GENERATORS

Digital audio is a serial signal with each bit transmitted sequentially. The boxes on each end have to agree which bit means what. Many devices today will delay an incoming signal until it matches their internal clock, but if things get too far out of sync, clicking can result. Most equipment lets you select the input as a clock source; this prevents clicking, but any time variation (*jitter*) in the incoming signal can cause distortion. A better solution, found in most professional audio setups, is to distribute a more reliable *word clock* signal on a separate wire. This is a constant heartbeat at the sample rate, or occasionally 256 times the sample rate (*superclock*). Word clock generators vary from a few hundred to a few thousand dollars, depending on their precision and ability to work with high-resolution audio formats. They can also be free—some devices have a word clock output along with their digital audio connections. Word clock is a 75Ω signal that can be carried on standard video cables, and—with a little tweaking—can even use video distribution amplifiers.

Most professional digital video decks need the audio sample rate to be synchronized with the frame rate. If a serial audio word doesn't start at exactly the right time relative to a video frame, the deck won't record. Good word clock generators have a video reference input for this reason. Connect it to the same blackburst or house sync as your video equipment, or to the sync reference output of the video deck.

A separate SMPTE timecode generator used to be an essential in audio post, but isn't any more. Most devices that read or sync to timecode can also generate it. But if you're going to be using a timecode generator to keep audio and video together, be sure it's also locked to a video reference signal. Otherwise the timecode words will drift relative to the frame rate, causing massive problems down the line. (This rules out using most MIDI equipment as a timecode source for digital video.)

 Gotcha

Digital audio syncs like analog video. If you've worked in an analog audio studio, you may be used to the idea of SMPTE timecode controlling the audio playback speed to keep it in sync with picture. Digital audio doesn't work that way; it needs a more stable reference. Instead, timecode is used to cue audio until it agrees with picture, and then the speed is controlled by a video reference or word clock. This is essentially the same way video editing decks are controlled in an online suite.

An audio tone generator also was once essential to create pure and steady signals for equipment testing and level calibration. These days, most desktop audio programs generate tones as files and then play them. Test tones on audio CDs are also useful as real-time test signals or can be ripped as audio test files; feel free to use this book's disc that way.

 Hear for yourself

Not really for your listening pleasure. Tracks 9 through 11 are steady tones, 30 seconds each, at −20 dBFS (network standard lineup level): 100 Hz, 1 kHz, 10 kHz. Track 12 is a 1 kHz tone at −12 dBFS, the standard level for miniDV formats.

Recorders and Players

Some filmmakers use DAT or MiniDisc in the field. But miniature consumer portables often have poor analog outputs, and you can lose quality just by dubbing from recorder to computer. If you're using this kind of recorder, consider investing in a full-size AC-powered deck only for playback, or sending your media to a properly equipped audio post house to be digitally converted to files.

Most of the newer field recorders store their sound as standard audio files which can be loaded directly into your editing system, either by copying over a

USB or FireWire port or by mounting their media on your desktop. Files transferred this way have no quality loss.

DAT, MiniDisc, file recorder, and CD speeds are usually locked to an internal crystal, which makes them stable enough to use for sync sound over the short term without timecode. Crystal quality varies, but it's reasonable to expect an accuracy of better than one frame in 15 minutes. High-end recorders let you lock their internal crystals to external video signals for perfect stability over performance-length takes.

Audio cassette and most open-reel tape decks are useless for sync sound because their speed isn't stable.

Timecode DAT and DTRS Digital 8 track (also known as DA-8) were the tape standard for film and video audio interchange until a few years ago, and are still found in most large studios. But tape is rapidly giving way to file exchanges on removable hard disk or DVD-ROM. If you need a tape deck with timecode, consider renting just for the project.

WIRING FOR AUDIO POST

The computer world has come a long way. Our first home computer used identical DB-9 connectors for mouse and printer, and you could find that same plug on a videogame's joystick, some modem cables, and VTR control interfaces. Nobody could tell just by looking at a plug what kind of circuit it would work with. Today you can take just about any FireWire- or USB-equipped peripheral—camera, disk drive, printer, mp3 player, multichannel audio, or anything else—plug it into a matching jack on a computer or hub and it'll probably work; if not, probably all you need is to download drivers from the manufacturer.

Audio is still in the dark ages. Physically identical connectors can be used for widely different kinds of signals. Even though two connectors might fit together, joining the wrong ones can result in damaged equipment, missing audio, and other problems that are mysteries to diagnose. You sometimes can't even tell, looking at a jack, which of several varieties of plug it's designed for. Occasionally, the only cure is to examine the equipment manuals.

Or check my Web site (dplay.com/gotcha). You'll find a guide to common audio connectors, with photos and how they're used.

Cross-Connecting Balanced and Unbalanced Audio

Balanced wiring won't do any good unless the equipment at both ends is designed for it. If either end is unbalanced, the noise resistance goes away. If most of your equipment is already balanced, or your facility is very complicated or includes long cable runs, it makes sense to consider everything balanced and adapt the non-balanced devices. This will keep the sound as clean as possible, preventing line-borne noise and ground loops. The most common

Table 3.1	Feeding an unbalanced output to a balanced input		
Unbalanced Output	**Balanced Input**		
	Wire	**XLR Plug**	**3-conductor Phone**
Signal (pin or tip)	+ (red or white)	pin 2	Tip
Ground (sleeve)	− (black or clear)	pin 3	Ring*
No connection	shield	pin 1	Sleeve

Most balanced phone jack inputs are designed so this connection happens automatically with unbalanced 2-conductor plugs.

Table 3.2	Feeding a balanced output to an unbalanced input		
Balanced Output			**Unbalanced Input**
Wire	**XLR Jack**	**3-conductor Phone**	
+ (red or white)	pin 2	tip	Signal (pin or tip)
− (black or clear)	pin 3	ring	No connection*
shield	pin 1	sleeve	Ground (sleeve)

This is appropriate for modern, electronically balanced outputs. Transformer-balanced outputs might not show any signal unless its conductor is connected to ground.

57

solution to balancing non-balanced equipment is an electronic adapter; these also compensate for the voltage difference between consumer unbalanced and professional balanced gear (described in the next section). Ask for something called a *balancing, impedance,* or *level matching* adapter—it goes by all three names.[4] Good ones cost $50 to $150 per channel, depending on features or whether they have screw terminals for permanent installations or jacks for portable ones. More expensive units aren't necessary.

But if your studio is small and not too complicated, without too much cabling, you can often mix balanced and unbalanced devices just by wiring them correctly. These direct connections don't compensate for level differences (that's in the next section). And of course they unbalance the entire cable, so you'll have to be careful routing audio wires around power or video cables. Tables 3.1 and 3.2 explain the wiring.

In Table 3.1, ground on the balanced input is not connected to ground on the unbalanced output. Most adapters are factory wired with a connection here, which also works. However, leaving it disconnected can provide a telescoping shield with a bit more noise immunity; see Guerrilla Problem Solving on page 62.

---

[4]Even though impedance usually has nothing to do with it, as you'll learn in a few pages.

> **Gotcha**
>
> ***The case of the occasionally disappearing signal.*** A weird situation can come about when a balanced mono signal is sent to a stereo unbalanced input. If the adapter is not wired properly, both sides of the stereo pair will hear the signal perfectly—except one side will be inverted. It'll have a negative voltage when the other side is positive. Casual monitoring over stereo speakers might not even show a problem. But if the result is played in mono, the signal cancels itself and disappears!
>
> The usual culprit is a premade adapter or cable with a three-conductor phone or mini-plug on one end, and either a similar plug or two RCA plugs on the other. Don't assume that just because an adapter ***fits***, it's doing the right thing to your signal. And always check stereo mixes in mono (see Chapter 2).

Voltage and Impedance Standards

LINE-LEVEL VOLTAGES

Much of what we have to deal with today dates from telephones and early network radio. Standards get set, devices get built to them, and then the next generation has to conform. Even when the standard doesn't make sense any more, it's still How Things Are Done. That's why there are two different analog line level standards: $-10\,$dBV (used in prosumer equipment) and $+4\,$dBu (for pro gear). The former, reasonably enough, stands for *Decibels referred to a Volt*. The latter means *Decibels referred to the voltage generated by a milliwatt over 600 ohms impedance, even though we're not paying attention to impedance...* which is why we use the initials instead. Prosumer equipment generates about a quarter the audio voltage that pro inputs are looking for.[5] That's why you often can't connect them directly.

Even though the measurements are different, both standards use the same physics and math, and there's a definite relationship. I crunched the numbers for you in Table 3.3. That table also shows a couple of other handy rules—cutting any voltage in half changes it by $-6\,$dB, doubling it is $+6\,$dB, and changing it by 10 dB means a voltage ratio of about 3:1.

CROSS-CONNECTING CONSUMER AND PRO LINE-LEVEL

Along with the differences in voltage, pro line-level connections are almost always balanced, and consumer ones are unbalanced. So the easiest way to deal with both incompatibilities at the same time is to use a level-matching adapter, described previously. But if you don't really need balanced wiring, you may be able to save some money.

---

[5]The story behind these standards is interesting. So is why "one-quarter the voltage" is a 14 dB difference here, when the first chapter says that should be a *12 dB* difference. You'll find both at *dplay.com/gotcha*.

Table 3.3	Comparing prosumer dBV and professional dBu			
	Prosumer or Consumer	Voltmeter	Professional	
	+6 dBV	2.0 v	+8.2 dBu*	
	+4 dBV	1.6 v	6.2 dBu	
	+1.78 dBV	1.228 v	+4 dBu	(Pro 0 VU)
	0 dBV	1 v	+2.2 dBu	
	−2.2 dBV	.775 v	0 dBu	
	−6 dBV	.5 v	−3.8 dBu	
(Consumer 0 VU)	−10 dBV	.316 v	−7.8 dBu	
	−20 dBV	.1 v	−17.8 dBu	

*Or dBm at 600Ω.

Professional inputs might have enough range to handle a −10 dBV signal without too much noise. Connect them according to Table 3.1, turn up the input volume, and see if you can get a decent meter reading. Resist the temptation to turn up the unbalanced output to compensate. This will almost always cause distortion. If you don't get appropriate levels by adjusting only the pro gear's input, use a level-matching adapter.

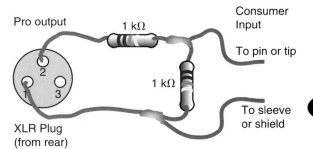

FIGURE 3.5
A couple of resistors can convert +4 dBu balanced to an almost perfect −10 dBV unbalanced.

Plugging unbalanced pro outputs into prosumer inputs is a little trickier. You need to lose some signal, and trying to do it with the equipment's volume controls almost always adds noise or distortion. You can buy attenuators for about $10 each, or might find them already built into balancing adapters you're using for other signals in the studio. Or save by building your own from a pair of 20¢ resistors: Follow Figure 3.5, which should work for most modern equipment. (If the pro gear has an output transformer and you don't hear anything, add a jumper from XLR pin 3 to pin 1 and change the top resistor to 3.3 kΩ.)

Timecode Wiring

SMPTE timecode (named for the Society of Motion Picture and Television Engineers, who devised the standard) is a digital signal to identify each frame. But in most applications it's put on an analog carrier—just like a fax machine signal—and carried on standard audio wiring (or recorded on an analog VTR's address track). This format is called longitudinal timecode[6] or LTC. Even digital

[6]Named this way because the track is parallel to the tape edge, instead of slanted like an analog video track.

59

pro VTRs convert their timecode data to LTC at the jacks. Since it's a squarewave rich in harmonics, SMPTE code loves to leak into unbalanced audio wiring. Keep its cables far away from others.

SMPTE timecode appears on just about any kind of audio connector or video-style BNC, at the whim of the manufacturer. It's usually unbalanced. There is no standard voltage for it. Devices made specifically for timecode, such as window generators, generally output around 1 v and can read anything from about 10 millivolts to 10 volts. Devices that have a different primary purpose, such as recorders, often keep timecode at the same level as its other audio: either −10 dBV or +4 dBu. Almost all modern timecode devices look at the digital component of the signal rather than its voltage, so it's very forgiving of mismatches. But if you're feeding +4 dBu timecode to a prosumer audio track, the extra level could cause leakage. Solve this problem with the pad in Figure 3.5.

Other versions of timecode don't travel on audio cables. *Vertical interval timecode* or *VITC* is superimposed on the video itself. Many DV cameras put timecode data on FireWire along with the picture. MIDI timecode runs on dedicated MIDI cables and doesn't follow the SMPTE format. SDI (Serial Digital Interface) video can have timecode, along with digital audio, embedded with the picture data. So-called RS-422 code isn't timecode at all but a bidirectional series of *where-are-you* queries and answers between an edit controller and video deck.

Digital Wiring Standards

In a world that cares only about ones and zeros, it's not necessary to worry about noise pickup or absolute voltage levels. But there's another concern: digital audio uses very high frequencies that act more like radio waves than like standard audio. If impedances aren't precisely matched, these signals can keep bouncing between input and output, making data echoes that can destroy the signal.

Fortunately, there are only two common electrical standards for digital audio. They use different connectors, so manufacturers can build the right impedance into the equipment based on which connector is used. To avoid problems, you have to use the right wire as well. Also, you can't mult or split a digital audio signal; that changes the impedance. Instead, use a distribution amplifier or transformer.

AES/EBU DIGITAL AUDIO

The AES/EBU standard[7] is found on virtually all pro digital equipment. It uses 5-volt squarewaves and 110Ω impedance, is balanced for noise immunity, and almost always has 3-pin XLR connectors wired the same way as analog audio ones. Standard XLR audio cables may work for AES/EBU digital, but only for

---

[7]The initials stand for Audio Engineering Society and European Broadcast Union, who set the standard. It's also known as AES3.

short cable lengths. Most wire manufacturers make a 110Ω balanced version specifically for digital audio. It's only a bit more expensive than standard analog cables, so use it any time reliability is important.

Some facilities save money by using RG-59 75Ω video wire for AES/EBU. This is cost-effective for long runs, but needs a $40 transformer at each end—available from pro audio suppliers—to unbalance the signal and convert the impedance. Word clock connections usually appear on BNC connectors at the equipment, for RG-59 wire.

S/PDIF DIGITAL AUDIO

The s/pdif standard[8] is found mostly on consumer and prosumer gear. It uses $\frac{1}{2}$-volt squarewaves and 75Ω impedance, usually on phono connectors. This happens to be very similar to consumer video, and video cables from a chain electronics store are perfectly acceptable for s/pdif. If you're making your own, use RG-59 video wire.

TOSLINK AND MINI-PLUG OPTICAL

Digital audio can use fiber optics instead of wire. Toslink optical connectors (Figure 3.6), developed by Toshiba, are frequently found on consumer

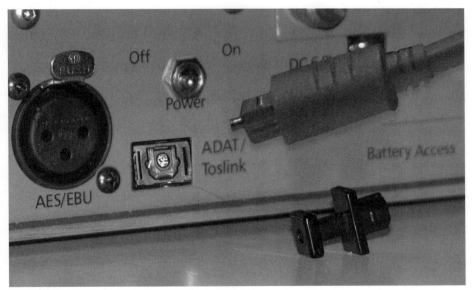

FIGURE 3.6
Toslink plug and jack, with the blocking plug that protected that jack from dirt.

---

[8]Sony/Philips digital interface format is always abbreviated lowercase (s/pdif). Also known as IEC958 or IEC60958 when an equipment manufacturer doesn't want to promote Sony's or Philips' name.

equipment; they're stable and latch in place, and if kept clean are reliable. The fiber optic cables provide isolation so ground loops can't form; however, length is limited to about 30 feet, even with high-quality fibers. Toslink jacks usually ship with a snap-out blocking plug to keep them clean.

Toslink just substitutes bursts of light for standard s/pdif signals, so converting between the two formats is electrically very simple. Powered adapters start around $30, and let you extend the optical signals over almost unlimited lengths of RG-59 video cable. Toslink connectors are also used by Alesis ADAT recorders to carry eight simultaneous audio signals in digital format. These can also be converted for standard copper wiring, but the converters are much more expensive.

Some equipment uses combination optical/electrical mini-jacks. They work just like standard analog ones for normal consumer analog signals. If you insert a Toslink/mini adapter (about $2 at audio suppliers), the circuits use the optical signal instead. However, the springs on a mini-jack aren't very secure and there's nothing to keep dirt from getting into an empty jack, so these connections are often unreliable.

 Gotcha

AES/EBU as consumer? s/pdif as pro? We've discussed standards for the **electrical** connection between devices because at digital audio frequencies, wiring can get tricky. But AES has also specified two **data** standards: consumer and professional.

In general, the differences between the data formats are minor. Most have to do with things like copy protection (ignored in pro equipment) or pre-emphasis (obsolete). One specifies the number of bits in the audio sample—pro can handle 24 bits, consumer only 16 bits—but other than bit depth, there's no difference in audio quality. A 16-bit signal will sound exactly the same in both data formats, and the formats are so similar that for many purposes most equipment will accept either one.

GUERRILLA PROBLEM SOLVING

Generally, audio wiring problems show up with three kinds of symptoms: hum, other noises, and intermittent audio. Once it's there, none of these can be eliminated from a track without affecting dialog.

Hum

The dreaded 60-cycle hum is inaccurately named. It's actually more of a buzz with harmonics much higher than 60 Hz. They extend through voice and music frequencies and are almost impossible to remove. It's most common in unbalanced setups where shield and equipment grounds are shared with the signal. Tiny audio currents loop around these multiple paths, acting like antennas picking up noise … particularly the low-frequency noise radiated by the high currents in standard electrical wiring. Even worse, the three-prong AC plugs on most gear tie these *ground loops* to hundreds of more feet of wire inside the walls.

So the first step in cleaning up hum is to unplug every non-audio cable. That includes the video cables in your audio/video editor, data cables on CD-ROM drives that also have audio connections, and even shielded RS-422 control cables on a video deck. (Before you start unplugging, make sure the wires are labeled with their corresponding jacks.) Go all the way back to your monitor amplifier. Then reconnect the wires one at a time, starting at the monitor amplifier and working down the signal chain from output to input. Listen for hum after each connection. When you hear it, you'll know which cable is causing the loop and you can apply some of the following cures.

 Gotcha

Ground loops without wires. Sometimes loops form because two grounded equipment chassis are making electrical contact. This can be hard to diagnose if the equipment is mounted in a rack, where the metal screws and rack rails complete the circuit. But if nothing else seems to be the culprit, suspect this.

It's easy to cure. Large audio dealers can sell you low-cost kits of fiber tabs or insulated shoulder washers and nylon screws. These isolate the gear while still providing support.

63

Two of the most common hum culprits are cable TV feeds and grounded power cords. If a VCR or monitor/receiver is connected to both cable TV and your audio system, you can get giant ground loops, even when the video equipment is turned off. It's easy to diagnose; just unscrew the cable TV and listen. To diagnose power-cord ground problems, use a three- to two-prong molded AC adapter from a hardware store. Don't connect its metal grounding foot to anything. But use this only as a temporary diagnostic! It defeats an important safety feature, and makes any line noise filtering less effective. There are better solutions.

Once you've located the offending connection, you have to break its loop. You can often do this by disconnecting one of the grounds in an audio, video, or control cable. Turn your monitor down before trying this with audio cables— while breaking the ground may fix the hum, it might also raise it to speaker-rattling levels. If an audio cable uses RCA connectors, just pull the plug partway out so the center pin connects but the outer shield doesn't. If the cable has phone plugs, use clip leads or plug a short phone-to-phone patch cord into the jack and

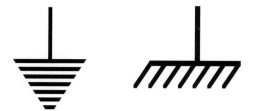

FIGURE 3.7
An icon like this indicates a grounding screw on equipment.

touch the tip of its other end to the cable being tested. If this eliminates the hum, rig up a more permanent way to disconnect the ground and you're done.

You may also be able to reduce ground loop noise by providing a better, lower-resistance audio ground. Run a heavy cable—such as 14-gauge speaker cable or automotive primary wire—from a grounding point on each device to one central point in your studio (often a mixer or computer audio input). For just this purpose, most audio equipment has a screw on the back marked with one of the icons in Figure 3.7. If you don't see a ground screw, connect your ground wire to the exposed metal shell of an input plug. However, this "better ground" strategy often isn't as effective as actually breaking the ground loop.

Of course, some grounds can't be cut. Power line third-pin grounds are there for safety reasons. Cable TV systems won't function without their ground. In these cases, you'll need a transformer to pass the signal while not letting the grounds through: in effect, this balances a tiny part of the unbalanced wiring. If the loop is on a TV cable, the cure is trivial: get a pair of 75Ω/300Ω antenna transformers and wire the 300Ω sides back-to-back. If the loop is because of a power-line ground, you can get AC-power isolation transformers at electronics suppliers. They're used for servicing TV sets safely, and start around $75 for a unit capable of 300 watts. Bigger ones—including systems capable of providing balanced AC power to an entire studio—are also available.

Ground loops in audio cables can be broken the same way. Electronic dealers sell small isolation transformers with RCA jacks, designed for car stereo systems, for less than $20. They're not really hi-fi, but it's surprisingly good for the price. Or get higher-quality transformers from a pro audio dealer for about $35 per channel. Ground loops can also affect analog video, usually appearing as a darkened horizontal band that slowly crawls up the screen. If that video cable is also forming an audio ground loop, fix both problems at the same time with a video hum-stopping transformer—about $150 at pro video houses.

The ultimate solution is to use balanced wiring exclusively. When done right, ground loops can't form.

Random Noise

You might also encounter some mystery hummers that sound like loops but aren't. The audio heads in an analog video or audio deck can pick up hum, particularly if there's a big power transformer nearby. All dynamic and some condenser mics have tiny transformers that can pick up hum from other equipment (or even the power wiring in walls). Moving things a few inches—or turning them 90 degrees—usually helps. Defective or badly designed AC supplies in AC/battery equipment can also cause hum: run the equipment on batteries until things get fixed.

Audio heads and transformers may also pick up high-frequency noise from CRT video monitors. Turn off the monitor if you think this is the culprit. The only long-term cure is to move things around, or use an LCD display.

Sporadic high-frequency noise can leak from building wiring into audio cables, particularly microphone and unbalanced line-level ones. The problem frequently has to be cured at the source, so it may need some detective work and might require an electrician to fix. Large electric motors in elevators and oil burners have tiny sparks that can radiate through the building power. Wall-mounted light dimmers work by slicing up low-frequency electric power and create nasty harmonics throughout the audio band. This radiation is the worst when the lights are only partially on. The easiest cure, if dimmers in an edit suite are causing problems, is to replace all the bulbs with lower-wattage ones and stop dimming. Or look for low-noise dimmers at large electric supply houses.

Sudden Death

Your room has been working perfectly. Then you start hearing clicking, bursts of static, or nothing at all. First do a little deductive reasoning:

- Have you changed anything? New software might require new drivers for your hardware. If you used borrowed equipment on the last job or patched in a client's camera, have you returned everything to its normal condition?
- Can you isolate it to one piece of equipment? Are some meters bouncing even though you don't hear anything from the speakers? Work backwards from your monitors or forwards using headphones. If you've got a patchbay, it's a great diagnostic tool; patch around suspect equipment until you determine which is causing the problem.
- Can you isolate it to one place in the project? If a certain part of your mix always has static, it's probably an overload or bad media. Lower the levels or insert a replacement.
- Did it fail overnight? Something that worked last night but not this morning probably died on power-up. It could be as simple as a user-replaceable fuse—but if a replacement fuse immediately fails, call for service. Some equipment hides user-replaceable fuses in odd places (on a circuit board, or hidden in a battery compartment) so check the manual.
- Are any tiny buttons in the wrong position? Pressing the wrong solo on a mixer can turn off the output. Selecting the wrong reference in a piece of digital audio gear can create clicking mixed with the sound.

One of the most common failure points in prosumer equipment is the input and output connection. Mini-jack springs stop making contact, and the inner sleeves in phono jacks start to let go. If you suspect this is the problem, try wiggling the plug in its jack and listen for anything. A bad jack will frequently respond to manhandling, if only for a moment. If this seems to work, you can often temporarily fix things by flexing the cable in different directions until you find a position that produces sound. Then tape or tie the cable to keep it there. Ultimately, you'll have to replace the jack.

Modular power supplies—wall warts and line lumps—are popular with a lot of equipment, because they can be mass produced. But they're often sealed, and an internal fuse or rectifier can burn out. If you suspect that's the problem, unplug the supply from the equipment and check its output with a voltmeter. It should be at or somewhat higher than the rated voltage. Otherwise, contact the manufacturer or take a trip to your local electronics store for a replacement.

One of the best pieces of problem-solving advice I ever heard was, "Walk the dog." Get away from the problem, ideally out of the room, for a few minutes. A fresh outlook always helps.

Some problems might be beyond your ability to diagnose or fix. But before you call a tech, write down everything you know about the problem: when it developed, what the symptom is, any unusual meter or panel readings, and what you've done so far to fix it. Gathering that information first can save hours of repair time.

CHAPTER 4

The Studio: Audio Software

REMEMBER THIS:

- NLEs are powerful software. But they're not the best places to edit or mix a track. A few audio-centric programs can make your project sound better.
- Moving sync elements from one program to another—even on separate computers—should be painless. Just follow some simple rules.

Nonlinear editing is nothing new. Hollywood was doing it almost a century ago, long before computers existed. When you're cutting film, you can add or delete shots in whatever order you prefer. The rest of the movie will ripple[1] automatically. Random-access editing is just as old: when you're working on a film scene, you first hang all the selected shots in a trim bin, a large cloth-lined barrel with tiny hooks suspended across the top. Then you grab whichever ones seem appropriate, try them in different orders, and generally juggle until you're happy.

Audio editing used to be done the same way. Because I came from a film background, my first tape editing studio (Figure 4.1) had a "trim bin" of its own. Since audio tape doesn't have sprocket holes to hang individual clips from, I used plastic clothespins instead. The editing itself was as nonlinear and random-access as today.

Today's NLEs have adopted some of the older film concepts. Many organize selected clips in "bins," even though any other software would call them folders. Your timeline shows strips of still frames—it sure looks like film—which you "physically cut" with a razor tool. But in many programs we've lost one of analog tape's most valuable features for editing sound: automatic cross-fades.

---

[1]Editor-speak for having later scenes automatically move to accommodate the earlier ones. It's an issue when cutting videotape, but you might not even have to deal with it in an NLE.

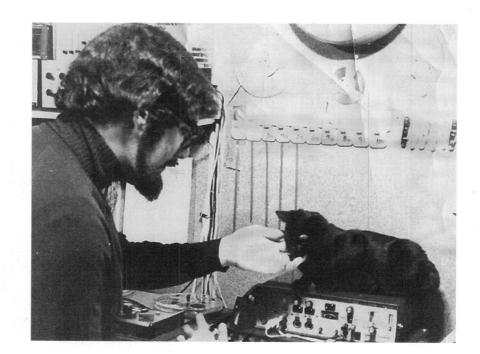

FIGURE 4.1
"Confurring" with a studio friend, circa 1970. Note the tape trims—individual phrases—hanging from plastic clips behind the cat.

68

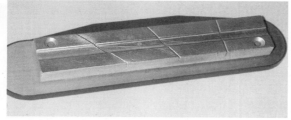

FIGURE 4.2
A well-worn audio splicing block. Tape fit in the long groove down the middle. The various angles were for different length cross-fades.

SPLICES WERE CROSS-FADES

Audio used to be cut in a splicing block, like the one in Figure 4.2. You'd lay two strips of magnetic tape in the long shallow channel, with the tapes' edit points lined up at the deep diagonal groove. Then you'd pull a razor blade through the diagonal groove, cutting both strips identically. You'd discard the scrap, and join the remaining pieces with sticky tape. I made this series of movements a few thousand times a week for decades.

The angle of the groove is no accident. It slows down the transition from one sound to the next. When you join two waveforms, there's a good chance the voltage won't match at the cut point—creating a jump, like the one in the middle in Figure 4.3. A vertical rise like that has infinite harmonics, which creates a click. You can avoid the click with a quick cross-fade. The middle of the edit then becomes an average of the two waves.[2]

If you looked at analog audio tape in a magnetic viewer—a device we used for analyzing recording problems—it looked a lot like the drawings in Figure 4.4.

---

[2]You can also avoid the click by cutting only where the waves match. Since every wave goes through zero, some programs automatically snap their edit marks to the closest zero crossing.

The vertical stripes along the tape were areas of high and low magnetic force, representing voltage changes in the original waveform. The tape was pulled across a coil, where it created a varying voltage which was amplified and sent to a speaker.

Each of the tapes in the drawing starts with a low frequency on the right, followed by a higher one on the left (remember, the tape is moving toward the right). Notice how the splice between tones on each tape is at an angle. As the splice passes a magnetic gap in the head, it picks up just the low tone at first. Then it's gradually replaced by more of the high tone as more of that tape covers the gap. In other words, we hear an audio dissolve.

It's a *fast* dissolve. The 45° created a 16 ms cross-fade at the usual tape speed,[3] about half a frame in film or video terms: short enough to sound like a cut while avoiding a click. This angle was the most used, and you can see that the 45° groove in Figure 4.2 is the most worn. Professional blocks like the ones in the picture frequently had other angles as well, for different transitions or tape speeds. If you look carefully at Figure 4.2, you'll notice some very long scratches: the 1.5-inch ones were equivalent to 3-frame dissolves.

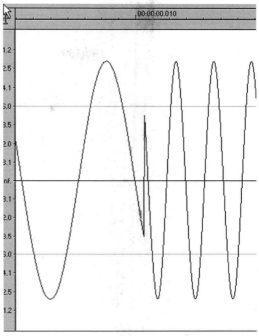

FIGURE 4.3
A jump in a wave because of an edit.

69

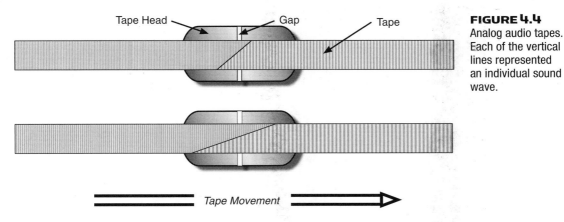

FIGURE 4.4
Analog audio tapes. Each of the vertical lines represented an individual sound wave.

---

[3]How fast the tape is moving, of course, affects how long the dissolve takes to cross the tape head; this figure is for 15 inches per second. That timing also assumes a mono track 1/4″ wide, which is what we used whenever possible.

Gotcha

Clicking with your NLE. Almost every NLE does a hard cut when you join two clips in the timeline. If you want to edit where there's no silence—such as in an interview or piece of music—there's a chance of a click. On most setups with limited monitoring, you might not even notice the click until that piece is mixed.

Some NLEs let you apply a 1-frame dissolve at the cut point; a workaround for other NLEs is to put the clips on separate tracks with a 1-frame overlap, and draw fades on each. Both techniques will fix the click… but might also harm the edit (see the next "Gotcha").

 Gotcha

A single frame can be too long. One of the biggest barriers to sophisticated audio editing in almost every NLE is their insistence that edits snap to the frame line. One frame is a very long time for sound. Critical consonants like /t/ or /d/ may be only a third that length. In fast-paced music, a frame can be almost 1/32 note: enough to make an edit sound wrong.

Film sound *used* to be more flexible: you could cut 35-mm mag sound on any one of the four sets of sprocket holes per frame. Computers have taken this capability away from film editors.

The software used for audio post doesn't have this restriction. You can cut on framelines, trim to precise fractions of a frame, or make your cuts on individual samples.

AUDIO SOFTWARE

Nonlinear Video Editors

Today's NLEs come with basic audio capability. Almost all are suitable for track layouts and simple mixes. Trying anything more complex can range from being a time-waster to a disaster. Even if a program has a pretty on-screen mixer, the audio filters[4] supplied with most NLEs are often clumsy, lack important controls, or don't let you tune them while listening. You can get third-party plug-ins for some editors, though even the best can suffer in an NLE environment because of limited bit depth or short preview memory. Audio programs also have more capable mixers (with surround, subgroups for dialog or music stems, flexible ways to add special effects like reverb), and many more built-in processors. Most important: they make audio editing faster and more precise.

Audio-Centric Programs

Just about every audio program today has some picture capability. Simpler programs will put a QuickTime or AVI window on the computer screen; more

---

[4]In the audio realm, a *filter* is a specific kind of equalizer, as you'll learn in Chapter 11. To an audio operator, calling a compressor (Chapter 12) or reverb (Chapter 13) a "filter" is just silly.

elaborate ones can feed a large external monitor or have elaborate timecode and serial video deck control systems. But picture isn't the focus. In these sound-and-picture programs, audio is definitely the main event. You can expect to find:

- Smooth audio scrolling and marking down to a single sample (1/1600 frame). You're never forced to pay attention to this kind of resolution, but it makes precise editing and dialog cleanup possible when needed.
- 24-bit signal flows with as much as 56-bit processing, for cleaner finished mixes. While some NLEs brag of 24-bit audio file capability, it's seriously limited for anything more complex than a simple cut.
- File flexibility, supporting all audio formats. Narrative film projects are recording more tracks in the field, to keep separate mics isolated for post. Eight-track shoulder-mounted portables are common, as is recording multiple channels on a laptop. But many NLEs can't sort out multi-track audio or handle it conveniently.
- High-quality algorithms for things like time compression and sample rate conversion.
- Tighter integration with more processing plug-ins than you'll find in a NLE. Most plug-ins are tunable while you listen to long previews or jump around the timeline. Many are real-time and don't require rendering. A few audio programs can use add-on processing chips (either in the computer, or connected by FireWire) for even more power—something that can be essential when mixing the dozens of tracks in a modern film.
- Click-free editing with automatic fades and dissolves that are user-tunable, or automatic tweaking to find zero-crossings.

ABOUT SCRUBBING

A sound is not a blob on a screen. In Chapter 1, you saw how words are seldom related to a sound's envelope. The editing technique in most video sound tutorials—look for a spike or dip in the waveform display and mark it—is rough and limited. Experienced NLE operators rely on slow-speed audio scanning in a clip or preview window to locate precise edits. Good video software lets you choose between *jogging*, with which you directly control clip motion by moving the mouse from side to side, and *shuttling*, which changes speed in response to mouse movement.

In the audio realm, this scanning is usually called *scrubbing*. On the best audio workstations, scrubbing is smooth and precisely related to controller movement: it feels like you're rocking a reel of tape or scratching a DJ's turntable. Some programs offer choices of scrub modes. Fixed slow-speed playback may be handiest for seeing the relation between sound and waveform. Variable-speed motion, similar to shuttling, lets you navigate through a long sound quickly and then slow down to find the edit. Stutter scrubbing repeats very short sections of the sound—as small as 10 ms—to find transitions quickly. Stutter scrubbing is often the only way to find where two vowels join or mark where a note changes in some music.

Hear for Yourself

Track 13 lets you hear and compare different scrubbing options with dialog and two kinds of music. You'll hear tape-like scrubbing, slow scanning, variable motion, and stuttering with various sized chunks between 10 and 300 ms.

There is no standard way to scrub, a universal keypress equivalent to the "space-bar" stop command in most audio and video players. Some programs give you a tool that looks like a little waveform that you drag across the file; others expect you to drag the normal pointer with a specific key held down; some have a backwards/forwards speed slider; a few use video editor's convention of tapping the J, K, or L keys to control speed and direction. If you think a program doesn't scrub, don't give up until you've searched the manual and help files.

Gotcha

Rough Scrubs? If scrubbing seems jerky or sporadic when you move the mouse, try zooming in on the waveform, or turning off video sync. Some programs can't shuffle data from hard drives fast enough, and zooming in lets them load data into RAM for smoother scrubbing. A few programs jump to frame boundaries when scrubbing, but only when video is turned on.

A few older audio programs only let you edit visually, and you can't scrub at all. If you're doing serious editing in one with that limitation, it's worth upgrading to newer software. If an upgrade isn't possible, you can work around the problem by selecting a short loop of audio around the edit point, and then playing the loop while slowly moving its boundary until you find the precise edit. This is a time consuming technique, but does the job if you have only a few edits. Check the software's manual for specific instructions.

MULTITRACK SOFTWARE

These usually have unlimited audio tracks arranged along a timeline. Many have something equivalent to a clip window for scanning and marking edit points, or you can select *regions* of a clip right on the timeline. The regions can then be trimmed, split, or dragged around the timeline, just as you would in a NLE. Like NLEs, multitrack programs are generally *nondestructive*: files that have been cut into regions aren't really changed. Instead, a database is built showing where each part of a file should appear on the timeline. There is no capture window; if you want to add something new, select a track and record directly onto the timeline. You can listen to any combination of tracks and watch synchronized picture while recording.

Gotcha

What you see isn't what you get. Even though audio professionals had been doing perfectly acceptable edits by ear for half a century, computerized sound editing evolved as a visual medium because that's the best early desktop machines could do. But don't swallow some programmers' and marketers' assertion that it's the right way to edit.

You have to hear what you're marking. Except for the convenient examples in NLE tutorial files, the spike of a drumbeat rarely matches the bar line—lots of music doesn't have loud drums at all. It may be easy to cut on pauses in scripted dialog, but interview and other real-world voices usually don't have convenient pauses where you want to make an edit. Some audio transitions, such as notes in a smooth musical line or the seven distinct vocal sounds in the word *trial*,[5] don't change the envelope at all. Experienced editors learn to cut them by ear. You will, too.

Unlike NLEs, you don't have to edit on frame lines. You can turn on an optional grid that constrains edits to any convenient unit, or edit freely. Using a multi-track to fine-tune and mix gives you other advantages as well:

- Tracks can be mono, stereo, or surround at will. This makes it easier to create interesting mixes.
- Almost all programs have a mixing panel with virtual faders, routing switches, and extensive metering. Fader movement usually can be controlled by hardware controllers with real faders—a big time-saver—and movements can be easily automated.
- Transport controls usually include multiple locate points and loop play, and can also be remoted to hardware controllers.
- Mixing is usually real-time for any number of tracks and effects, without rendering. Pre-programmed mixes can be many times faster than real-time.

Figure 4.5 (on the next page) shows some of the windows in one multitrack program.

INTERCHANGE FORMATS

Most multitrack programs let you import edited audio directly from a compatible NLE; the NLE's clips show up as regions on the proper track at the right time. The principle is fairly simple: both types of programs are essentially database managers, tracking parts of media files on a timeline, so there should be a way to translate one database to another. The two most common interchange formats, *Open Media Framework Interchange (OMF or OMFI)* and *Advanced Authoring Format (AAF)*, work this way.

That's the principle. If the two programs aren't sharing storage space, things are more complicated. The relevant media has to be transferred as well.

---

[5]You'll learn how to manipulate phonemes—and do impossible edits—in Chapter 9. Meanwhile those phonemes are /t/, /r/, /ah/, /ih/, /y/, /uh/, /l/.

73

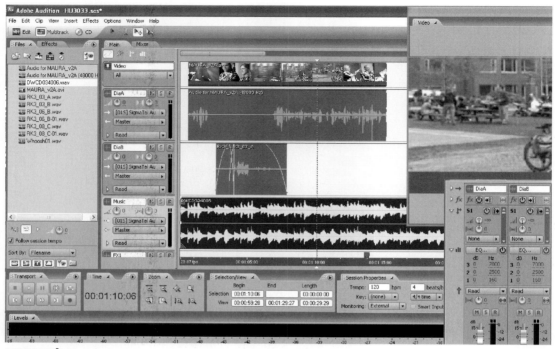

FIGURE 4.5

A typical multitrack audio program, Adobe Audition.

Some interchange protocols copy folders of entire audio and video files as well, giving you lots of flexibility to re-edit. Others just copy the smaller chunks of the original files that actually appear on the timeline, throwing away things like slates and outtakes; these large *consolidated* files make transfers faster. Consolidated files for long projects can get so big they come up against limits in the underlying operating system, and you have to transfer the project in reels or sections instead.

Most consolidation schemes let you specify *handles:* short extra pieces of each file that extend for a few seconds beyond the actual in- and out-points used on the timeline. These let a sound editor refine an edit or smooth over abrupt cuts without having to refer to the large original production files.

Most of the times, these interchange systems work. Sometimes they don't. Problems happen when the audio and video software don't handle timecode, sample rates, or even file names and formats the same way. They can also happen when manufacturers change standard database specifications to take advantage of specific program features.[6] The result can range from mysterious sync drifts to a total failure. Sometimes an exported file won't work because the video editor interrupted the computer when it was compiling: start over with a fresh transfer, and everything works.

---

[6]Or to make it harder to move to a competitor's program.

Manufacturers sometimes modify their interchange systems when they make minor software updates, and a workflow that worked last month might not work today. It's a good idea to always test to make sure a particular combination will work, even if you're moving among programs from the same manufacturer. If you're sending tracks to a separate audio post facility, ask if they've issued specific instructions for your NLE. Or use one of the more-or-less universal interchange methods discussed next. These aren't as efficient or flexible, but evolved over the history of film and video and always work. Or purchase one of the translation utilities discussed in the next section.

 Gotcha

Sync slip. Some programs use timecode numbers to fire off regions on their timeline and trust the common sample rate to keep things in sync. This works unless you have to change timecode formats, which is sometimes necessary during post. If that happens, it affects the sync between two clips that are already playing.

Sophisticated audio software bases its timeline on audio sample numbers rather than timecode numbers. This prevents these problems. The programs then translate sample numbers to timecode as needed for on-screen displays.

75

EDL

The most basic way of moving an edit database from one system to another is the EDL, Edit Decision List. This is a form of the data that can be read by a word processor (or a human operator), without any of the source audio or video. In fact, EDLs grew out of the original online editing systems that controlled the movement of separate video decks, and reflect the way those systems' text-only displays looked to the operator.

A typical EDL entry will look like Figure 4.6.

EDLs are usually passed from the picture editor to audio post as a piece of paper, or as a text file. Some software can read the text files and automatically assemble a program from them. If the last colon in a timecode is replaced by a semicolon, it indicates *drop frame* timecode (described in Chapter 6).

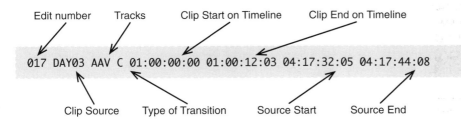

FIGURE 4.6
An EDL entry, with what the columns mean.

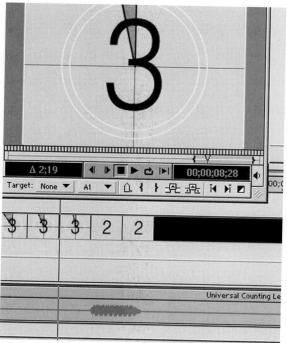

COUNTDOWN AND 2-POP

Before computers became common, sound editors would assemble individual reels of dialog or effects or music on sprocketed magnetic film, with a beep at the start of each reel. When it was time to mix, the beeps were manually lined up in multiple players and synced to the number 2 in the picture countdown. Then the sprockets kept everything running at the same speed, keeping things in sync. Editors and mixers could look at the leader, listen for the beep, and know immediately if there was a sync error and how much was needed to correct it.

Digital audio files will always run at a stable speed, determined by the sample rate and the playback software's internal clock. So sprockets aren't necessary. But the beep, a 1 kHz tone lasting exactly one frame and affectionately known as a *2-pop*, is still the best way to assure the files start together. In fact, 2-pops are still used as the ultimate sync check even on projects that are synchronized by timecode or other means,

FIGURE 4.7
Approaching the 2-pop. The audio beep should start exactly on the frame that has a big 2.

and almost all NLEs have a way to generate them with matching visual countdowns. Figure 4.7 shows how they should look when things are in sync.

The old Hollywood method of preparing individual reels with 2-pops can bail you out when there's no other way to transfer sync material between NLE and audio software. Either edit a countdown leader onto your picture, or cut in an all-white frame exactly 2 seconds before the film or reel starts. (Video editors frequently put the pop at timecode 59:58.00 so the program can start at exactly 1 hour.) Then put a pop on every audio track, directly under the white frame or the 2. A variation puts a pop at each number counting down to two.

When you're ready to move to an audio program, export entire individual tracks as files that include the pop, and save a reference copy of the video with the flash frame. Load the files onto different tracks of an audio program, and slide tracks until the 2-pops match.

Saving individual tracks with 2-pops usually results in much bigger transfers than an interchange system like OMF. If a track is mostly silent, you still have to export the silent passages as full-resolution data. This generally isn't a problem for short-form videos, but can be a real waste of time and space[7] over the length of a film.

---

[7]Fortunately, you can save some space by using a compression utility like PKZip or Stuffit. These usually aren't very effective on audio files, but they do a great job compressing silence!

If you have any doubts about your system's ability to hold sync long-term, put a *tail pop* and flash at the end of the program or reel as well. If the ends don't line up, you can calculate the error and apply a speed correction.

Hear for yourself

Track 14 contains a 9-blip countdown ready to line up against visual leaders. The first eight tones are at 1 kHz, for the on-screen numbers 10 through 3. The last is at 2 kHz as an audible warning the program is about to start. Or use just the first 1 kHz blip as a 2-pop.

TIME-STAMPED FILES

A few audio file formats, including.bwv or Broadcast Wave, include timecode data indicating when the first audio sample should play. The playback software can then compute the desired timecode for any moment in the file by counting samples, multiplying by the frame rate, and adding the result to that start time. These time-stamped files are often used by high-end field recorders, but currently most editing programs ignore the stamp and treat the file as if it were a standard .wav. If you're using .bwv files as the transfer medium between video and audio, it's a good idea to add a 2-pop for safety, or manually note the starting timecode.

EDITING SOFTWARE

Sometimes you need to make a lot of edits in a single sound file, as when you want to rearrange a voice-over narration or trim music to length. Rather than deal with dozens of tiny clips, *editors* let you work word-processor style: select individual sounds or phrases, delete, copy and paste on a single file. It means far fewer mouse clicks.

Unlike most multi-track programs, editors make permanent changes to a file. If you're not sure you like that idea, work on a copy. On the other hand, once you've finished a sequence, there's no need to render or mix anything. The job is done.

Editors often have more extensive built-in effects. Effects can be applied just to a selected area, or to the entire file. Some let you preset conversions or effects and then batch-process multiple files at once. Most provide a pencil tool that lets you redraw the audio waveform, smoothing over occasional clicks or rounding out an overload.

In general, editors are great timesavers. If I already had video software and could buy only one other program, I'd specify an editor (and mix in the NLE). Figure 4.8 shows a typical one.

If you don't have an editor, check into *Audacity* (Figure 4.9). It's free and has versions for Windows, Mac, and Linux. It's also open-source, which means

FIGURE 4.8
Editors like Sony's
SoundForge are often
better and faster
than a multi-track
for manipulating
complete files.

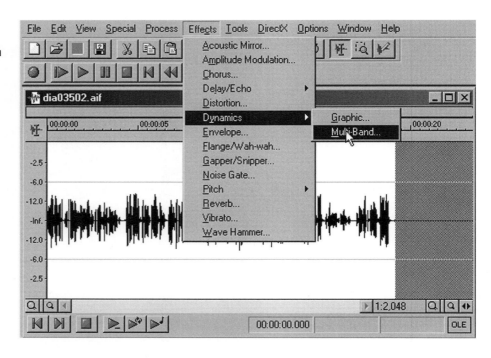

78

FIGURE 4.9
Audacity, a very
capable cross-
platform editor. And
it's free.

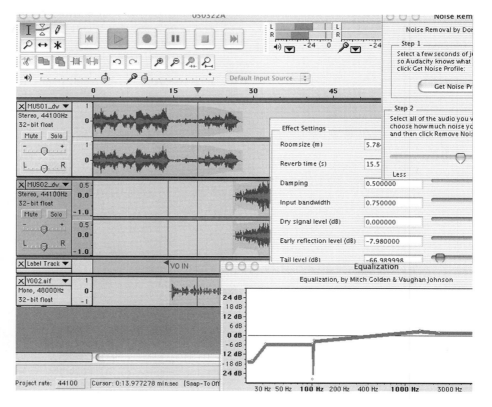

programmers all over the world are continually adding new features. Find the latest version at audacity.sourceforge.net.

 Gotcha

Time-consuming saves. Multi-track programs and NLEs can spoil you. Saving a project in one of them involves updating an internal edit list, which is usually small and can be written to disk easily. Editors save the actual audio file—as much as 11 megabytes per stereo minute—and that can take a while. For fastest saves, make sure there's a large defragmented area on your drive. Don't waste data and disk access time by recording mono sources in stereo.

Music Software

MIDI sequencers evolved in the mid-80s as a way to record and edit keyboard performances. The musical sounds themselves weren't recorded; just instructions about which note to play and when, how loudly, and on what instrument. The files could then be played on external synthesizers, creating a perfect musical performance. Today sequencers are the standard tool for music composition and creation, and often play through samplers to create new songs from recordings of non-electronic instruments or voices, or a sequencer can print full scores for orchestral performance. But with today's more powerful computers, they can manipulate audio files as well as MIDI commands. If you've got musical talents and like to score your own films, one of these programs will probably be more useful than an audio-only multi-track. Figure 4.10 shows a typical one, with audio on one track and musical notes on another.

LOOP MUSIC SOFTWARE

As computers have gotten more powerful, they've gained the ability to change the key or tempo of musical segments on-the-fly. *Looping* programs such as Sony's Acid or Apple's Garage Band are multi-track editors that rearrange musical building blocks—snippets of rhythm, solo instruments, and backing sections. When you combine these snippets, the program does its best job of making them sound good together … and the result can be good enough for a film score or pop song. They often have elaborate ways to search and manipulate the loops. A few programs, aimed primarily at the video market and bundled with NLEs, add basic loop functionality to multi-track mixing programs. Looping techniques and other scoring software are discussed in Chapter 9.

Audio Utilities

Here are some additional programs to make audio post easier. This section doesn't cover specific processors like reverbs or noise reduction, which have full chapters devoted to them later in this book.

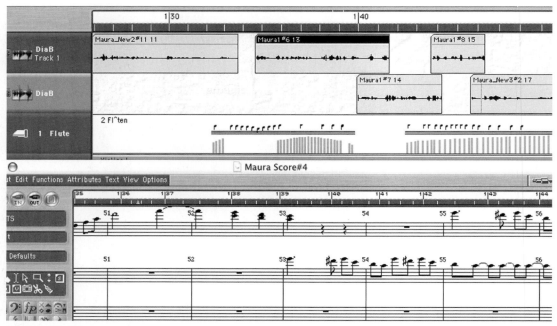

FIGURE 4.10
Most music sequencers now support simultaneous audio tracks.

80

EFFECTS SHELLS

There are multiple formats for audio plug-ins, and few NLEs support more than one or two. A standalone shell lets you run other plug-ins as applications on your desktop, you can open a file in one, preview and process through the plug-in, and then save a processed version. While most audio programs can also do this, it can be a needless expense if all you want to do is process.

One commercial shell, Bias's Vbox (Mac/Windows), gives you access to the whole world of VST.[8] There are hundreds of plug-ins in this format, ranging from high-quality professional processors to hacker-developed, freeware sound manglers in every imaginable style. Other shells may be available from plug-in manufacturers to let you use their products in different environments.

FILE CONVERSION SOFTWARE

NLEs can be flexible about accepting different sample rates and bit depths yet still do a poor job of actually converting the file. Periodic clicking is the most common symptom. It's almost always better to convert in a program designed for sound. If you don't have an audio editor, consider a separate conversion utility. Many are available as shareware, though quality varies. A reliable option is Apple's QuickTime Pro for Mac or Windows, a very low-cost upgrade to its free QuickTime Player.

---

[8]Virtual Studio Technology, a plug-in format invented and trademarked by Steinberg Media Technologies, is now an open standard.

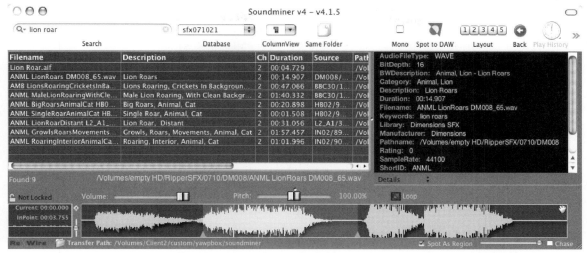

FIGURE 4.11
SoundMiner, an automatic sound effects searching program.

Most converters can import and export multiple file formats as well as different audio standards, but some can't convert audio to mp3, the most common Web audio compression standard. To do that, you may need a separate mp3 encoder. Quality varies, but generally the popular encoders, including both the official licensed Fraunhofer[9] engine and the open-source LAME library, do a good job.

INTERCHANGE FORMAT CONVERSION SOFTWARE

A few companies have translation utilities to bridge the gaps among interchange systems. Solid State Logic's *ProConvert* (formerly *EDLConvert*) claims to speak twenty different languages, ranging from OMF and AAF to product-specific protocols used in digital dubbers. These not only convert the audio where needed, but also maintain the timeline, handles, file names, and other important data. The products are aimed at professionals—and priced accordingly—but are a worthwhile investment for facilities that handle a wide range of workflows.

SEARCH SOFTWARE

It can be hard to find a specific sound in a large library. Commercial music and sound effect publishers often come with their own databases or let you search on the Web (see Chapters 9 and 10). But if you've assembled your own large collection, you may want software that lets you search your own hard drive by keyword and then audition a sound. BaseHead (Windows) and SoundMiner (Macintosh; Figure 4.11) are specialized audio search and audition programs.

---

[9]Fraunhofer IIS-A invented MPEG Layer-3 (mp3), as well as the emerging standard MPEG-2 AAC.

81

They're designed for busy effects editors, and rely on custom databases of searchable keywords that get linked to sounds on your hard drive. Setting up one of these programs can take time—particularly if you've got a lot of effects on audio CD that have to be transferred, or a lot of custom effects that require keywords added—but can be worth the investment. Once you decide you need an effect, the program presents a list of likely candidates, lets you audition and even select just part of a larger file, and then drops your selection right into supported multi-track software... virtually instantly, and exactly where you want it on the timeline.

Macintosh Versus Windows

I put this section last because conventional wisdom insists that you choose software first and then buy whichever platform it requires. Don't be confused by software that's supposed to be cross-platform; some features may be supported on one computer but not on another. Chances are you've already got a computer for your NLE, so this is a non-issue. Computer capabilities and operating systems keep changing—current Macs, for example, can be restarted as Windows machines—so check the Web for the latest details.

CHAPTER 5
Planning the Track

Communication is a two-way street. Some theorists say the meaning of a message isn't its words, but how you act when hearing it. They say this is the only way to account for factors like nonverbal cues, feedback, and existing ideas about the subject. So if I walk up to you and say, "Nice day," I'd expect you to smile, because I'd expect you to realize I was actually greeting you as a friend. But you could frown and say, "Nah, it's not warm enough for this shirt." In that case, the meaning of my message is getting lost.

Enough theory. For filmmakers, the practical side is that a soundtrack—whether it's commercial, corporate, theatrical, or event—doesn't have a life of its own. It and the visuals exist only to elicit a response from the viewer.[1] Unless you understand how someone will hear your track, you can't know what should go into it.

DIFFERENT MEDIA ARE HEARD DIFFERENTLY

I'm not saying they *sound* very different. The technical differences between broadcast television, home or office DVD, theatrical sound, and well-done computer tracks are fairly small. They all can do a reasonable job of carrying

---

[1]Even if the response is only, "Wow, what a great film!"

80- to 15-kHz stereo with little noise. The only real variations are in how many channels the formats carry and how much distortion accompanies the signal.

Unfortunately, what viewers hear is seldom the best a medium can do. It's limited by realities of playback equipment, room acoustics, and everyday psychology. Because of the way we listen to film and video, a track can work beautifully in one medium and fall flat in another.

Broadcast

Don't expect much from conventional analog TV. While the transmission system is capable of reasonably good stereo, few viewers ever hear it that way. The majority of sets—even large-screen ones—have limited-range speakers and considerable distortion at typical listening levels. Low-cost sets often have resonant peaks as well. This means you also shouldn't expect too much from digital broadcast or cable: for a lot of viewers, the signal eventually has to pass through analog gear that's at least a couple of years old.

Here's the sorry fact: Manufacturers don't bother putting better speakers in sets because few consumers will pay for—or even notice—the difference. The average living room or office has the kind of acoustics that hurts intelligibility and destroys musical balance. Background noise is usually fairly high. Both these problems are compounded by viewing positions that are often closer to reflective surfaces than to the set. Savvy commercial and program producers try to counter this with processing to make their tracks seem louder. Broadcasters use different processing to keep their stations' average loudness constant. The result of these physical realities and processing games is a total loss of subtlety.

 Gotcha

Multiple tracks in a mono world. A significant part of the TV audience watches on mono sets. Another part may have stereo or surround, but it's consumer-level equipment that's never been aligned properly, with randomly placed speakers, and proprietary surround matrixes that do unpredictable things when faced with a complex signal.

Unfortunately, some stereo and surround sources depend on polarity reversal tricks that aren't compatible with real-world equipment. When the channels are matrixed, sounds can come from unusual places. On a mono system, some sounds can completely disappear!

Bottom line: unless you're absolutely sure how things will play back, check your surround mixes as stereo (*left total* and *right total*) mixdowns. Then check the stereo as mono.

Stereo and surround can also get mangled before they ever get to the viewer's equipment, particularly if your film is shown on a cable channel. Their master control rooms are seldom built or staffed to the highest standards, and there's no way to predict what a local cable operator will do to the signal once they snag it from a satellite; some condense all but the premium channels to mono to save money on equipment. Even local broadcast stations on the big networks are playing catch-up, trying to build new facilities that'll properly handle network tracks, let alone local origination. And since the vast majority of programming is legacy from analog days, it'll be decades before the market forces everybody to upgrade.

A few practical tips to help TV tracks survive this hostile world:

- Start with elements that are noise-free and undistorted. Station processing will emphasize flaws.
- Don't plan for more than two or three layers of sound: dialog and important sound effects (centered and loud); ambiences and background effects (stereo and medium loud); and music (stereo and variable).
- Don't make accurate stereo a part of the plot; most people will never hear it. Forget about notions of left and right; these won't exist for many viewers.
- Be careful any time voice is mixed with wide-range music. Few viewers will hear the ratio between voice and music the same way because speakers and acoustics vary so much. Often, music will seem lower in the field than it did when you mixed. Multiband compression (Chapter 13) can help keep things predictable.
- Be *very* careful about meeting level and lineup tone standards. Most broadcast operators never listen past the tone when they're setting up a tape, and some don't even listen to the tone… they just look at it on meters.[2]

Subtlety is wasted on TV. Many viewers won't be in a position to pay attention to what you've done. Broadcast TV is often accompanied by conversation, chores, and background noises—or is the background itself.

 Gotcha

But what about quality? When conditions are just right—good equipment and acoustics, no competing noises, and a station that uses little processing—TV sound is capable of subtlety and beauty. If you're of an artistic bent, you may prefer to design a track just for those lucky viewers who might actually hear it all, and not worry about the rest.

It's your choice. Personally, I consider it a greater art to create interesting and engaging tracks that respect the reality of a mass medium.

---

[2] Some producers try to cheat by making their tones a few dB softer than normal, so operators will turn them up on playback and make the program louder on the air. Trust me: it doesn't work. Station limiters will squash and distort that tape's program. The same thing happens if you record tone at a proper level but then exceed standard maximums in the mix, except there's also a chance the station will reject the tape and never play it at all. Standard levels—and ways to make a show seem louder without exceeding them—are discussed in the chapters on processing and mixing.

Educational Video

Classroom playbacks can sound worse than living room ones. It's not strictly the medium's fault. Schools can have VHS hi-fi or DVD players, and good presentation monitors (though with student use, they're usually not in the best of shape). The real problem is acoustics. Very few classrooms sound good. Hard parallel surfaces are the norm and ceilings are often low and hard. The resulting echo hurts intelligibility.[3]

Educational films generally have simpler tracks than entertainment ones, both to keep the message clear and to save money. Often there's just a dialog or narration track, a few key sound effects, and sparse music. Slowing down the narration can help compensate for poor acoustics.

Fortunately, most classes can be expected to quiet down while a film is being shown—at least they did in my generation. And the threat of a quiz may force students to pay attention.

Home Theater and Auditorium Presentation

Things start to get a little better here. Systems are wired to take advantage of stereo or even surround, which can present a very detailed sound field. Speaker quality is often much higher than that in consumer TVs, though it too can vary widely. Be aware that "surround in a box" setups usually compromise accuracy to cut costs. Those very small, easy-to-mount speakers with subwoofers popular at mass marketers have problems at dialog frequencies. Auditorium systems don't have dialog problems if they're well-designed, but sacrifice non-dialog frequencies to save power.

Acoustics are also variable. Home theater setups range from hard-walled living rooms to mini theaters. Large auditoriums may be designed for intelligibility, but architects usually have other constraints. General-purpose meeting rooms and hotel ballrooms often don't have any acoustic treatment other than a fissured tile ceiling. They may even rely on small ceiling speakers as their only playback.

On the other hand, viewers are usually motivated to pay attention. If they've paid for a home theater system, there's a good chance they actually like watching movies. If they're in an auditorium, it's probably part of a social or work-related event they care about. This attention also raises the "shh!" factor; audience noises and other distractions are minimized.

A good home theater or auditorium track can have a wide dynamic range and take advantage of stereo or surround spread. Dialog can vary in loudness and position. You can have many layers of effects going on and still hear the music.

---

[3] It's become a cliché: if you want to make dialog sound like it's in a classroom, add hollowness and reverberation. I wonder how many children have trouble in school just because it's hard to hear what Teacher is saying.

For best results, plan to mix with speakers at about the same volume as the audience will hear—usually just below 85 dB SPL for average dialog.

Theatrical Soundtracks

Ahh. Every now and again I get to work on one of these. Count on reasonably good acoustics, reliable stereo (usually with surround), and—in a well-maintained theater—wide-range speakers with low distortion and little electronic noise. There's very little environmental noise as well, though multiplexes frequently have low-frequency rumbles from the auditorium next door. Once the movie starts, people usually pay attention.

So you can plan for a rich, dynamic track with multiple layers of sound coming from every direction and music recorded in surround formats. Theatrical mixes and sound systems are supposed to be standardized with an average dialog level projected at 85 dB SPL—but producers and theater managers keep pushing this to raise audience adrenaline levels. Yes, movies are getting louder. Plan to mix accordingly.

 Gotcha

Wide screen, narrow dialog. Theaters want to sell as many tickets as possible. So seats extend the full width of, and can be very close to, the screen. This creates problems if you try to spread dialog realistically across the screen. For front-row viewers sitting at the sides of the theater, the inverse square law dictates that dialog on their side of the screen will be too loud and dialog on the other will be too soft.

The standard practice is to keep dialog centered, or only slightly off-center, no matter where actors appear on the screen. This solves the side-seating problem and also makes the track easier to follow for everyone in the room. (If audio positions jumped every time the camera position changed, the result would be disorienting.) Off-camera characters and crowds can come from any direction that makes dramatic sense.

Internet and CD-ROM Audio

The only rule is there aren't any. Streaming audio quality varies from worse than telephone (because of swooshy artifacts) to better than FM radio. The quality depends on what choices you make in data-compression method and settings. CD-ROM audio is capable of CD quality, or can be compressed to near-CD quality, but is often limited to save disc real estate.

What is much worse is that there's absolutely no control over how the track will be played. It could be played on a laptop with a speaker hidden under a keyboard, that barely covers 200 Hz to 6 kHz. It could be played in a tower with a loud fan and single small speaker, underneath the viewer's desk. It could be played on small nearfields designed for gaming, not dialog. Those nearfields might come with or without a subwoofer, and might be wired properly or have left and right channels reversed. Or the track could be played through high-quality headphones, tiny earbuds, or a cell phone.

Forget about trying to predict noise and other potential distracters. You have no way of knowing whether a track will be played in a quiet office, a noisy family room, a quiet carrel, a busy classroom, or on an airplane.

The only solution I've found is to plan tracks with nothing critical outside the midrange and no more than two things going on at once. If you want complexity, make the elements sequential instead of simultaneous. Just as with broadcast TV, Internet and CD-ROM elements must be free of noise and distortion; you know the quality will get much worse before it's heard. But a wide frequency range isn't important, and extensive highs can even hurt you by robbing bits from the midrange during Web encoding.

Putting It Together

Of course, these categories aren't absolute: a corporate piece may be shown in an auditorium at the home office, then over the Web to branch managers at their desks, then on a tiny all-in-one DVD player for the employees. Even theatrical features get cut down for classroom use. You have to use your own judgment about the potential audience and what they'll hear. The rules summarized in Table 5.1 are just a starting point.

The bottom line is, "Put yourself in the viewer's place." Imagine watching your film in a real situation, and pay attention to how it sounds *there*. What's important is how much of your message reaches the viewer's brain, not how much you recorded on the track.

SPREAD THINGS AROUND

The best Hollywood tracks are planned so that sounds don't compete in space (the *soundstage*). Sound effects may come from the left, right, or behind you. But you rarely hear them in the center of the screen when there's dialog going on. That area belongs to the voices.

Simultaneous sounds usually have different frequency ranges as well. Composer John Williams chose low notes for the ominous theme in *Jaws*, so ocean sounds would also be heard. But he felt free to use the full orchestra in *Star Wars* to underscore the Death Star, which didn't make its own noise in space. Leonard Bernstein learned this the hard way some years earlier with his score for *On the Waterfront*. He composed a beautiful orchestral crescendo, timed perfectly to the peak of an important scene. But the scene's emotion was based on dialog and the film was in mono, so director Elia Kazan had to turn

Table 5.1   Technical and human factors influence how different media are heard.

	Broadcast TV	Educational	Home Theater and Auditorium	Theatrical	Internet
Speaker quality	narrow frequency range, distorting, often peaky in mids	consumer TVs or slightly better	quality varies: some full-range, some lack mids	usually very good by consumer standards; varies by pro standards	often lacking bass; subwoofer-equipped systems often lack mids
Dynamic range	very little	very little	medium to high	very high	depends on codec
Room acoustics	poor	poor to horrible	poor to good	good to very good	poor but usually nearfield
Tracks	up to 5.1, but most people will hear mono	mono or stereo	up to 5.1, but difficult to predict	usually 5.1, almost always shown as mixed	can be stereo, but plan for a large mono audience
Consistency	none	none	slight	medium to high	none
Competition	life continues while TV is on	little to none	most people concentrating on screen	just a few inconsiderate patrons; some bass leakage in multiplexes	computer fans, office distractions
Viewer attention	depends on content	somewhat high	motivated	high	variable
Track layers	few	few	medium	many	few

89

down the music as things went along. The final mix preserved the voices and killed the crescendo.[4]

Spreading things out in the frequency spectrum makes sense for sound effects as well. If there's going to be a car crash, don't have a woman screaming at the same time the tires squeal. One of those sounds will surely get lost.

Or spread sounds out in time. If you hold her scream until after the crash, it can still make dramatic sense and not compete with other sounds. Or have her scream in anticipation of the crash—then squeal those tires and follow it up with a child crying. While all that high-pitched stuff is going on, you can still use a low-frequency crash or fireball. And the midrange is wide open for shouts or musical stabs.

And if the medium supports it, you can spread things around in space. That's what stereo and surround are for. Don't forget the dimension of distance as well; it can translate better to the small screen. Plan to move some elements farther back by using a combination of volume, equalization, and reverb. Manipulating distance should usually be saved for postproduction; with few exceptions, field recording should be done with the mic as close to the subject as possible.

About Stereo

Most people have been exposed to the idea of stereo through consumer electronics, radio, and TV. But I've found many filmmakers don't really know what it means or appreciate how it can vary.

Stereo *doesn't* have to mean two tracks. The first Bell Labs experiments (and most early stereo film epics) used separate channels for left, center, and right. It wasn't until the format reached home listeners that two channels became the norm, because that's all vinyl records could deliver. The point of stereo isn't how many speakers are used; it's the ability to reproduce an infinite number of points between speakers. Stereo relies on localization mechanisms that evolved as part of human hearing. It creates an artificial space that's different from the room you're listening in. Listen to just part A of Track 15 on a pair of good speakers at fairly close range, and forming an equilateral triangle with your listening position. This track was properly produced in stereo. You'll hear piano in the center, violins to the middle left, and woodwinds to the middle right. The percussion enters in the center. Then you will hear brass on the far left. All this from only two speakers.

Your brain supplies these phantom locations—sounds from places where there aren't any speakers—because the volume and timing of each instrument is slightly different in each of the channels. This reflects the acoustics of the recording studio. For contrast, compare what you just heard with part B of

---

[4] Bernstein followed 1954's On the Waterfront by writing Broadway shows, a third symphony, an opera, a mass, numerous smaller pieces, and four books … along with a beautiful concert suite based on his cues for Waterfront. He also had time to lead the New York Philharmonic, perform as a concert pianist, and host television shows about music. But he never scored another film.

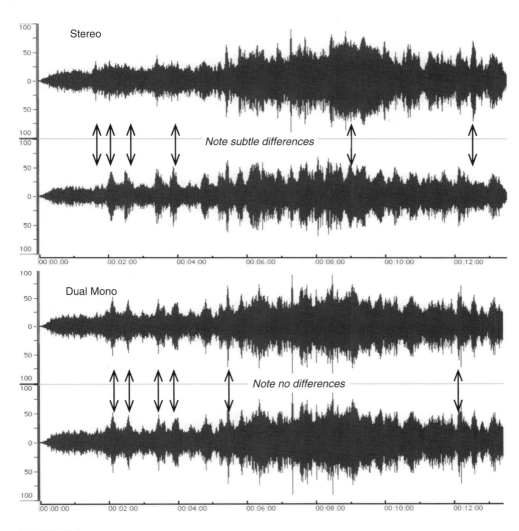

FIGURE 5.1

Track 15. It's a two-channel recording of the same music, and looks almost the identical in a waveform display (see Figure 5.1). But those critical timing and volume differences have been eliminated, and every instrument appears in the center. Even though this book's CD is in stereo and you might play it on two speakers, the sound is *monaural* (single ear) or mono. Engineers call this kind of track *dual mono* because the same information is on two tracks. If it were a computer file, 50 percent of its data would be redundant. In an NLE, mono audio should stay in mono file formats, panned to the center[5] or set to play through both tracks. This saves disk space and makes the system run smoother.

---

[5] Depending on software, the function may be called *pan, fill,* or *take*: in each case, the idea is to have a single track play equally from both speakers, so it appears in the center.

Hear for yourself

Track 15 starts with true stereo, in an orchestral recording from the DeWolfe Music Library.[6] You'll hear piano in the center, violins to the middle left, and woodwinds to the middle right. Then, part B of the track plays the same music as part A, but with all the directional information removed.

Gotcha

If that's right, then what's left? It's possible you'll hear directions reversed in the CD example. They were correct when I mastered the disc, but computer and NLE speakers sometimes have their wires crossed. This is a good opportunity to fix things.

In film and video, the distinction between mono and stereo is primarily a post-production issue. Field-recorded dialog is almost always mono because that's how it'll be mixed; if two or more channels are used for dialog, they're to give the sound editor a choice between microphones. Events and ambiences are usually recorded in stereo. Now, while you're planning the track, is the best time to decide whether to use mono or stereo for each element:

- Many CD sound effects and even some music cues are actually mono. They don't need to tie up two tracks in your NLE.
- Voiceovers should always be mono for a single announcer; there's no point to using two microphones on a single mouth. If two people are having a conversation in voiceover, it's often a good idea to record them to separate channels so you'll be able to process their voices separately. But unless you're looking for a special effect (which won't survive broadcast), don't plan to leave those voices separated that way in the mix.
- Foley sound effects (Chapter 10) should be mono and placed where appropriate. This usually means they're centered with the dialog.
- Walla crowd sounds (Chapter 7) should usually be recorded and mixed in stereo.

When it's time to mix, you'll have to choose where each mono sound (other than dialog) gets placed across the stereo field. You can also turn mono into simulated stereo using various techniques, most of which are fairly simple and

---

[6] "Voyage of Destiny" (F. Talgorn) DeWolfe CD 272/1, protected by copyright and used by permission.

some of which are appropriate for film tracks. We'll discuss and demonstrate them in Chapter 16.

Using Different Elements for Texture

Some of today's action films have nonstop tracks. Everything is loud. When there's no excuse for gunshots or explosions, pounding music takes over. These are films you often see described as a "nonstop roller-coaster ride." Real roller coasters don't work that way. What makes the amusement park ride exciting isn't just the long fast plunge; it's also the anticipation while the cars are being slowly dragged to the top. The best roller coasters even have a couple of breaks in the middle of the ride: cars go up a stub of track, slow down as they near the top, and then reverse and come screaming down again.

Give viewers a break. Let different kinds of elements take turns dominating the track. You've got a lot to choose from:

- Characters are usually on-camera, talking to each other. But for a more intimate sound, consider treating parts of some scenes as voiceover. You'll be able to record these with much closer mics and more acoustic treatment.
- Don't keep on-camera voices in the same acoustic surrounding for too long. Let your actors move around the room or walk into a hallway or next to an open window, so the reflections and ambience change. Do similar processing to on-camera dialog you've replaced in postproduction studio sessions.
- Additional voices can be added in post to make a scene busier and give it a richer texture. Crowds can be from a stock library but work better if you also record specific phrases appropriate to the scene.
- Voiceovers are almost always intimate and close up. It sounds like the announcer is talking directly to us. But that's a fairly modern conceit. Until the mid-1950s, announcers usually projected as if they were trying to reach a crowd and sometimes artificial reverb was added to simulate a theater. In the earliest films, voiceovers were treated as oratory and declaimed like a political speech. In the future, voiceovers may be yelled or whispered. Feel free to experiment.
- Some sound effects, such as doorbells or car crashes, may be called for in the script. You'll add these in post. But don't stop there. Exteriors and busy interiors almost always need additional background sounds. Quiet interiors do also, unless you'll be using a limited medium like broadcast TV.
- In real life, standing in one place usually means hearing a continuous background. Movies don't have to work this way. If characters are on a sidewalk, vary the traffic noises. Plan to make them quieter as the audience gets more involved with the dialog. Or add occasional things we can't see but could exist off-camera, such as children playing or a distant siren.
- Sound effects don't have to be realistic. Consider designing sounds from the characters' point of view, emphasizing things that would be important to them.

93

- Vary the music as well. Few films benefit from a constant underscore. It won't hurt to let some scenes rely on dialog and effects. Or consider having some scenes use only music, with no dialog or effects.
- Music doesn't have to sound like it was added in post, even though it almost always is. Let some of it be *diegetic* (also known as *source music*), taking place naturally in the scene. This could be dictated by the situation—you'd expect a nightclub or party to have music, even if we don't see the band or stereo system. But source music can also be used to help set up a location: stores and restaurants usually have canned background music playing. Choose an appropriate style—rock, country, classical, ethnic, or elevator—to help the viewer identify what kind of place it is.

CONSIDER THE WORKFLOW

I've been a sound guy for a long time. I've worked on movies, TV shows, interactive games, telephone response systems, meditation CDs, you name it. Some years ago I was asked to develop a tutorial column for a new magazine, *Desktop Video World*. In those distant days, *video* sound was something totally different from *film* sound. It had different specs, production styles, and aesthetic. In fact, the whole idea of *desktop video* was revolutionary: most videos were posted in analog multi-machine suites that looked like something out of *Star Wars*.[7] If a project had a big enough budget, the track would be sweetened by dubbing between ¼-inch stereo and 2-inch 24-track analog tape, and then mixing on a large analog console. Film tracks, on the other hand, were almost always done by splicing thousands of pieces of 35 mm mag stock, playing them on banks of 35 mm transports, and then mixing on an even larger console. Computer video was a low-quality scratch pad, where producers tried out ideas before moving to online.

Most of those online video suites are out of business, and the 35 mm mag transports largely obsolete, both replaced by more efficient digital setups. The majority of film and video tracks are created entirely within desktop computers. Ready for the surprise? I wrote that first magazine column in late 1995. A little more than a decade later, everything has changed.

Computers took over quickly for a lot of good reasons. But ways of working that had been developed for 35 mm mag are still valid for movies. Similarly, tricks and shortcuts from the 24-track suite still make sense for video. In fact, within the city of Los Angeles there are neighborhoods where everybody is using film workflows, and others where everybody is emulating the 24-track way… all on the same desktop computers and software. The biggest change isn't that things are digital; it's that you can choose the best way of working on each aspect of a project no matter what medium it's on. Telling a story with actors, to play on a large screen? You'll get a better track if you think about

---

[7] Literally. The first *Star Wars* movie used recognizable shots of standard analog TV switching equipment for the Death Star control panels. It became an in-joke.

it film-style. Presenting a documentary or recording an event? You'll save time and money without sacrificing quality if you treat it as a video track.

Theatrical Workflows and Techniques

Talking films evolved as high-budget entertainment, with production costs amortized over hundreds of thousands of tickets. So there's an expectation of quality in a theatrical soundtrack. Minor audio flaws that wouldn't be noticed on a network show are not only heard in a theater; they're dissected and discussed by critics and theorists. Casual viewers—who might not know what a timbre shift is or pay attention to tiny clicks—pick up on these standards. People expect a good movie to *sound* like a movie. This spills over into any narrative storytelling. Videos with acting have a higher sound standard than presenter or event videos; otherwise we're pulled out of the characters' world and lose the story.

Talking films also evolved as a big business, with studios employing thousands of people and turning out dozens of titles a year. A factory system was necessary. Tasks were broken into manageable chunks and standardized methods. Some sound editors specialized in splitting mono dialog into multiple mag films, others cut effects, and still others cut music. Since the editors didn't need to make processing decisions, the studios gave them different setups than were used for recording or mixing. Even the final mix had its own tasks and specialists. The split dialog tracks were mixed first, by the head re-recording mixer, into a smooth dialog-only soundtrack. Then sound effects and music were added, usually having been premixed by assistants who never touched dialog. The workflow was smooth, predictable, flexible enough to satisfy directors, and efficient enough to satisfy studio heads. Today most of those tasks are done by freelancers and small companies, but the workflow and division of labor survives. It's how movies are made.

Video-style Workflows

Maybe it's an East Coast/West Coast thing, or maybe it has to do with the budgets, but even sophisticated video sound evolved differently. A picture editor would assemble the images, with sync sound on two tracks of videotape. A sound engineer would then copy those tracks in real-time to a 24-track tape, where they became the dialog source. If a line had to be manipulated, it would be dubbed to another track for effects or to a completely different tape for physical editing. Music, sound effects, and razor-blade cut voices would be played on smaller decks and dubbed to the 24-track. Then all those tracks would be mixed to an audio master, which was then dubbed onto the master videotape.

Because it was all being done on the same few tape decks, in the same room, one engineer took responsibility for every aspect of the track: editing, special effects, processing, and mixing. Sometimes the engineer had an assistant to load tapes, but it was primarily a one-person show. So it made sense to do as many operations as possible simultaneously. This saved both time and generation losses. Need to process the voiceover? Do it while you're dubbing the edited announcer to the multi-track. Want reverb on an effect? If you're sure the reverb will work, print it right to the tape.

This way of working meant just a couple of people could turn out a complicated national spot in one morning, or completely edit and mix a 1-hour dramatic track—with effects and custom-cut music cues—in less than a week. It also meant that the giant monitor speakers, console, and multi-track would go unused for a few minutes, while the voice track was being edited on a ¼-inch deck with a cue speaker. It was all too casual for the Hollywood studio system, but it was the best way to handle post-production sound for video.

Pick and Choose

If you're comfortable with both workflows, you can use the best pieces of each. You don't need an army of dialog editors to split a disjointed scene into multiple tracks for each mic setup or actor, or a dub stage to re-combine those tracks into a smooth whole. You don't need a re-recording mixer to test whether a noisy line can be cleaned electronically; you can do it while you're deciding which take to use. On the other hand, you can decide to handle your product video's track in two totally separate sessions: Critical monitoring isn't necessary for editing, so you can do that at your kitchen table. Then move the files into a proper studio for equalization and mixing.

PREPRODUCTION FOR POSTPRODUCTION

Sounds like an oxymoron, doesn't it? Actually, you should start planning for post in the earliest stages of filmmaking. It definitely saves time and can also save a lot of money.

Before You Shoot

Know what you'll need from the shoot. This includes technical considerations, such as what sound formats you or a post facility will require, and what kind of mic technique will work best for the way you'll be mixing. Getting this wrong almost always means extra steps converting, processing, or rerecording.

Don't assume a scene doesn't need sound. Even if it will be covered by voiceover and music, or you're going to replace all the sound effects, plan for recording natural sound if at all possible. If you're shooting DV, it's free: point a good mic at the shot, and you'll have additional elements for the mix or a guide track to use when syncing new effects. Even a built-in camera mic can be useful for this kind of sound. If you're shooting film, it doesn't cost very much to have a small digital recorder, set to automatic mode, hidden somewhere on the set. You can pull effects from it for post, or—if you slap a slate—have a record of what happened for sync reference.

Do some research before assuming you'll be able to replace dialog. *Automatic Dialog Replacement* (ADR, Chapter 7) is complicated and time-consuming. Rethink the sequence to eliminate most of the lines that would need to be replaced or choose a different location. A little ADR is often necessary in dramatic films, but each line takes time and money. Unless you've got Hollywood budgets and very strong contracts with your actors, don't expect to ADR an entire film.

Make note of *nonsync* (*wild*) sound effects and voiceover dialog that can be gathered easily at the location, such as extra character lines or prop noises. A few minutes of extra recording while actors and props are in place can save you hours in post. (Make this commitment before you start shooting; nobody ever seems willing to do anything non-visual once they arrive on the set.)

MAKE NOTES

If you're working on a scripted project, take the time to read the script slowly, hearing and seeing everything in your head. Make a note for anything that may present a sound issue or opportunity (Figure 5.2). This includes warnings about lines that might be off-mic or have to fight noisy props, but also suggestions for wild sounds to pick up at the shoot, and ideas for the post-production sound design.

Then gather the notes that have to do with shooting, and *use* them. If you're sound designing and someone else is directing, review them all with the director. Bring them up at the pre-pro, so the DP and sound mixer know what to expect... instead of having to wing things at the shoot. If you're wearing all those hats, make a list to remind yourself of sound concerns at the shoot.

Before You Edit

It's tempting to just load in the footage and start cutting, but this can be a mistake unless you've done other films in the same format. Spend a few minutes making some basic decisions about sound to avoid problems later.

ANALYZE THE BUDGET

There's a tendency among hobby filmmakers to buy new toys before starting a project. Audio software, an effects library, a voiceover mic, or high-quality speakers for mixing may seem like a good idea. But first, ask yourself if you'll be able to amortize their cost over other projects. You may find that it's cheaper to rent equipment just for this use, or hire a studio for specific functions like ADR and mix. Business-oriented filmmakers should be making this kind of decision already.

Consider the cost of your time as well. Even if you're doing this as a labor of love and not paying yourself professional rates, your time is a limited commodity. You can spend time debugging and then learning how to use new software or special sound techniques; or you can concentrate on things you

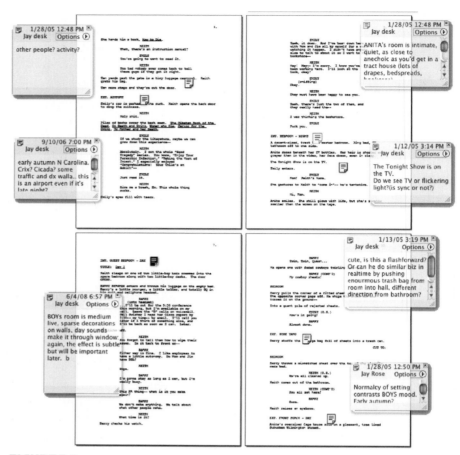

FIGURE 5.2
Make sound notes before you shoot the script. This one uses electronic notes, but the paper stickies work just as well.

do best, possibly storytelling or visual composition, that will make a bigger contribution to the film.

BUDGETING OUTSIDE AUDIO SERVICES

In large cities, a good audio-for-video or narration studio with experienced engineer will cost $125 to $250 per hour plus stock. A lot of the price variation isn't related to quality, but glitziness: ad agency clients are willing to pay extra for services like a dedicated traffic department, or amenities like a kitchen staff and well-appointed lobby. You can save some money, if you don't need to see picture while doing a narration, by hiring a studio that specializes in radio. Many narrators have their own studios and throw that service in for free.

A film-style dub stage uses more real estate and personnel, so prices start around $250/hour. It doesn't make sense to book this kind of room for editing or voice recording, so these facilities are used to picking up projects when they're ready to mix. But choose the stage before you start editing sound, and make sure they're happy with the workflow and techniques you plan to use.

A narration session can take about an hour for each twenty minutes of finished audio, but a lot depends on the script, the narrator's experience, and your own directing style. Add at least an hour if the client is in the studio for narration or mix. But this may be more efficient than having to come back for changes.

Full audio post takes a lot longer. If you want the studio to start with your tracks and clean up voice edits as necessary, then add well-timed music and appropriate sound effects, process everything for proper impact, and mix, figure between 4 hours and a day for a 20-minute video. A lot depends on what shape your tracks are in to start with, how much prep you've done, and how experienced the engineer is. It also depends on what kind of equipment the studio has. Typical mouse-driven computer systems are much slower than audio workstations with dedicated control surfaces and built-in mixers designed for media production.

Mixing a theatrical film on a dub stage takes a while, primarily because you're going to be working to theatrical expectations. A week is the minimum for a feature-length project, and most films take a lot longer. It's a good idea to figure at least another half day for final review and tweaking, after you think the mix is done. If you're doing surround for theatrical distribution, it could easily take another full day just for operations to turn your mix into stems and the various processed files that Dolby or DTX require.

Even if the studio is providing music from their library, you can often save time and expense by booking a separate session to select the music. Library music costs between $15 to $125 per selection, or about $100 to $500 for unlimited music in a 20-minute video, for basic corporate or educational use. The lower end covers basic buyout music, often performed by a single musician on keyboards. The higher end covers the same sources Hollywood features often rely on, with hot session players, top composers, and vocals or symphony orchestras when appropriate. Costs rise depending on how many people are likely to see a production, so they'll be slightly higher for local broadcast, much higher for national broadcast, and easily up to $5,000 per selection to use stock music in a film that's going to be shown in theaters, possibly broadcast, and sold as home video.[8]

Original music is negotiable. Composers who specialize in video scoring will charge $100 to $1,000 per screen minute, depending on their talent and experience, what kind of instrumentation is necessary, and how soon you want it. But you may be able to find a band or young composer who's willing to do it

---

[8] Fortunately, most libraries will let you create your opus with a limited license for film festivals, at a few hundred dollars per song. They'll expect you to upgrade to full theatrical when a Hollywood distributor discovers you.

for free, in exchange for the exposure. Follow the tips in Chapter 9 about rights, licenses, and written agreements.

Existing music—pop songs that would make sense in particular scenes—are *very* negotiable. Even oldies that haven't been hits for years can easily go into the five figures. Local and undiscovered acts can be a lot more flexible. Remember also that there are two sets of rights involved—one for the composer/lyricist, and another for the recording—and you can often save money by licensing just the notes and words on paper, and having another group cover the recording with their own version.

 Gotcha

They call it "temp love." In Hollywood, editors will frequently grab a song from another project—or even a commercial CD—to suggest a rhythm and mood for a sequence. The intent is to use this *temp track* while the piece is being worked on, and then replace it when the final score is available.

But music has a way of getting under your skin. Producers or advertising clients can get used to the temp track and decide that no other song will do. Sometimes there's an unexpected scramble to secure rights—usually for more money than was originally budgeted.

This may be okay for features and national ads, but I've seen it happen on corporate films and local spots. If your music budget is limited, it can be a good idea to choose—and have the client approve—the actual piece before you start cutting picture.

Sound effects are free if you gather them yourself. Commercial ones, with full rights to use them in your film, are fairly cheap: You can download them from reputable suppliers for a few dollars per minute. Most audio post facilities have immense sound effects libraries already on-hand. Costs may be negotiable even if it shows up on the studio's rate card (a standard is $15 per effect); the studio needs to cover the cost of buying the libraries but doesn't have any incremental expense when using them.

TECHNICAL DECISIONS

Before you start cutting picture, you also have to make some basic sound choices:

- How are you planning to use the tracks in your NLE? If you use a consistent layout, with specific tracks dedicated to on-camera dialog, voiceover, sound effects, and music, you'll make subsequent processing and mixing go a lot faster. Don't be afraid to assign lots of tracks for each, so you can separate characters or voiceovers, or keep plot-critical effects different from backgrounds. It'll save a lot of time later.
- What sample rate should you work at? If all your footage is being imported via FireWire, 48 kHz is probably the most efficient. It's the primary standard for DV cameras, and the alternate standard—32 kHz—is

easily converted to match. But music and sound effects CDs are 44.1 kHz, and many NLEs don't handle the conversion between 44.1 kHz and 48 kHz well (see Chapter 6). If you're redigitizing source footage through an analog connection and dubbing the final output as analog, it makes sense to set everything at 44.1 kHz.

- Do you need timecode? If so, what format? This may be dictated by how the video will be used—TV stations often insist on dropframe for long programs—or by the production contract. In most software, it's difficult or impossible to change the timecode format after you start.

WORKFLOW DECISIONS

Making smooth dialog edits—particularly in adlibs and interviews—takes longer in an NLE than in an audio program. A good audio person can often join two words smoothly in a few seconds, even if the video editor struggled for ten minutes and couldn't completely eliminate the jump: different tools, different skills. The same thing applies to music. So it can make sense to quickly do rough edits, and then pass them with handles[9] to audio post. On the other hand, a low-budget production might not be using an audio editor, or may be planning to bring everything to an outside studio just for the mix. In this case, it can be a lot faster and more rewarding to do those edits along with the picture.

The same thing applies to processing. Tricks like noise reduction, reverb, or equalization are better when done with the right gear and with proper monitoring. Trying to do those in your NLE not only wastes time; it can even make further fixing impossible unless you redo without the effects. If you're not planning to use an outside studio, and have to do everything in the NLE, it can still make sense to put off those processes until everything is cut. These are best heard in context with other tracks, while your mind is concentrating on sound instead of sequence.

Before You Start Audio Post

Films don't become real until they're edited. While a straightforward training video might follow its script exactly, the script is just a jumping-off point for most projects. The editor's first assembly, following script and on-set notes, usually has little relationship to the finished film.

That's the art of picture editing. A character's entire attitude can change with just a few mouse moves on the NLE. Lines—and entire sequences—should be deleted or rearranged if they don't advance the story. Characters and even entire locations can end up on the cutting room floor.[10] Of course this is true

---

[9]Hidden overlaps that let audio software take apart your edits and tweak them. See Chapter 4.

[10]Which is why it's so hard for a writer/director to edit their own film. A scene might have taken days to write, rehearse, and shoot; it might get laughs or be thrilling; you could be incredibly proud and want to keep it for your demo reel. But if it's not helping the movie, it's got to go. This, of course, is a subject for a whole shelf of other books. It's also why there's never a shortage of deleted scenes for the DVD release of a theatrical film.

101

◇	A	B	C	D	E	F	G	H	I	J	K	L	M
1	reel	min	sec	cue	scene	by	dan e	de f	e f x	foley	clh d		note
167	4	4	19	paper slap									soften sound at end of scene
168	4	4	52	Emily's pen							1		leads Barry's 'how's it coming
169	4	5	15	4M3 Mr. and the Boys									will be score
170	4	5	17	car drive and stop					1				prodn track not usable
171	4	5	17						1				Walkup to bank: more city n
172	4	5	17	downtown Wilmington					1				similar to courthouse 3.14.4
173	4	5	17										BANK EXT MORE SYNC SOUND
174	4	5	27	**You ready? Let's go.**	79	j	1	1			K		face not seen.
175	4	5	29	car doors					1				possible prodn track, probab
176	4	5	44	**if you hear gunfire, make sure the engine's...**	79	j	1	1			K		
177	4	5	57						1				In bank: paper rustling, foot
178	4	5	57	bank interior					1				Computer fan at desk, walla
179	4	6	49	bank manager									in mix: add verb to match 3-
180	4	7	38							1			Rabbi/Rabbit scene, playing
181	4	7	38	kitchen, group eating Chinese					1				foley Matt in bg, boxes and
182	4	7	55	matthew eating						1			spoon in shallow casserole
183	4	8	41	barry chopstics						1			
184	4	8	55	**Interview questions**	85	s	1	1			K		
185	4	10	4	4M4 Emily Takes Pill									Heitor and Jay must coordina
186	4	10	4	Em: scrapbook | pills | 'let go' | panics									subtle grow during scene: He
187	4	10	4										AT 4.11.20 CHECK FOR MOA
188	4	11	23	replace sally's last moan in scene with ADR (was done to pix) cut with scene rather than carry over									
189	4	11	25	Bridge to ext raining									thunder clap (ext perspective
190	4	11	25										rain and keen is big!!! just c
191	4	11	26	ext raining					1				add more rain for surrounds,
192	4	11	38	doorbell									double for mix options
193	4	11	42	int hallway					1				rain, int perspective; also fill
194	4	12	17	int LR splitting up stuff					1				birds through window, contra
195	4	12	41	Em takes tray									cover upcut prop noise with f
196	4	12	41										emily takes tray has been a

master design list / wild fx / To Do / foley / ADR

FIGURE 5.3
Spreadsheets aren't just for the business office. They can help you keep track of audio operations as well.

of documentaries and event videos, and other ad-libbed films. It's just as true for fully scripted ones.

So now is the time to start ignoring the script, and look at the film. Keep your original notes handy, but be ready to reject some and apply others. Watch the film and note lines that might need technical fixes or replacement, opportunities for sound effects or music cues, and anything else that might need some audio help. The best way to keep track of this all is with a spreadsheet (Figure 5.3).

Use separate columns for which characters will be needed for ADR, what kind of effects have to be found or recorded, which music has to be sourced or cleared and what has to be composed, and anything else that applies. This will make it easy to compile other lists later, sorted by operation or resource. Note the timecode for each note in minutes and seconds columns (and hour or reel for longer projects). That not only makes it easy to find the appropriate point when you're working; it also means you don't have to make notes in sequence. You can watch a couple of times, making notes on anything that strikes you, and let the spreadsheet sort the time columns later.

I've always found it helpful to add a column for additional ideas and queries, go through the list with the director, and put their responses in a separate column. Then, as deadlines approach and you're wondering if a particular operation is necessary, you can judge which ones are most important. A complex film will have a lot of small audio edits and effects inserts that don't have to be done in order, so you'll be skipping around the list while you work. Add a column for a checkmark after the task is done. Then you can see at a glance what's left. You can also use spreadsheet macros and conditional formatting to compile to-do lists, or gray out a line once it's been completed.

Some of your spreadsheet notes will suggest picture edits, so it makes sense to start compiling them even while the film is still in rough cut. And therein lies a conflict: when is a film ready for sound work?

THE IMPORTANCE OF LOCKED PICTURE

Film and video editing deals with shots and sequences, but audio is a continuous arc. Sounds in one scene are influenced by those that came before. While it may be easy to delete a few video frames here and there if a sequence feels too slow, it gets very hard in the audio world. You have to cut the dialog to keep lipsync, but that also affects other elements. Sound effects can seem disjointed if you cut them parallel to picture or dialog cuts. Music seldom wants to be cut "a few frames here and there"; that destroys its rhythm. Leaving music uncut isn't an option, because that throws it out of sync later in the scene. There are ways to finesse both effects and music to make them match the edit—you'll learn them in Chapters 9 and 10—but they take time. They can also be frustrating, not just because of the extra work but because they compromise the sweep of the original audio edit.

So unless you've got a lot of time, money, and patience, it doesn't make sense to start serious editing of the track until the picture is finished. Sound design starts when you're writing the script, and a sound designer should be involved before the shoot… but few audio editors want to actually load files into their computers until the picture is *locked*.

Locking picture isn't as rigid as going gold with a software release, or accepting the final proof on a printing job. There can still be changes. But you can't let them affect timing, even by one frame. Picture can be considered locked even if color correction hasn't been done, titles are missing, or animations and video effects are represented by placeholders. Then you can start fixing audio for the film, even if you'll have to go back to add sync sounds under the animations or music on the end credit.

Unfortunately, locking can have different meanings in the film and video worlds. If you're making a TV show or sales video, postproduction happens on a schedule: picture gets locked, sound gets completed, job gets done, everybody gets paid, the end. Movies don't work that way. Directors want to keep fine-tuning their story, almost until the moment it gets shown on a screen, and that can mean building a finished track even though the picture will still change. Some of this is artistic, and it's up to the director and producer to decide how much money they want to spend opening up and remixing the track. But some of it is practical: festival and test run reactions might suggest useful changes;

103

distributors might require changes before a film can go to theaters; clearances and copyrights can fall through at the last minute. I recently worked on an indie with a $2,000,000 budget and name stars. A year after the final mix, a couple of scenes still had to be changed.[11] This same director had told me, early in our careers, that "a film is never finished … it's just taken away."

There are some ways to handle finished movies that need changes, in Chapter 18.

Choosing an Outside Studio

It's not enough to decide to take some audio operations to a professional studio. You'll have to find a studio that can do a good job for you. While your town might have a lot of music studios, the techniques and philosophy of audio post are different. So is a lot of the equipment. Even a simple voiceover requires a different kind of mic, room acoustics, and processing than a pop vocal. ADR is a completely different process from anything done in a music studio; it can even be beyond studios that specialize in radio and TV voiceovers.[12]

This isn't to say that a music studio can't do the job or have an engineer who knows the proper techniques. But I've found the crossover to be rare, except in very large facilities that can devote separate operations to each kind of recording.

A good way to find an appropriate studio is to ask local ad agency producers. A video post facility can tell you where their clients get tracks done. If you have to rely on a Web search or the Yellow Pages, look for a studio that specifies this kind of work as a specialty and can show you past projects.

If you can, check the facility itself. If you're going to be recording voiceovers, a large studio isn't critical, but you should be able to clap your hands in it and not hear any echo. The control room should have room for a producer to spread out scripts and other notes, and—if you're working to picture—have a prominent high-quality video monitor centered between the speakers. Look for a large, licensable music and sound effects library, even if you'll be supplying your own elements—this is usually a sign that the studio does a lot of this kind of work. Look at what's hanging on the wall as well: Emmys, Clios, and other media awards are usually given for creative reasons rather than technical expertise, but having them around suggests the studio's got experience.

Make your final judgment based on actual final soundtracks the studio, engineer, or composer has worked on. Any professional will have a demo reel available, and most also post segments of representative projects on their Web sites. When you're watching a reel, forget the picture: Close your eyes and see if the sound makes sense.

---

[11] One of the nice things about working in computers with automated mixes is that it's relatively easy to make a change a year later, and have the new scene match the surrounding ones perfectly.

[12] There are techniques for doing ADR in non-ADR surroundings, in Chapter 7.

CHAPTER 6

Getting Audio into the Computer

Our business is often accused of a lack of originality. Critics complain that almost every new film or TV show is a copy of something else.

That's certainly how soundtracks used to be created: by copying. Movies had their field audio tapes, with sync signals, copied to 35 mm mag stock. This was then edited, and copied to a premix. The premix got copied along with other elements into a magnetic master, which was then copied to an optical master, and then to prints (with possibly some intermediate copies along the way).

Video wasn't any better. You'd put blank videotape into a master recorder and copy individual scenes and camera angles to it, along with matching dialog. Then you'd copy the videotape's track to a multi-track audio tape. If precise editing was required, you'd copy from there to ¼-inch audio tape and back. Then you'd copy the tracks into a mix, copy the mix back to the video master, and make copies for release. If this was a spot going to a TV station, it would then get copied to a compilation reel or server before it went on the air.

I'm not talking ancient history; just a little more than a decade ago. Most of what's on the air or available for DVD rental was created that way. This was a problem, since each analog copy was a chance for noise or distortion to creep in. We all worked very hard (and spent a lot on equipment and maintenance) to keep these problems controlled. But they couldn't be completely eliminated. Once it was there, the junk could never be removed.

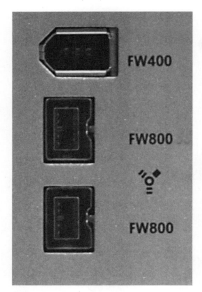

FW400

FW800

FW800

FIGURE 6.1
FireWire connectors come in different configurations with different capabilities, but for filmmaking purposes you can cross-connect them.

106

Today, sound is digital and you can copy or mix with no loss of quality in a desktop computer. But first you have to copy it *into* the computer. If you do this through an analog connection, most of the old bugaboos are back. If you do it digitally, traditional noise and distortion isn't a problem—but you can introduce other problems. Because this is the easiest place for gremlins to sneak in, getting a signal onto a hard drive can be the most important technical step in postproduction.

TRANSFER TECHNOLOGY

Apple's FireWire,[1] a high-speed serial protocol, is now the most common way of capturing audio and video from the original footage. It can also control tape movement and pass timecode. FireWire comes standard on most computers, and can be easily added to others with low-cost cards. Most DV cameras also have FireWire jacks. There are two flavors of connections on the computer—6-pin jacks are the most common, but 9-pin ones are appearing—and a 4-pin version on the cameras. For most filmmaking purposes, they're all the same: All you need is a simple adapter or cable to cross-connect them. They're usually even *hot-swappable*—you can plug or unplug without restarting the equipment—but there are exceptions.[2] It's safest to check the manuals or shut down if you're not sure about specific equipment.

Analog video decks don't have FireWire connections. But you can capture footage from these by using a powered converter box, also known as a FireWire interface or media converter; it has conventional audio and video inputs and outputs on the analog side, and a FireWire jack on the other. The computer sees it as a digital camera. Some very high-end NLEs also accept AES/EBU audio directly; its issues are very similar to those with FireWire.

> ⚠️ **Gotcha**
>
> ***One way street.*** FireWire is bidirectional—data flows in both directions simultaneously— but most FireWire media converters aren't. You have to flip a switch to determine whether the box will turn analog signals into digital for capturing, or convert the computer output back to analog for a deck or video monitor.

---

[1]Apple invented it, trademarked it, and opened the standard up to other manufacturers. But until the middle of 2002, Apple charged a license fee to use the name, so companies often called it IEEE 1394 to save money. Sony gave the standard its own handle, i.Link. It's all the same thing.
[2]The differences include whether the plug carries power as well as data. Some equipment can get damaged if you change a power connection while it's turned on.

Digital Audio Transfers

When a DV signal is carried from camera to computer digitally, there is no audio loss. Unless there's a setup problem, the computer file will be a clone of the DV tape. There's no need to adjust levels. In many cases, there's no *way* to adjust levels.

SAMPLE RATE

The most critical part of the setup is making the sample rates match. DV audio runs at nominal 32 kHz or 48 kHz s/r. Your capture setup controls should be set to the same rate as the source, or audio is likely to get damaged. Problems range from sound at the wrong pitch, to periodic clickings, to silence.

If most of your project's audio is coming from the camera, the project or sequence should be set to 48 kHz. That's also the rate you're most likely to use when printing the final project to video. But if most of the sound is coming from 44.1 kHz sources, and you'll be outputting for the Web or CD-ROM, use 44.1 kHz for the project. The goal is to minimize times when a clip's rate doesn't match the project. Each mismatch requires on-the-fly conversion for previews—which can sound bad—or a separate rendering at the new rate.

Even when sample rates match, there can be problems. Some NLEs require precise sync between the digital audio words and the video frame rate, and a few cameras don't have this precision. When this problem occurs, you may hear momentary dropouts in the track. The only cure is to transfer the audio as analog. (This isn't the same kind of sync problem as having sound and picture drift apart, which is covered later in this chapter.) Going in the other direction—printing the finished master to tape—also requires precise sync. Most professional digital decks won't accept a digital audio signal that isn't locked to the picture.

107

CHANNELS

A lot of dialog is recorded in mono with a single mic. There's no advantage to capturing this kind of footage in stereo. Stereo material, of course, should be captured in stereo. If the footage has a boom and lav on separate tracks, capture it as stereo with one mic on each channel. You don't want to combine the mics yet and possibly never will. Edit them as stereo, and be ready to sort them out at the mix.

Many cameras give you the option of adding extra audio tracks by setting a 32-kHz sample rate and 12-bit format. NLEs convert this to 16-bits as the file is being transferred. If footage has four tracks, most NLEs let you capture only two at a time; you have to go back, capture the others, and then sync them on the timeline. But since those extra tracks are intended for adding narration or music in the camera—something you're better off doing in a computer—it usually makes more sense not to shoot at this rate in the first place.

Some digital double-system recorders capture multiple audio tracks, and are usually hooked up to give each wireless mic its own track. But these devices record to files that can be inserted in the NLE, so real-time multi-channel capture isn't an issue.

Gotcha

Digital quality loss. Many filmmakers use pocket digital recorders in the field, as an alternative to wireless or the poor audio circuits in some cameras. While the format itself can provide acceptable audio,[3] the players' analog outputs usually aren't high quality. I have measured more than twice the noise and reduced high frequencies when comparing some devices' analog outputs to the actual files they recorded.

If you're transferring material from MiniDisc or DAT, you'll get better results if you use a deck that can connect to your NLE digitally. Or take the tracks to a studio or dub house that can transfer them digitally, and have them turned into files.

Direct File Transfers and Ingest

Many of the newest portables let you mount their media on your computer and copy directly to their internal drives. This not only saves time, but assures the best audio quality since error correction can be used. Sample rate and bit depth are specified in the file header, so there's little chance for setup error. Many of these recorders use mp3 or other compressed formats. Even so, a direct file copy usually sounds better than playing in the recorder and copying as real-time audio. Even if you then need to run a utility to covert back to standard format, the process will also be faster.

A similar process happens when you capture (*rip*) music or effects from an audio CD in your computer's CD-ROM drive. It's usually a perfect-sounding digital transfer, as fast as your drive can spin. Ripping functions are available in most audio programs and NLEs, and directly on many computer desktops. CDs are always at 44.1 kHz, so sample rate conversion might be necessary before you use the file.

 Gotcha

Too hot to handle! Many pop CDs are recorded at extreme levels, sometimes louder than your computer's audio output can play without distortion. In my experience, it's a good idea to soften these files by a decibel or two in an audio program before importing them to the NLE.

INGEST

Unlike digital or analog dubs, file transfers can carry more than audio. Sound file formats can be expanded to include all sorts of useful information in their

---

[3]There's no guarantee a particular $300 recorder will sound better than a $3,000 camera, but most do.

headers. The information is invisible to software that isn't expecting it—other applications just play it as a normal audio file—and adds only a few hundred bytes to the files. But because it allows so much more to happen at the transfer, and it's a fairly new workflow concept, it gets a new word: *ingest*.

At the very minimum, ingest maintains the original filename on the NLE's timeline. Organized productions often include the reel, scene, and take number as part of the filename (many audio field recorders do this automatically), so it makes subsequent audio operations easier. Looking for isolated mic channels that aren't on the OMF? Pick up the sound log and see if they were recorded. Need a word or two to cover noises? Alternate takes will have almost identical filenames, with just the take number changed.

Ingest also captures a file's *timestamp*: camera- or self-generated timecode noted in the field by properly equipped recorders. Many NLEs can use this to automatically sync takes against picture, either directly or by using a third-party plug-in.

An emerging standard for this audio file *metadata* is iXML, invented by the Institute for Broadcast Sound in 2004. It's now supported by many recorder and software manufacturers. iXML embeds all of the information that would be in a sound log, plus sync and other data, into normal .wav files. Figure 6.2 (next page) shows a little of what can be included.

Ingest can be a great timesaver. But it comes with a warning: When you transfer audio from a tape, the original stays intact and is always there for backup. But when you mount a camera or recorder's DVD-RAM or memory card, the original appears on your desktop. There's a very tiny chance it will get corrupted by the operating system, but a much bigger chance that it will get accidentally changed by the user. Copy the file onto another drive, and remove the original as soon as possible.

ANALOG AUDIO RECORDING

It's called *digitizing* in the NLE world, and *recording* in audio-only programs. The process is the same. You connect an analog audio signal to a jack on a sound card, module, or NLE connection pod, and press Capture or Record on the computer. Even though the original recording may have been digital, the transfer is analog. Each time audio jumps from digital to analog and back again, it picks up a little more distortion and noise.

Despite this, transferring via analog can sometimes be helpful. Nonstandard or badly synchronized sample rates are easily handled. You can adjust audio levels as you digitize. Doing this once, with properly adjusted equipment, isn't a problem. But you have to set levels properly.

Headroom and Noise

Analog circuits have a limited range between their own internal noise and the loudest signal they can carry accurately. Unfortunately, that upper limit

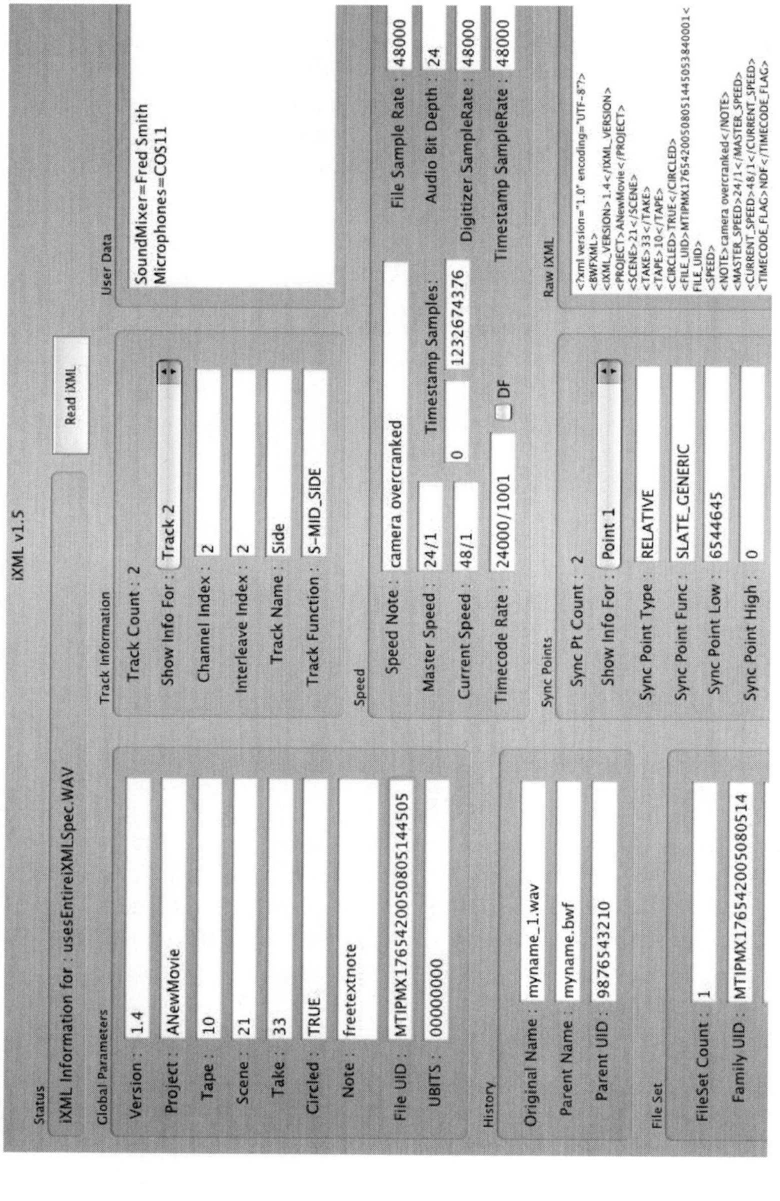

FIGURE 6.2
Some of the data that can be ingested along with audio, shown in Gallery Software's free iXML reader.

is a slippery concept. Unlike digital audio, which has negligible distortion below full scale and then fails utterly, analog begins to add distortion as the signal approaches 0 VU. It then increases the distortion for signals above 0 VU—a volume range often known as *headroom*—until things reach a maximum volume. This is not only true for analog recordings, but also for the analog circuits in your digital sound card.

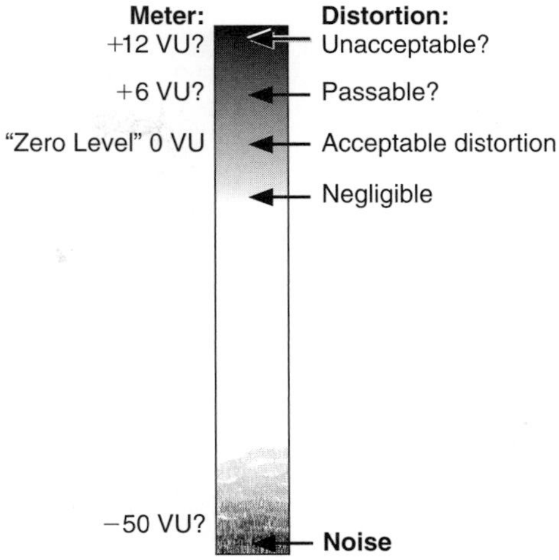

How much distortion happens or headroom is available depends on the circuit designer. Figure 6.3 expands the analog part of the level graph from Figure 3.1 (page 48). It represents the full range a circuit can carry, with the upper gray area as increasing distortion. Someone decides how much distortion is acceptable, and the volume at that distortion level becomes 0 VU.

You can reduce the possibility of unacceptable distortion by lowering the volume, but the downside—literally—is system noise. The softer the signal, the worse noise gets by comparison. While this kind of noise can be made less annoying (Chapter 15), it can never be eliminated.

You have to compromise, making things loud enough that noise isn't a problem but not so loud that distortion is noticeable.

Meter:	Distortion:
+12 VU?	Unacceptable?
+6 VU?	Passable?
"Zero Level" 0 VU	Acceptable distortion
	Negligible
−50 VU?	Noise

FIGURE 6.3
The range between analog distortion and noise. The question marks are because actual values depend on the specifc equipment.

111

CREST FACTOR

Professionals typically line up their equipment using a tone at the nominal or average level. But this doesn't tell you how much louder the peaks might be. The ratio between average and peak (the *crest factor*) depends on the material.

- A dialog recording with dynamic acting can have peaks 12 to18 dB above average. But recording of a neutral on-camera spokesperson might never reach 6 dB above average.
- Many background ambiences are fairly even. But sound effects can be unpredictable. A recording of a gunshot may have peaks 30 dB louder than its average.
- Pop music is usually processed to stay within a 6 dB crest factor.[4] Older recordings may have higher dynamic range. Some newer dance music can stay within 2 dB. Classical music ranges can vary even more than pop.

Production sound recordists and studio engineers rely on their experience. They try to guess the best and safest recording level. Getting post-production levels right is easier: You can scan the entire take before you set the volume, or undo if you've guessed wrong.

---

[4]That's not an official spec, just my observation of current styles.

Gotcha

Don't trust things at the top. Some forms of pop music tolerate a lot of distortion. Many of today's prosumer analog audio mixers and processors are sold for this kind of music, so the peak-reading meters on this equipment may extend beyond +10VU before turning red. Dialog is more sensitive—even a little distortion hurts intelligibility—so filmmakers should check anything above +6VU.

Level Setting and Meters

Back in analog days, the VU meter made level-setting easy. Its timing was calibrated to the way humans perceive analog distortion. You'd adjust so occasional peaks were just above zero, and everything would be fine. If a sudden overload was too fast to be caught by the meter, chances are nobody would notice it. You could even set the meter using a lineup tone. Its crest factor, of course, would be different from the program you're recording. But any differences could probably be ignored.

Things aren't as simple at the interface between analog and digital. Digital distortion is easier to hear, even when it's only for a very short time. Circuit designers are in a bind. If they assign a high average analog level to a high digital value, sudden peaks might cause noticeable distortion. But if they make that level too low, it'll be close to noises from both the analog circuits and from subsequent digital processing. All they can do is compromise and hope for the best.

Designers tend to be conservative with professional broadcast and film equipment. They design their analog circuits to be very quiet and use high bit depths to avoid processing noise. So they set the nominal at −20 dBFS. That's the level that relates to +4 dBu on the equipment's analog connectors. It leaves 20 dB for a crest factor, but still puts the average signal roughly 60 dB above the equipment's analog noise.

But desktop and semipro equipment generates more noise internally. So to keep the signal clean, the nominal level is usually raised to −12 dBFS. That's what matches line level on the equipment's analog side.[5] It leaves less headroom for sudden peaks, so setting levels is actually more critical in the semipro world than on a Hollywood shooting stage.

WAVEFORM LEVELS

Of course, setting a precise level is possible only when you're dealing with steady tones. Dialog levels keep changing depending on the words that are

---

[5]Which is usually −10 dBV for unbalanced connections, and +4 dBu for balanced ones. The difference has nothing to do with the −12 or −20 dBFS digital standards; it's an historical accident from pre-digital days.

112

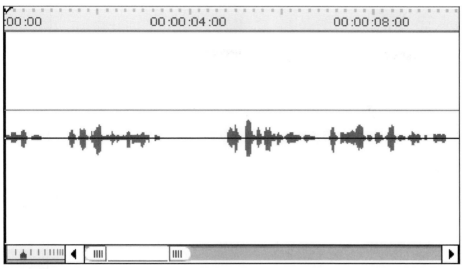

FIGURE 6.4
Typical pro dialog recordings average −20 dBFS and peak around −14 dBFS. But showing them accurately in most NLEs makes them look too small for editing.

being said. Fortunately, there's another way to judge volume when a project gets to post: look at the envelope in your NLE's waveform display.

A recording at −20 dBFS actually looks kind of small in a program that has linear displays—as almost all of them do—since it's only about an eighth of the total possible voltage (Figure 6.4). Inexperienced editors often complain that professionally recorded dialog is too soft because of this.

Many desktop NLEs specify −12 dBFS for a nominal level, both so the waveform looks better (Figure 6.5) and to avoid processing noise. But this level might not provide enough room for peaks in a dynamic theatrical track.

There's a danger in digitizing at too high a volume. Figure 6.6 shows original dialog with an average level of −6 dBFS and peaks at −0.2 dBFS. While it's acceptable for a processed or mixed file to become this loud, if original footage looks like this, there's a good chance that short peaks—too fast to show in this waveform—have gotten distorted.[6]

So what level should you digitize at? In a desktop environment, I recommend −12 dBFS for average signals. But you have to be flexible and lower the digitizing level if the meter is coming close to 0 dBFS, or if the waveform comes close to filling the clip display. That's the approach used in music production as well, where standards range between −20 and −12 dBFS, based on the program material.

---

[6]These very fast overloads create clicks that may even be too soft to hear at a typical editing station. But *boy!* do they jump out at you in a theater.

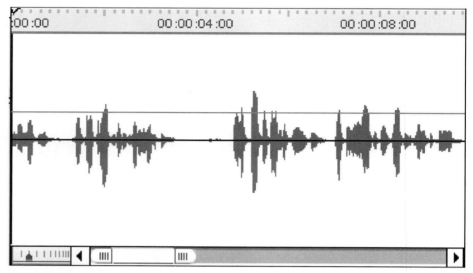

FIGURE 6.5
This recording averages −12 dBFS and peaks around −6 dBFS, probably as high as an original capture should ever go.

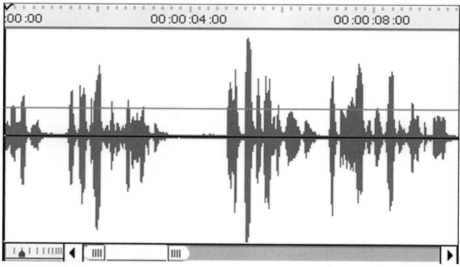

FIGURE 6.6
Dialog with average level around −6 dBFS. This is living *very* dangerously.

If you're preparing material for broadcast, you can still work at this slightly elevated level. Just turn the final mix down to −20 dBFS nominal before making digital tapes for the stations.

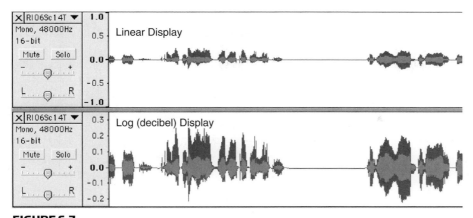

FIGURE 6.7
A properly recorded clip (top) looks easier to edit (bottom) when you boost the display, even
though this doesn't affect the sound quality.

And if working at a proper level means the waveforms look too wimpy to
edit, see if your program has a way to boost the display without changing
the file. Figure 6.7 shows the same clip displayed normally on the top, and
with roughly a 50 percent visual-only boost below it. Better yet, learn how
to edit by ear instead of by eye. It's faster and much more flexible. See Chapters
8 and 9.

115

Metering

You can't automatically trust the meters. Presumably, the hardware meters on a
mixer or analog video deck equal 0 VU when the device is putting out its nominal line voltage. But there's no standard for how that voltage will show in any
software's meter. It depends on the input hardware, and can be influenced by
system-level settings before it ever gets to the app. Calibrating the meters isn't
hard, and needs to be done only when you change your hardware or system
settings. I've posted instructions at dplay.com/gotcha.

Once the signal has made it to the software, you can usually trust any
meters that are calibrated in dBFS. The meters in Figure 6.8 are; you can tell
by the fact that zero is at the absolute top. These meters are also somewhat
logarithmic: -6 dBFS, or 50 percent of the maximum signal voltage, is fairly
high in the scale. A meter calibrated this way will encourage you to digitize at
safe levels.

The meter in Figure 6.9 is also calibrated in dBFS. But note how -6 dBFS is at
the middle of the scale. This meter is calibrated in linear volts and will tempt
you to digitize at too high a level. If your software has meters like this, avoid
letting unprocessed dialog get above the midpoint.

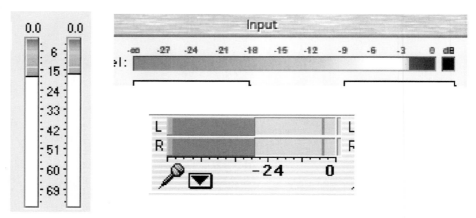

FIGURE 6.8
These meters are calibrated in dBFS: you can tell because zero is at the absolute top. They're also based on logarithms, with −6 close to the top.

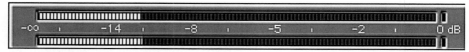

FIGURE 6.9
This meter also reads dBFS, but it's not logarithmic. Even though it's reading −12 dBFS, a good level for recording dialog, it's lit up only a quarter of the way.

 Gotcha

The mysterious overload. Note how the two horizontal meters in Figure 6.8, and the one in Figure 6.9, have an overload warning light to the right of 0 dBFS. Digital audio values can't exceed zero—there are no bits to express a higher voltage—so what are they doing there? A signal can never get loud enough to cause this overload!

A flashing light can be a valuable warning. There are a couple of standard ways to trigger one. Many systems count how many samples in a row reach *exactly* 0 dBFS; when there are a bunch, they give you a warning. Others simply blink at some level *near* 0 dBFS. How close that level has to be—I've seen some as far as −6 dBFS—or how many samples get counted is up to the programmer.

So in some software, you should trust the bar graph more than the blinking light. But in others, the bar graph response time has been slowed down to more closely match VU meters... so the light might spot problems the graph would miss!

Bottom line: until you're sure how a particular meter behaves, check the actual files to make sure they're not too soft or too loud.[7]

---

[7]And be glad you're working in post instead of location recording. You get a chance to re-digitize. Those folks have to look at the meters and get it right the first time.

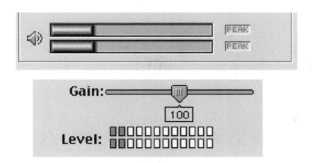

FIGURE 6.10.
Meters with no calibration marks aren't much good at all.

LEVELS YOU CAN TRUST

There are level-setting tones included in this book's CD. If you rip them into your NLE with no volume adjustment selected in your ripping software, they should give you files with accurate levels. Use these for comparison with your recordings, and to judge how your software's waveform display and meters react.

Hear for yourself

Track 16 consists of steady test tones for checking a level meter. It has a 1-kHz sine wave, with 5 seconds at −20 dBFS, −12 dBFS, and −6 dBFS. Be aware that tones on a CD are recorded at 44.1 kHz. A particularly sloppy conversion algorithm might affect their level. If you convert these tones to 48 kHz to match your NLE's timeline, check the result in an audio program to verify that the level hasn't changed.

AVOID SOFTWARE-BASED RECORD LEVEL CONTROLS

A record volume adjustment, either in a program or at your computer's system level (Figure 6.11), can pollute the sound. While they do adjust levels, they can only work after a signal has been converted from analog. So raising them doesn't solve existing signal/noise problems; it just raises the noise along with the signal. And lowering them doesn't cancel the distortion on a signal that's already run out of bits. Furthermore, any volume adjustment requires additional math, which in a 16-bit desktop system can make things sound a tiny bit worse. Always leave these adjustments in their neutral position. Look for these adjustments in your software, and make sure they're set to neutral.

If you're dealing with pro equipment that has 24-bit digitizers and excellent analog input stages, a software volume control can be helpful before converting a signal to 16 bits. But in a desktop world, with most sound cards or input devices, you should leave these controls at their neutral positions: There should be no change of level at all. A few systems let you disable them completely, which is the best idea.

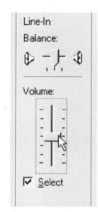

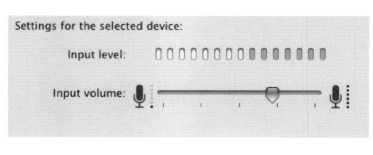

FIGURE 6.11
System-level input volume controls should be left in their neutral position, or have their checkboxes turned off.

Using Small Mixers

While low-cost mixers can be helpful in a digitizing setup, they don't have the noise and distortion performance of a studio recording console. A few extra steps will help you get the best sound out of them.

- Many mixers have small *trim* controls near each channel's input jack. Follow the adjustment procedure recommended in their manual to reduce distortion and noise.[8]
- Each input generates a little noise of its own, even if the device plugged into it is turned off. Reduce this by turning all unused channel faders down. If the mixer has effects return controls (usually small knobs above the master), turn those down as well.
- Avoid using the mixer's equalizers. You can do a more controllable (and undoable) job in software. Leave equalizers at their midpoint or neutral position.

Digitizing from Analog Tape Decks

Analog tape is a simpler technology than DAT or computer backup tapes, and its performance is more subject to variations in the playback equipment. Couple that with the likely age of any playback deck you'll be using—few analog decks are manufactured any more—and it's reasonable to assume some adjustment will be necessary to get the best results.

Three mechanical steps are necessary before any critical transfer from analog tape: clean the tape path, demagnetize the heads, and adjust the azimuth.

---

[8]Very briefly, this means setting the channel and master faders to nominal (marked 0 or U), playing a nominal test signal like that −12 dBFS CD track, and adjusting the trimmer for a zero reading on the mixer's meter.

None of these is particularly hard or requires advanced test equipment, and there are step-by-step instructions at dplay.com/gotcha. If you skip them, it means more than just a poor transfer. There's also a chance your deck can permanently hurt your tape.

One electrical adjustment is also necessary, even if your deck is in perfect condition: check the noise reduction settings. Both cassettes and open-reel tapes may have been recorded with one of the many flavors of Dolby or dbx noise reduction. These are *double-ended* systems, which means that processing during playback has to match what was used during the recording. Getting them wrong can affect frequency response and dynamics as well as noise levels. If you can't tell what was used from a tape's label, try all the options your deck offers.

 Gotcha

Ten years from now, who will notice? It's worth taking the time to adjust analog decks before you digitize valuable tapes. A badly adjusted deck will hurt the sound in ways that subsequent software processing can't fix. Since analog recording is a dying art—decks are hard to find, and older tapes are deteriorating—this might be your last chance to convert things to a preservable format.

119

SYNCHRONIZATION

If you're capturing sound and picture simultaneously from the same videotape, the resulting file should be in lipsync.[9] But if you're using double-system sound, with audio coming from a different playback deck than video, you'll have to synchronize manually. Double-system is the standard when shooting film. Videographers use it as a way to avoid wireless mics—hiding tiny recorders on talent or the groom in a wedding video—and as a workaround for what can be poor internal sound recording in camcorders.

Speed Issues

DV cameras, film cameras with crystal or AC motors, and digital audio media are all inherently speed stable. The crystals in all but the cheapest units should hold sync within a frame for at least 15 minutes. Most will go longer. But crystal stability is influenced by temperature, and there is some variation between units. If in doubt, transfer to your computer using the same recorder at about the same temperature that was in the field. Once double-system is transferred into your NLE, the computer's internal clock should keep audio and video rolling at the same speed.

---

[9]A few cameras record the sound slightly ahead of the picture, because their internal video processing takes time. There's more about this in my book *Producing Great Sound*.

Gotcha

Sinking sync. I've used the qualifier "should" twice in the previous paragraph. Here's one more: Crystal-driven materials will stay in sync when everything is done exactly as the equipment designers and programmer assumed it would. But with all the variation in system-level drivers, third-party cards, and recording systems, a lot of things can get in the way. If transfers don't look like they're in lipsync, or things seem to drift as you play or output a file, check the troubleshooting tips at the end of this chapter.

If you're shooting performances or other long events and require perfect double-system stability, you'll need a common reference between sound and picture. This has to happen both at the shoot and during the transfer. Check Chapter 3 for advice about blackburst and audio word clock.

Establishing Sync

For most of the past century, double-system sound was synchronized by lining up a sudden sound with a one-frame event on the film. That's what Hollywood's familiar slate was for: two pieces of wood would be slapped together in front of camera and microphone. Diagonal stripes on the wood made it easy to see the precise frame where the wood met. An editorial assistant would match this film frame with the *crack* sound, and sprockets or code numbers would be used to keep things together for the rest of the take.

It works just as well in the digital world. In fact, slapped slates are often used as a backup even on productions that have timecode. Slates are available at film and video suppliers. Or focus on an assistant's hands as they clap or tap the mic.

For very long takes, put a slate at the tail as well as the head. Sync the front slate manually in your editor. Then jump to the end. If the tail slate isn't in sync, count how many frames picture and audio have drifted. Then divide by the number of frames in the shot and apply a correction using the clip speed setting. If your NLE distorts the sound on tiny speed changes like this, try tweaking the video speed instead.

SLATELESS SYNC

Because DV tape records a soundtrack, you can use a camera's track for sync reference even if its quality isn't good enough for the final mix. Send the same audio to the double-system recorder and to the camera. Slip the double-system track in a NLE until it matches the DV track. If there's subsequent drift, you'll hear it immediately as an echo between the two tracks. Once you're satisfied things are in sync, delete the reference and lock the remaining audio and video tracks together.

It's possible to use a camera mic for this, but room echoes and delays because of the speed of sound can make it a lot more difficult. On the other hand, the feed from your double-system recorder to camera doesn't have to sound particularly good. Even a cheap wireless from an electronics chain store will work.

Timecode

Most films and high-end video projects use SMPTE timecode for sync. Crystal-controlled code generators are provided on the camera and sound recorder. A few times a day these generators are jammed to synchronize their clocks; the rest of the time, internal crystals keep things together. Traditional slates have been replaced by ones with internal timecode generators and large counting displays. The picture numbers are shot on film and read visually during postproduction, or encoded as a digital pattern along the edge of the film, or recorded on a high-definition videotape timecode track. The audio numbers are recorded as a time stamp on digital files or at the start of DAT tapes. Once things are aligned, the picture's frame rate and audio sample rate are locked together and keep everybody marching in sync.

If film takes are being transferred to video for broadcast editing and release, new continuous timecode is added to the video master. At the same time, the production DAT or file is played in sync, and copied with timecode matching the videotape. This dub (often called a *simulDAT*) becomes the audio master for postproduction. Because it's a digital clone of the original, there's no quality loss.

TIMECODE TYPES: LTC AND VITC

Timecode was developed by the Society of Motion Picture and Television Engineers (SMPTE) back in analog days, as a way to put a unique number on every frame of a videotape. At first, it was an audio stream around 2.4 kHz[10] bi-phase serial data, sounding very similar to a fax transmission. This audio stream could be recorded on any conventional audio channel, though lower-quality *address tracks* were often used instead. Conventional audio wiring carried the signal to timecode readers and other equipment.

While analog video is always recorded at an angle to the tape movement, audio and cue channels are parallel to it. So timecode was also called LTC or longitudinal timecode. (The name also refers to the signal itself, when it's on a wire.) LTC is great at play speed or fast wind, but doesn't work when the tape is jogging or paused. Once it became possible to still-frame a videotape, an alternate code was added that uses flashing lights in the black band above the video picture. VITC (Vertical Interval Timecode) could be read when the tape was at play speed or less, but got jumbled at faster speeds. Modern pro analog video decks—yes, such things are still being used every day—support both code types internally, and switch between them as appropriate. Pro digital video decks and DAT tapes use a separate data stream, but output the signal as LTC for compatibility.

---

[10]The precise frequency depends on the frame rate.

TIMECODE TYPES: DROPFRAME AND NON-DROPFRAME

Timecode identifies each video frame with integers for hour, minute, second, and frame number. This works perfectly when there's an integral number of frames per second—24 fps for film, 25 fps for PAL video, and 30 fps in some HD. The math is simple. For example, PAL timecode counts 00:00 (seconds:frames) through 00:24. Then it adds one second and resets the frame counter for 01:00.

But NTSC video, still used in most of the Americas and the Pacific Rim, runs at (approximately) 29.97 frames per second. This tiny difference—for all practical purposes, 1/10 of a percent slower than 30 fps—causes problems. You can't simply count 0 through 28.97 frames and then increment one second. The system doesn't know what a hundredth of a frame is. It's counting frame edges as they go by, and has no way to align tiny fractions to those edges.

So they fudge the numbers, counting 30 fps for most of the time, but once per minute, they *skip* two frame numbers. The frame after 1:29 (seconds:frames) is 2:00. But the one after 59:29 is 1:00:02. In that first second of the new minute, frames start counting with 2 instead of 0.

Confusing, huh? Figure 6.12 fits it all together.

The scheme almost works. But we're still doing a little rounding off, and that introduces another error. This error is smaller, 2 frames every 10 minutes, but in the other direction. To make things come out even, once every ten minutes we *don't* skip frame numbers.

Got it?

That's *dropframe* (also *drop* or *df*) timecode, used by broadcasters for program production. Timing is critical for them, and they rely on timecode to insert commercials or join network smoothly. *Non-dropframe (ndf)* code is easier to deal with and used when running time doesn't need to be as precise, such as sales or event videos or feature films edited as NTSC. Broadcast commercials also have to be tightly timed, but 30 seconds isn't long enough for the uneven numbers to introduce a significant error, so the simpler non-drop format is usually used for spots.

- It's important to remember that dropframe doesn't actually drop any frames. Every image of your precious picture is put on the screen. It's just that some of them are numbered strangely.
- Dropframe and non-dropframe are indistinguishable during most of a minute while they're being run. You can even sync audio that was recorded one way to video that was shot the other. Unfortunately, after a minute goes by the sync will appear to be off by two frames. Some systems avoid this issue by not letting you import clips that aren't in the right format. Better ones let the operator choose to ignore any errors—sometimes things really are still in sync—or modify the speed until the numbers match again.

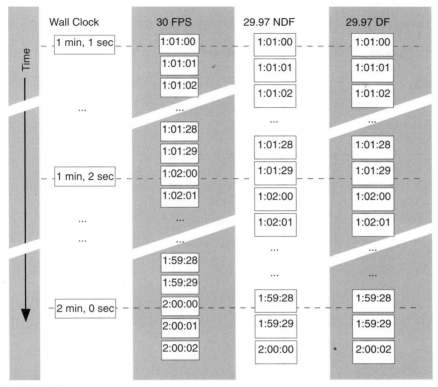

FIGURE 6.12
Dropframe demystified. If there were exactly 30 frames to a second, timecode would always agree with the clock on the wall. You can see that by checking the first two columns at 1:02 and 2:00. But NTSC frames (third and fourth columns) are slightly slower. When nondrop (col. 3) thinks it's two minutes, the clock says two minutes *and two frames*. Dropframe (col. 4) catches up by skipping two numbers at the asterisk.

- Most NLEs and audio programs start clips based on timecode numbers. If you change a project's timecode format after you've started editing, long clips might not line up properly with those starting later. There is no cure for this other than manually resyncing. Again, most systems avoid this by not letting you change the format after a project is started. But sometimes changes are necessary, and the best audio programs use a very precise internal timecode and translate it to the desired SMPTE format on the fly. This completely fixes the problem.
- LTC and VITC carry a 1-bit flag to indicate whether timecode is dropframe or non-dropframe, so a device can tell immediately which it's dealing with. Most programs and decks substitute a semicolon for the final colon when displaying dropframe time data. 01:00:00:00 means nondrop; 01:00:00;00 means drop.

Gotcha

Hope for the future. Dropframe is necessary only for NTSC color television, the system used in the United States for the last half-century. An all-digital television system—the kind the we're starting to adopt—doesn't need it.

Unfortunately, there are going to be a lot of NTSC users around for a long time. So it's going to take quite a few more editions of this book before I can tear out these confusing pages.

TIMECODE SUMMARY

Table 6.1 shows the common video timecode formats. There are others, which are used outside the film and video industries.

Table 6.1	**Timecode formats**		
Type	**Frame Rate**	**Counting Format (seconds:frames)**	**Used For**
24 fps	24 fps	00:00, 00:01, 00:02, 00:23, 01:00, 01:01	Nonlinear editing of film
25 fps	25 fps	00:00, 00:01, 00:02, 00:23, 00:24, 01:00, 01:01	PAL video
29.97 non-dropframe	29.97 fps	00:00, 00:01, 00:02, 00:28, 00:29, 01:00, 01:01	NTSC video, shortform and nonbroadcast
29.97 dropframe	29.97 fps	00:00, 00:01, 00:02, 00:28, 00:29, 01:02, 01:03 (minutes ending in 0 count like non-dropframe)	NTSC video, longform broadcast
30 fps non-dropframe	30 fps	00:00, 00:01, 00:02, 00:28, 00:29, 01:00, 01:01	Some film and PAL double-system audio; music production
30 fps dropframe	This rate and format combination is very rarely used; it's found only in some film-for-video applications.		

All of these formats count hours (0–23) and minutes (0–59) as well as seconds and frames. Common practice is to start each video and audio tape, and each reel of a longform film, with a new hour number. Be careful during that 23rd hour; most timecode equipment can't deal with code that keeps counting past 23:59:59:29.

TIMECODE TRANSMISSION AND DECK CONTROL

LTC over an audio cable used to be the standard in analog video editing suites. But it's largely abandoned now, outside of some audio applications. Its high frequencies can jump into nearby unbalanced audio circuits, causing a chirping noise. Besides, other methods of transmitting time information are more reliable and convenient.

RS-422

While the name refers to a standard computer interface, most video people use RS-422 to identify the high-speed control protocol originated by Sony and now found in almost all pro video equipment. Commands—sent as efficient strings of Hex bytes and not humanly readable—include obvious transport instructions like play or rewind, but there are also commands like "what frame are you on now?" or "play at 1/32nd speed" for decks, or "start a 60-frame dissolve" for switchers. Responses from the device are usually a simple acknowledgement or status report. This protocol is also sometimes called P2[11] or simply Sony 9-pin. While the RS-232 connection on PCs also uses a 9-pin jack, the wiring is different and usually doesn't work. USB or RS-232 to RS-422 adapters cost under $50, and RS-422 jacks appear on many FireWire-connected video i/o boxes.

Since there's no timecode signal in this format, precise sync requires that the controller or NLE and video deck also share blackburst or a video reference. Otherwise, sync can be as much as a frame off in either direction. This is an important consideration when you're hooking up a tape deck via 9-pin in a small NLE suite.

RS-422 data is also used by the *ES Bus* protocol, an open standard developed by the European Broadcast Union and SMPTE. Unfortunately, it appeared about the same time as Sony's P2 and got buried by market forces.

RS-232

The RS-232 electrical standard is unbalanced but otherwise similar to RS-422; the data protocol is almost identical. Because the circuits are cheaper to build, RS-232 is found on semipro analog video equipment. The command structure is similar to P2, though it's more limited.

---

[11]In the 1980s, Sony decks could accept two different remote control plugs simultaneously: one for a conventional system, and one for their new-fangled RS-422 controllers. A front-panel switch let you choose which would be active, and *Plug 2* or *P2* was the newer format.

125

FIREWIRE

The FireWire high-speed data standard, described earlier in this chapter for digital audio and video transfers, can handle simultaneous timecode and transport instructions as well. It's become the most common control protocol in DV setups. Additional LTC, sync, or serial wiring isn't necessary. There are two standards with different levels of control; good NLEs let you choose the one that matches your deck or camera.

LTC VIA AN AUDIO CHANNEL

Some NLEs can interpret LTC that comes in over one of the soundcard inputs, or through a dedicated timecode audio jack on the video i/o box.

SDI

Serial digital interface, used for high quality video and audio distribution in high-end systems, also supports timecode and transport control. Separate wiring isn't necessary for those functions.

MIDI

The Musical Instrument Digital Interface serial format, used to control synthesizers, can also handle limited timecode and machine control. Wiring is more complicated because the data flows in one direction only, and it often is augmented with LTC. But the technology is familiar to music studios, and most studios already have the interfaces, so MIDI control may appear in smaller audio post suites.

V-LAN, VISCA, LANC, AND OTHERS

These are proprietary communication and control schemes, that were popular in prosumer analog gear. They've been mostly replaced by FireWire in DV.

Using Film with Digital Audio

Sound for film—we're talking specifically about the 16 mm or 35 mm stuff with sprocket holes—is largely a hybrid today. While the picture may be acquired through traditional photographic methods, the sound is recorded and edited digitally. (The picture is usually transferred to digital for editing as well.)

Most film cameras today are driven by internal crystals, and their speed is as stable as digital video. A few cameras plug into the AC wall current for similar accuracy. Some use DC motors and their speed is unpredictable; instead, they generate a *pilot* signal based on their speed, which is then recorded along with the audio. Pilot recordings have to be treated specially, and I devoted two pages to the process in the first edition of this book. Today the equipment is so rare that I cut those pages to save space. If you need the information and can't find the earlier book in a library, drop me a line.

TOTALLY WILD SOUND

If the film camera didn't have stable speed control for some reason, or either sound or picture got dubbed without paying attention to speed, there is no way to mechanically recover sync. You have to do it by eye. This is not an exercise for the faint-of-heart. It takes a long time, even if you have years of experience. There are sync-spotting tips in Chapter 8 to get you started.

Or if you have control over the project, you might find it best to rethink the footage and edit it mostly as voice-over.

SYNCING FILM ON VIDEO

If your film camera has stable speed, a clapped slate is all that's necessary to sync it with digital audio… but only if you're going to stay in the photographic film world. If you're transferring to video for editing or distribution, things won't stay in sync. That's because the video transfer process usually changes the speed, and the film doesn't stay at its nominal 24 frames per second.

In Europe video runs at 25 fps, so film is sped up 4 percent when it's transferred to that medium. Audio is sped up to match. This used to result in a noticeable pitch change, but now it can be shifted back digitally. Or as an alternative, the film is shot at 25 fps. It raises stock and processing costs by 4 percent, and may require special equipment for flicker-free lighting, but assures perfect sound and video with no speed change necessary.

In the Americas and the Pacific Rim, NTSC video runs at *almost* 30 frames per second. Converting 24 fps film to 30 fps is easy because those two speeds are a perfect 4:5 ratio. NTSC actually uses two interlaced images (called *fields*) per frame, so the transfer equipment simply alternates between copying one film frame to three fields and the next to two video fields (see Figure 6.13). The process

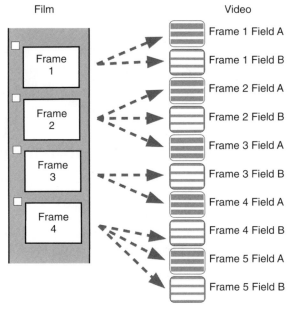

FIGURE 6.13
A 3/2 pulldown turns four film frames into five video ones.

is known as a *3/2 pulldown*. Overall speed isn't affected, though very fast motion can appear uneven.

But remember, the video is slightly slower than a true 30 fps (that's why we went through the whole dropframe weirdness earlier). So the transfer equipment also slows the film down an additional 1/10 percent. It's too small a difference to be noticed visually. Sound is usually slowed to stay in sync; it's too small a change to notice aurally either. The cleanest method is to lower the sample rate slightly, and all digital timecode decks have a " −0.1%" switch for this purpose. If your equipment doesn't have this option, transfer the audio into your computer at its normal speed and then apply a speed change in software.

Cameras can also be adjusted to shoot at 23.97 fps, making the 0.1 percent correction unnecessary. If you have to deal with any nonstandard settings for film or digital audio, you need a copy of Wolf Seeberg's self-published *Sync Sound and the New Media*. Seeberg is a Hollywood recordist and equipment consultant, and his 280-page manual is constantly being updated to cover the latest techniques.[12]

MUSIC VIDEOS ON FILM

Many music videos, and other projects that are lipsynced or danced to a playback, take a different approach. Rather than slow down the song in post, the music is played 0.1 percent *faster* at the shoot. Portable timecode DAT decks often have a setting for this function; if not, a special playback tape is prepared.

 Gotcha

Don't let the tiny details getcha. If any part of a project involves film, every aspect of camera speed, sample rate, and sync technique should have been written down on both the camera report and the sound log. This is the standard in all professional production. Trying to work any other way wastes money.

TROUBLESHOOTING TRANSFERS AND INGEST

In a well-designed digital editing suite with a knowledgeable operator and good source material, audio transfers are clean and sync is perfect. Believe it or not, that's how things often work in professional situations.

But desktop systems can develop trouble. There are three ways to deal with this: you can develop a hacker's mindset and diagnose problems technically; you can look for solutions in a book like this or online; or you can hire a tech.

---

[12]See www.wolfvid.com for details.

All three methods may be appropriate. A little of each can get you through most problems smoothly.

The first step is to figure out exactly what's wrong.

- Noise and distortion are usually caused by improper levels. If the source material sounds good but the transferred version doesn't, follow the advice in the first section of this chapter. If the tape sounds bad, try it on another deck or camera. If that fixes it, get your deck checked.
- Changes in timbre—sound that's too thin, bright, or dull—can be a configuration issue. But note the next bullet, as well.
- Ticks, pops, and *splats* (very loud signals lasting for about a frame) can have multiple causes; so can timbre changes. Follow the steps in the next section.
- Loss of sync can be hardware or software incompatibilities, operator error, or in some cases, a mystery you can correct but never understand. See "Loss of Lipsync" on page 132.

Other than for loss of sync, the terms used to describe these problems can be subjective. So I've put samples of most of these problems on Track 17. Listen to them to see which sound matches your troubles.

 Hear for yourself

Track 17 includes samples of most of the gremlins that can sneak into a transfer.[13] It's not great party listening but can help you diagnose a problem.

Missing Tracks or Absolute Silence

I'll assume you've already verified that something was actually recorded, and can hear it when playing back on other systems.

- Compatible cassette doesn't necessarily mean compatible tape. There are some proprietary digital audio formats that use standard VHS, Hi-8, or DAT tapes. But they can be played only on specific equipment. Check how the material was recorded.
- Standard tapes that play perfectly on one deck or camera can have problems on another. This is usually because of an alignment problem. Changing decks will probably get you through this project, but see a technician before you shoot another. In extreme cases, a technician may be able to tweak a properly aligned deck to play a non-standard tape.
- Missing sound during file ingest is usually a format question. This can also show up as one or two channels being usable on a multi-channel

---

[13]I had to simulate some of them since my equipment isn't broken.

file, with the others silent. Updating your software to the latest version usually helps. If a format isn't supported at all in your software, look for a conversion utility. It can also be a resource question, so check the next item.

Sound that goes missing when you're transferring from an NLE to audio software usually has one of the following problems:

- The audio might not have been carried from one hard drive to another. Some formats, including OMF and QuickTime, can be saved either with actual audio data, or with references to data elsewhere on a disk. The latter results in much smaller files, but you have to make sure the referenced material also gets copied and the file path is still accurate.
- File formats and names might not be compatible between systems. A few punctuation characters don't translate between Mac and Windows.[14] Some channel arrangements or sample rates work in one program but not another, even if they're on the same computer. These bugs are all well known; a simple Web search should get you the latest info.
- Many programs keep drawings of audio waveforms in special files. If you can hear something but can't see its waveform, use the program's redraw function.
- Some two-channel files sound okay in stereo—and look great on the waveform display—but are silent or significantly quieter in mono. One of the channels has had its polarity reversed. This is sometimes called a *phase error*. Most audio applications have a function to fix this.

Thin, Overly Bright, Spitty, or Dull Sound

These are usually problems with wiring or improper digital settings, and most can be fixed easily. But they may be inherent in the medium or a particular track and have to be worked around rather than fixed.

- Transformer-balanced circuits, found in some high-end studio equipment and field XLR adapters, are sensitive about proper termination. Highs get boosted when they're connected to typical computer inputs. It shows up as too much treble or as extra hiss. Put a 680Ω or 820Ω resistor across the output.
- Some transformers in field XLR adapters show an extreme loss of low end with unbalanced signals. This can happen if you put a standard mini-plug into a balanced mini-jack intended for wireless mics. There's not much that can be done for this after the fact—boosting the bass just adds noise.
- Sample rate directly affects high-frequency limits. If a transfer sounds duller than the original, make sure the new files are at the right sample rate.
- Inadequate filters in a digitizing circuit (Chapter 1) can cause aliasing distortion, which adds spittiness or jangling extra notes to high-frequency sounds. This can happen in some soundcards when you need to digitize

---

[14]Never put a question mark, colon, or slash in a filename if there's any chance it'll be moving to another operating system.

at a low sample rate. If it does, digitize at a higher rate and then convert the file in software.

- Inexperienced sound recordists may apply equalization at the shoot. They think they're solving problems but are actually creating bigger ones. Don't try to compensate while you're transferring. Try to fix the file later, when it's possible to experiment and undo… and tell the recordist to be more hands-off in the future.
- Early digital audio equipment included a pre-emphasis equalizer, and a matching de-emphasis equalizer had to be used for playback. While modern circuits make this technology obsolete, you may come across it on old tapes or recorders.
- Band-limited analog media such as audio cassettes or analog FM use pre-emphasis also. Matching de-emphasis is built into all players and FM radios. But the media get boosted so much that loud, high-frequency sounds are pushed into distortion. A multiband limiter or de-essing processor can help a lot during recording or before broadcast. If a track already has the problem, an equalizer set to the offending frequency (usually somewhere between 3–6 kHz) can make it a little less annoying. See Chapter 11 for tuning tips.

Ticks, Pops, and Splats

ARE THEY PERIODIC?

If ticking is relatively rhythmic and repeats at once per second or slower, it's probably a digital audio sync issue. Periodic ticking can be masked by loud sounds or hard to hear on NLE speakers, so it may seem intermittent.

- Make sure the sample rate you're recording or saving to a file is the same as the source sample rate. If the pitch also seems wrong, a sample rate error is the most likely cause.
- Make sure the digital input card or recorder is set to lock to its input, or that all equipment is locked to the same word clock.
- If nothing else works, transfer through an analog connection.

IS IT REPEATABLE?

The ticking doesn't have a rhythm, but it always appears at the same place in the source material.

- You could have level problems. These can be in your NLE's output even if the file is okay; try lowering the playback level. If parts of a tape are too hot for a deck's analog output, but are clean on the tape, a FireWire or AES/EBU transfer may be more successful.
- Some tape damage can also cause clicking. If switching between digital and analog outputs doesn't help, try the tape on a different deck.

Many of these problems are intractable, and the best you can do is edit from alternate takes.

IS IT ABSOLUTELY RANDOM?

You're plagued by ticks, but can't predict when they'll happen.

- There could be equipment damage. Try a different deck or soundcard.
- Your computer could have fragmented memory or cumulative errors. Try rebooting.
- Your computer could have been distracted. Make sure it's not being accessed over a network, and that automatic backup or virus scan software isn't actively using the system.
- Defragment your hard drives.
- Make sure FireWire or USB busses aren't hobbled by slow devices. If there's a SCSI chain, make sure it has proper termination.
- Record to a different hard disk.

Loss of Lipsync

LONG-TERM DRIFT

Individual clips are in sync when they start. But as you get into a long clip or play from the timeline, sync gets progressively worse. This can happen during previews, or it might not appear until you're printing the final project to tape or DVD.

- Is there a dropframe/non-dropframe conflict? Some NLEs insist that NTSC projects be dropframe, even if you want to work in non-dropframe.
- Is there a break in timecode? This can happen if a camera or DAT tape was improperly wound between takes, if you're doing a long transfer to the NLE, or have transferred in batches.
- Are your FireWire drivers the latest version? Surprising things can happen to sync if not. Check your card manufacturer and system software vendor's Web sites.
- NLEs expect precise 32 kHz or 48 kHz sample rates. Some camera designs are known to be slightly off. Check NLE settings to see if there's an automatic sample rate adjustment when capturing longer clips. Or transfer the sound as analog.
- Is there a speed compensation issue because you're using both film and tape in the workflow? Check the previous section of this chapter.
- If drift appears only when printing to tape, and you can't find any other cure, try printing in small sections. Some machine-to-machine video editing might be necessary afterwards. Or try exporting as shorter AVI or QuickTime movies and assembling those in other software.
- If an AVI or QuickTime is out of sync, try rendering it again at a different frame rate.
- Some third-party capture cards have known issues. Check with the manufacturer.

If nothing else works, measure the amount of drift over the length of the show and apply a speed correction to compensate.

ERRATIC SYNC PROBLEMS

A clip may appear out of sync from the start. Or it may be in sync and then suddenly jump out. Some clips might be affected more than others.

Before you try any of the other cures, ask yourself if this particular setup—source, system software, system hardware, and NLE software—has ever given you reliable sync. If not, you'll have to trace things down through the manufacturers involved. Some FireWire cards might not be supported by system or NLE software. Some memory or hard disk configuration problems might not appear until the system is stressed by the demands of full-size, full frame rate video with lipsync.

- Have you tried the suggestions listed in the section "Long-term drift"?
- Are you sending audio and video to the same output device? Some NLEs have a problem directing picture to FireWire and audio to a standard output at the same time. Check software for a compensation setting.
- Dropped or stuttered video frames can appear to be an audio sync error, even though it's a video problem. Make sure no other programs or processes are running, and direct memory access is enabled on your hard drives. Adding RAM can help, too.
- Are you using the presets suggested by your video card manufacturer?

When All Else Fails ...

- Check the manufacturers' Web sites.
- Check user forums. Others may have already solved this problem.
- Look for answers in the rec.video newsgroups (searchable at groups. google.com).
- Call the manufacturers' tech support lines.
- Ask a local audio or video facility to recommend someone who fixes equipment.
- Walk the dog. I've said this often: it's one of the most helpful pieces of debugging advice I ever got. If a problem seems intractable, get away from it for half an hour. Do something else entirely. When you come back, you might have a fresh insight.

Or at least you'll have calmed down enough to call tech support without screaming.

 Gotcha

Where's my problem? Noisy locations, mumbling actors, hum in the microphone, camera hiss, and lots of other gremlins can sneak into a track. Sound effects can be great when you're mixing and wimpy in a theater or on the air. But these aren't transfer problems and don't belong here. You'll find many more troubleshooting hints in the gray pages at the end of this book.

133

CHAPTER 7

Voiceover Recording and Dialog Replacement

> **REMEMBER THIS:**
>
> - Voiceovers should usually sound different than dialog. That's why they're recorded using different techniques.
> - Your recording space's acoustics are as important as which mic you use.
> - The more directional a mic, the stranger things sound coming from the sides or rear.
> - Low-budget ADR is possible...but it needs thought and preparation.

Surprisingly few films are made using only dialog recorded at the shoot. Many people don't realize that most feature films and TV movies replace at least some of the production dialog with voices recorded later. It's common practice on bigger projects to *loop* or *ADR* scenes where location problems or noisy effects interfered with the production recording. When it's done right, the studio tracks fit the actors' lips perfectly and the sound is completely convincing. There are techniques for ADR later in this chapter.

But ADR is always time consuming and can be stressful for the actors. It shouldn't be considered unless the production dialog is absolutely unusable. Recording, editing, and mixing replacement lines is tricky … and if you don't get things right, the film will suffer.

Of course, some projects don't need studio voices at all. Event videos, short or low-budget narrative films, sketch comedies, and a lot of other projects may use nothing but production dialog. If that's what you're working on, feel free to skip this chapter.

VOICEOVER PERSPECTIVE

The goal of production sound is to get dialog that sounds like it belongs to the picture. Boom operators position their mics to pick up some of the location's acoustics and background noise, which becomes part of the dialog track. One of the reasons Hollywood frowns on using lavs in feature films is because they're *too* clean; instead of hearing the actors in a proper perspective, it sounds like we're leaning our ears on their chests. Extra time is spent in post to make lavs sound like booms.

There's no such thing as a voiceover that's too clean. A good voice studio doesn't contribute sound of its own. The narrator should come from right inside the playback speakers, talking directly to us, not performing in some other room. This makes us part of the conversation, something that doesn't happen when one actor talks to another. Cleanliness refers to technical quality as well as acoustics. A track with no noise, echo, or distortion can be processed more, which is one of the secrets behind those rich-sounding Hollywood trailer voices.[1]

 Gotcha

What about character voiceovers? On-camera characters frequently have off-camera lines, part of the dialog while the camera is aimed at someone else. Obviously, they should be recorded on the set using the same mic as the rest of the dialog.

Occasionally a character will deliver voiceover lines directly to the viewer. The voiceover tradition that started with film noir was based on radio, and should have the same acoustic intimacy as a good narration.

WHAT'S NEEDED FOR VOICEOVER RECORDING

Sure, you need a mic and a performer. But the most important factor can be the room… and some non-electronic accessories may be very important.

Acoustics

My favorite announce booths are designed to have no noticeable reverb. The back and sides are soft, and the front has only a moderate reflection. This reflection is important; it lets announcers hear themselves in the real world as well as in their headphones, which helps them control the voice. If the room were completely dead, there'd be a tendency to speak too loudly. Because the reflections come from in front of the announcer, they hit the back of the mic where it's less sensitive.

The booth in my studio was designed as a compromise between perfect sound and real estate costs (see Figures 7.1 and 7.2). Walls and the true ceiling are sheetrock on RC-1[2] channels for soundproofing. Three walls are covered with the foam and fiberglass absorbers. The front is a thermal glass sliding door. It's more reflective than ideal, but comparatively far from the mic so the inverse square law keeps echoes at a low level. Good glass doors provide about the

---

[1]The other secret is, of course, the talents' ability.
[2]Construction details are in Chapter 2.

same isolation as solid wooden ones, and you can't beat glass for preserving sight lines. Even though this front of the room is reflective, it isn't parallel to the back wall, so resonances don't build up.

The ceiling is special thick fiberglass tiles, rather than common fissured tile, to absorb more reflections from the floor. With a ceiling height of 8 feet, the room has about 336 cubic feet of space—comfortable for one or two performers but just barely large enough in acoustic terms. As rooms get larger, critical resonant frequencies drop, and these can support deep voices at greater distances. If I'd had room for a bigger booth, I'd have built one. (The BBC likes to specify a minimum of 1,500 cubic feet. As it happens, that's just about the size of my mixing room … and it sounds great.)

Guerilla Acoustics

Most filmmakers have to live with even smaller booths or none at all. This isn't necessarily a problem. If you've followed some of the suggestions in Chapter 2 for your editing room, it's probably adequate for recording. Turn off computer towers and other noisy equipment, and use a directional mic as described in the next section.

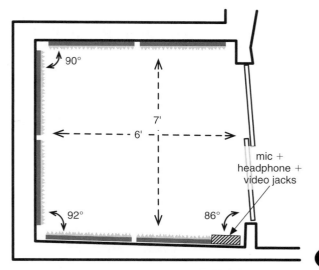

137

FIGURE 7.1
A typical voiceover booth (mine). There's a lot of absorption, and no two walls are parallel.

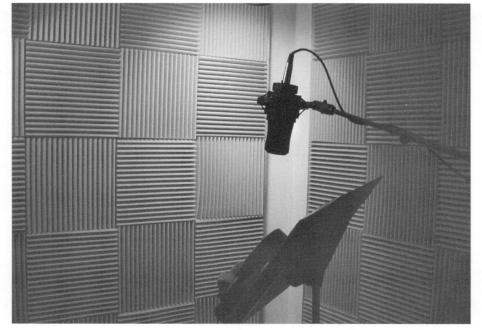

FIGURE 7.2
The absorbers are low cost foam tiles over fiberglass, described in Chapter 2.

Soundproofing is important for voiceovers. Audiences can forgive some noise in a location shoot because they see the noise source; it makes the location seem authentic. But those same noises are distracting in a voiceover. Close all the windows and doors and turn off HVAC systems. (If a ducted air system can't be shut off, temporarily remove the grill. Getting those metal vanes out of the way cuts the noise down significantly.)

Echo control is just as important. Most rooms have lots of echo. You might not hear it as reverberation, but it colors the voice by reinforcing random frequencies. If you can't mount permanent absorbers, put up sound blankets, furniture pads, or slabs of Owens-Corning 703 fiberglass wrapped in cloth.

Echoes are influenced by surface treatment, angle, and distance. Once the absorbers are up, walk around the room. Stand in different positions and face different directions, while speaking in a moderately loud voice. Listen to what the room does to your voice. The best positions are usually a couple of feet from a corner and face diagonally into the room. Some corners sound better than others. Once you find the best place for your voice, you'll know where the talent should stand.

Microphones

I used to shill for AKG, an internationally-respected microphone company.[3] I'd say nice things about their products, and in return I'd be sent to trade shows in Geneva, Amsterdam, and other nifty cities. One time, I lost the ID badge to let me onto the show floor. The product manager said he always ordered a spare, with a fictitious name. So for the rest of that show I was *Mike Rafone*. It was an honor to wear that badge, since few gadgets are as essential to audio work. To choose the right one, you have to understand how mics create a signal and how their pickup pattern works.

MICROPHONE ELEMENTS

There are three basic kinds of mics suitable for voiceover work: dynamic, condenser, and ribbon. Each has its advantages.

Dynamic

The simplest voice mics used regularly are really tiny electric generators. Just like a power plant's dynamo, *dynamic* mics have a coil of wire suspended in a magnetic field. Dynamic mics can't be as sensitive as the condensers used in production, and don't create enough voltage to be plugged directly into most camcorders. On the other hand, since dynamics convert sound directly into electricity, they can have very low distortion and no electronic noise. Many announcers prefer their sound.

---

[3]That's an AKG C-414 mic in Figure 7.2, one of my favorites for voiceovers in good acoustic surroundings. (I wasn't working for AKG when I bought it.)

Condenser

A *condenser* mic doesn't turn sound into volts; instead, it modulates a voltage coming from elsewhere. A metalized plastic diaphragm with an electric charge on it is mounted close to a rigid plate. As sounds vibrate the diaphragm near the plate, varying amounts of electrons can jump across. This tiny current is much too weak to send to a recorder—even a few feet of extra cable would destroy it—so a low-noise preamp is mounted in the mic itself. Since condenser mics don't use a magnet, they can be smaller and lighter than dynamics. That's why most location mics are of this type.

Traditional condenser mics are *externally polarized.* The diaphragm is charged up to a couple of hundred volts at a tiny current. This means the mic can be very sensitive, so this design is preferred for the highest-quality mics. An alternative is to charge the diaphragm chemically, using a process similar to that used in static-charged dust mops. The result is the ubiquitous *electret* condenser found in cell phones, lavs, and most studio or boom mics under $400.

All condenser mics require power for the preamp, but there are different and incompatible ways of getting power to it.

- Cameras and consumer recorders with mini-jack inputs put a low DC voltage on the audio line. You can buy compatible mics, but they're seldom good for voiceover use. The voltage may cause trouble with standard mics.
- Studio condenser mics are usually *phantom powered*, which puts a low DC voltage on both wires of a balanced audio cable and returns it through the cable shield. Most mixers and preamps supply this voltage, nominally 48 V (though some models work with much less). Battery-equipped phantom adapters are also available from film and video suppliers.

Because the DC is applied equally to both signal wires, balanced circuits don't see a voltage difference and it doesn't affect the audio.

When power is first applied to a condenser mic, it can produce a loud *thunk*. As a general rule, turn the mic's volume down before you change the battery or plug it into a phantom supply.

Ribbon

Ever notice the large jellybean-shaped mic on Larry King's interview desk? It's a classic RCA 77DX, one of the all-time greats for making a voice sound both warm and natural. These mics can be more than 50 years old, but good ones (and modern recreations) cost a few thousand dollars each. This and other ribbon mics use the same basic principle as dynamics, but without a diaphragm. Instead, sound waves vibrate a delicate foil strip that's suspended in a very strong magnetic field. This produces a tiny electric current. Because the foil has so little mass, the ribbon can be extremely accurate—particularly on relatively loud sounds that lack extreme highs, like the human voice.

The low output of a ribbon requires a sensitive, impedance-controlled preamplifier with an input transformer. Prosumer mixers usually aren't good enough; if you've got one of these classic mics, treat it to a good preamp. A few contemporary versions include an internal preamplifier that uses batteries or phantom.

The tiny ribbons are physically fragile. A strong wind or other shock can knock them out of position, requiring an expensive repair. The mics themselves tend to be large and heavy because of their big magnets. For these reasons, ribbon mics are almost never used for location dialog.

 Gotcha

Beware the phantom! Theoretically, phantom voltage should be invisible to a balanced ribbon or dynamic mic element. But a damaged cable or connector, or the wrong adapter, can let the voltage through. The result can be audio problems or even a damaged mic.

Most devices that provide phantom power have a way to turn it off. On the other hand, some modern ribbons look for that phantom voltage to power their internal preamps. Safest bet is to leave phantom off unless you're sure a mic requires it. If you're using a ribbon mic, be *darned* sure.

MICROPHONE DIRECTIONALITY

Few things are as misunderstood as mic pickup pattern. In fact, the very term is misleading: a mic's pattern isn't a template, with sounds from inside the boundary being picked up and others rejected. No matter what the pattern is called, all mics are somewhat *omnidirectional* and hear from every direction.

A mic is not like a lens.

- You can't point a mic at one person in a crowd and exclude someone nearby.
- You can't narrow the focus of a mic to pick up a distant object.
- Even the best mics are far less directional than your own ears.[4]

However, some mics are more sensitive in particular directions than in others. This can make objects directly in front seem slightly louder, or closer, than those to the side. The effects can be pictured visually. Consider what we see in Figure 7.3 as what an *omnidirectional* mic—one that picks up equally from all directions—hears.

If we wanted to concentrate on the happy bride, we could use a shotgun mic from the same distance. The visual equivalent is Figure 7.4. Notice how she's a bit bigger than she used to be, analogous to the mic picking her up a little louder.

---

[4]Most people locate sound sources based on tiny timing variations at different frequencies, in an automatic process that you learn starting from birth. The variations are based on the convolutions of your outer ear and the shape of your head, so are slightly different for each person.

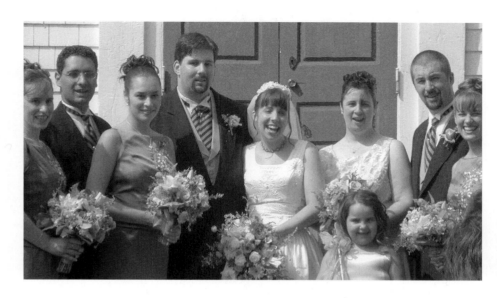

FIGURE 7.3
A nondirectional mic would pick up all the members of this wedding party evenly.

141

But notice also that people right next to her are also bigger. And other members of the party are still in the picture; they're just slightly smaller. From this distance, no microphone made could pick up just the bride and ignore everybody else.

There's another consideration; mic directionality varies with frequency. Most mics aren't very directional at the low end. Even the best shotgun mics have varying sensitivity from the sides or rear. If a wide-range sound comes from the wrong direction, this acts like an equalizer. The sound's timbre becomes tinny, tubby, or otherwise wrong. Figure 7.5 updates our analogy to include this. The groom is only partly affected because he's near the center. But others in the party seem like cardboard cutouts. It's an interesting effect—and may even be what the bride experienced that day—but doesn't lend itself to accurate or natural sound.

 Gotcha

Spherical world on a flat page. These wedding photos are only a partial analogy. Mics pick up sound from all three dimensions—above, below, and behind—as well as from the front. Since I couldn't print the pictures that way, you'll have to use your imagination.

Polar patterns

Microphones are categorized by their directionality. *Cardioid* mics are named for a theoretical heart-shaped pickup pattern, which lowers sounds from the rear but not from the front and sides. Since they're directional, there's a little coloration from the rear, but because they're not too directional, it rarely causes problems. *Short shotgun* mics, used frequently on video shoots, can also be useful for voiceovers. But because they're very directional, voices or room reverb from the sides can sound strange. Film professionals generally reach for a *hypercardioid*—a cross between cardioid and very short shotgun—for interiors because of this.

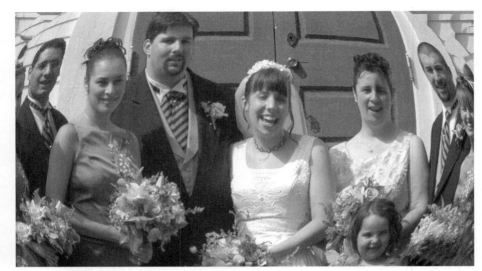

FIGURE 7.4
A shotgun mic makes the bride seem bigger or closer, but it doesn't exclude the rest of the group.

142

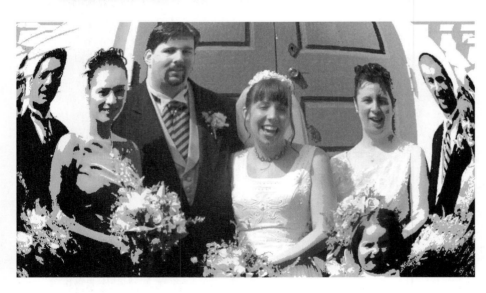

FIGURE 7.5
Directional mics tend to color sounds that aren't coming from directly in front.

   Hear for yourself

Track 18 is a short piece of orchestral music,[5] played as it would sound from the front of a good mic, then from the rear of a cardioid, from the side of a short shotgun, and from the rear of that shotgun. Pay particular attention to the sound of the sustained string choir, and how it balances with the other instruments.

---

[5]"Fingal's Cave" (Mendelssohn, DWCD70/11). Performance from the DeWolfe Music Library, protected by copyright and used by permission.

CHOOSING A VOICEOVER MIC

- If your recording space has good acoustics, use a cardioid. This will give you a smooth sound even if the talent moves around a little, and reject reflections from the studio glass.
- If your space has a larger reflective area, use a hypercardioid to reject it.
- If the acoustics aren't very good, add extra absorption—even if it's something temporary like sound blankets. Then use a short shotgun, close to the mouth and aimed to avoid reflections from the sides. Be aware that the rear of this kind of mic doesn't reject as well as the sides.

Omnis are not on this list unless you have absolutely perfect acoustics. Lavs are almost always omnis and should be rejected for the same reason. (Cardioid lavs are sometimes used as hidden mics on a set, but they're hard to mount for a voiceover.)

If you can't afford a really good mic, choose condenser instead of dynamic. Modern electret cardioids in the $150 range are quite respectable. Low-cost dynamic mics are generally designed as handheld mics for singers, have a restricted frequency range, and may lack sensitivity. More expensive condenser and dynamic mics—starting in the $300 range—often have larger diaphragms, which can be flattering to voices and sound warmer. But the difference isn't significant on small projects.

Voiceovers shouldn't have any noticeable hiss or other noise. Cheaper condensers generate their own hiss. Dynamics and ribbons don't, but require a more sensitive preamp; standard preamps can get noisy when their sensitivity is raised. Mics with internal transformers—all dynamics and ribbons, and some of the better condensers—also pick up hum from power panels, large transformers, or nearby video monitors. Moving the mic or rotating it 90° can help.

Unless you're specifying a top-notch studio mic with a good reputation, it's not a good idea to buy a mic without listening to it. Even recommendations from a professional can be misleading: they might prefer a certain mic because of how it flatters their voice, or only have experience with a limited selection. Professional dealers are usually willing to lend you mics for a short evaluation period, or you can rent the mic you're considering buying. When you're auditioning, listen through good monitors and value a smooth, natural sound. Some mics add high-frequency boost and distortion which make them sound brighter at first listen, but this becomes fatiguing over time.

Mic Placement

There is no magic place to put a mic that will always assure a good recording. The exact spot varies with the talent's working style. Over the years, I've found some basic positions that give a clean, intimate sound with a minimum of problems. So I start with one of these, and then adjust to fit the talent.

You'll need a flexible way to position the mic. The most common is a floorstand with a short boom; these usually sell for about $50 at broadcast suppliers and

143

music stores. You don't need a shockmount or heavy windscreen; the clamp and foam supplied with the mic should be sufficient for this purpose. While some engineers prefer pop screens—4-inch circles of nylon mesh that clamp in front of the mic—I've never found them useful for voiceover work. They don't stop pops any better than using a good mic position, and are one more large item in the talent's face to break their concentration.

Ask the talent to start reading, and see where they hold their head when working with a script. Then try one of the positions below. Listen through speakers and adjust as necessary. Closer will be more intimate but can pick up more vocal problems. As you move off-axis from the mouth, sibilance and pops decrease but so can warmth. The best compromise is often off-axis but close, with the working end of the mic about 9 inches from the talent's mouth. Don't get so close that you'll hear differences when the announcer's head turns to read the bottom of a page.

For a small diameter cardioid or hypercardioid, start with the mic angled down toward the mouth from just below eye level. Since the mic comes from the side, it won't get in the way of reading the script. This position seems very good for getting an intimate sound without pops or sibilance. Figure 7.6 shows it from three angles.

This position also works with large diaphragm cardioids. Or as an alternative, try them at mouth level and slightly toward the side. The front of the mic, of course, should be angled toward the mouth. Figure 7.7 shows this placement for a large cardioid that accepts sound from the side. If the mic accepts sound from the top instead, just rotate 90 degrees.

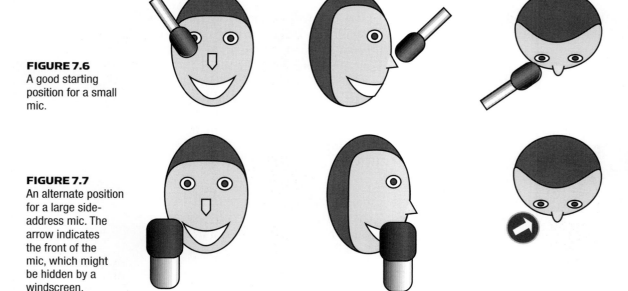

FIGURE 7.6
A good starting position for a small mic.

FIGURE 7.7
An alternate position for a large side-address mic. The arrow indicates the front of the mic, which might be hidden by a windscreen.

You can use a short shotgun in the same position as a small cardioid, though a couple of inches farther away (Figure 7.8). Angle things so nearby reflective surfaces are about 90° from the mic's axis (direction A), and as far from the mic as practical. For best results, the talent should be facing the largest dimension of the room (direction B). The dashed lines indicate walls at least 3 feet away from the mic. They also show how the best position might be diagonal.

These drawings are intended as starting positions. Take time to learn how your mic works best with the talent you use. As you're experimenting, there are a couple of positions to avoid:

- Don't put a large diaphragm mic directly in front of the talent's mouth (Figure 7.9A). Some announcers assume this is the only way to work—it's popular in radio—but it's also most prone to picking up pops and clicks.
- Don't put any mic at chin level or slightly below, pointing up (7.9B). As the talent breathes, you'll hear blasts of air.
- Don't point a mic directly toward the mouth from in front, unless you're at least 16 inches away (7.9C).

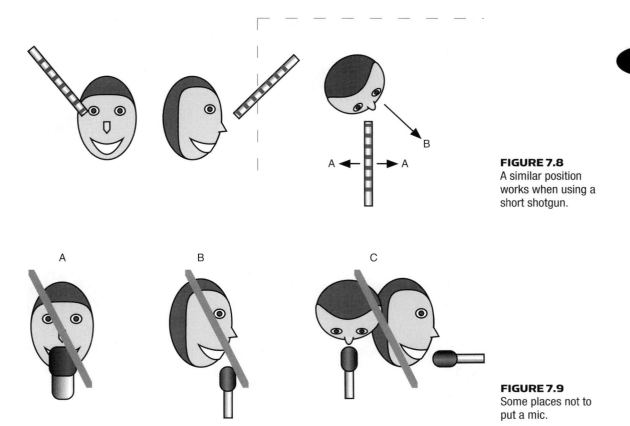

145

FIGURE 7.8
A similar position works when using a short shotgun.

FIGURE 7.9
Some places not to put a mic.

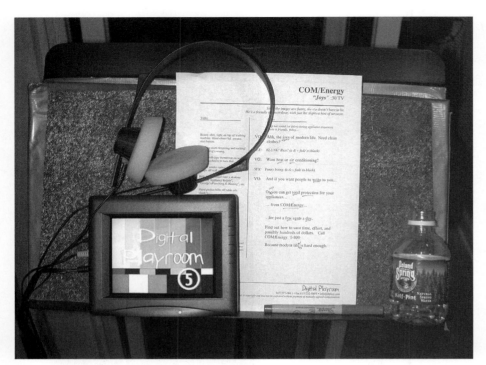

FIGURE 7.10
All these accessories
can make a voiceover
recording better.

146

Other Necessities

Obviously, you need to record onto something. But a couple of other items (Figure 7.10) can make a voiceover session go smoothly and help talent give you a good performance.

- Headphones are a must for professional talent. Voice actors like to hear their own voice accurately and comfortably, and slightly louder than they hear it acoustically in the room, with no delay through the computer. Open-air phones like the ones in the photo are okay if you won't be playing music or other cues to the talent; otherwise, use ones that seal to the ear to avoid leakage. Some amateurs find headphones distracting and prefer to work without them.
- You need a tall script stand that talent can read from without having to hunch over. Solid metal orchestral stands—about $40 in music stores—are convenient and provide good support for a multipage script. But these also reflect sound back to the mic, which can add a hollowness to the track. That's why I've taped a piece of fiberglass ceiling tile to the stand in the photo. Other echo-free alternatives include a wire-frame portable music stand, a lighting flag in a C-stand, or a small clamp on a gooseneck mic stand (Figure 7.11). Since these don't provide a surface where talent can make notes on the script, make sure there's a table handy.

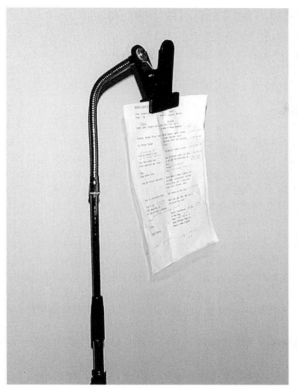

FIGURE 7.11
The little script stand that wasn't there. A gooseneck mic stand with a clip from a stationery store: script stays put, but doesn't cause any echoes.

- If talent is working to picture, they'll need a monitor. I like a small LCD on the copy stand itself. This way they can glance between video and script quickly, without having to refocus. If you're using a CRT monitor, be aware that it can radiate electrical and acoustic noises.
- Water is essential. As the narrator's mouth dries out, saliva thickens and can cause a snapping sound. The water shouldn't be ice-cold; that can tighten the throat.

Some narrators prefer to sit for long scripts, but sitting in a regular chair compresses the diaphragm and makes it hard to take a full breath. A bar stool is usually the right height.

You also need a talk-back system, if you're not right in the room with the talent. Sessions flow more smoothly when there's immediate communication and feedback about a performance. Recording and broadcast consoles have this function built-in, but small mixers rarely do. You can assemble your own with a push-to-talk microphone and a small amplifier and speaker, but the easiest solution is an FM wireless intercom, about $60 at electronics chains.

THE HUMAN FACTOR: DIRECTING

Film directors often concentrate on the look of a scene—dressing, lighting, and blocking—and trust the actors to interpret the script based on guidelines and rehearsals. This can lead to a hands-off attitude when directing voiceovers. Professional narrators are okay with this, and many give a credible performance on their own.

But a narrator can't know as much about your project as you do, and even the best can't interpret every sentence of a script properly without some help. Narrators are trained to *read cold*—glancing a few words ahead, and relying on conversational patterns to sound plausible. But sentences can miss the mark. Even if they all sound good, the talent might have missed a logical flow in the script. The result can sound polished while not communicating exactly what the writer or director wanted.

It's easy to direct a voiceover session properly, giving the talent just enough guidance to do the best job without getting in their way or slowing things down. Good narrators welcome this kind of direction: it makes them sound better, which leads to more jobs. They also hate bad direction, which just wastes everybody's time. So it's worth mastering the technique.

Directing from a Distance

Another benefit of the digital revolution is that it's totally changed the meaning of "local production." Your voice talent can be anywhere there's a mic and good acoustics—in a room next to you, or across the country.[6] With the right equipment, you'll hear every nuance of their voice in full fidelity, and can record every take on a hard drive for editing. Even without specialized equipment, you can direct by phone and then get selected takes via Internet. This has become so common that many voice actors now have their own studios—often in their homes—available for no extra charge.

ISDN

The first practical digital hookup was ISDN (Integrated Services Digital Network, but nobody uses the full name), a phone company invention that allowed direct dial-up connection between two studios. After a few shaky years in the early 1990s it was reliable, reasonably priced, and fast! Or, at least we thought we thought it was fast then: a basic ISDN hookup supports 128 kbps in each direction—that's kilobits, considerably slower than today's DSL or cable modems.

A full-fidelity mono recording of a voice needs at least five times that data, so studios and some actors invested in *ISDN codecs*. These boxes digitized the mic signal, and compressed it using techniques like mp3, all in real-time. They also

---

[6]We also used to do cross-country hookups in analog days but they were expensive, difficult to set up, and never sounded quite as good as a local recording. All three of those objections have disappeared with digital.

presented a simple user interface to the actor, not much harder to work than a standard telephone. Most models could handle simultaneous stereo in both directions, at good enough quality for broadcast. It was far beyond what desktop computers could do at the time.

While a few competing companies made the boxes, they were mostly compatible. Telos's *Zephyr* codec was the most popular and became synonymous with the process. It's still fairly common to book an "ISDN session" or a "Zephyr session" between actors and a studio, or interview guests and a broadcaster. I keep a free database on my website with some 600 U.S. actors and studios who have this technology, and there's probably at least one near you. Check it at www.dplay.com/audiobahn.

IP CONNECTION

We used ISDN because it was fast and reliable. Since ISDN was dial-up point to point—you made a physical connection between the two studios—there was none of the latency or unpredictability of the Internet. (The Internet breaks your message into packets, and copies them router-to-router until they find their destination. You can't know how long individual packets will take, or even if they'll arrive in the right order.) While you might not mind—or even notice—a 5-second pause waiting for your daily newspaper's front page to arrive, a 5-second hole in a voice performance would be deadly.

But the Internet is getting faster, data compression algorithms are getting more sophisticated, and computer memory is cheap enough that it's no trouble to keep plenty of packets in a *buffer* until they're needed. So IP codecs (Internet Protocol) are starting to appear. They look and act like the ISDN boxes, and allow the same stereo bidirectional connection. There can be a few seconds delay between when the talent talks and when you hear it, but the connection is smooth and usable most of the time. These boxes are even smart enough to momentarily switch to a lower audio standard when the connections get flakey. If a few words get mushy because of this, just ask for another reading.

PHONE CONNECTION

ISDN and IP became popular because they're fast. This can be essential for broadcasters and projects with tight deadlines, which is why studios pay a few thousand dollars for the equipment. The techniques are also bi-directional: you hear the actors in full fidelity, and they hear your direction or music cues the same way.

But most of the time, the actors don't need to hear you with that quality. If you don't need the immediate delivery of a direct digital connection—and trust the actor to do a good job recording themselves—you can do satisfactory long-distance recording over ordinary telephones. Then have the actor send you a compressed audio file electronically, or overnight a CD or DVD for longer projects.

It helps to have direct connections to the line at both ends. A lot of the "awful telephone sound" comes from the phones themselves, not the line. If the talent's good microphone goes directly to the phone company, and that signal

149

goes to decent monitors in your studio, things will sound a lot better than handsets or speakerphones. *Phone couplers* to do this start at less than $50 at broadcast suppliers, or you can build your own for under $10.[7] Most studios have more elaborate phone *hybrids* which do an even better job—that's how radio call-in shows are handled.

Cellphones and VOIP sound much worse than landlines because of their data compression. If at all possible, use a standard landline.

Script Preparation

The first step in directing a voiceover narration is often overlooked: a few days before the session—when there's still time to fix problems—read the script *aloud*. Make sure the wording is conversational and that sentences aren't too long or express too many concepts. It should be obvious from the context which words are important in every sentence.

You can ignore the formal rules of written punctuation. If a sentence is too long, and it's not obvious where the pauses should be … break it up with ellipses. Or like this (sentence fragments are acceptable). If a paragraph tries to express too many thoughts, split it in half. Or turn it into a bulleted list. Use ellipses, hyphens, and italics liberally. The worst that may happen is the talent sees these marks and reads with too much emphasis. But you'll spot that in the first couple of sentences and can tell them to pull back.

While you're reading through the script, mark it into sections. Be aware of subject breaks and changes of emotion. Put double paragraph breaks where these changes occur, so the talent can see a new thought is starting. Don't be afraid to tell them, during the session, where each section is trying to go.

Note any difficult-to-pronounce words, and make sure you know how to say these properly. If there are just a few, add phonetic spellings in the script: "As diakinesis (DIE-uh-kuh-NEE-sis) sets in….". If there are a lot, warn the talent ahead of time. They'll probably ask for either a separate list of the words with pronunciation hints, or a recording of an expert saying the words.

Pay attention to readability. Use a large font and short line length, with at least a half line of space between lines and double spacing between paragraphs. Use upper- and lowercase. And number the pages—they're sure to get out of order sometime during the session.

Session Flow

Master shots of narrative films are usually done in full takes, repeating a scene until it's right. This also makes sense for very short narrations, like commercial voiceovers. But if a script is long, it's most efficient to record straight through: start at the top, and stop when there's a problem.

---

[7]Instructions on my website.

Start by giving the talent some direction about the tone you're looking for. Descriptions like *proud, conversational*, or *formal* are helpful here. If a style is particularly demanding, ask them to read a few sentences for you to evaluate. Otherwise, slate the first take and start recording.

 Gotcha

Why slate? The Hollywood slate started as a way to identify scenes in silent movies. At first the scene and take number were just written in chalk, but when sound was added, someone would also speak that data. This technique is just as useful for identifying pieces of a session. Even if you're using timecode or numbered files, a verbal slate—something as simple as, "Take two"—can save time when you're editing.[8] If you don't have a slate mic, say it into the talk-back so it's picked up on the talent's mic. Hearing that slate also lets the talent know that you're recording and ready for their performance.

During the first paragraph or so, pay particular attention to the pacing, energy level, and intimacy. If it's right, keep going. If not, stop and give notes. It's not unusual for even a good narrator to do the first paragraph four or five times before hitting the proper style. But once the narration starts sounding the way you like, *let them keep going.* Don't interrupt with directions like, "That's good. Please continue." A nod or smile are sufficient.

On the other hand, if you hear something wrong or the style is starting to drift, stop as soon as the sentence is finished. Explain what you need, back up to the paragraph or line before the error, reslate, and continue recording. Keep notes on your copy of the script of where each new take starts. Recording continuously like this, interrupting only when there's a problem, keeps the style consistent and makes editing easier.

If you don't know exactly what you want for one or two paragraphs, it's okay to stop and ask for an alternative reading. If you think something was read properly but aren't sure, it's usually best to keep going. Put a question mark in the margin. After the script is finished, play back that paragraph and check it. If necessary, record a replacement to drop in during editing.

How to Talk to a Narrator

Directing is not a zero-sum game or an adversarial process. A good narrator will take direction happily, knowing that you're going to make their part of the project more effective. The key is giving meaningful directions.

---

[8]Much longer slates—"This is the third paragraph of page twelve, starting with the announcer"—just waste time. Writing that take number next to the script's paragraph accomplishes the same thing.

Strike a balance between insufficient feedback and too much direction. "I don't like it, do it again," isn't very helpful. Ask for something once, make sure they get it, and continue recording. If you don't get what you want on the next take, *don't repeat the direction.* It didn't work. Try different words, or better yet, a completely different method of directing. There are at least three:

- Actors generally give a better performance if you tell them what they should be thinking and let them translate it into a performance. ("I need more awe when you say, 'The moment had arrived.'")
- Some actors need a little help solving the problem. ("Please slow down and deepen your voice at 'The moment had arrived.'")
- As a last resort, do a line read: say it exactly the way you want to hear it, and let the talent mimic you. This often works best with announcers as opposed to actors. It can also be helpful when directing novices. But use line reads only when you hear a problem, and if you're sure you have the skills to say it properly yourself (see next section). Reading the whole script to an announcer wastes time and accomplishes little.

To err is human. Admitting your errors can be a powerful directing technique, putting you and the narrator on the same side and enlisting their help to solve problems. If there's a technical problem, admit it and go on to the next take. If you ask for a particular kind of reading and get it but it's not having the effect you hoped for, let the announcer know it's not his or her fault that you want a different approach.

How to Talk *Like* a Narrator

If you're going to give line reads or narrate your own film, take some time to improve your reading chops.

BREATH CONTROL

The *vocal folds* are two flaps of skin in your throat. As you push air past them, they vibrate like a reed. This creates the buzzing that is the basis of your voice. It takes a lot of air to make these folds vibrate properly and to sustain that vibration during a scripted line. The only way to get enough air into your lungs is to expand the chest cavity and create a partial vacuum. Children usually learn to take big breaths by forcing their ribcage out and their shoulders up. But that's not efficient because chest muscles are puny compared to the *diaphragm*, a thick domed wall just above the stomach and intestines. You need to move that diaphragm to get a decent lung's worth of air.

Here's how: Stand up and put the palm of your hand on your stomach. Open your mouth and inhale in a very quick gasp. You should feel the stomach press out as the diaphragm pushes down on it to create a vacuum above. Do this a few times to get used to the feeling, then slow the movement down until it's smooth. Practice breathing this way. Your diaphragm will get stronger, and you'll be able to take in more air at a time.

AVOIDING STRESS

Involuntary muscles around the vocal folds clench when you're nervous, changing the way the vocal folds vibrate. As the folds get tighter, the natural reaction is to force more air past them, stressing those muscles even more. As humans, we learn to recognize this sound as fear—probably not the ideal emotion for a narration. Yawning is a great cure; the physical act stretches the muscles in question and you get a nice slow breath of air. Professional announcers learn what a yawn feels like from inside and consciously repeat the motion to open their throats.

There's also good advice in the western movie cliché, "Smile while you say that, pardner." Vowel sounds are made by filtering the buzz of vibrating vocal folds through resonators in the mouth and sinuses. Smiling changes the way these resonators work, making a brighter sound that comes across as friendlier. Unless the copy is somber, it's worth forcing a smile while you read.

CREATING STRESS

Part of the announcer's skill is adding emphasis to appropriate words. Unfortunately, most people stress words by making them louder, which isn't a good idea in a narration. It wastes breath, makes the words harder to record, and gets defeated by postproduction compression. Instead, add emphasis by slowing words down, putting a slight pause before the important word, or raising its pitch slightly. Or use combinations of these techniques simultaneously. Try them on the examples in the next three paragraphs.

There's a simple logic to deciding what words to stress. Information theory says the most intelligence is contained in the least predictable part of a message. So in general, the most important words in a sentence are the ones that don't repeat what came before. "Take some *shallots*, chop the *shallots*, and then sauté the *shallots* in butter," sounds like you're producing Cooking for Idiots. But "Take some *shallots, chop* the shallots, and then *sauté* the shallots in *butter*," makes sense. Better yet, replace the second and third "shallots" with "them." We already know what's cooking.

When you stress a word, you're also reinforcing that its opposite isn't true. "I was *hoping* you'd call," means you're really glad to hear from a person. But "*I* was hoping you'd call," suggests nobody else cared, and "I was hoping *you'd* call," sounds like other calls have been from telemarketers. "I was hoping you'd *call*," means you're unhappy they showed up in person.

It's almost never appropriate to stress prepositions or conjunctions. There's a famous outtakes tape where actor/director Orson Welles is asked to give more emphasis to the first word of *In July, peas grow there*. He reacts with scathing anger.[9] And to say, "Our employees are smart *and* loyal" implies the two characteristics aren't usually found in the same person; anyone with brains would be long gone.

---

[9]As of this writing, you can hear it as streaming audio at my Web site, www.dplay.com/humor. But if anybody ever figures out the copyright—I had it passed to me 35 years ago by another engineer—I might have to take it down.

ADR

Hollywood cheats. When you hear beautifully clean dialog in a horribly noisy setting, like the middle of a windstorm or a busy public building, it's not because magic microphones were used. It's because the track was actually recorded in a quiet studio, sometimes months after the picture was shot. Dialog replacement is so common that its name is usually abbreviated to ADR—the A stands for "automatic," though it's a labor-intensive process. ADR is also still called *looping*, after the original method used to create it. The film was cut into individual loops for each line of dialog. The loop would run continuously while an actor tried to match the lip movements.

> **Gotcha**
>
> ***ADR avoidance.*** If looping is difficult in Hollywood, where there are experienced technicians with the right equipment, it's even harder when you have to do it ad hoc. The best strategy is to do as little as possible. Some of this has to take place long before post.
>
> - Strive for the best production sound. Renting better equipment or hiring a good boom operator is usually cheaper than rerecording later. Ten minutes of extra setup time at the shoot can save a day of ADR. If you must replace dialog, the session will go smoother if you have decent guide tracks. If the original was recorded indoors with a camera mic, ADR can be long and painful because the guide track will be blurred by echoes.
> - If you think ADR will be necessary because of a noisy setting, block the scene so lip movement isn't too obvious. Have extras mime their conversations. If you can, rewrite the scene with a lot of back-and-forth dialog, short lines are easier to replace.
> - While you're shooting, pay attention to intermittent noises like car horns or airplane flyovers. It's cheaper to retake a scene immediately than to try to record it later. Even if the second performance isn't as good, you may be able to lift just enough dialog to save the first one. Or forget about picture. Have the actors record problem lines as audio-only, right after the bought take. They'll still be in the right mood, and the acoustics will match.

While ADR is an accepted practice, it's frowned upon by feature directors and sound supervisors because the acting is seldom as good as the original performance. Producers don't like ADR because it's expensive. Many actors hate the process. They have to read the scene line by line without other performers to work against. It's difficult to recall the original emotions or motivations for a reading and to keep an appropriate projection level. It can also be intimidating to have to perform while listening to cues in a headphone and watching yourself on a screen.

ADR Equipment

You'll need an A/V playback device: a NLE is ideal because it can cue quickly. If you can't isolate its fan noise or run from a laptop, use a camera or a VCR instead and prepare a tape with each line repeated multiple times. You'll also need a separate audio recorder with at least two tracks, so you can record the original audio on one channel as a sync reference. Timecode helps but isn't necessary, so a consumer recorder may be adequate for this. You'll need the same kind of mics that were used at the shoot. For the actor, you'll need headphones, ideally isolating ones so that cue tracks aren't picked up by the mic.

Hook everything up as in Figure 7.12. Studios that specialize in ADR have more complicated setups and specialized software to drive it, but this will do the job for casual sessions.

You'll also need a quiet room with little or no reverberation. Even though the production dialog has natural room reverb, every room sounds different.

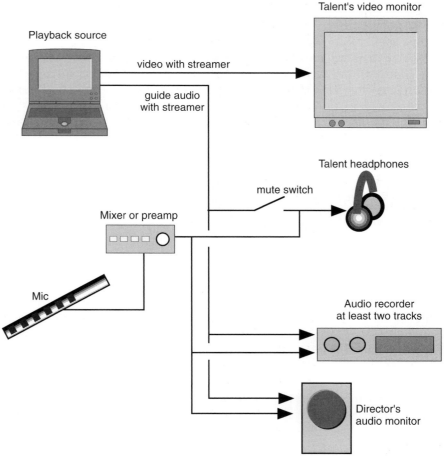

FIGURE 7.12
A setup for casual ADR. (Streamers are described in the next section.)

You don't want replaced lines to stand out. If the new audio is echo free, you'll be able to simulate reverb at the mix to match the shoot. If the new audio has its own echo, you probably won't.

The room should be larger than a typical announce booth, unless the production track used lav sound and was low-key. New dialog should be recorded at the same mic distance and with the same energy as the original, and most booths aren't big enough to support this. So plan on a lot of sound blankets or other absorbers. If you have to simulate exteriors, the room must be absolutely dead. Outdoor echoes are nothing like the ones you get indoors.

Some ADR recordists prefer two boom mics, one slightly closer and one slightly farther. Each is recorded to a separate track, and the most appropriate one is chosen in post. If the shot originally used a lav, of course use a matching lav for occasional ADR lines in that scene. (If the entire scene has to be looped, you may want to use a boom mic.)

ADR Technique

The first step is to do your homework. Watch the edited project with a script handy and mark which lines need replacing. Jot the line's timecode on the script, along with why you're replacing it and anything else that might be useful. Knowing whether a shot was interior or exterior and how it was miked will save time at the session. Then check for alternate takes. You may be able to lift a few words from a cleaner track and slip them under the existing video.

If you must loop, turn each line into a separate A/V clip. If characters overlap, make two clips. Record each separately and mix them later. Besides, it's better to book each character for a separate session: ADR skills vary, and there's no sense making one actor wait while another blows takes.

VIDEO-DOMINANT ADR

There are two principal ways to record ADR. The traditional method is to make picture dominant. Each clip should start a few words before the desired line and end a few words after.

You'll need to add visual *streamers* to each clip, lead-ins that stop on the frame before the target line. Originally, this was done by scribing a diagonal line across a few dozen frames of the film itself; when the film was projected, the streamer would appear as a white line moving across the screen from left to right. These days, streamers are usually generated in video by the ADR equipment, which may be part of a specialized audio workstation. If you're trying ADR on a desktop NLE system, it's easiest to superimpose the streamers from another video track. Also add an audio streamer to the track: three short beeps about 20 frames apart, forming a rhythm that ends as the new line starts.

The actor watches a playback of the clip on a large monitor, with production audio in headphones, to get comfortable both with the delivery and with the way the streamer leads into the line. Then the guide track is muted. The actor records a new version while watching the screen but without hearing the original. (The director may want to listen to both tracks, with production audio at a slightly lower volume, as a guide for sync.) Multiple takes will probably be needed, and it's important that the takes form a predictable rhythm. Start-and-stop ADR, when it takes a random time to cue each pass, puts extra stress on the actor. Eventually, the new performance will start to match the guide track. You don't have to achieve perfect lipsync: small errors can be fixed by editing.

The advantage of this method is that actors can feel freer to experiment with delivery because the original version isn't being played in their headphones during the actual ADR take.[10]

AUDIO-DOMINANT ADR

Traditional ADR can be intimidating to an actor. A modern alternative is to make sound dominant. Set the playback device to play the clip and streamer in a continuous loop. Let the actor hear the rhythmic beeps and line over and over, and then record him or her speaking along with the original until the new and old voices match. The advantages to this method are that it can be faster with performers who aren't used to looping, it often produces a tighter match, and since it isn't necessary to concentrate on picture—you don't even need the video monitors—the actor can be looking at a script instead.

157

Whichever method you use, make sure your actors' energy and pitch match the original. It can help to give actors a little small-room reverb in their headphones, so their voices sound similar to what they heard at the shoot. But don't record with echo. This will make editing more difficult and rarely matches the original without a lot of fine-tuning.

ADR Editing

While you're recording, mark which take of each line was the best match. If you're recording in multitrack software, it's helpful to put a copy of each best take on a single *hero* track, while the choices are fresh in your mind.

Capture both the new audio and its guide track to your NLE. Slide them together on the timeline until the guide track matches production audio. Then delete the production audio and the guide track. Lock the new audio to picture. It's a good idea to keep ADR on a separate track from production audio, since you'll be processing it differently during the mix.

---

[10]It's said the reason Brando liked to mumble on-camera was to force producers to let him polish the performance later, in a looping session.

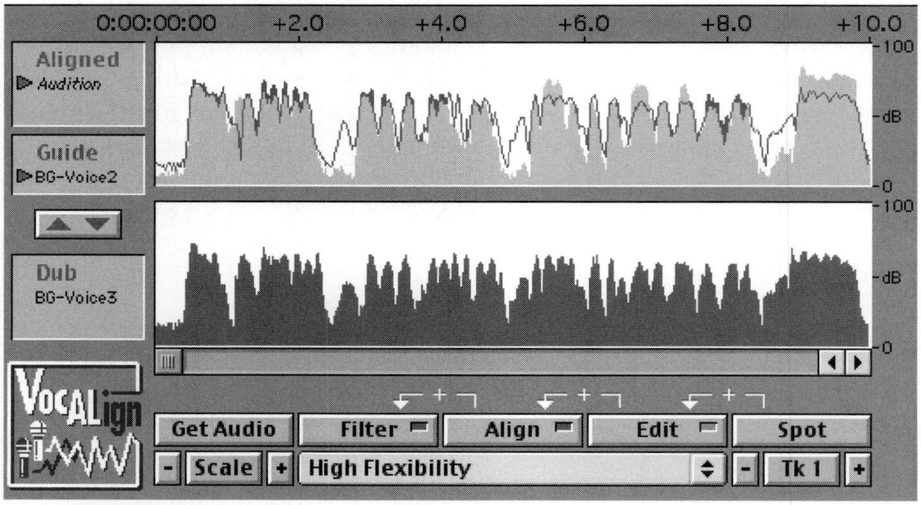

FIGURE 7.13
VocALign software automatically tweaks ADR takes to match the guide track, within reasonable limits.

To fine-tune ADR, you can use software like VocALign (Figure 7.13); it analyzes the guide track at critical frequencies, then makes tiny edits in the new track to make it match. A few modern audio programs have a similar feature built-in. Or do it yourself using the techniques in the next chapter. Either will be less painful than demanding perfection from an actor.

CHAPTER 8
Editing Dialog

159

THIS CHAPTER IS IN THREE SECTIONS

The first section is what dialog editing is really about: the ability to patch individual words—or even tiny syllables—together to make a seamless whole. It's how you avoid noises or mispronunciations in an otherwise perfect take, how you combine two less-than-perfect takes to make a better final result, and how you tighten up an interview to keep the meaning but make a better documentary or commercial.

For this book, I'm considering *dialog* to be any time a human talks: scripted lines, on-the-street interviews, voice-overs and narrations, animation voices, historic clips. Film theorists might break these into smaller categories, and they're usually treated differently when it's time to mix, but when you're editing it's mostly all the same.

The key word is "seamless." Properly cut dialog doesn't sound edited at all. It sounds like the person talking said exactly the right thing. When dialog editing isn't seamless—when you can hear a click, or awkward jump in pitch, or strange pacing—it momentarily kills the message. It reminds you that what you're watching has been manipulated.

If you've ever cut a film or video, you're aware of the need for smooth dialog. But if you've ever watched a good dialog editor, you were probably amazed that all these seamless edits happened quickly, without trial and error or multiple undos. The first section of this chapter teaches you how to work that way: read it, and you'll know exactly where to place the cursor, and which tiny sounds work together when others won't. While it's based on speech science, it's grounded in reality and actually pretty easy. I've taught hundreds of picture editors to work this way.

The second section has to do with workflow, and what happens to a track between picture edit and the mix. These evolved differently for film and video. Each has advantages and drawbacks. But the historic differences don't exist anymore: You can use both techniques on the same project, and accomplish a lot more.

There's a third section, at the end, on restoring lost sync for dialog. It has nothing to do with editing technique or workflow, and is usually necessary only when someone has made a technical error. But this seemed the best chapter to put it into.

DIALOG EDITING TECHNIQUES

Here's the approach to cutting dialog that appears in most NLE manuals and is taught in some film schools: look at the waveform, find a pause where it drops to zero, and edit during the silence. This kind of editing is simple, easy to describe, and somewhat appealing to visually oriented filmmakers. Cutting in pauses may be fine for some edits—if you're lucky, and there isn't any background sound getting in the way. But it limits where you can cut, and may cause you to discard an otherwise perfect interview clip or even a full take that has noise on a couple of words. It might even make your editing more obvious, if pitch and projection don't match on both sides of the cut.

Lots of what you hear won't show up on waveforms. That's why professional sound editors mark their edits while scrubbing and listening, and use the waveforms just as a guide. It's faster, more flexible, and can be more precise. It's also easy to learn, with just a little ear training and an understanding of how sounds fit together.

 Gotcha

Why bother? Some editors are put off by this methodical approach to editing. They've taught themselves by ear, and are quite happy cutting by trial-and-error. For them, it's easiest to try an edit, then undo if something doesn't sound right.

If that's you—if you're already cutting accurately and quickly even on difficult edits, without paying attention to the science—you have my admiration. (It's a lot like jazz. Some great musicians have so much natural talent that they play by ear, without ever learning to read a score or understand chords. This doesn't mean music lessons aren't an important part of training most musicians.)

But even if it does describe you, glance through the rest of this section. Find out what you might be missing.

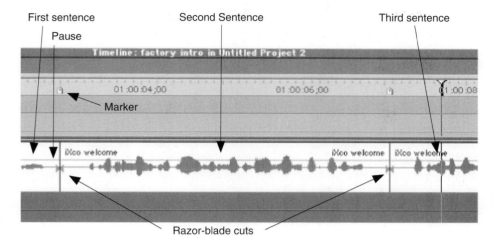

First sentence
Pause
Second Sentence
Third sentence
Marker
Razor-blade cuts

FIGURE 8.1
A basic, almost brainless edit of a narrator recorded in a quiet studio.

Waveform Editing

We'll start with a quick review of the most basic technique, the one taught in NLE manuals. Track 19 of the book's CD contains audio from a typical narration and a talking-head sequence. Let's start with the narration, recorded in a quiet studio. The woman is saying three sentences; we'll take out the middle one. If you want, load the first part of Track 19 into your NLE and follow along—though this example is so trivial, you'll understand it easily from the pictures.

161

1. Put the clip on a timeline, set so you can see its waveform.
2. Visually locate the two pauses between the three sentences.
3. Put the cursor in the middle of the first pause and plant a marker. Repeat for the second pause.
4. Using the razor tool, cut at the two markers. It should now look like Figure 8.1.[1]
5. Delete the middle section and slide the other two together. Or do a ripple edit, dragging the second razor cut over the first.

This edit works fine if the background is quiet. But the method starts to fall apart when there are constantly changing background noises, such as traffic or machines. That's because there's a good chance the noise will change abruptly at the edit point.

Hear for yourself

Track 19 contains source audio for this example and the next.

---

[1]This picture is from Final Cut Pro. But it should look about the same in most NLEs and many multi-track audio programs.

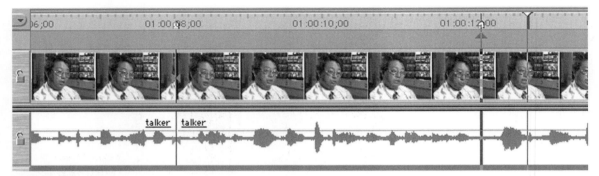

FIGURE 8.2
Razor cuts in a location interview. The background noise will cause problems.

COPING WITH LOCATION NOISE

Unlike the previous exercise, which can be understood from the figure, this one is worth actually doing. Load the second part of Track 19 (a location interview in a moderately noisy medical lab) into your editor. Cut out the middle sentence using the steps above. The razor cuts should look similar to Figure 8.2.

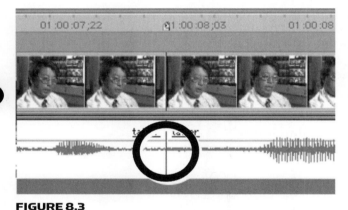

After you do the deletion or ripple edit, look closely at the cut (Figure 8.3). That tiny change in the background noise, exactly at the edit point, can sound significant. Listen to it in your version or play the first part of Track 20.

You could apply a long cross-fade, but that takes time to render and still might not sound natural. In fact, as a general rule:

FIGURE 8.3
You can hear room tone jump at this edit point.

> ### *Rule*
>
> Cross-fades longer than a half frame have very little place when joining dialog clips.[2] They can be useful in track splitting, but that's a different technique.

For a better, faster fix:

1. Grab the cut with a rolling-edit tool.
2. Drag the clip right up to the start of the next sentence (Figure 8.4).

That tiny shift, eight frames in this example, hides the jump in the background sound. Hear the difference in the second part of Track 20.

---

[2]You'll learn about ¼-frame cross-fades later in this chapter.

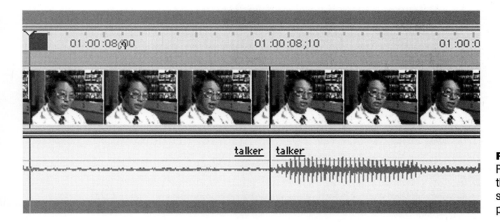

FIGURE 8.4
Rolling the edit to
the start of the next
sound fixes the
problem.

 Hear for yourself

The first part of Track 20 lets you hear how the background noise jumps, as in the edit
from Figure 8.2. The second part of Track 20 fixes it with a rolled edit.

Rule

Edits in the middle of a sustained sound are often obvious. Moving them to the beginning
of the next loud sound almost always helps because the new sound distracts the ear.

Audio-Based Editing

Spotting where that next loud sound started was easy in the last example: the
"And" starting the third sentence makes a large blob on the waveform display.
But if the sentence started with "So" or "For" spotting would be harder, since
/s/ and /f/ are softer. And if the sentence started with "However," it would be
almost impossible to mark the edit visually. That's because /h/ is the softest
consonant, and while you could definitely hear it, you might not be able to see
it under the room tone.

Professional sound editors rely on programs that let them *hear* where they're going
to edit, instead of just look. There are a couple of ways a program can do this:

- The easiest is to let you drop markers as you play the audio in real time;
  every program can do this. Then you edit from marker to marker. This is
  fine for creating a dialog rough cut, though speech moves too quickly to
  fine-tune edits this way.
- Most NLEs let you jog forward and play one frame at a time, as you press
  a control (often the → key) or move a jog slider. It's the best way to find
  the /s/ or /f/ in the examples that started this section.

- Also handy are the scrub algorithms in many audio programs and the similar shuttle function in many NLEs. They let you cruise forwards or backwards through the audio at a controlled speed. You can slow down to find an exact edit point.

 Gotcha

Quotes? Italics? Slash marks? Bars? I've tried to stay consistent, using italics to introduce technical terms and quotes to set off dialog that might be spoken in a track.

But if you're going to be a good editor, you also have to pay attention to *phonemes*—the smallest units of sound the mouth can make. These combine to make words. Standard convention is to indicate phonemes with slash marks, like the /s/ or /f/ above.

Phonemes have a written alphabet as well, *IPA (International Phonetic Alphabet)*. It's got some strange looking characters because phonemes don't necessarily match letters in the alphabet. IPA is overkill for the sound editor. I'll use dictionary-style equivalents instead, like /ay/ for the "a" in "play." I'll also use double vertical bars || to indicate where an audio edit takes place.

A few older versions of some editing systems don't support scrubbing directly in the waveform. There's a workaround, setting a short loop to surround the likely edit point, then playing the loop while you move one boundary to the exact point. This is so cumbersome, that unless you do only a few edits a year, it's probably faster to upgrade your software.

 Gotcha

Backwards forwards? In most programs, jogging consists of playing a frame's worth of sound in a forwards direction. Even when you jog backwards (usually the ← key), the frames are still played forward. It makes sense because many editors alternate between tapping ← and → to find the start of a sound.

It also leads to a curious effect. If you hold down → in most programs, the audio plays relatively smoothly, usually at a low speed. If you hold down ←, you hear a succession of one-frame slices, each playing forward, but stepping backwards through the clip.

BREAKING THE FRAME BARRIER

Most NLEs force you to edit on frame boundaries, or use clips that are an integral number of frames. But a few tenths of a frame can make the difference between a perfect edit and a poor one. Listen to Track 22: it consists of three short audio clips. In the first, an announcer says, "Tired of living life in the slow lane?" In the other two, the third word has been deleted: "Tired of || life in the slow lane?"

But the first edit was done in a NLE. You can hear a click at the edit point because it was impossible to mark the precise start of the /l/. I did the second version in an audio program. It was easy to mark exactly where the /l/ starts, so this one sounds like the announcer actually read it that way.

Hear for yourself

Track 22 lets you compare dialog editing in a NLE and an audio program using the examples described previously.

While the difference is immediately apparent to the ear, you can hardly see it on the waveform. Figure 8.5 shows the two edited examples, zoomed in fairly close. If you look closely, you'll see a tiny spike at 0.400 second in the NLE example on the left. That spike doesn't exist in the audio program's smooth-sounding version on the right.

FIGURE 8.5
The same dialog, edited in an NLE (left) and an audio program (right). The circled spike in the NLE's version is a very noticeable click.

165

SPIKES, CLICKS, ZERO CROSSES, AND CROSS-FADES

The click in the above example is caused by a sudden jump in the waveform, visible when you zoom in (Figure 8.6). In just a couple of samples, the wave goes from almost perfect silence to around −18 dBFS. The waveforms didn't match at the edit: The out-point of the first clip was very low, and the in-point of the second was much higher. The sudden voltage jump creates a click.[3]

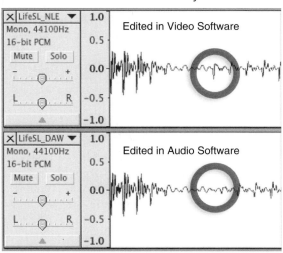

If you're cutting from silence to silence, there won't be much of a jump. But if you have to cut within a word, voltages at the edit point are a matter of luck. A lot of NLE edits have clicks like this. They go unnoticed on desktop speakers but can be atrocious in a theater. There are two ways to avoid them, and good audio software often lets you turn one of them on for automatic click-fixing.

---

[3] Clicks can also happen on edits if DC voltage is getting into your signal chain because of a hardware problem. The best cure is to fix the hardware, but you can diagnose the problem by rendering a suspect clip through a low-cut (also known as *high-pass*) filter and then re-editing. If DC was present, the filter will remove it and there'll be a lot fewer pops. Some audio software includes a Remove DC Offset function to compensate.

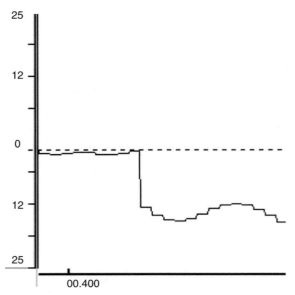

FIGURE 8.6
The sudden jump was caused by editing together parts of two waves at different voltage levels. The result is a nasty click.

Most waves pass through zero—the center line in our screenshots—once per cycle at the fundamental frequency. If you mark all your edit points at *zero crossings*, the voltages will match and there won't be a jump. Some audio software automatically snaps to the closest zero crossing when you make a selection. Depending on the fundamental frequency of the sound, this can be as much as a half frame away, but it's usually much less. If the software doesn't snap to zero, you can zoom in and see a zero crossing, then nudge the edit to it.

Or you can make the jump smoother by applying an audio cross-fade. It works like a video cross-fade, gradually moving from the first piece, to a blend of both pieces, to the second piece. This eliminates the possibility of a sudden jump. The fade doesn't have to be very long; a few milliseconds—less than a quarter frame—is enough. Good audio software lets you apply *automatic cross-fades* or *blending* at each edit.

> ⚠ **Gotcha**
>
> **My NLE doesn't let me do this!** No, it might not. Frame-based NLEs can't nudge edits to zero points because those points seldom line up against frame boundaries. The shortest audio cross-fade in many NLEs is two frames, or 60ms—long enough to eliminate clicks, but much too long for precise dialog editing.
>
> Another reason to fire up your audio software.

Figure 8.7 shows both of these click-reducing methods applied to an extreme edit, from silence to a fairly loud 40-Hz wave. The version on the left is the untreated original; it clicks because of the sudden jump from silence to the wave's peak. The version in the middle used automatic snapping to a zero crossing; the program moved the edit 1/80 second from where I put it, eliminating the click by cutting at the start of a whole wave. That's about a third of a frame and not noticeable as a sync error, but if you're doing a lot of editing in a single shot, the error can add up. Fortunately, another technique doesn't affect sync at all: The version on the right uses an automatic cross-fade. A 2-millisecond blend is enough to ramp the voltage up, so there was no click. But it's still short enough (1/15 of a frame) that it's heard as a cut.

You can also eliminate clicks manually by using an audio program's pencil tool to smooth them out—essentially making a cross-fade by hand. But this is so labor-intensive, it's hardly worth the effort.

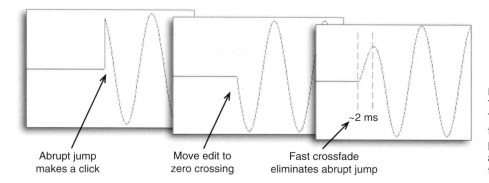

FIGURE 8.7
Three different edits. The first one clicks; the other two use program features to automatically avoid the click.

| Abrupt jump makes a click | Move edit to zero crossing | Fast crossfade eliminates abrupt jump |

> **Rule**
>
> If an existing NLE track clicks at an edit, move it to an audio program, select a couple of milliseconds around the click with snap-to-zero or blending turned on, and erase. Or use the program's pencil tool to manually smooth over the click.

Learning How to Listen Quickly

Film and video work because your eyes blur those very fast still frames into an illusion of motion. But you can easily hear individual sounds that are shorter than a single frame. The click in Figure 8.6, only a couple of samples, takes about 1/1000 of a frame. Meaningful sounds don't have to be much longer.

Consider two phrases, "the small pot" and "the small tot." I recorded them both and lined them up on two channels of the stereo file in Figure 8.8. The /p/ from "pot" is called out on the top track, and the /t/ from "tot" on the bottom. The two vertical dashed lines are exactly one frame apart. You can see the critical difference, changing the meaning of the phrase, takes only about half a frame.

> **Gotcha**
>
> *I should mumble at my desk?* This chapter uses spoken-word exercises to improve your short-term audio memory. The goal is to help you learn to analyze what you're hearing. Say the words out loud, not just in your head. If this upsets your office-mates, tell them you're becoming a better editor because of it.

Most of us are born with this ability to hear and understand fast sounds. If you want to edit, you just have to learn to recognize what you're hearing. It takes a little bit of acoustic memory. Musicians and actors usually have this talent. But even if you can't carry a tune, you can still improve your listening skills.

1. Say, "the small pot" aloud, and listen very closely to your own voice while you do.

167

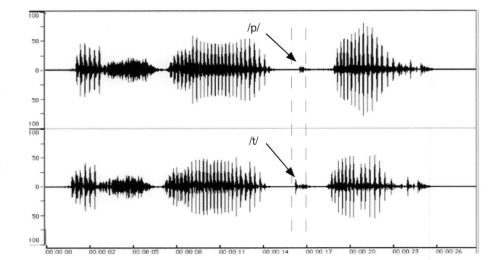

FIGURE 8.8
"The small pot" on the top track; "the small tot" on the bottom. The difference is only about half a frame long.

2. Immediately afterwards, try to remember exactly what your voice sounded like. If you can, hear those three syllables again in your head.

3. Repeat this a few times, and you'll find that you can recall the actual sound of your voice more and more accurately.

Try saying the phrase with different intonations and timings, and hear those versions in your head as well. Try saying slightly longer phrases until you can recall those also. Then try listening to playbacks of very short dialog clips and practice until you can recall them as well. Now do one more thing.

4. Slow down what you're hearing in your head, so you can hear the tiny changes inside each word. In "the small pot," you should be able to hear definite transitions between /th/, /uh/, /s/, /maw/, /l/, /p/, /ah/, and /t/. Those are the phonemes.

Don't give up if you aren't hearing individual sounds immediately—this is a skill that can be difficult at first, particularly for someone who's visually oriented. But I've found that most video editors catch on in fewer than a dozen tries. After that, it's easy.

EIGHT SOUNDS FOR ONLY THREE WORDS?

Most meaningful syllables contain at least one vowel and one consonant sound. But some syllables have more than that. Take my name, Jay. It's a single syllable, but has four distinct phonemes: /d zh ay ih/. Track 23 is me saying "My name Jay." First you hear it at normal speed, then slowed down to 1/6 speed. You should hear 11 phonemes in those three syllables: /m ah ih n ay ih m d zh ay ih/. Almost any of them can be used as edit points.

Some common sounds are always made of a pair of phonemes, called a *diphthong;* my name has two of them. The *j* sound is always a /d/ followed by a /zh/ (that second phoneme is what you hear in the middle of "leisure"). The vowel

Table 8.1	The consonants of standard English. The groupings are based on how you edit them	
	Unvoiced	**Voiced**
Stop Consonants	/p/ (punt) /k/ (cut) /t/ (tot)	/b/ (bunt) /g/ (gut) /d/ (dot)
Friction Consonants	/f/ (food) /s/ (silly) /sh/ (shoe) /th/ (thin) /h/ (horse)	/v/ (very) /z/ (zebra) /zh/ (leisure) /TH/ (then) –
Nasal Consonants	Nasals are always voiced	/m/ (mighty) /n/ (nap) /ng/ (lung)
Glide Consonants	Glides are always voiced	/w/ (willing) /y/ (yes) /l/ (locate) /r/ (rub)
Diphthong Consonants	/t-sh/ (church)	/d-zh/ (judge)

in my name always includes an /ih/ at the end. If you try to say just the /ay/ sound, my name sounds clipped.

 Hear for yourself

Track 23 contains the previous example. The second part might sound like I'm on drugs,[4] but it's actually the first part slowed down in software, so you can hear individual phonemes.

Phonetic-Based Editing

We could predict exactly which tiny sounds made up "the small pot" or "my name Jay" because there aren't very many ways humans move their mouths during speech. Standard American English has only about four dozen of them, to cover the entire vocabulary.

Tables 8.1 and 8.2 show them organized into groups based on their usefulness to editors. Note how there's no phoneme for *c*, because that letter is sometimes said as /s/ and sometimes as /k/. But there are 15 phonemes and diphthongs for the five vowels. That's why, when you're scanning a script or transcript to find replacement sounds or likely edits, it helps to say the words aloud.

---

[4] I ran it through a phase vocoder, a specialized pitch shifter that's worth adding to your arsenal. You'll learn about it in Chapter 14.

Table 8.2	The vowels of standard English	
Single Vowels		
/ee/ (eat)	/ae/ (hat)	/eh/ (lend)
/ih/ (sit)	/aw/ (all)	/ah/ (father)
/o/ (note)	/u/ (bull)	/oo/ (tool)
/uh/ (about)	/UH/ (up)	/er/ (worker)
Diphthong Vowels		
/ay-ih/ (play)	/i-ih/ (high)	/aw-ih/ (toy)

The two columns—*unvoiced* and *voiced*—have to do with how the sound is generated. You'll see why this is important later in this chapter.

Using Phonemes

People slide words together when they're speaking, so you can't always tell where one word ends and the next begins. But you can almost always hear when one phoneme ends and another starts. Consider Track 24: two takes of "This is a special occasion." While the first is usable, the second has more emotion. But the second has a noise under the first few words. The only way to get a performance that starts cleanly and ends enthusiastically is to use a few words from each: "This is a," from one and "special occasion," from the other.

 Hear for yourself

Track 24 is the audio for this exercise. It will look like Figure 8.9 when you capture it.

The line was delivered at normal speed and there's no pause between "a" and "special," so you can't cut in silence between those words. But the /p/ in "special" is a stop consonant; it creates a pause *inside* the word. You can scrub through the two takes, easily hear and mark that pause in each take, and edit from one to the other: "This is a sp || ecial occasion." The whole process shouldn't take more than ten seconds and should sound perfect.

This principle also works when the words aren't strictly identical. If you had the right words from elsewhere in the clip, you could join them to the first phrase to say, "This is a spectacular show," or "This is a specious argument."

Phoneme-Based Editing Rules[5]

Cutting the way we just did is fast, precise, and usually undetectable. First, hear the phrase you want to edit, slowly, in your head. Identify any phonemes that

---

[5] It really *does*, man. But what I meant was, "Here are some rules for using phonemes when you edit."

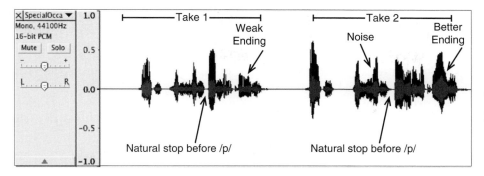

FIGURE 8.9
Two takes of "This is a special occasion." The first is cleaner... but flatter. Read how to combine the two seamlessly.

might be useful for the cut you want to make, using the rules below. Then scrub through the clip to find those points.

All the *stop consonants* are created by storing air pressure in your mouth and then releasing it in a burst. There's a moment of silence in the middle of each stop consonant, right before the pressure is released. It can be as short as a third of a frame.

> ## Rule
> Stop consonants will always give you a moment of silence.

- If a stop consonant is followed by a pause, it usually has two distinct sounds: one when the pressure is cut off, and another when it's released. But the second part isn't important and can be deleted to shorten the pause, or edited to some other word.
- If two stop consonants are next to each other (as in, "fat cat"), they're usually *elided*; the closure comes from the first consonant, and the release from the second. But when people are self-conscious, they often pronounce each stop separately, making four distinct sounds. Editing out the middle two stops will make a nervous speaker ("the faT Tcat") sound more relaxed ("the fah..Tcat").

With the exception of /h/, *friction consonants* are created by forcing air through a narrow opening: between the lips for /f/ and /v/, between the tip of the tongue and back of the teeth for /th/ and /TH/, and so on. This always makes a high-pitched sound that's easy to spot while scrubbing.

> ## Rule
> Friction consonants give you a high-pitched cue.

Air pressure also creates /h/, but air is flowing through an open mouth. There's very little friction, so this phoneme can be very quiet and not even show up on a waveform display. Be careful you don't accidentally delete it.

- You can usually edit from the start of one friction consonant to the start of a completely different one.
- Friction consonants are frequently stretched when a speaker is talking slowly. You can usually speed things up by cutting a little bit out of their middles.

For the three *nasal consonants*, air comes out of the nose instead of the mouth: Try saying a long "nnn" as you pinch your nostrils together—it'll feel as if your head's about to explode. If your performer has a head cold, nasals may sound wrong and need to be replaced from elsewhere in the dialog. But be aware that nasals are always voiced (see the following section, "Cognate Pairs"); the replacement sound will have to be at the right pitch.

> ### *Rule*
> Nasal consonants might be mispronounced.

The /ng/ phoneme is written that way because it's heard at the end of words like "ring." But it's a phoneme on its own, not a diphthong made up of /n/ and /g/. Many people add a /g/ anyway, as in the New York regionalism "Long Guyland." Feel free to delete the /g/; it'll make your performer sound more polished.

The *glides* make the transition between sounds on either side. This means glides are influenced by adjacent sounds, and their own sound changes while they're being pronounced. This can make them very difficult to mark or match.

> ### *Rule*
> Glide consonants may be impossible to edit.

- In general, the only successful glide edits occur when both the consonant itself and the leading or trailing sound are identical.
- The /l/ glide involves lifting your tongue from the ridge behind your upper front teeth. If the speaker's mouth is dry, saliva can stick and cause a tiny click in the middle of this sound. Feel free to delete the click—it won't hurt the sound.

Even though we hear *consonant diphthongs* as a single sound, they're actually two separate and predictable phonemes. If you scrub through them slowly, you can hear the transition and mark them separately.

> **Rule**
>
> Diphthongs can be cut in half.

The /d zh/ at the front of my name (Track 23) can be cut into two phonemes. Go ahead and try it. Delete just the /d/, and my name sounds French. Delete just the /zh/, and my name turns into the opposite of night. Similarly, you could borrow a /t/ from the front of someone saying "chicken" if you needed one to use elsewhere.

Cognate Pairs

There are two columns of consonants in Table 8.1 for a reason. The paired sounds in each row use exactly the same tongue and lip movement. The only difference is that the first in a pair relies on air pressure alone (unvoiced), while the second adds a buzzing from the vocal cords (voiced). The pairs are called *cognates.* Not all consonants have them.

Try saying "gut" and "cut" aloud, with your hand loosely on your throat. The tongue movement is the same for each. But you'll feel the buzzing in your throat start before the /g/. It doesn't start until after the /k/ in "cut."

Every aspect that we interpret as a voice's *pitch*—from what note is being sung, to the vocal difference between me and James Earl Jones—is based on the fundamental frequency of those buzzing vocal cords.[6] Unvoiced consonants simply don't have that buzz.

> **Rule**
>
> You don't have to worry about pitch with the unvoiced consonants.

- Unvoiced phonemes tend to stay consistent even if the speaker has a lot of tonal variety. This gives you more choices when editing.
- Unvoiced phonemes don't carry much that's identifiable as a specific voice. You can often substitute one person's voice for another's.

You can even substitute a male voice for a female one. Grab the first part of Track 25. It consists of a woman asking, "Have you read Jay's book?" and me responding, "I've written a couple of books." Merge the sexes to correct

---

[6]While pitch differences are based on the fundamental, character differences are often based on *formants*—harmonics of that fundamental. You'll learn more about formants in Chapter 11 and some ways to manipulate them in Chapter 14.

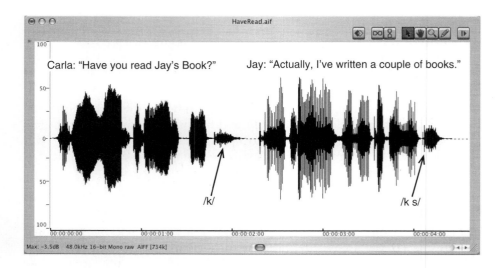

Carla: "Have you read Jay's Book?"   Jay: "Actually, I've written a couple of books."

/k/   /k s/

FIGURE 8.10
Amaze your friends!
Learn to make this
sex-changing edit!

174

her question. Because both /k/ and /s/ are unvoiced, the edit "Have you
read Jay's boo || ks?" works almost perfectly. Unless you listen very closely,
you're not aware that the sources have completely different voices.[7] In fact,
because /k/ is a stop consonant, there's a convenient silence for you to edit
in (Figure 8.10).

 Hear for yourself

Track 25 is the two voices from the above example, first in the original readings and then
edited together.

Because the mouth movements are identical, you can occasionally substitute
one cognate for its brother. This may be the only way to save an edit, or create
a new word.

Rule

You can sometimes substitute one cognate for another.

- Depending on the context, this may add what seems like a slight accent
  to the voice. That's because foreigners often confuse cognate pairs when
  they first learn English.

---

[7] You could make the edit absolutely perfect by applying about a semitone's pitch shift up.
See Chapter 14.

- When the voiced stop consonant /b/ begins a word, some people start their vocal cords humming a fraction of a second or so before the release. This turns a word like "baby" into "mmmbaby." Deleting the hum, or replacing it with room tone, makes it sound better.

When *s* is added at the end to pluralize a word, its pronunciation is influenced by whether the vocal cords were buzzing on the phoneme that came before. There are two different *s* sounds in "cat's toys." The unvoiced /t/ at the end of "cat" leads to an unvoiced /s/, but the voiced /aw ih/ at the end of "toy" forces a voiced /z/. Be aware of this when looking for replacement sounds; the presence of an *s* in the written script doesn't guarantee a /s/ on the track.

Rule

A final /s/ might actually be a /z/.

The Vowels

Learn to recognize individual vowel phonemes in dialog. You can't substitute one for another. In Table 8.2, the unstressed /uh/ in "about" and the stressed /UH/ in "up" are separate entries. Even though they're made the same way, the difference in projection is critical.

- Vowel diphthongs can sometimes be separated into their component phonemes and used elsewhere. This is a lot harder than separating a consonant diphthong.
- Vowels and voiced consonants carry the pitch of a voice, which varies a lot during normal speech. After you edit, make sure the pitch doesn't jump unnaturally. If it does, try moving the edit to a nearby unvoiced consonant instead.
- Vowels carry most of the pacing of a voice. If a word is said too slowly, you can often make a small cut in the middle of a vowel to pick up speed—but this works only if the pitch is constant.
- When nervous performers pause before a word that starts with a vowel, they often build up pressure in the back of their throats. When they release it to say the word, the result is a *glottal shock*—a tiny click, almost like a stop consonant. It sounds tense. Calm things down by deleting the click.

Some More Tips for Great Edits

Speech is continuous, and the end of one word is influenced by the word that follows. If you say, "Mary grabbed the knob," the end of "the" will be slightly different than if she grabbed "the doorknob." The stop consonant /d/ changes the /uh/ in ways the nasal /n/ doesn't. A lot of interview edits feel subtly wrong because a producer put the words together while reading a transcript, without paying attention to how the edits sound in context.

175

> ### Rule
> You can almost always cut from the start of a phoneme in one word, to the start of the same phoneme in a different word.

On the other hand, you could easily take a different /n/ word and replace the "knob" with it. So she could grab "the || knocker," "the || needle," or "the || neighborhood cat."

Because the stop consonants cut off sound entirely, there's more flexibility when editing between them. If Mary originally grabbed "the doorknob," it wouldn't be hard to have her grab "the || bagel," "the || gavel," or "the || cat" instead.

> ### Rule
> You can often cut from the beginning of one stop consonant to the beginning of a different one.

It's almost always best to hide a voice edit in the middle of a visual cutaway rather than right at the cut back to the speaker's face. That's because the visual discontinuity calls attention to the aural one. Similarly, it's almost always better to edit *inside* a word rather than at its start. The mind tries to complete words based on their context and beginning, and that helps you hide the edit.[8]

Say you wanted to combine "Mary grabbed the neighborhood cat," and "She liked her neighbor's car," to suggest she's also a car thief. The best place to make that cut is at the stop inside "neighbor," as in "Mary grabbed the neigh || bor's car." This also works when combining identical words, as we did in the "This is a special occasion" example of Figure 8.9.

> ### Rule
> Try not to edit where it's expected.

People change pitch while they're speaking. Sometimes two syllables you're trying to join are at different places in the musical scale. If this makes an edit sound wrong, try a small amount of vari-speed or clip speed adjustment. But don't use more than a 3% change or else the voice will sound artificial.

---

[8]This is one reason the she/he cut in Figure 8.12 works so well.

> **_Rule_**
>
> Use room tone to extend abrupt cuts.

Sometimes you have to cut from a word to silence, even though the speaker had kept on talking in the original recording. This happens frequently when pulling interview bites or when deleting a /s/ to turn a plural noun into a singular one. Cutting to room tone instead of silence can fool the ear into thinking the subject paused naturally. The same trick works when a bite starts abruptly; add a little room tone in front.

> **_Rule_**
>
> Make sure the sound quality matches.

Sound quality can also change across an edit, because the two pieces had differences in mic placement or performance. That's just as easy to fix. Since feature films are usually shot with a lot of different camera setups and performances within a single scene, the necessary technique is the basis for film-style dialog editing. Which brings us to the next part of this chapter.

TRACK SPLITTING AND FILLING

A rare thing happened in Hollywood a number of years ago: something originally done to save money actually improved the art. You know how scenes are shot: A dialog line might extend from a master shot to a two-shot to a close-up, get a response from a character in a different close-up, and then go to another close-up or back to the master. Eventually, all these little bits of picture have to be cut together. What we see as a continuous scene might have had three or four different boom mic angles, performances, and background noises. Unless something is done in audio post, they'll all sound different on the screen.

TV sound doesn't worry about this. The medium grew up with continuous performances, shot with multiple cameras and switched in real-time. It made audio post a lot easier… if there was any at all (remember, TV started as a live medium). As videos moved out of real-time studios and began to be assembled in editing systems, the aesthetic and philosophy stayed. Video editors would assemble single dialog tracks on their masters, and audio post would do things to sweeten them, usually at the same time as adding music and sound effects.

Part of this also had to do with playback. Until recently, video usually stayed on small screens with small speakers. Movies, of course, are heard through big speakers. Any sudden shifts in voice timbre or noise level jump right out, destroying the mood. Since films are shot and edited in pieces, there are dozens of shifts in each scene. It takes good monitors and proper processors to fix

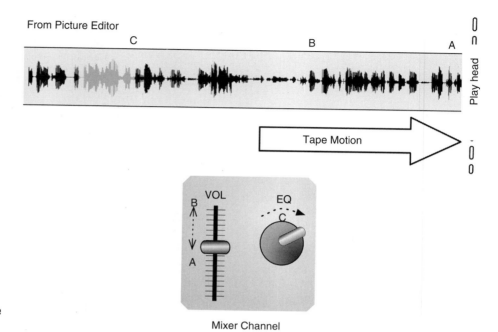

From Picture Editor

C   B   A

Play head

Tape Motion

VOL   EQ

B   C

A

Mixer Channel

FIGURE 8.11
A typical TV dialog workflow. The imperfections (at B and C) can be easily fixed by tweaking the level or equalization.

178

them. But film dub stages are big and expensive, so studio bosses didn't want to take any longer than necessary in those rooms.

The answer was brilliant: Take the film editor's single track, and split it into pieces depending on what needs to be done.

Splitting: Why and How

Figure 8.11 shows how dialog fixes typically happen in TV production. A single audio track arrives from the picture editor, drawn here as a piece of moving tape with waveforms. Most of this scene's waveform is of a consistent quality (area A on the tape). Once the console has been set up, it can be pretty much ignored; the engineer can easily tweak overall dialog levels while mixing the ambience and music.

On this particular tape, the area starting at B is too soft. And C has the wrong timbre (drawn as a non-matching gray). But the engineer has plenty of time to raise the level just for B, then grab the equalization knob in time to fix C.

Now look at Figure 8.12, a typical scene of the same length from a film production. Because it was built from multiple takes, there are many more shifts in quality. And since it'll be heard on giant speakers, smaller changes in timbre are more obvious. That's why they're shown in two different grays.

The film's re-recording engineer might be able to catch all those changes on-the-fly, but it's harder. It will take a lot of rehearsals or automation programming to get all the cues and adjustments just right. Since a whole movie's dialog is usually made up this way, this could slow mixing down to a crawl.

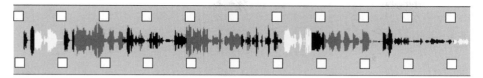

FIGURE 8.12
A typical film scene has a lot more variation.

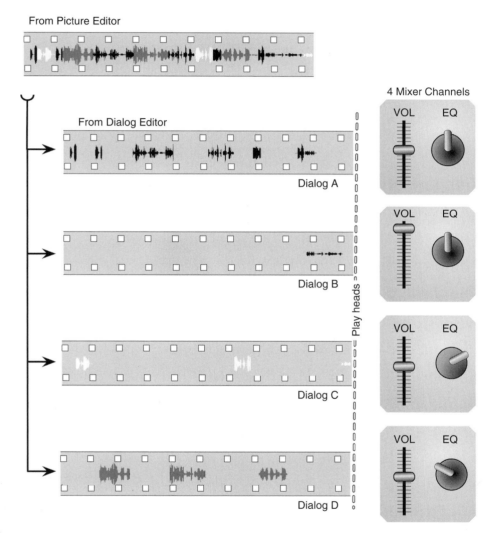

FIGURE 8.13
Splitting the film into multiple dialog tracks will make the mix a lot easier.[9] All four tracks are run simultaneously, so a piece of the original dialog is playing at all times.

179

Instead, the film goes to a *dialog editor* first. That editor splits the picture department's one track into four separate ones, sorted by sound quality and separated by silence (Figure 8.13). Each needs its own kind of processing. But the engineer can preset four console channels with the proper settings for each, rewind the whole scene, and let it rip.

[9]The actual process involves separating pieces of the original dialog with silent, non-magnetic leader. I left those splices out for clarity.

What made the bean counters happy was that dialog editing is a lot cheaper, per hour, than mixing. Editors earn less than re-recording mixers, and they can work in a small room with just a flatbed or Moviola and midsized speaker.

But there's also a creative benefit: since the re-recording mixers weren't worrying as much about mechanical details, they could concentrate on the smoothness and emotional flow of the dialog. Those factors are so important that features often spend half their mixing time just fine-tuning the splits into a single *dialog pre-mix*.

WHEN WORLDS COMBINE . . .

If you were mixing video sound in the early 1990s, you probably wouldn't bother with—or even know about—track splitting. There was no practical way to do it. Audio tape doesn't have sprocket holes, so it's almost impossible to physically split one tape onto four reels and have them maintain sync. Besides, a video post room's console is smaller than those used for film, and you couldn't squander a dozen or more channels on dialog.

Today we edit in audio workstations. Splitting a clip into multiple tracks is just a question of marking and dragging. It can be done on simple setups, even using a laptop and headphones.

Similarly, a film re-recording mixer in analog days would never consider trying to fix jumpy dialog from single track. Even with automation, it was too time-consuming. Today's audio workstations make this much faster: precise, repeatable cues are as simple as drawing a rectangle. If dialog doesn't need a lot of fixes, it makes sense to wait until the mix; it's more efficient overall and won't slow the process down significantly.

 Gotcha

Sound effect of jaws dropping. This is really a radical change, made possible only by today's systems and software. I spent decades editing and mixing tape for TV, and I have friends who spent just as long mixing film dialog. Over the past five years or less, we've all started borrowing each others' techniques. It makes us all more efficient, and lets us do better work.

You've gotta love this twenty-first century!

Cross-Fades and Overlaps

I left one vital step out of Figure 8.13.

- If you play those tracks as shown, the dialog will be smooth. But background noise is also affected by the volume and equalizer knobs. The background will sound normal on Dialog A, suddenly be boosted on Dialog B, and then switch to being brighter or duller during C and D.
- Fortunately, people's sensitivity to noise is easily distracted by dialog. If we slow down those changes just a little bit, viewers can ignore them. So

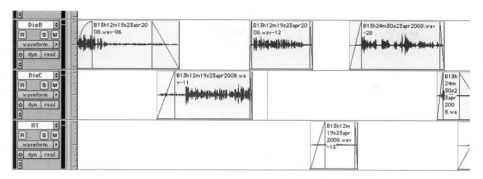

FIGURE 8.14
Tiny fades at the start and end of each dialog segment will hide abrupt jumps in the background noise. Here, Dialog B blends smoothly into Dialog A when they're both played back.

the dialog editor stretches each segment, on each dialog track, to include a short fade in or out from the background noise. Depending on the program, they either apply a fade function or drag the end of the volume line down. These fades don't have to be very long; frequently a half-second is sufficient. Figure 8.14 shows how they look. When these tracks are mixed, they'll automatically make a smooth cross-fade between their channels.

Most dialog is continuous, and doesn't have convenient half-second pauses for each camera cut. In a lot of scenes, stretching a segment to make room for the necessary fade might expose an unwanted sound, such as another word or a sudden prop noise. Anything other than the expected background noise will call attention to the cross-fade. That's why you always keep a stock of spare background noise recorded during the shoot: *room tone*. Paste a bit over the offending sound, and use it for the fade.

Room Tone or Presence

Every shooting location has a unique sound. It consists of the obvious background noises such as distant traffic, clocks ticking, and HVAC systems. But it also includes the room itself—its size, shape, and surfaces—and how those acoustics affect the background noise. A recording of that room sound can be very useful.

I recorded film dialog on location early in my career. Back then it was customary to capture a minute or so of a location's background before striking. I'd yell, "Room tone!" and the crew would stand still while I taped. We did this right after the takes, because a room's sound can change during the day. We did it while the crew was still there, so their breathing and subtle movements were recorded on the dialog takes as well. The procedure remains common in feature production today. Sometimes it's called *outdoor tone* or just *presence*, since it also exists during exterior shots.

Room tone has to match the existing background that's already under dialog takes. For this reason it's almost always in mono, recorded with the dialog mic, and treated as a dialog element at the mix.

FARMING FOR ROOM TONE

If a production hasn't captured room tone, you might still be able to find some. You can often grab a few usable seconds between "Action!" and the start of dialog, before the camera stops after a take, or while an interview subject is thinking about an answer. A loop of that sound may be all you need. If you're planning to collect room tone this way, here are a few tips.

- Be sure you're hearing only presence. Voices will echo for a second or more after dialog stops, depending on the room. Wait until the echo has died out before grabbing the presence.
- If you're taking presence from pauses in an interview, make sure you're not hearing the subject inhale, which can be fairly loud if picked up by a lav. A looped breath sounds like Darth Vader.
- If the presence includes constantly changing elements, like ocean waves, there can be a noticeable jump when you transition from the end of one pass to the start of the next. Use a *C-loop*, described in Chapter 10.

Even if you're not splitting tracks, room tone can be used to fill pauses during cutaways, or to cover noises during a take. If a character has a long voice-over, tighten things up by replacing breaths with somewhat shorter clips of presence—usually, about 2/3 the length of the breath you've removed. Room tone is also necessary for matching studio ADR to location dialog.

There are times when room tone isn't needed at all. A well-designed narration studio is so quiet that its presence disappears on TV; you can't even hear it in theaters if there's music or effects playing. You can edit faster by using silence instead of room tone.

 Gotcha

When room tone isn't your friend. Novice editors sometimes try running an extra, continuous room tone track during dialog. The idea is to hide the jumps in existing room tone because of dialog edits.

This doesn't work. All it means is that in some places there'll be twice as much background sound, cutting in and out with the dialog edits.

Specific ambiences (Chapter 10), such as restaurant or office backgrounds, usually can't be used as room tone. They're too busy to cut in and out just during pauses, don't match existing set noises, and almost always are mixed in stereo or surround and won't appear to come from the same place as dialog.

ROOM TONE AND DIALOG SPLITS

It's common, when editing dialog, to separate out lines that'll be replaced by ADR or be "futzed" for special effects like a phone filter or PA echo. Similarly, useful prop noises that were picked up along with dialog, such as phone slams, are moved to a *production effects (PFX)* track. That way they can be treated separately, or easily replaced. And of course there's almost always something on the dialog track—shouted directions, crew movement during a pause, or an assistant feeding lines—that has to be deleted.

The holes left in the dialog track, after these sounds have been moved, should be filled with room tone. That way it'll receive the same processing as dialog, and keep the main dialog sounding continuous. If a production effect is kept in the final mix, it'll have its own tone. In that case, the mixer will cross-fade to it from the fill.

Going Deeper

You could fill a book just about track splitting, what's expected in Hollywood workflows, and how to handle specific situations like phone calls. In fact, dialog editor John Purcell did exactly that, in his *Dialog Editing for Motion Pictures* (Focal Press, 2007). If you're ever given dialog chores on a big feature—or just want to learn more about the art—get a copy.

RESTORING LIPSYNC BY EYE

You've got a clip with picture and no sound and a different clip with sound only, and you need to sync them up. If both clips are exactly the same length, chances are they were originally captured together and all the job needs is to place their starting points together in the timeline.

But if the clips are from separate media, or if they were digitized separately, it will be much harder to match the track with the right mouth movements.

- It helps if both audio and video were recorded in media with stable speeds. This usually happens when both are digital. But if the film was shot with a noncrystal camera, or audio was recorded on analog tape without pilot or timecode, restoring sync can be impossible.
- It helps if both audio and video start on the same word. If the audio track has a few extra syllables that don't appear on the picture, you'll find it difficult to link mouth movements to their sounds.
- Check the clip's statistics to make sure there are no dropped frames. If there's a problem that slows down the software when digitizing or capturing, most NLEs will skip a video frame or two to catch up. But each dropped frame knocks subsequent audio out of sync and has to be treated as a separate resyncing operation. There are tips for avoiding dropped frames in Chapters 6 and 18.
- It's essential that audio and video are of the same event. I was once asked to resync a scene, only to find out later that the client had inadvertently used picture from one take and sound from another. It was an expensive learning experience for the client.

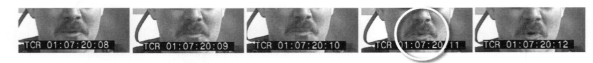

FIGURE 8.15
Find where pursed lips just start to open after being closed, and you've located a /b/ or /p/.

It also helps to make your editing setup as sync-friendly as possible. Use a large picture monitor and play at full frame rate. Make sure playback is smooth, and be sure to allow enough time for preroll and synchronization if your system requires it. The best software environments give you *bump* or *nudge* controls—single key commands that let you slip selected regions against picture in controlled increments of a frame or less, while both are playing.

There's a general procedure to make sync matching a little easier.

1. Play the audio clip and locate the first plosive /b/ or /p/ sound. Find the silence right before that sound—it can last a frame or two, and unless there's a lot of background noise you'll be able to see it on the waveform—and place a marker on the first frame where the sound returns.
2. Note approximately how far that marker is from the start of the speech.
3. Find the first frame of video where the subject's mouth opens.
4. Move forward the same distance you noted in step 2, less a few frames.
5. Shuttle forward slowly until you see the lips close. Then jog forward and find the first frame where the lips start to open again and put a marker there.

That step requires a good eye because the movement can be subtle, but it's always there. Figure 8.15 shows a typical /p/: note how the lips are just starting to part at 1:07:20:11, after having been closed in the previous frame.

6. Line the two markers up and things should be in perfect sync. If they look slightly off, move the sound a frame forward and check again. If that makes it look worse, go back the other way. If moving helps but doesn't fix things, add another frame in the same direction. If sync didn't look right at all when you first checked, you found the wrong lip movement in step 5. Try again.

If the speech doesn't have a /b/ or /p/ sound near the front, listen for an /m/ followed by a vowel. Follow the same steps—lip movements for an /m/ looks almost the same as those for a /p/—but mark the audio clip on the start of the vowel sound after the /m/

You may be able to skip steps 2 and 4, and just match the first sound with the first picture where the mouth is open. Sometimes this works, but often it doesn't. I've found it faster to always go for the stop consonant.

CHAPTER 9
Finding and Editing Music

REMEMBER THIS:

- There's no reason a film can't have a fully professional-sounding score, even on a limited budget. But doing it the wrong way can get you into serious legal and financial trouble.
- Today's music libraries and other tools have an incredible range of good music. If you take some time, you'll find exactly what you need.
- Music editing isn't difficult once you apply a little ear (and finger) training.

Even before they learned to talk, movies had music. Every theater had at least a piano player; bigger houses had elaborate organs that could also make sound effects, and some even had small orchestras. While the choice of music was often at the whim of theater management, the more important feature films came with original scores on sheet music. You could even say silent films inspired the singing commercial: As new technologies like the Victrola and radio became popular, movie producers commissioned ballads that just happened to include the film's title. (The old standard, "Janine, I Dream of Lilac Time" was actually written to promote the movie *Janine*.)

But film music didn't take off until the synchronized soundtrack was possible. Many early talkies followed the musical tradition of silent films, with somewhat random instrumentals playing under dialog. Then Hollywood began importing European composers with a tradition of orchestral *program music*—music designed to tell a story. Movie scoring became an art form. Some of the greatest classical composers of the twentieth century, including Prokofiev, Copland, and Bernstein, also wrote for films.[1]

---

[1] A suite from Prokofiev's *Lieutenant Kijé* score is now part of standard symphonic repertoire, as is Copland's score for *Our Town*. Copland even won a best-scoring Oscar for *The Heiress*. Leonard Bernstein wrote one film and vowed never to repeat the experience (see Chapter 5). For what it's worth, someone with the same name but no relation—Oscar-winner Elmer Bernstein—is credited as composer on 238 different film and TV projects in his 50-year career.

If you're making a narrative film, you're probably already thinking in terms of music. But even if you're producing documentary, corporate, or event video, music can be used the same ways: to set the mood, underscore emotions, provide a rhythm for visual sequences, and comment on what we're seeing. The techniques for spotting, obtaining, and applying music are the same for any film, whether it's a drama or a factory tour.

SPOTTING NOTES

You don't need to be a musician to figure out what kind of music your project needs. It does help to be familiar with a wide variety of musical styles, but even that isn't essential. What's critical is that you know your project and its goals.

The music selection process should start before you hire a composer or even search online libraries. Read the script or watch a rough cut and see where music is needed. Most likely, you'll want a main title and ending, even if it's just under "Installing Your New Ultra-Crunch" in front and a corporate logo at the end. But there are probably other places where music can help.

Find places for music by making spotting notes, even for something as simple as a 10-minute sales film. For each scene or segment, write down what the music could be doing. It doesn't need to be in musical terms. Terms like *music swells with inspiration*, or *exciting sports music* are useful. If music is just there to tie testimonials together or support a narrator, it should still reflect the mood of the piece. Be aware of any emotional or subject shifts: that's where the music should change. Of course, if something suggests a particular style or tempo—a period piece under historic footage, for example—write that down as well.

Break your list into cues of music linked to specific on-screen sequences. They might last for a few seconds, or for a few minutes. This lets you deal with music pieces efficiently when searching libraries, talking to a composer, and putting the music in place. If there are only a few cues, give them descriptive names. If there are many, numbering helps.

If a scene doesn't suggest music, perhaps silence is more appropriate. Hold back from time to time, and alternate scored sequences with just dialog or with sound-effects driven sequences. One common approach for documentaries is to score narrated sections but let the interviews stand on their own without music. Some short films work best with continuous music; longer films often benefit by dropping the music for a while, so we're aware of its return. Don't forget *source* (also known as *diegetic*) *music*, cues that are presumably coming from something in the characters' world. On-camera radios or TVs, or settings like a restaurant or supermarket, probably need source music.

Spotting notes are important even if you're the only one who'll be seeing them, because they provide a structure for music selection. If you're searching through existing music, it'll make the search more efficient. ("I'll know it when I hear it," just wastes time.) If you're using original music, the notes help you decide who should create it, and are essential when you start discussing the project with them.

GETTING THE MUSIC

Music is subject to the Golden Triangle of Production: You can have it excellent, fast, or cheap—pick any two. If you're on a limited budget, it's worth taking time to find great music that doesn't cost much. One place you *won't* find great inexpensive music is at record stores or their online equivalents. Law and common sense both get in the way.

Copyright Considerations

Students and other low-budget filmmakers sometimes ask why they can't use songs from their personal CD or mp3 collections; after all, they paid for the disc or download. Copyright law takes a different view. When you buy a song that way, you get the right to play it for yourself and close friends, or to make a backup copy for your own personal listening. Syncing it with images or playing it outside your immediate circle is forbidden. Copyright violation might not bother you—and a low-profile infringement might never get noticed—but if the lawyers come after you, they'll win.[2] If you're not sure about any of this or think it doesn't apply in your case, talk to an attorney before you use the music.

- You can't defend yourself by claiming Fair Use. That doctrine allows criticism, parody, and commentary on the music itself—not the use of the music as an underscore. Also, Fair Use is just a set of principles, not a guarantee. It's always up to the judge in your specific case.
- You can't defend yourself by claiming you couldn't afford the song, so its creator isn't losing money because of your use. Economic loss is only one of the factors. Paupers and nonprofits are subject to the same laws as professionals.
- You can't argue you're promoting the music by giving it exposure in your film, unless the copyright owner already agreed that they *want* that exposure in return for use.

A couple of copyright myths are based on misunderstandings of when usage *is* legal. TV stations pay fees to ASCAP and BMI to broadcast music as entertainment. Those fees pay the composers and lyricists for the public performance of their songs. They have nothing to do with using a specific recording, or syncing the notes or words to images.

Also, at one time courts accepted that copying fewer than eight bars of a song was not plagiarism. But that 8-bar rule—eliminated years ago—applied only to the notes on paper, when two different songs were similar. It never applied to recordings.

187

---

[2]It's possible your attorney could build a convincing case for letting you use the music under existing U.S. law. But the copyright owners have statutory protections and the possibility of big awards, so they're going to throw their best lawyers at it. Even if you do win, you'll probably end up paying your attorney more than permission would have cost.

Gotcha

But it's the bride's CD! Some wedding videographers believe they avoid copyright issues by using music from the client's personal collection. It's not true.

While it's unlikely a record company will pursue a bride who scores an amateur video of her wedding on a home computer (even though it's clearly an infringement), professional producers are considered fair game. I've heard of wedding videographers being put out of business because they used a copyrighted song. It turns out one of the happy couple's neighbors worked for the giant corporation that owned the rights. Some companies even reward employees for spotting these infringements.

I personally believe many large record companies exploit their artists shamelessly. A band can have two or three hit albums before it sees a penny. Unfortunately, some of the money that doesn't pay the artists goes to large legal departments instead. Karma isn't a factor: As a professional, I have to follow the rules.

But there are other reasons for not stealing pop music. Well-known songs get tied up with viewers' personal memories. Unless the music is incredibly appropriate, those memories may draw the viewer away from your message. You also don't have as much editing flexibility. If viewers know the original well, they'll be distracted by cuts. Even if you're not worried about legal or creative issues, using unlicensed music limits your options for a film. Exhibitors, festivals, and networks won't touch it unless you guarantee it's fully cleared.

Rights and Licenses

Most music, no matter how old or obscure, is protected. While songs fall into the public domain after a while, old standards get modern arrangements, and classical music often gets new copyrights by the scholars who edit it. Besides, public domain applies only to notes and lyrics on paper. There's a separate copyright on the recordings, even for public domain songs. It usually belongs to the musicians or record company.

To make things even more complicated, there are four different kinds of permissions to consider.

SYNCHRONIZATION AND MASTER LICENSE

A *synchronization license* lets you match your images or other sounds to a recording of a copyrighted work. It's controlled by the composer or publisher and has to be issued by them.[3] Oddly enough, sync rights don't include the right to use the recording itself; that's a separate *master license*, usually controlled by the

---

[3]You used to be able to get sync licenses from the Harry Fox Agency in New York, but it dropped that service in 2002.

record company. Music libraries always combine these licenses, but if you're negotiating for non-library recorded music, you'll have to get the licenses separately. If you're having music exclusively recorded for your film, be sure to specify all the rights the musicians are giving you in your letter of agreement.

There is such a thing as a *mechanical license*, which automatically gives you the right to record a cover version of a song upon payment of a preset fee. But this applies only to recordings sold just as music for listening, not to film or video tracks.

PUBLIC PERFORMANCE LICENSE

The *public performance* license gets tricky, but can be important. Any time you play a song for anyone other than family and friends, the law says you're performing it in public and the composers must be paid. Obviously, this applies to public commercial performances like TV broadcasts and theatrical releases. But it also covers free performances, the Internet, trade show booths, factory tour videos, and college viewbook DVDs. This isn't a part of the sync or mechanical license.

The performing rights societies—ASCAP, BMI, and SESAC in the United States—grew up to track these performances. Different composers and publishers belong to each, but ASCAP is by far the largest. Broadcasters and trade show promoters often purchase annual licenses from the societies to cover all the music the societies control. If you're creating a TV show or theatrical release, the station or distributor usually requires a cue sheet (Figure 9.1). This reports

FILM TITLE: Three Hits!   DATE OF RELEASE: 3/1/07
COUNTRY OF ORIGIN: US

PRODUCER/PRODUCTION COMPANY: Triple Jeopard LLC
MUSIC EDITOR: JAY ROSE, CAS
CUE SHEET PREPARED BY: JR

TOTAL MUSIC TIME: 00:12:59

USAGE LEGEND: VV=Visual Vocal, VI=Visual Instrumental, BV=Background
                              Vocal, BI=Background Instrumental, SRC=Source

PRODUCER'S   MUSIC
PUBLISHING ENTITIES: (BMI) (ASCAP)

CUE #	TITLE	ARTIST	MASTER OWNER	COMPOSER(S) Performing Rts Society & %	PUBLISHER(S) Performing Rts Society & %	USE/ TIME
1	Fan Time	Catalonies	Aspect Records	Bill Warriner (ASCAP) 100%	D&D Music (ASCAP) 100%	MT 01:03
2	Hijaquer	Livelib Orch	LiveLib Inc	Jon Valentine (BMI) 100%	Livelib Music (BMI) 100%	BI 0:11
3	Steve's Montage	David Bender	TripleJeopard	David Bender (ASCAP) 100%	Bendit Mus (ASCAP) 100%	BI 01:32
4	What's Next	Rach... Tropp	Liv... Inc	Rachel Tropp (BMI) 100%	Livelib Music (BMI) 100%	BI

FIGURE 9.1
A cue sheet goes to the broadcaster or theatrical exhibitor, so they can report the performance.

the information to the societies, who then pay the composers a tiny share of the annual fee. The societies' formulas are heavily weighted in favor of pop music, but film scoring and library composers are starting to have an impact. You can download cue sheet forms at the rights societies' Web sites, or prepare your own that covers the same information.

Commercials don't use cue sheets, but are sometimes tracked by the first line of copy. A composer or music library may ask for the script so they can report uses themselves.

Even a point-of-purchase video or attract loop running at a kiosk requires a license. It may be covered by a store's or venue's blanket license. If not, skip the giant societies: you can usually negotiate these special performance rights directly with the composer for less money.

Music libraries can also supply performance licenses if needed. Depending on the use and your relationship with the library, the cost can range from zero to a few hundred dollars. Performance licensing is often ignored when using library music in training or sales videos, and many producers have never even heard of the concept. But there's no guarantee the copyright-owning corporations won't start asking for it in the future.

REPRODUCTION LICENSE

Whoever else owns the original recording and gave you a Master License isn't done yet. They also control a separate right to copy parts of their recording when it gets mixed into the soundtrack of release prints, DVDs, or VHS tapes. These *reproduction licenses* are usually negotiated and issued with the Master License, but their cost can vary with the number of copies, and whether any copies will be sold at retail.

Clearing Non-Library Music

While you can't just take a song without getting into trouble, there are accepted ways to get the music you want.

USING MUSIC LEGALLY, FOR FREE

You might avoid paying if you enlist local musicians to perform their own songs or public domain standards, in exchange for a screen credit. Some very fine scores have been done this way. You can occasionally find musicians eager for scoring experience, offering their services in user groups on the Internet. Just be sure you're happy with their musicianship, you understand any production costs, and you have a written agreement. If either the film or the band gets successful and there's nothing in writing, someone is going to want to sue somebody.

If your cause is noble enough, you may be able to get well-known musicians to let you use their recordings for very little money. Check with the record company first, or whoever owns the master recording. You may have to then negotiate separately with the composers for performance rights. But it's worth the legwork: I've done PBS promos using Beatles songs, and a recruiting piece for a music school with recordings of the New York Philharmonic, and the rights didn't cost a thing.

Or check the Web. Musicians' collaboratives and some stock libraries sometimes offer legitimate producers a single license for free, as enticement to buy more. Some let you use their recordings in broadcast projects, and only require that you report the performance so composers get paid under the ASCAP and BMI licenses. But don't assume that any song on the Web—even those you can download legally—can be used this way. Many bands give away music to build a fan base, but they still keep the copyright. Even the free "broadcast-performance-only" sites have the right of prior approval.

TEMP TRACKS

While not legal, it's very common for editors to drop a commercial recording onto a timeline as temporary music. It serves the same emotional purposes as a score while a film is being developed, and then can be an example for a composer or music search. This illegal music is deleted before the film is released.

The real danger here is *temp love*: A director or client gets so used to the temp track that nothing else will do. If this happens in a big-budget production, there's a possibility of licensing the original recording. On lesser projects it usually leads to frustration. Use temp tracks sparingly and make sure everyone understands the score's status.

GETTING CLEARANCES

191

Finding out who owns a particular recording involves some legwork. You can often locate the publisher through ASCAP or BMI's website, but not always. And unless you've got a physical recording with a ℗—that's the symbol for a recording copyright—it can be very hard to find who owns the master. It might be the band, the label, or a third party entirely.

There's some gamesmanship in negotiating the rights. Some bands have the clout to tell a record company to let you use a recording. Some record companies get offended if this happens—many consider the recordings to be their exclusive property—and might demand extra money out of spite. There are no rules, no fixed schedule of fees, and no standard package of what rights are conveyed. You might pay tens of thousands of dollars to use a song in your movie, only to discover later that you can't put the song in a trailer or broadcast spot. But this licensing-in-pieces can also work in your favor: sometimes copyright owners issue low-cost *Festival Licenses*, to let independents make just a few copies for the festivals. Then, if a distributor picks the film up for theaters, the music company gets the rest of their money.

Because of this, many producers leave the contacting and negotiating up to entertainment lawyers. Or they hire a *clearance company* who already knows the players and is experienced in negotiating. The clearance companies might ask as little as a few hundred dollars for their service, and they're often skilled in getting partial clearances if that's all you need.

> ## *A Day in the Life of a Negotiator*
>
> (Excerpted from one clearance specialist's Website. With her permission, of course.)
>
> What did I do today?
>
> You mean besides negotiating music copyright clearances so my clients could use *Born to Be Wild*, *Start The Commotion*, *Dream On*, *The Girl from Ipanema*, and *Fight Fiercely, Harvard*? Or something unusual, like *Happy Trails* by Roy Rogers? Or recordings by Celine Dion or Moby or Fleetwood Mac?
>
> When you choose the perfect piece of recorded music, the fun has just begun. Intellectual property laws are stern, and copyright permission for a single item requires signed releases from all its owners: composers, publishers, record companies, and sometimes even the heirs of a recently departed artist. Where do you begin? It's enough to give you a brain cramp.
>
> And then what do you ask for? Budgets can have constraints, and while we can't work miracles, we've sometimes been able to negotiate $10,000 asking fees down to $1,000. But never forget it's a seller's market, and *You Can't Always Get What You Want*. After all, a well-known rock star once refused to grant permission to a U.S. President for the use of a song.
>
> —Cheryl Cooper, www.firstlightclearance.com

Original Music

Working with a composer on a score is an artistic collaboration, and there are as many ways of working as there are artists. But some things are essential for a successful relationship. David Grimes (www.davidgrimesmusic.com), a highly regarded Boston-based scoring composer, stresses communication:

> "I expect to go over the project with the producer as soon as I'm hired. Usually I prefer that they be pretty specific... then, if I have an idea, I'll suggest it. If they want me to spot the project, it's going to be a lot more difficult. I don't have their vision.
>
> "The best producers use a musical or emotional language when they talk about individual cues. Temp music can be a problem if they get too used to it, but bringing commercial recordings to use as examples can be a good idea. Unless a producer has a good musical background, what they ask for and what you hear in your head can be different things.
>
> "What I don't like is people who only know what they don't like. I'll suggest something; they say 'no' but not much else. I'll respond by asking for negatives: 'You don't want a rock drum kit?', 'You don't want hand percussion?'. This is often the quickest way to narrow stuff down."

Grimes and other composers are often willing to produce demos, once they've agreed with the producer on basics about the sound and musical approach.

But unless you're working with big budgets and long lead times, composers may insist on picture being *locked*—no more changes that affect timing—before they work on final versions.

You and the composer will have to agree on contract terms, including not only licensing but who owns the basic themes and how extensive the production will be. Many composers aren't willing to write a score as *work-for-hire*, a legal term which assigns all ownership to you. They'd prefer to keep the musical ideas, give you nonexclusive licenses, and then sell rearranged versions to music libraries. Agreeing to this can save money.

You'll also have to agree on delivery media in both directions, though that's mostly a technical question. Composers might prefer picture reference as BetaSP with timecode, non-timecode DVD with a 2-pop, or short QuickTime or AVI files of individual scenes. Always give them sync dialog, without any music, on at least one track: they'll need that to make sense of their composition. Make sure what they give back to you is uncompressed (mp3 is fine for demos and during development), isn't mixed with effects or dialog, and has some way to sync.[4]

LOOP-BASED ORIGINAL MUSIC

Many filmmakers with moderate musical skills have been turning to loop-based software. These programs don't compose music, but do take care of musical details while you shuffle snippets of pre-recorded songs. These programs come with short chunks of musical elements—bass or drum pattern, bits of melody, or harmony parts—designed to repeat endlessly. You drag these *loops* onto tracks in a timeline, and they automatically snap into musical sync. The program adjusts the tempo and key of each loop so they play together nicely, making a complete song and complete band (or even orchestra). You can buy additional libraries of loops in different styles. By combining them, switching to alternative versions, changing the key or adding on-board studio effects, you can create a score of any length.

Sonic Foundry's Acid (now sold by Sony) was the first of these programs, and many competitors have now appeared. Most have similar interfaces and can share loop library formats. One example is Apple's Garage Band, included free with new Macs (Figure 9.2) and bundled as part of their low-cost iLife package. It looks like a toy, but can create credible scores quickly. Many multi-track programs now include this music capability as well.

Working with a loop program doesn't require composing or performing skills, just some creativity. The results really can sound musical, if you're not asking for something particularly sophisticated. Even though they use pre-recorded elements, there's so much variation that it's unlikely your loop-based score will

---

[4]If timecode or two-pops aren't practical, have them keep a few words of dialog on either side of the cue, muting it when the music's playing. Slide the file until it matches dialog in your timeline, then delete the reference dialog.

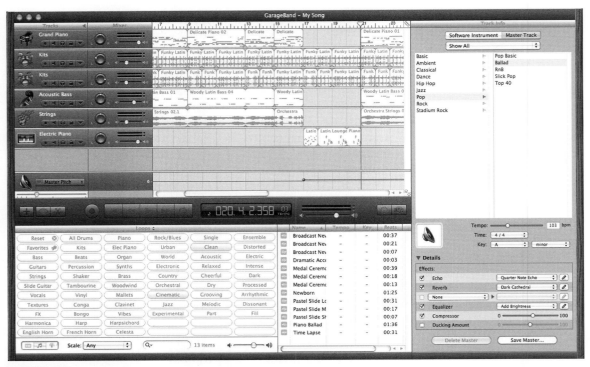

FIGURE 9.2
Apple's Garage Band is typical of loop programs that help non-musicians create musically credible scores.

sound like any other. They're also fun to play with. Many producers use loop programs as a scratch pad to set down rhythms and ideas for temp use; they then give the looped composition to a composer as a creative example. I've even done some spots where we remixed the producer's looped tracks, added a few custom flourishes, and put it on the air.

On the downside, creating loop music does take some work, it's hard to keep long cues from getting boring, and having a song actually end (instead of fade out) can be almost impossible. While you can buy loops in country or orchestral styles, the concept only works well on rhythmic and repetitive genres like contemporary dance, techno, or trance.

Most—but not all—loop libraries include a license you use for any compositions you create with them for any purpose, including film scores. But check the documentation for specifics.

Library Music

Library music has been around almost as long as movies. During the silent film era, British composer Meyer deWolfe started publishing generic sheet music for the house orchestras in large European cinemas. When the talkies came, he capitalized his name to DeWolfe, and he and a few competitors started offering pre-recorded versions of these pieces. The music was first supplied as optical tracks, then on 78 rpm disc, then on 10 inch LPs. By the late 1940s, newsreels and other low-budget films were using it extensively.

If you've ever listened to a corporate or classroom film from that era, the nicest thing you could say about that kind of music was that it sounded canned. Libraries didn't have much money for production. A handful of composers cranked out predictable songs, and recorded them in studio sessions so cheaply that instruments were sometimes out of tune. Film editors frequently had to remove *clams*—wrong or badly played notes that shouldn't have been on the disc in the first place. When I started producing tracks in the early 1970s, there were still only a few libraries to choose from, and those clams were still in the broth. It was unusual to find more than a couple of really good cuts on a new library record.

But by the mid-90s, cheap bad studio sessions had been replaced by cheap good digital instruments. Computers and sampling keyboards made it possible for composers to create well-produced music on their own, without a studio. Some sold cues to the established libraries, but many others started libraries of their own. Today, a Web search for "production music" yields close to one hundred publishers. Competition has raised the standards and widened the variety. Some still sounds canned. But if you pay attention while choosing and editing library cues, you can create an exciting, custom-sounding score for very little money.

Even Hollywood features often use library cues for source music, and occasionally to fill out an underscore. A mix of original and library music may be the best solution for some projects, hiring a composer for the major cues and then scoring the rest from existing pieces. A low-budget project can rely on library music exclusively. But you need the right music.

195

LIBRARY PROS AND CONS

The main reason to use stock music is economic. You can buy decent-sounding cues for as little as $8 each; these often compare to what a synthesizer-based composer might give you for $100/minute. Or you can get top-quality library productions with real orchestras, vocals, or hot session players starting at $75 per use—music that, if commissioned just for your film, would cost thousands.

Time is also money. An original score can take weeks, but any well-equipped audio post house has hundreds of hours of music waiting on the shelves. Or use your browser: Many publishers let you search and audition over the Web, pay for the music, and download it immediately or get it as an overnight-shipped CD.

A well-stocked library also gives you flexibility. You can switch from boogie to Broadway to baroque at the change of a client's mind—something that may not be possible if you've committed to one composer.

A minor problem is that stock music should be edited to picture. This isn't at all hard, even for musical klutzes; instructions start on page 199. A bigger problem is the lack of exclusivity. Libraries make their profit by selling the same songs over and over. Some years ago, I scored a big corporate project from a library... and a week later, heard one of the cues as background music in a supermarket.[5] Today, there's much more music available so this is less likely—but it's still possible.

COSTS AND LICENSING

There are two ways of paying for stock music, *needle-drop* and *buyout*. Buyout is sometimes called *royalty-free*, but that's misleading. Neither scheme charges royalties in the sense of continuing payments per copy or per viewing. Both charge for the licenses you need, but some charge when you buy the disc, and others after you've used the song. Despite the fact that a couple of libraries work both ways, these are different philosophies and can affect what the music sounds like.

Needle-drop was the original payment scheme. Newsreel editors would report a usage and pay a fee each time they dropped the phonograph needle to dub a song onto a track for editing; today, the term sometimes morphs to *laser-drop* but means the same thing. Discs are cheap—between $12 and $15—and may even be free for good customers. But the discs don't come with any rights other than to try the music. If you actually use a song, you report it to the library. They bill you and issue a license. Fees are based on the size of the potential audience, from about $75 for a local commercial or corporate video, to around $300 for films headed to a festival, to a few thousand for licenses that cover theatrical, TV, Internet, home video, and "any new media invented in the future."

Blankets are offered by almost every needle-drop library. Production blankets are licenses to cover all the music in a project, as much as you want from that source. The cost depends on the library, but is often close to the per-use rate for four drops every ten minutes. Many libraries also offer annual blankets: a set amount per year to cover all your productions, depending on the kind of media you produce. They might prefer this arrangement because it lets them predict income. Annual rates vary with the publisher and size of the library, as well as the media involved, but can be a real bargain for busy producers. Even if you have a blanket, most libraries still require individual reports for each use and issue specific licenses.

Needle-drop libraries don't make money unless you use their music, so it's in their interest to give you the widest choices. They tend to put a lot of good cues on each disc—usually 20 or more, plus variations—with very little filler or repetition. They also understand they're competing with other libraries every time you search, so standards can be very high. As a general rule, needle-drop music sounds better than buyout. (I'm basing this on overall experience. Yes,

---

[5]Fortunately, my client wasn't with me.

you might know of exceptions.) The downside of this flexibility and quality is that, in the long run, needle-drop music costs more.

Buyout libraries have been around a long time, but exploded with the development of good-sounding MIDI, digital desktop recording, and cheap CD replication. The discs cost $70 to $175 each, with discounts for multiple purchases, and include permanent licenses for anything you do in specified media. You can use a song over and over, for a price equivalent to a single needle-drop. You don't even have to report uses to most libraries. The disadvantage is there may be only one song on a $75 CD that you actually want to use.

Buyout libraries make their money selling CDs, so it's to their advantage to put just enough good music on each disc to keep you coming back. Other tracks on the disc are often simple loop-generated cues, or the library equivalent of an accompanist vamping to fill time. Buyout CDs usually include 8–12 themes plus shortened versions of the same material.

CHOOSING A LIBRARY

Some libraries are a waste of money. Others are incredible bargains. I keep library reviews in the tutorials section of my Web site and have tried to be as unbiased as possible. But your tastes might not agree with mine, and it's your money. Here's some help for making a good decision:

- Don't judge a library by its pretty site, brochure, or list of satisfied clients. Anyone can hire a designer, and the lists just show who bought (or were given) the discs—not who's actually using the music. Even network and feature-film credits may simply mean that a rushed producer grabbed something to put under an unimportant sequence.

- Don't judge a library by its listings. Some publishers describe every track with meaningless labels like, "A winner! Great for corporate, extreme sports, and romantic drama!" But cherish descriptions like, "Rock anthem with slow, inspirational start; builds to high-energy finish." It can make searching much easier.

- Don't judge a library by its online demo or CD. These narrated montages may hint at how many different musical styles a library has, but they can't tell you how good the writing and arranging is, or how much filler there is alongside the five minutes they used in the demo. For that, you have to hear complete tracks.

- *Do* judge a library by auditioning some of the discs along with the demo. Good libraries will send discs on approval, give you an evaluation period, or let you listen to reasonable quality full-length mp3s. Listen carefully. Is the music interesting? Even a narration underscore should have some development and changes, so you can move parts of it around to fit the mood. What about production values? Does the music sound rich and full? Does it sound like it's being played by real musicians (unless, of course, you're looking for techno styles)? Orchestras are particularly hard to synthesize well, but some composers manage. Don't be swayed by claims of live orchestras or choirs if they sound canned to you.

197

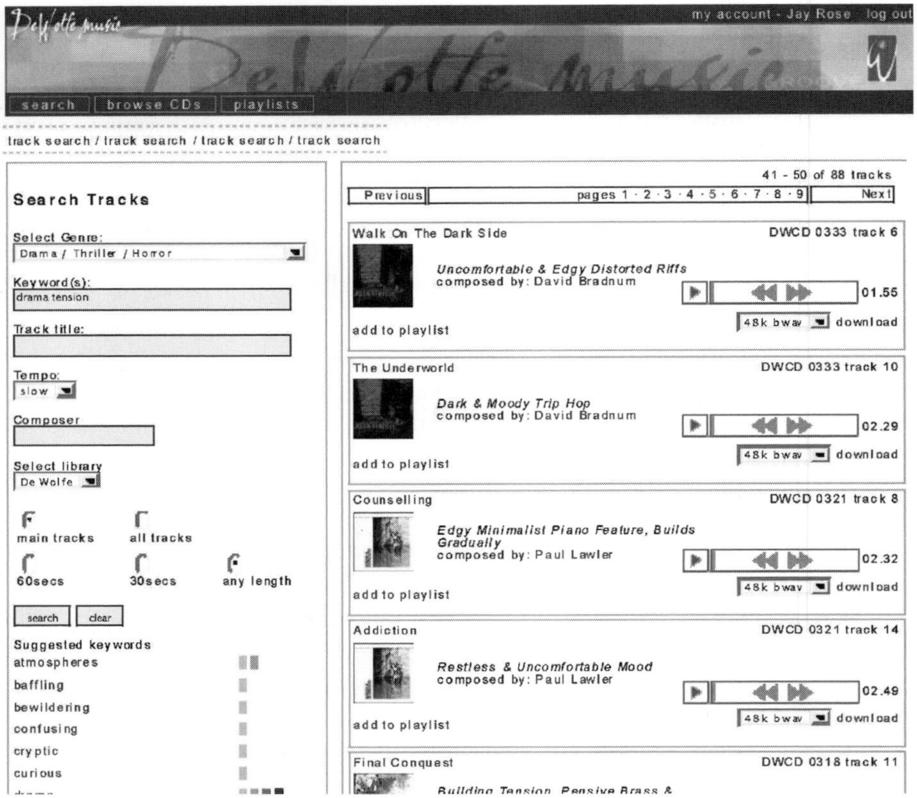

FIGURE 9.3
An online library search engine that lets you preview and download songs. This one's from DeWolfe.

- Give extra points to a library that has a CD-ROM or online search engine with meaningful categories and audio previews, such as the one in Figure 9.3. You might not need the search utility if you're buying just a few discs, but libraries grow and these programs can be a great time-saver. If you're assembling a large library from multiple sources, you can also use search-and-transfer software like SoundMiner (Chapter 4).

CHOOSING THE MUSIC

Grab your spotting notes and start to search. If you don't have a searchable database, flip through your collection and collect appropriate discs based on the track descriptions. If you do have a database, use it to make a short list—not the final decision. To pick music properly, you want to be able to scan through the whole song.

Play each candidate. If it's a reject, turn it off immediately. One key to a successful search is keeping your musical memory free from distractions, and every moment you listen to something wrong, that gets harder. If you think a piece is worth considering, fast-forward and listen to different parts. The melody often starts some ten seconds after the beginning, but a well-written piece will have variations or texture changes farther in. Check the ending as well, to make sure it's appropriate.

The "Mute Test"

When you find something you think will work, play it against the video or narration. Still like it? Then keep the other elements going but turn off the music! If a cue is just right, you should feel a loss when it goes away. This kind of love-at-first-listen happens surprisingly often. If it doesn't, don't despair; mark the track as a possible and move on. If a piece is almost right but you think it could be better, look for other tracks with similar descriptions by the same composer.

No matter what you do, don't forget music is an artistic element. No book, catalog description, or search engine can replace directorial judgment. Don't be afraid to go against type (I once scored a network sports documentary with Bach fugues), and don't be afraid to make a statement.

CHOOSING SOURCE OR DIEGETIC MUSIC

By and large, any library cue that's in an appropriate style should sound fine coming from an on-screen jukebox or television.[6] A good library will even include pop-sounding vocals designed specifically for source use.

If the music is supposed to be playing live in the scene—an off-screen band at a dance or club, for example—it'll be harder to find. Live bands seldom have the production polish of a recording. If you can't find something in a stock library, see if you can license a recording by a local group.

MUSIC EDITING

199

One of my clients calls it retrofitting. He chooses music from library sources. Then he has me move sections of that music around, changing melodic treatments when the scene changes, hitting musical peaks against the more dramatic shots, building in sync with the narrator, and reaching the last note perfectly with the final frame. Believe it or not, this kind of editing doesn't take very long. The result is a score that sounds original, but on a much friendlier budget.

The basic skill isn't difficult to learn, and doesn't require musical training. Actually, it's one of the handiest audio skills an editor can pick up.

Basic Editing

The main editing technique is shared by music editors throughout the industry. It doesn't require special equipment or software and can be adapted to virtually any program or editing system, even the online ones. It's faster and more accurate than looking for waveforms or scrubbing through a song. And it sure beats the "guess and trim" method some editors use.

If you can count to four while tapping your finger, you've got most of the skill already. It helps if you're also sensitive to chords and melody, but counting is the most important part. That's because almost all the music used in film and video has a structure based on groups of four beats.[7] Learn to hear those beats

---

[6]It'll need some technical mangling, of course. See Chapter 17.
[7]Some use groups of two or three beats. We'll deal with those later in this chapter.

and mark the groups. The chords and melody will often follow. Ignore the beats, and even the most elegant notes sound wrong.

TEACH YOURSELF TO COUNT ALONG

If you've ever studied an instrument, this section should be a piece of cake. If you haven't, but can tap your steering wheel in rhythm when you hear a favorite song on the car radio, you're almost there. Here are a few quick exercises:

Start by singing the "Marine Hymn" ("From the halls of Montezuma, to the shores of Tripoli…"). As you do, tap your index finger for each beat. In Figure 9.4, I've indicated each tap with a dot.

There's a tap for almost every syllable. "From the" is sung twice as fast as most of the other syllables, so those two words share a tap (I made them narrower to indicate this). The third syllable in Montezuma lasts twice as long as the others, so it gets two taps.[8]

Now sing it again while tapping. This time, note which syllables get the most stress. **Halls**, **zum**, and the final sound in Tri**po**li are emphasized. It might help to use Track 26 of the book's CD, an instrumental performance of the "Marine Hymn." Play it once or twice until you can tap its tempo easily. Then play it, tap, and count aloud: count once for each tap, and restart from 1 whenever you hit a stressed syllable. It all fits together like Figure 9.5. If you get totally lost, use Track 27 as a reality check.

 Hear for yourself

Track 26 is the "Marine Hymn" for you to tap and count with.[9] This track and the other examples in this chapter are excerpts of much longer pieces from the immense DeWolfe Music Library. They're protected by copyright and used here with permission. They've also given permission for you to load these tracks into your computer to practice these techniques. If you want to use any of their music in a production, of course, you'll need a license. For more information, and a few thousand other songs to choose from, visit www.dewolfemusic.com.

Track 27 is the same piece with me counting. My voice is on the left channel only, so you can mute it if you want to hear just the music.

tap ● ● ● ● ● ● ● ● ● ● ● ● ●
sing From the Halls of   Mon - te - **zum** - a,   To the shores of   Tri - po - li...

FIGURE 9.4
Each dot represents a tap of your finger, as you sing the song.

---

[8]For you musicians reading this: I'm not talking about stylized performances. Every note falls on a beat.
[9]"Marine Hymn" (arranged by J. Howe), DeWolfe CD 248/12. © DeWolfe Music.

count		1	2	3	4	1	2	3	4	1	2	3	4	1
tap	●	●	●	●	●	●	●	●	●	●	●	●	●	●
sing	From the Halls of			Mon - te - **zum** - a,					To the shores of			Tri - po - li...		

FIGURE 9.5
Counting with a *1* on the loudest syllable.

Note how there are always four beats before a 1. Those groups of four are mea-sures or bars, with 1 being the bar line. This four beat/one bar pattern is in so many songs that musicians call it common time.[10] Note also how each 3 count is slightly louder than the 2 or 4 count next to it. Almost every song with four beats to the bar has this pattern. Try tapping and counting along with other songs on your radio or mp3 player. Once you can count and spot the bar lines, you're ready for easy and accurate music editing.

TAPPING AND MARKING: THE TUTORIAL

Track 28 is a library cue that might be used in a high-tech documentary or cor-porate video. This kind of straight-ahead music is the easiest kind to edit. Load it into your NLE or audio software. Start playing the music and tapping while you play. Once you get a sense of where the bar line is, count along, but don't stop tapping.

 Hear for yourself

Track 28 is a typical documentary or corporate cue from DeWolfe. ("City Power" (D. Molyneux/R. Hudgson), DeWolfe CD 190/1. © DeWolfe Music).

Your software has a keyboard command that drops unnumbered markers on a clip (you might need to open it in a clip window, or drag it to a timeline first). Start playing the clip, and tap that marking key gently in time with each beat. Touch it lightly on most beats, so it doesn't drop a marker. But on each 1, tap hard enough to place a mark. Those light touches are important to keep your finger from tensing up right before the full-press 1. Tapping on every beat keeps your finger loose.

When you're finished, the markers should be regularly placed. Figure 9.6 shows how it should look for the piece we've been using.

---

[10]Also known as *4/4 time*. The first number means there are four beats to the bar; the second means that each beat is a quarter note. That quarter-note info is important if you're performing the piece, but not when you're editing it.

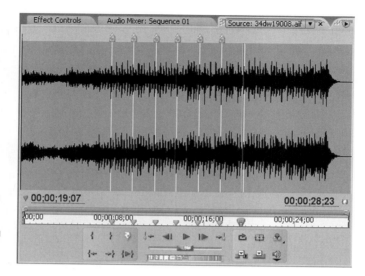

FIGURE 9.6
Markers placed on each bar line, from the piece on Track 28.

 Gotcha

I can't drop markers while playing! A few NLEs let you place a marker only when the transport is stopped. You can still edit in these programs, but it takes much longer. Music editing depends on marking bar lines precisely, and that's easiest when you let your fingers dance to the tune.

If you can't mark while playing, you'll have to use a two-step approach; listen and tap to the music at full speed until you have a good idea which note sounds on the bar line. Go back to the approximate location, and shuttle and jog until you find that note. Then stop and mark, and be prepared to undo if the note didn't land precisely on the beat. Or save your sanity, and move to an audio program for the music edits.

USING MARKERS TO SHORTEN MUSIC

Having regular markers on a clip, once at each bar line, makes the rest easy. For example, here's what you can do if you want to trim a piece of music by deleting some of the middle.

1. Put the marked clip on one track, starting where you first want the music to begin. For these tutorials, we'll start music at exactly one hour and refer to edit locations in seconds:frames past that point.
2. Count how many marked measures extend past the desired length. This is how much you'll have to delete. In this example, we'll cut five bars or just under seven seconds.
3. Play through the clip and find a likely starting place for the deleted section. This doesn't have to be the start of a verse, but it helps if it's the

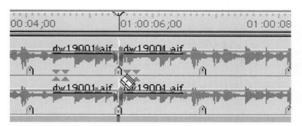

FIGURE 9.7
First, cut at the marker closest the start of the section you want to delete.

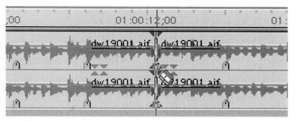

FIGURE 9.8
Go forward however many bars you want to lose, and make another cut at the nearest marker.

start of a musical figure within the melody. Make a razor cut at the closest marker there, as in Figure 9.7. Here, we're cutting at the marker near 5:14.

4. Move forward the desired number of bars and make another cut there. This will be the end of the deletion. In our example, that's at the marker around 12:16 (Figure 9.8).

5. Do a ripple delete, cutting out the middle segment and pulling anything that follows up to fill the gap. If you're using a two-track editing program, select cut—it's the same as a ripple delete in a NLE. Play back the edit. If things sounds right, you're done. If they don't, keep reading.

DEBUGGING 1: SYNCOPATION

If you followed our example and marked the bars accurately, things should sound *almost* right. But you'll hear a tiny hiccup at the edit point. You can also hear the hiccup in the edit I did, at about 5 seconds into Track 29. It's not our fault; it's the composer's!

 Hear for yourself

Track 29 has a double note at our edit point, even though we did everything right. It's the composer's fault, but it's easy to fix.

What happened is the composer placed a melody note slightly ahead of the bar line. Play the marked clip and count along, and you'll hear the note start before 1 or the marker. When we made the first cut exactly on the bar line, that note was already playing. *Syncopations* like this—and also those that delay the note—are common in music. In fact, even when the composer hasn't specified it, a performer may syncopate some notes as a matter of style.

At the second razor cut in our sample, the melody note started exactly on the bar line. So when we did the ripple, we picked up both the early start at 5:14 and the normal one at 12:16. You can't fix this by merely moving one of the razor cuts: That would distort the basic rhythm and make it sound wrong. Instead, use your NLE's roll tool to move *both* razor cuts by the same amount. In this case, rolling 21 frames earlier catches a place where the notes are more

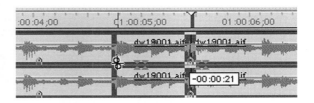

FIGURE 9.9
Rolling an edit to catch a syncopated note. We already know the cut is on the beat, so we can use the waveform display when fine-tuning this edit.

accurately timed. This is one of a few occasions you can rely is on waveforms (Figure 9.9) because you already know the edit will be on the beat.

This fixed the edit, moving it a little earlier to pick up a shaker sound. Your version should sound like Track 30.

 Hear for yourself

Track 30 is essentially the same as Track 29, but it's fixed by rolling the edit point a few frames earlier.

USING MARKERS TO LENGTHEN MUSIC

Sometimes you need to extend a piece of music. This is also easy, but you'll need two audio tracks.

1. Put the marked clip on one track, starting where you first want the piece to begin.
2. Put a second copy of the marked clip on another track, and offset the clip by the amount you want to lengthen it. In this example, I wanted to extend the music about seven and a half seconds. Since the first clip started at 0:00, I started the second one at 7:15.

If you prefer, you can simply slide the second clip until the song's ending is where you want it. The effect is exactly the same.

3. Now you have to fine-tune the two clips' relationship so they share the same beats. Slide the second clip until one of its markers is in line with a marker from the first clip. In this example, it means moving the second clip to start at 8:00 (Figure 9.11).
4. Play the timeline with both tracks audible. When the second clip comes in, its rhythm should be in perfect sync with the first. (If not, try lining up a different pair of markers. If that doesn't work, check that you marked the clip accurately.) The melody and chords probably won't be in sync most of the time, and may even clash in places, but both clips should have the same beat.
5. Listen again and find a place where both melodies are similar or create a pleasing chord. Make a razor cut thorough both tracks at the nearest

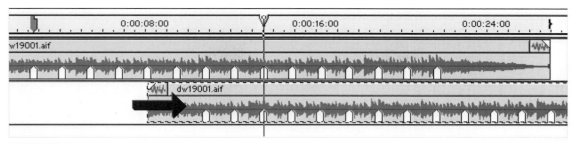

FIGURE 9.10
Slide the second clip so some of its markers line up with some of the first clip's.

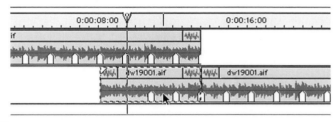

FIGURE 9.11
I'm about to press delete, to get rid of the first clip on track 2.

205

marker. Or, if there's a syncopated note on the second track at that marker, where the note starts. In this example, we used the marker near 13:15.

6. Delete the part of the first clip that falls after the cut (Figure 9.11) and the part of the second clip that falls before it. You can move the second clip up to the first track if you want.

7. In step 3, matching the markers extended the piece 15 frames more than we actually needed. But the fade at the end of this music is almost two seconds long. Use the rubber band to fade it half a second sooner, and the piece will end perfectly.

If you can't get exactly the length you need by fading the ending, use some of the fine-tuning techniques in the next section.

MAKING INTERNAL HITS

The above technique—with a slight modification—lets you fit a drum hit, key change, or any other musical detail in the song to a specific video frame.

1. Put the marked clip on one track at the point where you first want the piece to begin.

2. Put another copy of the marked clip on another track. Slide the second so the drum hit lines up with the desired video frame.

3. Follow steps 3 through 7 above to make a good transition between the tracks. It often works best to make your cut in the bar right before the hit. If this doesn't get you close enough, use the fine-tuning techniques in the next section.

You can do this as many times as you want in a song. Once you've done it a few times, it'll go very quickly. It's probably the most powerful technique in music editing, letting you customize an existing cue to fit your video perfectly. Of course, you can use the same technique to make music swell in sync with emotional peaks, complement fast action, or calm down under narration.

DEBUGGING 2: TOO LOOSE/TOO TIGHT

If you edit in the middle of a note, or mess up a key change, you'll know it immediately and can try moving the cut. But sometimes an edit just doesn't sound *right*, even though there's no obvious error. This is almost always because the edit changed the rhythm. It happens when bar lines aren't accurately marked.

This kind of problem will have different characteristic sounds, depending on where the mistake was made. Learn to identify them, and you'll know what needs adjusting. As you get more experienced with counting and tapping, you'll find these errors disappear for all but the most complex music.

Load Track 31 and mark its downbeats.

Hear for yourself

Track 31 is taken from a mellower cue from the DeWolfe Library.[11]

Using your marks, delete the two bars that fall roughly between 15:10 and 19:07. If it sounds right, congratulations. If not, see which of the next examples match your version: I deliberately did the edit wrong four different ways in Track 32.

Hear for yourself

Track 32 shows some of the ways that missing the beat can hurt an edit.

1. The first time, the marker at 15:10 was a little late, falling behind the actual bar line. This causes a double note. It also causes a slight delay in the rhythm, which is why this kind of double note can't be fixed with a rolling edit.
2. The second time, the marker at 19:07 was late. This clips the front of a note.
3. The third time, the 15:10 marker was too early. It makes the next measure jump in a hair too soon; something you may have to listen to a few times to recognize.
4. The fourth time, the 19:07 marker was early. It makes the rhythm hesitate a little at the edit point.

The fifth time, I marked the edit properly.

---

[11] "The Main Chance" (D. Molyneux/R. Hudgson), DeWolfe CD 190/8. © DeWolfe Music.

When you hear one of these problems, undo and move the incorrect edit point slightly off the marker to compensate. Or go back and re-mark the clip.

CHORD AND KEY CHANGES

The chords in a song change, often on bar lines but sometimes in other places, to add interest. That's why long cross-fades between sections of a song can sometimes sound awful: the two sets of chords don't work together. Cutting on bar lines—even if the chords aren't usually related—often works better than cross-fades because the changes sound intentional.

But some songs also change key, creating a totally different harmonic structure. Cutting from one key directly to another often sounds jarring. Before the song changed key, it probably had a bar or more of transition chords. They're important. If you have to connect two sections of a song that are in different keys, look for the bar where the key changes and be sure to include a couple of bars before that change in the final version.

THE ROCK 'N ROLL PROBLEM

There's a classic Chuck Berry song (covered by the Beatles and others), "Rock and Roll Music." If you remember it, you probably recall the lyric about "it has a backbeat, you can't lose it." A *backbeat* is used in almost all rock, pop, modern country, and dance music today. The drummer plays softly on beats 1 and 3, but hits hard on 2 and 4.

Don't let that backbeat throw off your count. Even though the drummer doesn't stress 1, the melody does. Load Track 33, a contemporary rock piece.

Hear for yourself

Track 33 is taken from a DeWolfe Library cue. It's somewhat reminiscent of a Sheryl Crow song about wanting to have fun.[12] Okay, *very* reminiscent.

During the 4-second intro, you'll hear hand claps on 2 and 4. The drum plays a 1-second riff, then a bass and melody part start. The bass enters strongly on 1. The slide guitar comes in around 7:15 on a 2 beat, but it's just leading up to a strong note on the next 1. And that bass keeps repeating its 1-based pattern.

Actually, the slide guitar is a tiny bit behind the bar line for emphasis, when it hits the 1 near 9:00. But the note clearly belongs to that beat. Syncopated melody lines are also characteristic of pop music.

Count and mark this tune, paying attention to the bar line. It should look like Figure 9.12.

---

[12]"Toot, Root, Shoot" (A. Hamilton/B. Lang), DeWolfe CD 225/11. © DeWolfe Music.

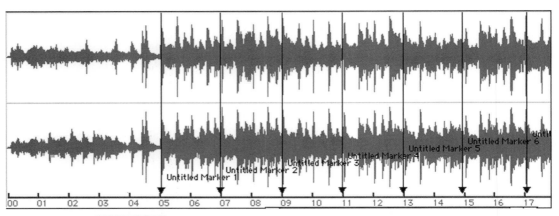

FIGURE 9.12
Track 33, properly marked. Note how bar lines *aren't* at the loudest drum beats.

Even though backbeats might be the largest things on a waveform display, counting and marking bar lines is the most reliable way to edit pop music. That's because melodies and chord changes are based around 1. However, pop melodies seldom start exactly on the bar line, so you'll probably find it necessary to roll the edit to catch the lead instrument.

THE ORCHESTRAL PROBLEM

The bar lines in orchestral music aren't always obvious, and the percussion section is usually doing something other than beating time. But you can still hear the beat. Load Track 34, a piece appropriate for an adventure film score.

 Hear for yourself

Track 34 is from a John Williams–style march in the DeWolfe library. It may remind you of the theme to *Raiders of the Lost Ark*.[13]

As you listen to the track, pay attention to the first three notes of the repeating figure. It's two unstressed short notes, followed by a longer stressed one. Mark that third note as beat 1, and everything else will count properly.

 Gotcha

Hey! What about John Williams' copyright? Or Sheryl Crow's, for that matter? Composers can get away with these seeming rip-offs because they borrow only a few actual notes from the original. They're called *stylealikes*—drawing on the same common pool of musical styles as the originals, along with similar arrangement and production.

---

[13]"Epic Movie Adventure" (F. Talgon), DeWolfe CD 272/11. © DeWolfe Music.

Fast marches like this are usually written with two beats to the bar instead of four. There's no reason you can't count them in fours, subdividing the beat. But you might find it easier to count "1, 2, 1, 2," still making a mark at each 1. (Each bar in this piece is a tiny bit longer than one second. Your marks should be that far apart.)

Try a few cuts on this music. Editing orchestral string sections can sometimes sound abrupt even if you mark them properly. That's because a little bit of one note keeps echoing while the next note is played. The part you're cutting to doesn't have the right echo. A two-frame cross-fade can help smooth things out; so can applying some reverb (Chapter 13). Sometimes the best solution is a much longer cross-fade on two tracks: hold the first theme on one track, bringing the second in over the course of one or two beats on another, then fade the first.

OTHER PATTERNS

Not all music moves in four or two beats. Waltzes move in threes and have to be counted that way. Load Track 35, a charming folk waltz.

Hear for yourself

Track 35 is an excerpt from a longer DeWolfe piece.[14] It sounds French, but is actually a traditional Scottish tune.

The first time you hear it, listen for the oom-pah-pah pattern in the accordion. The *oom* is always on 1. Then you can pay attention to the melody, which obviously stresses 1 as well.

Occasionally, you'll come across music in five, six, or even more beats to the bar. These are usually divided into repeating patterns of fewer beats. For example, a piece in six will usually break down to either two waltz-like sections per bar, or three march-like ones. In either case, the first beat of the first section—at the bar line—will always have a stronger stress than the first beat of the others.

FINE-TUNING THE LENGTH

Basing your edits on bars is almost always the fastest way to achieve smooth, musical edits. But even a single bar can last a while. Whole bars might not be precise enough to fit a piece of music the way you want.

There are some ways to deal with this. First, rough out the music using whole bars; get the tracks to about the right length. Then do one of the following:

- Make a half-bar edit. Open the second clip you've laid on the timeline and count with it again, but drop the markers on 3. Then line a 3-beat

---

[14]"Ranza Waltz" (arranged by C. Jack/D. Aran), DeWolfe CD 288/26. © DeWolfe Music. By now you've probably gotten the idea that DeWolfe covers lots of different musical genres. I haven't scratched the surface. Go to www.dewolfemusic.com to hear for yourself. (They gave me the music to use in this book, so they deserve a plug.)

marker on this clip with a 1-beat on the clip above it. You'll end up with a pattern of 4-4-2-4. It might be hard to dance to, but the melody usually hides the edit.

- Make a *fermata*—a musical pause that stretches a single beat longer than usual, and then continues counting. You'll need a part of the music where a one note or chord is held over a couple of beats, without any other instruments playing shorter notes. Make a copy of the clip lined up with the first, but slid a little later on another track. When you get to the held note, do a cross-fade between the clips. This can be particularly effective on cues with a high emotional content.
- Export your edited music to a single file, and move it to a program that lets you change duration without affecting pitch. Or use a clip speed setting with a pitch shifting plug-in to compensate. Both of these are covered in Chapter 14.
- If your software's speed adjustment doesn't keep a constant pitch, it will change the key as well as the tempo. Too much can also change the timbre. Acoustic instruments and vocals can rarely be shifted more than ±3% before they start to sound strange. Electronic music, including a lot of keyboard pop, can shift as much as ±12%.

Unless you're lucky, this kind of speed change will make the music fall into a nonstandard key. This may sound offensive if the piece is near a cue that's in tune.

Automatic Music Editing

Trimming library music to a desired length is easy, but it does take time when you're learning the process. Programs like Sony's Cinescore and SmartSound's SonicFire Pro give you an alternative. Select a song, tell the program how long it should be, wait a couple of seconds, and play back a perfectly timed version.

It happens so fast because music editors at the software companies have already marked phrases on the song, using the bar line technique above. The editors then write templates for how the phrases should link together. This editing information is saved as data along with the audio. When you run the program, it collects phrases to reach the length you want. But because the assembly is based on those editors' templates, the result doesn't sound mechanical.

If you want to further customize the result, you can tell the program where scenes change and give it some idea of what mood changes would be appropriate. The program will then try another phrase at the bar line closest to your request, or use another trick like slightly varying the tempo, or featuring individual instruments from the ensemble recording. The changes are far from radical: you still hear the original song; it's just played slightly differently. These aren't the kind of mood shifts you'd expect in a custom score for a feature, or even in a well cut library score. But they certainly can be appropriate under a corporate video. Figure 9.13 shows this fine-tuning in Sony's version.

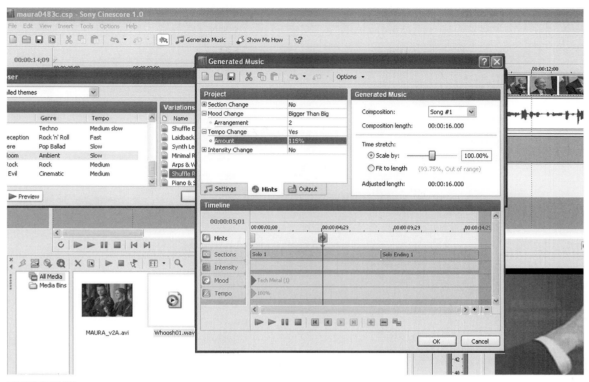

FIGURE 9.13
Cinescore lets you place hints on its timeline, for where the music should change.

The big limitation of these programs is that they work only with factory-encoded music.[15] SmartSound currently has a few dozen CD-ROMs, mostly versions of buyout music from a few mainstream libraries; Sony's selection is smaller. You can't add library or original music from other sources.

On the other hand, these programs can be perfect if you do a lot of very similar shows for different audiences, or for groups that aren't unhappy at the repetition. For example, Sony offers a wedding videographer package; it includes a few generic romantic songs plus all the traditional standards, ready to be automatically trimmed to each client's video's timing.

Embellishing the Music

After you've edited music to fit, you can customize it even more by layering other musical sounds on top.

---

[15]You can import a standard audio file into the program, cut it into pieces yourself, and juggle them manually. But I can't think of any reason you'd want to; this is faster and cheaper with other software.

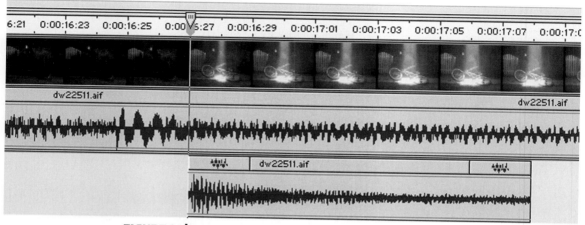

FIGURE 9.14
The song from Figure 9.12 is on Track 1. An extra drum hit—taken from the song's intro—syncs up on Track 2 against the spotlight frame.

Find a drum hit or cymbal crash elsewhere in the cue, and put it on a second track in sync with an important frame (Figure 9.14). Don't worry about the song's rhythmic structure. Your addition won't be on the beat, but it'll sound like the drummer was watching and playing along with picture.

If you can't find an isolated drum hit in the cue, look for an appropriate sound in an effects library. Most drum sounds aren't pitched, so you don't have to worry about tuning. When it's time to mix, you'll be able to blend the new sounds to match perfectly. (Kettle drums or *tympani* are pitched, but sound effects libraries often give you alternatives in different keys. Try each until you're satisfied.)

A harp glissando or cymbal ride mixed with the music can be a good accompaniment for title wipes or other transitions. Or add your own synth pads, piano chords, or synthesized or stock laser zaps to complement the video. Don't worry too much about playing them sync: Just digitize a few different versions and slide them on the timeline until one works. I've built client-specific libraries of these hits, which I use to customize and brand ongoing series.

CHAPTER 10

Working with Sound Effects

REMEMBER THIS:

- A kiss is still a kiss, but a sigh can be turned into a roaring monster.[1]
- There are limitless sources for sounds: camera tracks, commercial libraries, Foley, even mouth noises.
- Sound selection and placement is easiest if you follow some simple rules.
- When designing new sounds, it's best to start with well-defined palettes.

Sound effects have been part of movies almost as long as music. In silent film days, theater organs had collections of noisemakers—organists called it a toy counter— along with their pipes. Bells, birds, and even breaking crockery were at the touch of a finger; on bigger organs, you could also play car and boat horns, surf, and horses' hoofs with your feet. By the mid-1920s, Wurlitzer was building one of these magnificent machines a day.[2] Figure 10.1 shows part of the toy counter in a 1920s model by the Kilgen Organ Company; to give you an idea of its size, those slats in the bottom of the photo are a catwalk for technicians. Companies also advertised hand- or mouth-operated boat whistles, dog barkers, fog horns, and rain machines on the premise that they'd help a theater's box office. In Japan, humans replaced the toy counter: performers called *benshi* would stand next to the screen to provide dialog and vocal sound effects along with running commentary. The benshi often became more popular than the stars on film.

We have better ways to make sounds now, but the reasons for using them haven't changed. Sound effects are a way to direct the viewer's attention:

- They involve us with on-screen actions. The giant explosions in action pictures literally shake us in our seats. An actor's footsteps in an empty corridor, or a single unexpected cry from a baby, can be just as engaging.

---

[1] Sorry. Couldn't resist.

[2] Today, samplers are an important part of feature film sound design. Samplers assign digital recordings to notes on a keyboard, making the sounds easier to manipulate. The technology is different, but in one hundred years, the user interface hasn't changed very much.

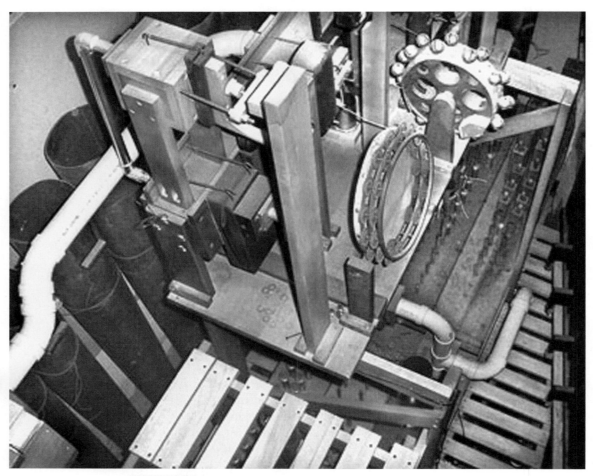

214

FIGURE 10.1
Movie sound effects before movies had sound: a toy counter in a Kilgen theater organ.[3]
Visible are sleigh bells, a tambourine, a siren, a wood block, and part of the castanets.

- They put us in the film's reality. A theater or living room can have lots of real-world sounds competing for our attention. Surf, jungle, or other backgrounds on the track help us forget where we are and imagine the location we're seeing.
- They complete the illusion. Closing a door on a plywood set, hitting a burglar with a rubber candlestick, or firing a quarter-load blank just doesn't sound right. Films need the *slam, bonk,* and *bang.*
- They provide continuity. An establishing shot of a busy mall with lots of extras can be followed by close-ups done days later on a stage. If we keep hearing the crowd, we'll know we're still at the mall.

---

[3]Now being restored at the Lakeview Congregational Church in Waltham, MA, by Eric Larson (who also took this photo).

- They can tell the off-screen story cheaply and quickly. An approaching siren, car door slam, running footsteps, and shouted "Police!" speaks volumes, even if all we see is the murderer's eyes in flashing red and blue lights.
- They help the on-screen story. A scene—say, a character lying in bed—can have different meanings depending on whether we're hearing children playing, a watchdog barking, or somebody hammering on the door.
- Even nonnarrative films use whooshes and zaps call attention to animations, title wipes, and other screen features.

SOUND EFFECT TERMINOLOGY

Background, BGs, ambience, and *presence* all mean the same thing: birds, traffic, machinery, crowd noises, computer fans, and the other sounds that surround just about everything we do. *Walla* is the spoken equivalent—background voices where only a few words may be distinguishable.

Hard effects are individual sounds in sync with on-screen (or scripted off-screen) actions. In feature work, they're separated into *editorial effects* such as telephone bells, which can be added by the sound editorial crew, and *principal effects* like explosions and crashes, which are usually done by a sound designer. *Foleys* are movements—footsteps, clothing rustles, chair squeaks and the like—recorded separately to replace small sounds that weren't caught by the dialog mic or removed during editing. *Stingers* are short individual sounds added to an ambience to make it more specific, like an ATM's beeps and whirrs in an otherwise generic bank lobby.

Production effects (PFX), sound on tape (SOT), and *nat sound* are sounds recorded along with picture; production effects are specifically those picked up by a dialog mic. They might not be usable as hard effects because of noise and mic distance, but can serve as a guide and sync reference when adding new effects, or even be mixed with their replacements. They're frequently sufficient for backgrounds.

Wild sounds are recorded without picture.

SOUND EFFECT SOURCES

An audio post house will have tens of thousands of sound effects on hand, often delivered to individual editors' workstations instantly from a server. But you don't need to amass that kind of collection to use sounds effectively. It's easy to find exactly what you need for a project.

Sounds from the Shoot

The sound picked up by a video camera's mic or recorded from a boom can provide usable backgrounds for documentary and event videos. Crowds, machinery, or traffic can be gathered from places where there's no dialog—don't forget to check the outtakes—and then looped to bridge scenes or link close-ups to the master shot. This kind of sound can also be mixed with library backgrounds to make the canned backgrounds sound more authentic.

215

Unlike traditional double-system sound, which needs a crew and separate recorder, video sound is free. Take advantage of this. Even if you don't think a scene will generate usable sound, it's a good idea to mic it. If you can't get a boom mic over the shot, use a camera-mounted shotgun—echo and room-noise pickup usually makes camera mics useless for dialog, but can be tolerable in backgrounds. If you're shooting inserts of small activities—handling a prop, dialing a phone, grabbing a doorknob—record the sound and keep it in your edit. Even if you're shooting dialog scenes double-system to get better quality than a camera's audio circuits, you can still record nat sound from other scenes with a camera mic. It'll often be good enough for effects use.

PRODUCTION EFFECTS (PFX)

A boom or lav that's set up to record dialog will also capture other sounds in the scene, such as door slams or telephone hang-ups. These have the advantages of being absolutely natural and already in sync. But they're seldom miked properly—it's more important to put the mic in the right places for dialog—and might not sound the way a director wants.

Even so, common practice is to move these sounds to a separate *PFX* track during the dialog edit. If you decide to use them in the mix, they'll probably need different processing or levels than the dialog; this way they're already isolated. When these effects are moved, the dialog track is often filled with room tone (Figure 10.2). This lets you blend a smooth sound if effects need radical processing, or if you replace them with other recordings. PFX clips usually have the same kind of fade-ins and fade-outs that you'd use for dialog clips (Chapter 8).

Commercial Libraries

In the 1930s, radio started using live sound effects to tell their stories. Realistic sounds were used to enhance dramas, and some comedies had signature noises (Fibber McGee's closet or Jack Benny's Maxwell). These sounds were performed live for the visual amusement of the studio audience; listeners at home heard both the effect and the studio laughter. Film started using similar techniques, with sounds created specifically for the scene. But while radio was live, film was

FIGURE 10.2
Sound effects that were recorded with dialog can be isolated onto PFX tracks. Fades and fills keep things sounding smooth.

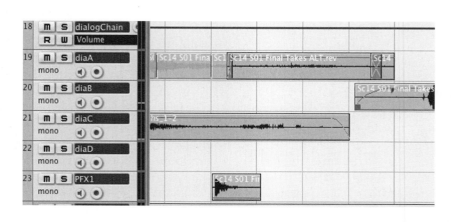

always canned: editors realized they could save time by reusing effects from previous films. At about the same time, radio dramas started using custom recordings of larger effects to simplify production. These private collections became organized by a few companies, and the sound effects library was born.

Today, you can buy complete libraries of beautifully recorded sound to use in productions. Or you can purchase sounds as needed over the Internet and have them delivered instantly. Sound effects are almost always sold as buyouts: You pay for them once and can use them forever in any of your films, with no additional licensing.

FULL LIBRARIES

These are collections of sounds on one or more CDs, usually sold together, though some publishers will let you buy individual discs. *General libraries* attempt to cover all the sounds commonly used in productions. They're usually organized with a disc for exterior backgrounds, another for interiors, one for cars, one for animals, and so on. *Specialized libraries* have multiple CDs in a single category (see Figure 10.3). For example, I have two separate libraries—about 20 discs total—just for human movements, and a 12-CD set of wind and other air sounds. General libraries usually sell for about $50 per disc; specialized ones can be as much as $100 per disc.

Many libraries are starting to appear on DVD-ROM. There's no perceptible quality difference between a standard audio CD (Redbook[5]) and the 16-bit,

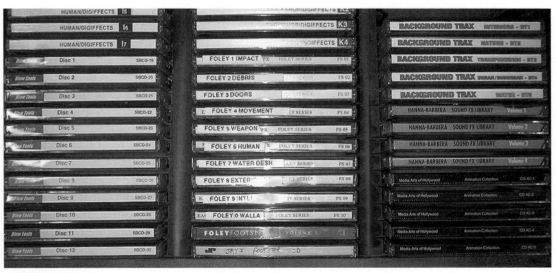

FIGURE 10.3
Some of the specialized libraries in my studio's collection. I bought these on the CDs shown, then ripped them into my server.[4]

---

[4]This is legal, so long as I keep the original CDs.
[5]The original specification for audio CDs had a red cover. Other formats, such as CD-ROM or video, had different color covers.

48-kHz computer files on DVD, but the data versions are more convenient. They can also include search engines with preview and automatic file copying, or databases for systems like SoundMiner (Chapter 4). They're not limited by an audio CD's insistence that everything be stereo or its 99-track limit. The DVD versions are generally priced about the same as equivalent libraries on CD. Very large libraries might be shipped on FireWire hard drives instead.

Some effects are also available on CD-ROM or DVD-ROM for multimedia and Web use. These are usually compressed with MP3 or proprietary formats, or limited to 22.050-kHz sample rates. It compromises quality but lets a publisher fit many more sounds on the same disc, and sell them for lower costs. Some are legal for Web or internal presentation only; others can be used for broadcast or theatrical exhibition. Figure between $30 and $100 per disc, depending on size and license.

 Gotcha

Go get it! Commercial sound effect libraries sometimes offer freebies, collections of high-quality fully licensed effects on CD or downloadable. Hollywood Edge's current collection (as of this writing) includes audience reactions, airplane flybys, explosions, and unusual urban sounds. It's a marketing gimmick, and it works; their samples have convinced a lot of us to buy Hollywood Edge libraries. Their contact info, and that for the other large sfx supplier, is in the list below.

The best place to buy a sound effects library is directly from these companies. Some video equipment dealers also sell effects libraries, but these two specialty operations have wider selections, knowledgeable staff, Web-based previews and demos, and occasional specials.

- Hollywood Edge, 800-292-3755, 323-603-3252, www.hollywoodedge. com. A corporate sibling of a giant audio post facility, Hollywood Edge publishes its own effects and represents other libraries—about two dozen total. Hollywood Edge was kind enough to let me reproduce some of its effects for this chapter's tutorials.
- Sound Ideas, 800-387-3030 (U.S.), 800-665-3000 (Canada), 905-886-5000, www.soundideas.com. This Toronto-based company created the first large, modern effects library, and now sells about 60 collections of its own and other publishers.

The worst place to buy sound effects may be a record or computer store. While some CDs or CD-ROMs are available cheaply, the quality is variable. A few seem to be sloppy copies of vinyl records sold in the 60s and early 70s—before copyright law protected sound effects—and include turntable rumble and groove noise. Others are more modern but still of limited quality. While some advertise as being royalty-free, their fine print specifies for home use only.

On the other hand, you may be able to find a few bargains with decent recordings and clear licensing.

INDIVIDUAL EFFECTS ONLINE

Despite my extensive collection, there are times when it doesn't have a sound I need. Those times are usually late at night when I'm working towards a deadline. That's when I go to the Dogs.

SoundDogs.com is probably the largest online effects library, with more than 100,000 high-quality sounds and music cues available (Figure 10.4). Sounds can be searched or browsed by category, then previewed in low resolution. The high-res versions usually cost only a couple of dollars per effect. Actual cost depends on how large a file you want. After you've selected effects, you select the specifications: mp3 or 16-bit linear, mono or stereo, a variety of sample rates, and how many seconds you want each to run. The Web site quotes a price based on that much data. Then you can modify or complete the order.

A few moments after you enter your credit card number, SoundDogs.com posts your sounds at a custom FTP or Web address for download. Since effects are sold on a buyout basis, you can add them to your personal library for future projects as well.

There are other professional effects libraries on the Web, but in my opinion none as comprehensive or reliable. Some make you wait hours for a human to

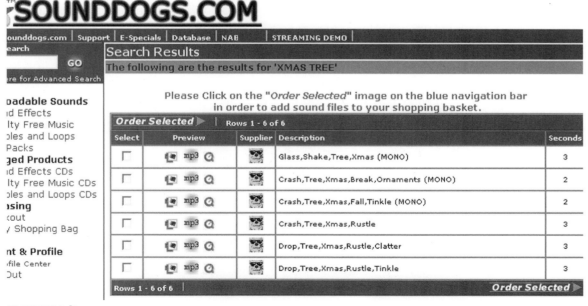

FIGURE 10.4
Finding a downloadable effect at SoundDogs.com.

transfer and upload the sound; one even announces, "If we fail to deliver, you get your money back." That's not much help.

There are also sites that offer free sound effects. These come and go, but a Web search will usually turn up half a dozen or so. A few, mostly sponsored by film and video groups, have pro-level effects. Others might not have any sounds at all: They're merely banner-ad cluttered indexes to hobbyist pages, where you'll find sounds copied from commercial movie and TV mixes. Copyright and quality are dubious.

Recording Your Own

Sound effects are also free if you make them yourself. Techniques include Foley, capturing hard effects and backgrounds in the field, using electronic sounds, and even manipulating mouth sounds. Unless an effect is very large, like an explosion or car crash, it's usually recorded in mono and panned as necessary during the mix. Backgrounds are usually recorded in stereo; sometimes in surround.

FOLEY

Jack Foley was a Hollywood second-unit director and editor. In the late 1940s, he became known for performing sound effects live while watching a projection. He'd mimic actors' movements to create footsteps, clothing rustles, and prop movements in time with picture. This was not a brand-new idea, but Foley popularized it among producers, and his name became attached to the technique.

Foley is still the standard for big productions, and it's a lot of fun to watch (or be part of). But it needs a specially built studio with video playback. A computer-age adaptation, *digital Foley*, may be a useful alternative. Instead of worrying about performing in sync, you just record the needed effects wild. Then, with a NLE or multitrack sound program, you trim the sounds to fit the picture.

While Foley is fun, it's also time-consuming. Build the rest of the track before you decide how much is needed. Scenes with music may need very little Foley. Ambiences may have random movements that, with a little editing, can match what's on the screen.

Foley is often recorded in multiple passes—once or twice for footsteps, once for clothing rustles, and once for prop movements or fights. Both the room and the recording chain must be quiet, or else hiss and noise will build up when all these tracks are mixed together. Theatrical Foley should be miked at boom distances, two to three feet from the action, so the perspective matches dialog. This means the room can't have audible echo of its own. If you're aiming for the small screen, you can get by with average rooms and close, directional mics. I often record clothing rustles and prop movements at about 10-inches with a short shotgun, in a reasonably echo-free space.

Foley doesn't start to sound realistic until you process it in the mix. The level, equalization, and amount of reverb have to be very carefully tuned to match dialog. Other processing, such as compression and gating, can change the character of some sounds—even turning male footsteps into female ones. There are specific suggestions in later chapters.

Foley Footsteps

Practice walking in place, keeping a constant distance from the mic. Practice different walking styles as well. Have a variety of shoes available to match the types of shoes the actors wore. There's not much difference between men's and women's steps, other than high heels. It mostly depends on how heavily you put your feet down. For best results, wear shorts and empty your pockets. If the character is supposed to have keys or coins jingling in a pocket, record them separately.

The floor is part of the equation. If the character is crossing or coming from a distance, the floor has to be big enough that you get some perspective as they move. The surface also has to be right: professional Foley studios have sections of floor with different coverings along with pits full of gravel, sand, or water for exteriors.

Some old-time radio tricks can replace dedicated pits:

- To simulate a hardwood floor in a carpeted studio, use a piece of half-inch or thicker plywood, about 2-foot by 3-foot. Tack strips of carpet on the bottom of the plywood to stop it from sliding around and to keep it from bouncing as you walk.
- To simulate concrete, sprinkle some sand on the plywood.
- For marble, walk on clean plywood and add gating and echo in the mix. Or get a large piece of slate or marble at a lumber yard.
- If your studio has a hard floor and you need carpeting, get scraps of carpet from a flooring dealer. Get some padding as well and glue it to the underside of the carpet scraps. It'll improve the sound and keep the carpet from sliding as you walk.
- To simulate grass, walk on carpet and mic it from a couple of inches away. The crunching fibers are fairly convincing.
- You can use a child's wading pool as an ad hoc Foley pit for water. You can also use it for sand or gravel, but it's cleaner to put dry materials in a large burlap bag. Fill the bag half way, seal it, and spread it flat for walking.
- If you don't need a lot of pit sounds, you may want to walk in miniature. Fill a large plastic dishpan with cornflakes, rice, or dry or semisoft pet food and walk with your hands.
- For snow, squeeze a cardboard box of cornstarch rhythmically. After a half dozen "steps," you'll probably have to shake the box a little to loosen things up.
- For wooden stairs, use a double-layer of half-inch plywood or very wide shelving, about 2-feet long. Prop one edge up with a couple of books or scrap lumber, so it's about 5-inches higher than the other; this adds hollowness. To walk upstairs on this board, scrape your foot slightly against the top edge as you step with your full weight. To walk downstairs, skip the scraping and land on your heels first, then your soles.

Gotcha

Look, Ma, no feet! Often you can't see the actor's feet in a shot. It's still important to capture the right rhythm for footsteps. You usually can do this by watching the actor's shoulders.

If the characters are walking at a normal pace or faster, one shoulder will rise slightly just after a step lands, as they push off for the next one. Put the sound a frame or two ahead of the shoulder rise.

If the character is walking slowly and pausing between steps, there may be a dip as each step lands. Put the sound on the first frame of the dip. There'll be a rise when they push into the next step, but it doesn't make noise unless they're wearing squeaky shoes.

Foley clothing noises You'll need an item made of the right material—cotton, silk, synthetics, and wool all sound different. For most clothing rustles, don't wear the item to mimic the actor's movement; this moves things too far from the mic. Instead, hold the cloth close to the mic and rub or crumple it as needed. If the character is actually putting on a piece of clothing, you'll probably have to do the same to get the necessary rubbing of arm or leg against cloth.

Foley prop movements These small sounds are best when you mimic the movement as closely as possible. It helps to work at a table, both to keep props handy and to have a hard surface when needed. You'll have to reposition the mic depending on whether an action is in the air (keychains or cigarette lighters) or on a table (tapping fingers, or writing on paper).

Experiment with different ways to hold each prop. Where you grab an object and how tightly you hold it makes a difference in how it resonates. Common objects like coffee cups, felt markers, or hand tools can create quite a variety of noises. The right way to hold a Foley prop often doesn't match what the actor was doing on-screen.

Make sure you've got the right props:

- Rustling papers need the right stiffness and surface. Newsprint, glossy magazine pages, and copier paper sound different.
- If the character is writing something, use the proper instrument and the right paper. A pencil doesn't sound the same as a felt-tip pen, and both change depending on how smooth the paper's surface is. Of course you also have to make sure your rhythm matches the words they're writing.
- If a character is working at a computer, type on a keyboard. It doesn't matter what you write—or even if the keyboard is connected—but remember that larger keys like spacebar or delete have different sounds than the letters, so be sure to hit them occasionally. A mouse or trackball has a distinctive sound when you press its button.

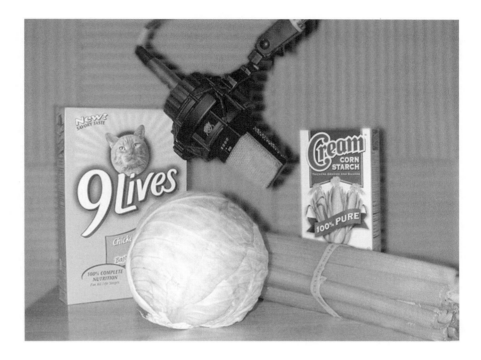

FIGURE 10.5
Important talent waiting for a Foley session. See text for how they're used.

- Modern residential telephones are lightweight plastic with a flimsy sound. I've found that heavier, multiline office phones make better noises. Old-fashioned dial and early Touch-Tone phones were very solid and had a mechanical bell that vibrated slightly with each movement. You can't fake these with a modern phone.
- An old briefcase can give you a bunch of suitcase and pocketbook sounds. The leather *creaks*, the hinge *squeaks*, and the snaps... uh... *snap*.
- Heavy cookie sheets can be flexed or struck. Depending on how you hold them and whether they're in the air or resting on the table, they can stand in for almost any metal object.

Foley fights Your body can be good for realistic sounds; just cup your hand slightly while you hit yourself on the trunk. Add a tiny echo in the mix. Many filmmakers prefer bigger—and sometimes wetter—sounds in fights. Useful techniques for this include wrapping two phonebooks in wet towels and slamming them together, or crashing a head of cabbage on a table. Twisting a bunch of celery works for broken bones. Body falls can be done by slamming both arms against a table, slightly out of sync with each other, or by taping a large phonebook closed and throwing it on the floor.

FIELD RECORDING

Some sounds can be captured only in their natural habitat. You can't bring a car or a horse into a Foley studio, and most background ambiences are impossible to fake.

You'll need a good recorder. Your camera may be adequate for this, but it's probably too bulky for convenient use. Consumer compact digital recorders can be okay for many sounds, but make sure you can turn off its automatic level control for anything other than calm backgrounds. As the circuit constantly adjusts the volume, it increases apparent noise. Slightly larger, professional file-based or DAT portables give you the best control and recordings.

You'll also need a good microphone—the camera's mic is useful only for loud ambiences—but what kind of mic to use depends on what you're recording.

Hard Effects

Background noise is a problem when recording effects in the field. The time of day is important—most places are quietest after midnight or very early on a Sunday morning. Relatively still air is also important. Wind noise can ruin exterior recordings; the more directional a mic is, the more likely it is to be affected. But don't throw away your directional mics: these can be ideal at very close range to a sound source, when you can't get a location quiet enough. If the sound is very loud, a dynamic mic will usually have less distortion than a condenser.

For maximum versatility, effect recordings should have very little echo. You can take a clean recording of a car door slam recorded in an open field with no wind, and add reverb to sound like it's in a parking garage. But you can't take a garage recording and make it sound outdoors. Be careful of this with animals as well: Indoor dog barks don't sound like outdoor ones.

Backgrounds

Noise is the point of an ambience recording, but it takes a little planning to capture it well. If your track is going to be broadcast or released on home video, mono compatibility is important. Use a single stereo mic to prevent flanging when the channels are combined. For best results, this should be an *m/s* (*mid/side*) mic; other stereo mics can work if their capsules are very close together. If compatibility isn't a concern, two omnidirectional mics a few feet apart can give you a very realistic sound. (I've even gotten decent results wearing a pair of lavs, one clipped to each shoulder.) If the project is mono, use a single omni to pick up the true ambience of an interior. Use a very directional mic if you have to avoid a specific noise source, but remember that these mics color the sound coming from their sides.

 Gotcha

Mono recordings, stereo mix. Don't worry if you don't have a proper mic for mono-compatible stereo. There are ways to simulate stereo with a mono recording (Chapter 16). Or you can take sections of a mono ambience track, recorded a few minutes apart, and put them on different tracks. When you mix, pan one mostly left and the other mostly right and add a little reverb.

224

Choose interior locations based on the size and shape of the room, and its floor treatment, as well as the level of its activity. Don't worry about matching the room's actual purpose. If the scene shows an old-fashioned bank lobby, a shopping mall branch won't work. But an older post office lobby—with some added bank-related walla or stingers—may be perfect. Watch out for background music: it'll restrict your ability to edit, and you may find it impossible to license.

Often, if you and your equipment aren't conspicuous, you can record public environments without worrying about permission. If voices aren't identifiable you don't need a release. Recording audience reactions in a theater or club usually requires permission from the venue, and the act may need a guarantee that you're not going to record its performance. Prior authorization is always needed in a casino, where guards are trained to spot electronic equipment.

Record at least twice as much background as you think you'll need, because you'll probably find some noisy parts that have to be edited out. Backgrounds can be looped, particularly if they're under dialog, but most shouldn't repeat more than once every minute or two.

You can customize any ambience by recording some specialized walla that's appropriate for the situation. You'll need a quiet and echo-free room, and the mic should be a few feet away from the sound source. Gather half a dozen friends (or union actors, depending on the project), pair them off, and give each pair a specific topic to ad-lib about. Record at least one minute of all three pairs talking simultaneously. Then assign new pairs, new topics, and have them ad-lib in slightly different voices.

225

ELECTRONIC SOUNDS

Sirens and bells used to be mechanical; now they're electronic. Microwave ovens and other household devices beep when you press their buttons. These sounds can be captured in the field, but it's faster to make them on the spot.

It takes a little playing around to make convincing electronic sounds, but you don't need a synthesizer or other special equipment. Many audio editing programs have an FM signal generator in their menus; this may be all that's necessary for anything from a siren to a spaceship. As an example, we'll make a telephone ringer. I'll list steps from SoundForge here, but just as a tutorial: the principles and techniques are the same in other programs. My point is how electronic sounds can be broken into component parts and rhythms.

1. Create a new mono document.
2. Open the Tools > Synthesis > FM panel.
3. Set the configuration (lower right in the panel) for a simple circuit with one operator feeding another. In other programs, the first operator might be called frequency and the second modulation.
4. Set the first operator *shape* or waveform to a sawtooth, and its frequency to 3 kHz.

5. Draw an envelope that's full on for about half a second, and off for the other half. Figure 10.6 shows how the panel will look for the first operator. This operator, by itself, can work for an alarm clock or microwave beep.

6. Now we'll add the warble of a telephone ringer. Set the second operator to a square wave around 10 Hz. Turn its amplitude down to about 1 percent. On another program, this might be called the *modulation depth*.

7. Preview the sound and adjust it to your liking. Then click OK to put the sound in the document.

8. This will give you a single ring followed by an equal-length silence. Select the entire sound, copy, and paste it for as many rings as needed.

By making subtle variations in the settings, you can create a variety of small beepers or a room full of phones. With larger variations and more operators, you can make science-fiction sounds, police sirens, and virtually any other kind of electronic sound. If you're using SoundForge, play with its presets. Try SFX Machine (www.sfxmachine.com), a versatile and relatively low-cost[6] Windows/Mac plug-in for sound mangling and synthesis. Or if you don't mind starting with an absolutely blank slate, download the free open-source program Sonic Birth from sourceforge.net. Here are some points as you're learning the technique:

- Start simple. Know what a single operator or oscillator sounds like with different frequencies and wave shapes.
- Sawtooth and square waves will sound richer than sines and triangles for the basic sound, since they have more harmonics; triangles and sine waves can be useful for the operators that modulate the sound.
- When you're trying to tune a basic tone, turn its modulators (or other operators, in SoundForge) all the way down. Create a preset with these off, and use this preset as a starting point.
- If an envelope has to turn on or off, give it a slight ramp to avoid clicks (as in Figure 10.6).

VOCAL SOUNDS

Wes Harrison is a genius at mouth noises. With no more than a standard microphone, he can create convincing explosions with debris falling; footsteps on just about any surface; and train rides complete with engines, passing warning bells, and the clacking of wheels as you cross between cars. He's mouthed off for Disney and MGM, and works his sounds into a very funny nightclub act as Mr. Sound Effects.[7] He has a unique talent for doing these live, but taught me some tricks that can be adapted for digital post.

---

[6]$75 with a few hundred variable presets; $150 for the version that also lets you program sounds and create new algorithms.

[7]You can get a hilarious CD of some of his performances: www.mrsoundeffects.com.

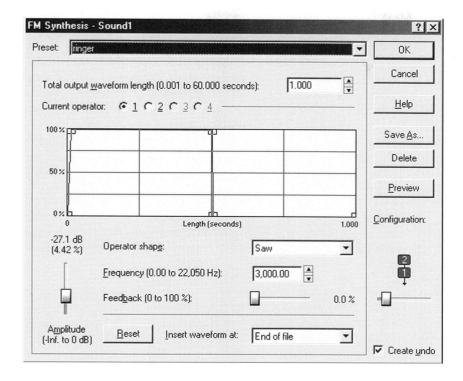

FIGURE 10.6
Creating an electronic telephone ringer in SoundForge. This is one of two operators; the other provides the warble.

227

Close-miking vocal sounds is essential. This means you'll need an omnidirectional mic, since that design is best at resisting pops. If you're making subtle sounds, hold the mic right against your mouth. Growls are best an inch or two away. You'll probably need a dynamic mic to avoid distortion.

Once you've recorded the sound, remove anything that reveals it was made by a human. Delete breaths, mouth clicks, and glottal shocks. Equalization can also help; there are some settings for this in the next chapter.

Further dehumanize a sound by radically slowing it down in a program that doesn't try to preserve pitch. Once you get beyond 50 percent of the original speed—an octave deeper than normal—resonances change and it won't be identifiable as human. Try the speed variation in a couple of different programs; some add aliasing that would be horrible in music but can enhance a deep effect. At around 10 percent of the original speed, friction consonants like /s/ become scrapes. Pitch bend can also help (Chapter 14), and so can playing the sound backwards.

For machine noises, start with short, unvoiced consonants and mouth clicks. Cut into them slightly so they start more abruptly, and then edit a bunch of these sounds closely together. Copy the entire set and paste it multiple times to form a mechanical rhythm; then use a pitch bend to vary the machine's speed.

Selecting Effects

Once you've got more than a few dozen sound effects in your personal library, you'll need a way to find the right one quickly. The most efficient method is an online database with audio previews and automatic spotting, like SoundMiner. Those programs are specialized and can be expensive (the configuration I use cost close to $1,000). They're worth the investment for professional because of the time they save. But you can get a basic program for searching sound effects CDs—without previews or spotting—for free. Figure 10.7 shows one downloadable from Hollywood Edge. It comes preloaded with data on every sound they sell. Sound Ideas has a similar download on their Web site.

These databases are actually FileMaker Pro files, with included run-only software for Windows or Mac. The files are protected against modification, and the software has limited capability. Since the publishers treat these as marketing tools, they don't let you customize their databases or add your own sounds.

But it's perfectly legal for you to export their data, and—using their file as a model—create a new version in your own copy of FileMaker Pro or similar. If you own libraries from both Hollywood Edge and Sound Ideas, you can export data from each and combine them in a single database. If you buy a library that isn't included in those files, ask its publisher for a text listing—most will provide it at no charge—or scan and OCR the catalog pages. When you collect your own sounds, enter them as well. This housekeeping pays off quickly in terms of time saved on your next production.

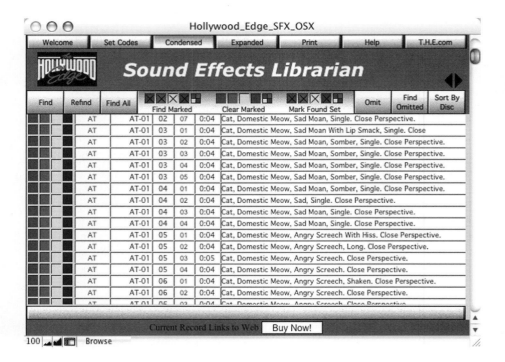

FIGURE 10.7
A searchable sound effects database. This one's free from Hollywood Edge.

SEARCHING

For the most efficient searches, you have to get used to how libraries describe their sounds.

- Search using the shortest possible terms. "Jet plane" will also find "jet airplane," but not the reverse.
- Libraries can be inconsistent about the words they use. Some Hollywood Edge libraries use "car" while others use "automobile." You have to try both. The high-price sound effects search programs include a thesaurus, and look for synonyms automatically.
- Limit your searches by including additional terms on the same line. "Dog bark angry" will get you closer than just "dog."
- If you can't find a particular sound, search for something that makes a similar movement. The small motor in a car's electric window can work well for any kind of servo. A fight bell, looped and repeated, can be an alarm.

Once you've performed the search, read each description carefully. Pay attention to words that might disqualify an entry: "dive, swimming pool (interior)" sounds nothing like the old swimmin' hole. Of course you'll want to audition the effect itself before deciding it's the one to use.

PLACING AND EDITING SOUND EFFECTS

The rule in Hollywood is if you can see it, you must hear it. Sound editors will spend a week fine-tuning effects in each 10-minute reel of a feature, syncing noises to every movement on the screen. Many of these effects will be thrown away by the director when the film gets to the dub stage. But as one sound editor told me, "You have to give them more than they could possibly want."

Hollywood works this way because music, dialog, and effects are prepared by different teams, and there's often no way to decide what's needed until everything comes together at the mix. More modest projects can avoid the wasted effort. It just means applying a little judgment as you work.

1. Lay the music in before you start editing effects. Listen to music and dialog or play them for the director. You might decide that plot-critical hard effects are all that's missing. This is often true for dialog-driven TV projects.
2. After those critical effects are in place, play all the tracks again. If scenes seem sparse or the hard effects seem to come out of nowhere, add an ambience track.
3. Listen again. The ambience may cover smaller sounds, saving you from having to put in editorial effects or Foley. Hits and other random noises in the ambience can be moved so they sync with on-screen actions.
4. Finally, add whatever small effects seemed to be missing.

It's a good idea to separate plot-critical effects, small editorials and Foley, and backgrounds onto different tracks or groups of tracks. Remember that Foleys and PFXs are treated similarly to dialog, and always mono.

Gotcha

Backgrounds, ints, and sitcoms. Sitcoms made in the United States generally avoid using presence tracks for interiors. They frequently skip them in even studio-simulated exteriors. Restaurants, backyards, and subway stations can be remarkably noise-free. It's a cost-saving measure, and nobody seems to mind.

British sitcoms sometimes do add backgrounds to indoor shots, which makes those settings more realistic. Unfortunately, the natural sound in most urban or suburban living rooms is often distant traffic coming through a window. It can be jarring for American viewers to watch a quiet Britcom conversation in a house, and hear cars and trucks in the background.

Hard Effects

Hard effects need to be placed exactly on the right frame. It's frustrating to do this on a timeline, since you have to keep bouncing between single-frame and wider resolutions, and it may be difficult to find a visual cue on a thumbnail-sized image. Instead, watch the scene in a preview window. When you get near an effect, jog to find the proper frame and drop a marker. Repeat for every effect in the scene. Then go to the timeline set for a wide resolution and drag the sounds to their markers.

In most cases, hard effects should start at the first frame where the action occurs and be trimmed to the length of the action. But there are plenty of exceptions:

- Percussive sounds like door closes and body hits should be placed where the action stops. Watch for the first frame where the door or fist is still, after it's been moving, and put a marker there. Many percussive effects are preceded by a lead-in sound, such as a hinge squeak before a door close (Figure 10.8). Mark the actual hit, not the start of the sound, and line that up with the video's marker. Then play the sequence to make sure the earlier sound doesn't start before the action does, and trim the front of the sound if necessary.

FIGURE 10.8
A lot of smaller sounds go into a 2-second door close. Line up the first hit (at 1:08 in this example) with the frame where the door stops moving, and everything else should fall into place.

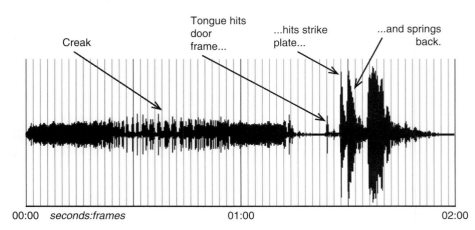

Creak

Tongue hits door frame...

...hits strike plate...

...and springs back.

00:00   *seconds:frames*   01:00   02:00

230

Hear for yourself

Track 36 is the sound from Figure 11.6. This and other sounds in this chapter are © Hollywood Edge and reproduced by permission.

- Explosions usually aren't on screen long enough to support their sound. Let them continue to decay after the camera is on something else. It's even acceptable in many cases to have an explosion extend half a second or so into a scene at a different location. By the way, it's a film convention that most explosions are followed by falling debris.
- If a gun is shot on-camera, there's almost always a barrel flash (Figure 10.9). That's where the sound should be.
- Sometimes there's no specific frame for an action. Figure 10.10 shows six frames of a golf ball bouncing off a tree. It's moving so fast that it becomes a blur. Even though we never see the ball hit, it changes direction between frames 3 and 4. The clunk should start with the fourth frame.

FIGURE 10.9
Look for the barrel flash (third frame), and put the gun's *bang!* there.

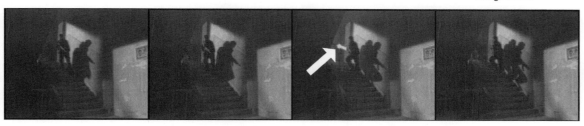

231

Golf ball heading towards tree...

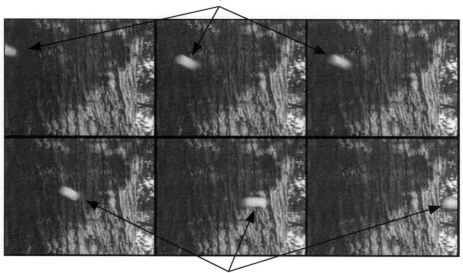

FIGURE 10.10
That blur is a golf ball bouncing off a tree. It's too fast for us to see it actually hit, but you can see where it changes direction.

...and away.

- Sometimes the frame for an action doesn't exist at all. It's fairly common to cut from the hero's fist flying in the air, to a frame where the villain's head is snapping back. The best place for the sound depends on the editing rhythm: Usually, the hit should start on the last frame of the flying clip; sometimes it wants to be right on the cut.

In narrative films, the speed of sound is often equivalent to the speed of light. We expect to hear things on the same frame that we see them. Things don't work that way in the real world, but they do in the movies. Even TV documentaries, supposedly based in truth, usually follow this rule when sound effects are edited.

Some sound editors working on theatrical features used to compensate for the speed of sound in an auditorium. They'd place sounds as much as a frame early, putting sound and picture in sync for people sitting 33-feet back from the screen, which made sense in the days of giant screens and orchestra pits. But with miniature multiplex theaters and home viewing so common, this isn't a good idea any more.

 Gotcha

Give them time to think. If the script calls for an off-camera sound, consider characters' reaction times before placing the sound. You can use this method to reveal more of the characters' mood.

For example, Mary might be working at her desk when the phone rings. If she picks it up on the first ring, we know she was easily distracted or eager for the call. If she lets it ring a few times before reacting, she was concentrating on something else.

Think it through, trim the sound to the right length to tell the story, and place its out-point where it belongs in terms of the reaction. Remember that phone bells like Mary's frequently get cut off in the middle of a ringing sound. It can seem more real if the last ring is shorter than the previous ones, and cuts exactly as she picks up the receiver.

Backgrounds

Ambience tracks should run the length of the dramatic scene, even if the scene includes close-ups and other angles that don't show what's making the noise. If you're dissolving in or out of the scene, extend the ambience a few seconds past the dissolve. Audio cross-fades are seldom as quick as video dissolves.

Many filmmakers like to extend ambiences a few seconds on both sides of a scene, even if the video cuts instead of dissolves. An early cross-fade can set up the scene and make a smoother transition. This can be very helpful if you're cutting to a scene that has dialog within the first few frames.

If an ambience isn't long enough, you'll have to loop it, repeating the effect over and over. Sometimes just putting multiple copies on the timeline, with a short cross-fade between each pair, is enough. But some backgrounds need a little help before they can loop successfully.

Gotcha

Don't need no fades. Many commercial effect recordings fade in at the start and fade out at the end. Looping the entire track would give you unexplained level dips at each loop as they fade. Instead, move the in- and out-points to where the track is playing at full volume.

LOOPING BY RHYTHM

Track 37 is a machine hum sequence. We hear a rhythmic cycle for about three seconds, then the cycles slow down and stop. Looping the entire effect, starting and stopping all over again, would be silly. Instead, we'll loop just one of the cycles.

Open the sound in an audio editor and select a cycle. Set the program to play that selection as a loop. If it sounds smooth, copy the selection and paste it as many times as you need.

 Hear for yourself

Track 37 is a mechanical, cyclic hum from Hollywood Edge. First you hear it as it was published by them; then you hear it properly looped.

It may be impossible to select an individual cycle by eye (Figure 10.11). The best way is to use the program's scrub feature to mark what you think is the beginning and end of a cycle, turn it into a loop, and then fine-tune. Play the loop while moving its boundaries, until things sound right. If you hear a click at each repeat of the loop, make sure the boundary is at a zero crossing. In this figure, about 17 frames are selected starting around 1:06; the result is the smoothly looped machine sound in the second part of Track 37.

A stereo effect may have zero crossings at different times on each channel, so finding a click-free loop can be difficult. A 10- or 15-millisecond cross-fade at each splice can help. Or convert the sound to mono, loop as needed, and apply a stereo simulation process (Chapter 16) before you mix.

FIGURE 10.11
It's hard to tell visually, but this is one cycle of the machine hum. Load the track into your editing software and hear for yourself.

233

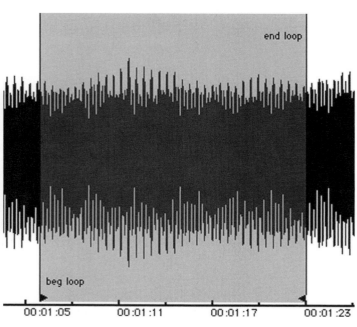

C-LOOP

Some sounds don't loop well because they change over time. The first part of Track 38 is a short traffic background in a city. Its timbre changes slightly during the length of the effect, so the end doesn't sound quite like the beginning. Looping it gives you the abrupt shifts in part 2 of Track 38.

When you've got this kind of situation, a *flip loop* or *C-loop* can work wonders.

1. Select the entire sound and copy it.
2. Move the cursor to the end of the sound, and paste. In many programs this will leave the newly pasted section selected; don't deselect it. In other programs you might need to select the second half manually. Since this needs to be precise, drop a marker at the end of the file before pasting and use the marker to select the pasted half.
3. Apply a *backwards*, or *reverse*, or *-100 percent speed* effect to the selection. This will turn it head for tail. Now the newly pasted version starts with the same timbre the first section ended with and should sound perfectly smooth at the splice. If it doesn't, look for zero crossings or use a short cross-fade.
4. Select the entire sound with both the forward and backwards version. Copy and paste as many times as needed.

If you're doing this in a NLE, it will want to render each backwards copy separately, wasting time. Instead, skip step 4. Export the single forwards/backwards pair from step 3 as an audio file.

Use the new file for conventional, straight-ahead looping.

Hear for yourself

The first sound in Track 38 is a traffic background from Hollywood Edge. Because its timbre changes, conventional looping can be obvious (second sound). But the C-loop works fine (third sound).

Sounds with foreground voices or percussive hits won't C-loop well; viewers can spot individual elements going backwards. But a surprising number of sounds work fine in reverse. Consider the echoey truck horn, about five seconds into our traffic track. When the effect is flipped, the echo comes before the horn, but still sounds like it's realistically bouncing off buildings.

SOUND EFFECTS DESIGN

The most creative use of sound effects are when a sound divorces itself from reality. Monsters, laser swords, and magic machines should have equally strange sounds; the magic castle or spaceship should have a unique background as well. Using manipulated or slightly wrong sounds in sync with real-world actions can help us appreciate a character's point of view.

Layering

Most real-world sounds are little symphonies. As we saw in Figure 10.8, even a simple door closing has different elements playing in sequence. Created sound effects can also have elements playing simultaneously. When you do this kind of layering right, they combine to create new sounds that are unrecognizable, but still familiar enough to be accepted as real.

Think about all the things that would be happening in the object you're trying to create, and then which individual sound-making objects work the same way. Need a robot walking? That's probably a lot of servos and mechanical actions, so reach for some electric car windows and mechanical toys. (If a toy seems too small, slow it down a little.) Add some gears from a CD-ROM drive, or squeaks from a playground see-saw. Be careful of continuous backgrounds— you don't want a car engine with that electric window—because stacking multiple continuous sounds can turn to mush. Think about whether sound clichés are realistic: the Jetsons' robot might make a random electronic beeping, but there's no reason a robot designer at Panasonic or GE would do something that annoying.

235

If you want simultaneous sounds to become a symphony, pay attention to things a composer would notice: timing and timbre. Things with very similar frequency ranges shouldn't usually play at the same time, because one masks the other. But you can combine multiple sounds to create new environments if you spread their frequencies around. This also gives you the ability to tailor the final frequency balance so it'll work well in the mix. For one film, I created a home hospice environment by building four separate medical machine sounds: one very deep, one medium deep, one in the midrange, and one just above the consonant range. I was careful to protect the areas around a few hundred Hz for vowels, and around 1.75 kHz for consonants.[8] It was actually a four-part choir. During the mix, I could change their proportions depending on other effects and music, or how intense the scene was. One of the sounds also had a mechanical in-out rhythm that sort of matched slow breathing; as the character's illness got worse, I was able to play with its timing.

Be careful about the soundstage when combining sounds. Putting some elements to the side or behind you makes a sound bigger, but might make the implied object too big for the film's reality. On the other hand, background ambiences can be as big as you want. Just remember that broadcast and home viewers might hear stereo or surround differently from what you mixed.

---

[8]These frequencies and ranges are discussed in the next chapter.

Which kind of sounds you layer also makes a difference. Pay attention to the palettes you're using.

Sound Palettes

Sound effects fall into three broad (and sometimes overlapping) categories. In most cases, it makes sense to think of these as different artist's palettes. Sounds within a single palette can often be substituted or combined successfully. Sounds from multiple palettes contrast and tend to be heard separately, even if you mix them. Of course, like all things artistic, these rules aren't absolute. The real key is how creatively you apply the sounds.

ORGANIC SOUNDS

These include human and animal noises, and naturally occurring sounds like wind and water. Monsters are presumably organic, so it helps to start their voices with organic sounds. Library recordings of animal roars can be slowed down, layered, or pitch shifted to be scary and inhuman. But the recording has to be clean, close-up, and echo free. Otherwise, you won't be able to apply realistic effects to it in the mix.

Wind can be made otherworldly by changing resonances with an equalizer or by layering multiple sounds. Wind-driven musical instruments, including the brass family and the organ, can be slowed down and pitch-bent (Chapter 14). Water works nicely at drastically changed speeds, with some reverb.

MECHANICAL SOUNDS

Machines are obvious noisemakers, but so are other objects that vibrate when they move. Nonwind musical instruments, random pieces of metal, scissors closing, and rocks rubbed together are all useful in a sound effects studio. As with the mouth-made machines described earlier, the key is to change the sound so its source isn't immediately recognizable, and then layer and loop things to form a rhythm.

Mechanical sounds tend to occupy wider frequency ranges than organic sounds, which makes it easier to build choirs of different timbres.

ELECTRONIC SOUNDS

The electronic palette can be the least versatile. While layering multiple organic or mechanical sounds thickens them and adds interest, synthesized sounds tend to blend into a single (and often bland) pudding when played simultaneously. Because synthesizers have such a wide range of frequencies, manipulation tools such as drastic pitch changes merely turn one synth note into another.

There are some uses for electronic sound, of course. A synthesizer or FM generator can create punctuations and science-fiction sounds as well as the telephone ringer described earlier. White noise, creatively filtered with multiple resonant peaks, can serve as a mechanical drone. Low square waves, with proper filtering to simulate vowel formants, can be an inhuman vocal drone. But both these sounds will be richer if they start with real ingredients.

Don't confuse synthesizers with the *samplers* mentioned at the start of this chapter. Samplers play digital recordings of real sounds from an electronic keyboard. These tools are tremendously useful in sound effects design, but they don't create the sounds they're manipulating.

237

CHAPTER 11

Equalization

Equalizers are precise tone controls, changing the timbre of a sound by making one part of the spectrum louder or another softer. But they didn't start out that way.

It began, as do so many other things in this book, with the phone company. Early radio broadcasters leased cables from the phone company, first for remote broadcasts within the same city, and later for intercity hookups and networks. But those wires were designed for phone calls, and lost too much of the high frequencies to sound good on radio. So a telco engineer would sit at one end of the hookup, and send test tones. A colleague would be at the other end with a voltmeter, clipping capacitors or inductors on line until the voltage was equal for each tone. When they were done, the phone company declared the line *equalized*.

A few years later movies started talking, and theaters started getting wired for sound. But no two installations were the same. A track could sound fine on the re-recording stage, but be muffled in one auditorium and brittle in another. So engineers used the phone company's technique to tune theaters. But instead of using jury-rigged collections of components, they put the parts in a box with switches and called the unit an *equalizer*. Someone tried one of the boxes to spiff up dialog and sound effects during the mix, and the idea caught on. By the mid-1930s, a couple of companies were building equalizers specifically for film mixing.

Today, equalizers are indispensable in audio post. But they're rarely used to make voltages equal. Instead:

- Equalizers improve intelligibility in dialog tracks.
- Equalizers remove some specific kinds of noise.
- Equalizers help a mix by keeping elements from competing with each other.
- Equalizers subtly change the character of a sound.
- Equalizers emphasize bass rhythms in a piece of music.
- Equalizers simulate telephones, intercoms, and other real-world speakers.
- Equalizers compensate for minor deficiencies in the playback system.

Despite all this usefulness, there are certain things an equalizer can't do. It can't eliminate most kinds of noise.[1] You can't use an equalizer to fix a distorted track either, even though one can make the track easier to understand.

Equalizers can't create sounds that weren't there in the first place. They don't put back highs that were lost to a low sample rate or add bass to a telephone recording. They can't turn me into James Earl Jones. They can't be used as a kind of spotlight either, to pick out a voice in a crowd or to eliminate a soloist or most orchestral instruments.[2]

FREQUENCY BANDS

The point of an equalizer is to raise or lower the volume in a specific frequency band, without affecting other frequencies. So before you can use an equalizer, you need to understand what's going on at different parts of the spectrum. That's easiest to do by ear.

Tracks 39 to 47 are a tour of the audio band. There are eight versions of the same voice-and-music montage. Each includes male and female narration, pop and orchestral instrumentals, a middle-of-the road pop song sung by a woman, and a hard rock piece sung by a man.[3]

Track 39 is the montage in full fidelity. The other tracks have been processed through a filter that passes only a single group of frequencies. I used lab-quality filters, with 24 dB reduction per octave. If you try to replicate this experiment with most desktop software you'll probably be disappointed; those filters seldom have more than 6 dB reduction per octave. Figure 11.1 shows this difference graphically.

---

[1]Chapter 15 explains the rules, along with other noise reduction techniques.
[2]Techniques for deepening voices are in Chapter 14 (though I'll never have Jones's acting chops). The one for eliminating the soloist in some recordings is in Chapter 16.
[3]The montage includes tracks we've worked on previously, plus "You Are My Fantasy" and "Hell Child" (DeWolfe CD 77, Tracks 9 and 13). Both are by C. Kiddy, © DeWolfe Music, and used by permission.

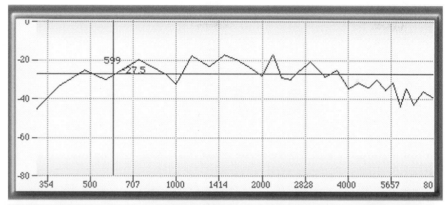

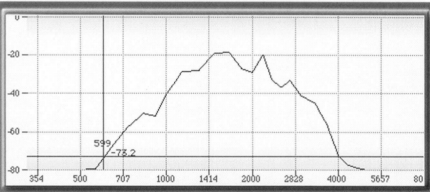

FIGURE 11.1
A tale of two filters. These are *spectragraphs*, which display signal strength at various frequencies. They're both from the same section of music, run through a high-pass filter at 1.2 kHz and a low-pass at 2.4 kHz. But the top one was done with filters from a popular NLE. The bottom one is an actual measurement of CD Track 44.

241

Hear for yourself

Tracks 39 through 47 are the examples for this section. You may be able to understand audio bands using just the text, but you'll get a much better feel for them if you actually listen.

Play Track 39 first as a reference, on the best speakers you've got. Then work your way through the others. Remember all that's changing is the filter frequency, not the volume or any other settings. If a track seems softer than others, it's because there's less going on in that band. Don't turn up your speakers to compensate.

Gotcha

It's not what I saw in Hi-Fi Weekly... If you're a stereo enthusiast or have spent time in music studios, some of the following descriptions of various audio bands may seem wrong. That's because they're based on the realities of film and TV sound, not on music recording (or advertising hype). You can verify everything I'm describing for yourself, by listening to the book's CD.

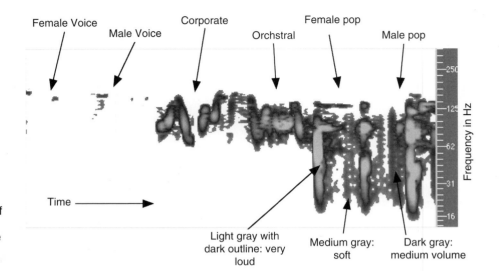

Female Voice   Male Voice   Corporate   Orchstral   Female pop   Male pop

Time ⟶

Frequency in Hz

Light gray with dark outline: very loud

Medium gray: soft

Dark gray: medium volume

FIGURE 11.2
A spectral analysis of track 40 shows how little deep bass there actually is in many sounds.

DEEP BASS

Track 40 is the band between 10 and 100 Hz. Most of this band is often deliberately filtered out during dialog recording to avoid noise. A lot of this band can also be thrown away in post. The first four seconds of silence are the woman's voice—it's quiet because she has almost no vocal energy in this band. But there's also very little of the man's voice in the next four seconds. Even the corporate and orchestral music are sparse, with only occasional notes that deep.

Figure 11.2 is a spectral analysis of the track, shown in a *spectragram:* a kind of three-dimensional graph of time as well as volume and frequency. The horizontal axis is time, roughly the length of the montage. Frequencies are plotted along the vertical, and volume is reflected by the amount of color. You can see how quiet things are during the voices. Note how there's virtually nothing below 60 Hz for even the orchestral music.

MIDBASS

Track 41 (Figure 11.3) is the band 100 to 300 Hz. These are the fundamental frequencies for most spoken voices. Hear how both male and female voices have about the same amount of energy here. But you can't make out which vowels are which—that depends on higher harmonics, created by resonances in the mouth. The music uses these frequencies primarily for accompaniment, rather than rhythm or melody. The singers also have fundamentals in this range, but they're masked by instruments so you hardly hear them.

Low Midrange

Track 42 (Figure 11.4) is 300 to 600 Hz. These are lower harmonics of the voice fundamentals. When you speak, your tongue and mouth form differently shaped hollow spaces. These act as filters—almost like an ocarina—emphasizing

FIGURE 11.3
Track 41 shows how much busier things are between 100–300 Hz, both for voice and music.

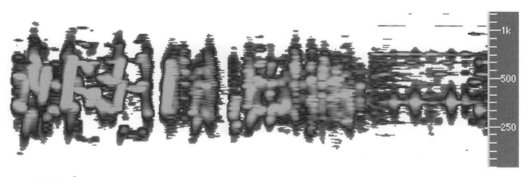

FIGURE 11.4
Track 42 has about the same amount of activity in the 300–600 Hz range for both voice and instrumental music. Notice how the instrumentals calm down during the vocals so we can hear the lyric.

243

different harmonics with each position. We hear those combinations of harmonics as vowels. Those combinations extend upward, and vowels can be recognized even if this band's specific frequencies are lost.

This band and the next contain most of the energy of the human voice, as well as the fundamental and most powerful harmonics of most melody instruments. That's why voice and melody sometimes compete when mixed together. You can hear how the melody instruments in the two pop songs hold back when the singers are belting. Advertising jingles and most other songs that depend on lyrics are arranged this way.

Mids

Track 43 (Figure 11.5) covers the 600 Hz to 1.2 kHz range. Now we're entering harmonic country, where much of the energy is generated by harmonics (Chapter 1) of lower fundamentals. Notice how the female voice, naturally brighter, is stronger in this range. Neither voice is fully intelligible, though. That's because

FIGURE 11.5
Track 43, covering the 600 Hz to 1.2 kHz band. Things don't look very different from the previous octave, but you'll hear a big difference because the ear is sensitive to subtlety here. This is where you can start to identify different instruments in the band.

FIGURE 11.6
Track 44 shows the band 1.2 to 2.4 kHz. This is also a critical range, particularly for dialog.

unvoiced consonants don't start until the next octave. This band is also important for music: while lower mids let you hear the melody, these harmonics help you tell instruments apart. Most instruments have significant energy here.

High Midrange

Track 44 (Figure 11.6) is the octave 1.2 to 2.4 kHz. This is an important range for dialog: There's enough harmonics to tell most vowels apart, and all of the consonants are covered. It's also important for brass instruments, which have loud upper harmonics. The singers are particularly strong in this range because they're singing *in the mask*, using natural resonators in the front of their faces to emphasize harmonics.[4] But despite all the activity in this octave, volumes aren't as high. Only the orchestral material has about the same energy as it did an octave below.

---

[4]The same thing starts to happen if you force a smile while you're speaking, an old announcers' trick.

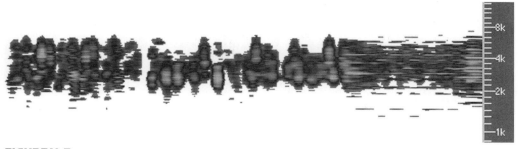

FIGURE 11.7
Track 45. When you get to the octave starting at 2.4 kHz, things start to calm down ... except for the rock music at the end.

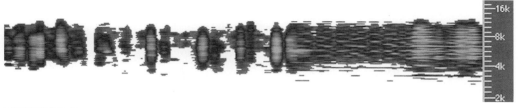

FIGURE 11.8
Track 46, between 4.8 and 9.6 kHz, has very little activity. There are loud sounds but they're less frequent than in other octaves.

245

LOWER HIGH FREQUENCIES

Track 45 (Figure 11.7) is the octave 2.4 to 4.8 kHz. You might not think of these numbers as being high frequency, but take a listen. While most vowels have appreciable harmonics up here, those harmonics only establish presence and aren't important for intelligibility. (Telephones cut off at 3.5 kHz, yet retain enough of a voice for you to identify who's speaking.) There's also very little of the synthesized industrial theme. The orchestral brass is strong here. Most brass is very rich in upper harmonics, and that's what helps us differentiate one brass instrument from another. The laid-back song is mostly just strings in this range. On the other hand, the rock number has a lot going on, typical of dance and rock music production.

Middle High Frequencies

Track 46 (Figure 11.8) is the 4.8 to 9.6 kHz range. Even though we haven't yet hit 10 kHz, this is definitely high. You can hear just a little of the female, and only friction consonants from the male voice. The synthesizer is almost completely gone. But the orchestral brass is still going strong because of its harmonics. About the only thing left in the two pop songs are the top of the strings, the guitar wail, and the percussion.

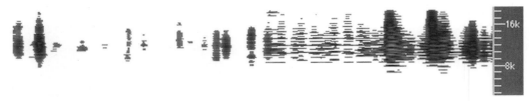

FIGURE 11.9
Track 47, the top of the band. There are very few spoken word sounds here, and not much in
the music (until you get to the pop).

HIGH FREQUENCIES

Track 47 (Figure 11.9) is the top octave of the audio band, 9.6 kHz to 20 kHz.
For most of the track, you might not hear much at all. There's still some
orchestral brass at these frequencies, but what's left of the pop music is mostly
unidentifiable sizzle.

 Gotcha

Magic ranges? Most of these examples are an octave wide. Since we hear logarithmically, this width makes the most sense—each band contains the same number of musical
notes. The two lowest bands are significantly wider, not because our hearing is less acute
there,[5] but because there's less going on that's important to soundtrack equalization.

The actual frequencies involved are fairly arbitrary. I chose them to reveal interesting things
about voice and music, not because you should be using them to set an equalizer.

EQUALIZER CHARACTERISTICS AND TYPES

Just about every equalizer has a frequency knob. But good software gives you
a choice of equalizer types: cutoff filter, shelving equalizer, peaking equalizer,
parametric, or various forms of graphic. You can't choose the best one for a
specific purpose until you understand their differences. But that's fairly easy
when you look at characteristics beyond frequency.

Slope and Filters

A filter is an equalizer that passes part of the band perfectly, while rejecting frequencies beyond a cutoff point. How it makes the transition between pass and
reject depends on its design. Glance back at Figure 11.1 on page 241. It com-
pares how much music was left at various frequencies, with two different filters
set up exactly the same.

---

[5]Though it is.

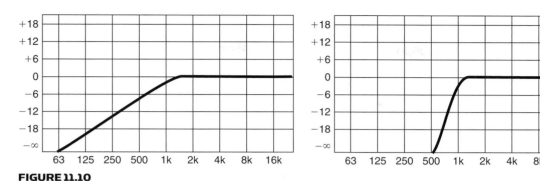

FIGURE 11.10
Two high-pass filters set to 1 kHz. The left is like the one in most NLEs; the right matches lab filter used for those CD tracks.

The average level of that music was -20 dBFS. The crosshairs in the figure show how loud the audio was an octave below the filter's low-frequency limit of 1.2 kHz. In the top screenshot, the signal was -27 dBFS, just about half the strength of the original signal. In the bottom one, it was -73 dBFS, less than 1/200 of the original.

Figure 11.1 can be impressive, but it's a little misleading. What we see also depends on what the music was doing when I grabbed the screenshot. There's a better way to visualize filter performance. Instead of showing the volume of an arbitrary signal at different frequencies, we draw a graph of how much *any* signal would be rejected. Signal loss is in dB along the vertical, and frequency in Hertz along the horizontal. The result looks like Figure 11.10.

A theoretically perfect filter would have a vertical line at 1 kHz; 999 Hz falls to the left of the line and gets infinite attenuation; 1001 Hz is on the right and isn't affected at all. But real-world filters—even the best digital ones—start working gradually, with a gentle transition between passing and reducing the signal. So to make some sense of this, we define a filter's *cutoff frequency* as where the signal is reduced -3 dB.

Even with that gradual transition, there's a big difference between the two filters in Figure 11.10. You can see it in the angle of the line below the cutoff. The top filter, with roughly a 45 degree angle, loses 6 dB per octave. At 1 kHz, the loss is -3 dB. At 500 Hz, it's -9 dB. At 250 Hz, its -15 dB. This is a *first-order* filter, and is what you get in most NLEs. The filter on the bottom has a steeper line of 24 dB per octave; this is a fourth-order filter.

More is not necessarily better. Filters with steeper slopes have more *phase shift*—a form of distortion—around the nominal frequency. It's a subtle side-effect that changes timbre. This shift is inherent in all filter design. Generally speaking, very sharp filters are reserved for special effects or eliminating noises. More gentle filters are used to preserve sound quality.

247

These drawings show high-pass filters, rejecting sound *below* a cutoff frequency. But the same rules apply to low-pass filters, which reject sounds *above* their frequency setting.

- High-pass filters are often used at a fairly low frequency, for example to remove room rumble below 80 Hz. Since high-pass filters appear on the low end of the spectrum, it may be simpler to think of them as *low cut* rather than high pass.
- Similarly, a low-pass filter at 12 kHz, which could remove hiss from dialog, can be called a *high cut* filter.
- To create Tracks 39 to 47, I used a high-pass filter followed by a low pass. This left a clearly defined band between two filter frequencies, and rejected everything else.

Most high- and low-pass filters have only one control, which adjusts FREQUENCY. While a few studio and lab filters also have a SLOPE control, this characteristic is properly determined by the circuit or software design and usually not variable. However, you can create a higher-order filter by stacking multiple first-order filters in series, all set to the same frequency. Each additional filter adds 6 dB per octave (and more phase shift). Figure 11.11 shows how you'd stack filters in Premiere to make them sharper.

Boost or Attenuation, and Shelving Equalizers

Sometimes you don't want to completely reject sounds; you merely want to adjust their volume.

SHELF FILTERS

A *shelving equalizer* (sometimes called a "shelf filter") has a slope like a filter, but the slope stops at a preset amount of boost or cut. The volume adjustment is applied from the nominal frequency all the way to the end of the spectrum. A low-frequency shelf will boost or reduce sounds below its nominal frequency; higher sounds aren't affected at all. A high-frequency shelf does the reverse.

Shelving equalizers can be set to any boost or cut value within their range. This can be helpful for reducing noise at either end of the spectrum, without totally losing the signal.

The slope of a shelving equalizer is fairly shallow and can extend more than four octaves. This gentle, low-distortion action, coupled with the lack of an obvious peak, makes shelving filters very useful for subtly brightening, warming, or filling out a sound. But be careful: when a shelf is boosting, it will also emphasize noises at the extremes of the band.

Shelving equalizers have two controls: FREQUENCY and AMOUNT of boost or cut.

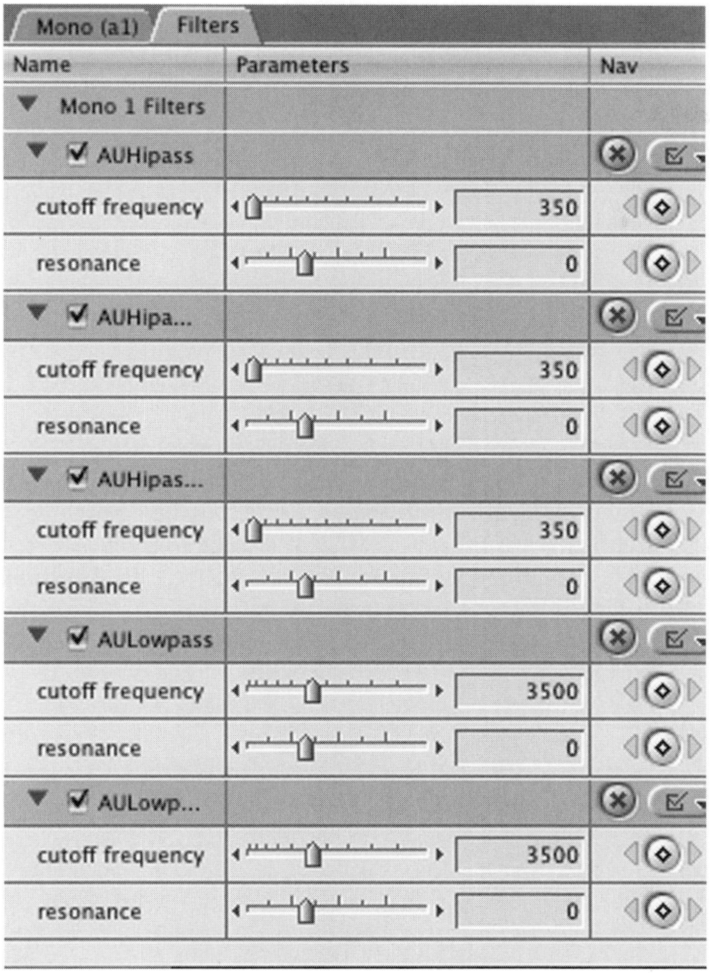

FIGURE 11.11
This may look redundant, but stacking multiple filters at the same frequency has the same effect as using a single filter with a steeper slope.

BANDWIDTH OR Q, AND PEAKING EQUALIZERS

The most common use for an equalizer in audio post is to fix something, such as reducing camera whine or boosting intelligibility. This kind of fix requires lowering or raising just a specific group of frequencies in the band, while leaving others alone. *Peaking*[6] *equalizers* also let you select FREQUENCY and AMOUNT of boost or cut, just like a shelving equalizer, but peaking equalizers work on a narrow range of frequencies. Figure 11.12 shows how peaking equalizers affect a sound.

---

[6]Peaking equalizers also dip, though it's not reflected in their name.

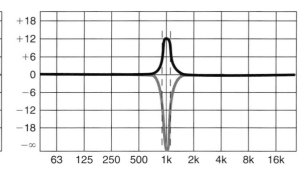

FIGURE 11.12
A peaking equalizer set to boost (dark line) or cut (light line) by 12 dB at 1 kHz. The dashed vertical lines indicate its bandwidth.

FIGURE 11.13
A sharper equalizer, with a Q of about 5.

You can see that the equalizer in Figure 11.12 has a slope of roughly 6 dB per octave, appropriate for gentle timbre correction. But if we tried to remove a 1 kHz whistle with this gentle slope, we'd muffle dialog between 500 Hz and 2 kHz. A more precise equalizer is needed. This concept is so important that there are multiple ways to specify it.

 Gotcha

Plus 18, minus infinity? You'll notice the graph is not symmetrical. It's reasonable to want an equalizer to reduce parts of a signal below audibility, so many designs offer 24 dB or more of cut. But boosting a signal that much can cause problems with noise or oscillation, so practical equalizers are often limited to +12 dB or +18 dB.

There's also an existential reason for this asymmetry. I have no problem making a signal infinitely soft; that just means turning it off. But how do you make a signal infinitely loud, without involving all the energy in the known universe?

An equalizer's *bandwidth* is defined as the range where its output is within 3 dB of the specified frequency. In Figure 11.12, that's shown by the two dashed lines at roughly 700 and 1400 Hz. So the bandwidth of this equalizer is 700 Hz. But that's a clumsy measurement. Because frequency is logarithmic, an equalizer with the same slope would have different bandwidths depending on where it's set. If we dialed in 250 Hz, the 3 dB points would be roughly 175 and 350 Hz— a bandwidth of 175 Hz. If we dialed in 4 kHz, those points would be around 2.8 and 5.6 kHz, and the bandwidth would be 2.8 kHz.

Instead, we use the concept of Q: the center frequency divided by the bandwidth. In each case above, the Q is roughly 1.4. This is a gentle-sounding equalizer. Contrast it with the one in Figure 11.13. This one has 3 dB points at roughly 900 and 1100 Hz, for a Q of 5. Practical equalizers can have Qs many times that. A Q of 15 or higher lets you surgically remove a constant-frequency sine wave without noticeably affecting anything around it. Some of the special-effects equalizers in my studio go up to 100 Q; at that high a Q, an equalizer can start oscillating as it boosts its own internal noise. The Q is sometimes expressed as a fraction of an octave centered around the nominal frequency. Most peaking equalizers have some form of Q CONTROL.

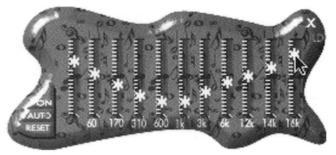

FIGURE 11.14
A not-very-serious graphic equalizer.

A *comb filter* is a particularly high-Q collection of harmonically related notches, handy for noise reduction. But it's actually created with a small delay, and is discussed in Chapter 13.

GRAPHIC EQUALIZERS

An equalizer doesn't need user-settable Q, or even user-settable frequencies, though this seriously limits its usefulness in audio post. The *graphic equalizer* found on most boom boxes and in simple software is actually a bank of low Q, fixed-frequency peaking equalizers with their outputs combined. Figure 11.14 shows a typical graphic equalizer. The choice of one that looks like a toy was intentional.

 Gotcha

Beware of Mr. Smiley! It's just too easy to misuse a graphic. Most boom-box owners know that if you slide the knobs so they look like a grin, as in Figure 11.14, music has more impact. The bass seems stronger, and there's more sparkle to the highs. So some producers ask for *smiley equalization* on their entire track. It really does make a mix more exciting on good monitor speakers, if the original track was clean to begin with. But that's where the good part ends.

While boosted bass and treble may sound great on good monitors, they can turn to distortion on other kinds of speakers. The track will still seem loud, but with a muddiness that gets in the way of the message—something hard to spot in a production environment but damaging on the air. The cheap, narrow-range speakers in most TV sets won't carry the hyped frequencies, but the distortion still comes through. Besides, unless you monitor a smiley track on very good speakers, you're apt to miss noise at the extremes of the band.

Even though the boost isn't heard on small speakers, it shows up on station's meters. An engineer or transmitter processor might turn down the overall volume to compensate, making a smiley track seem softer than others on the same station.

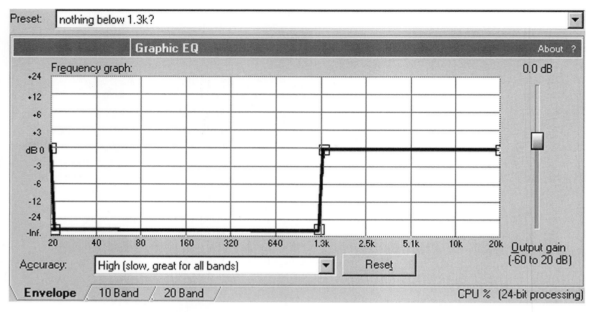

FIGURE 11.15
A different kind of graphic equalizer lets you draw an idealized curve, but probably won't sound like it looks.

The problem with graphic equalizers is their lack of precision. Not only do the sections have a low Q, but the frequencies are arbitrary. Sometimes they're an octave apart, centered around 1 kHz; sometimes they're two or more octaves wide. Sometimes their logic is a complete mystery.

Graphic equalizers do have a place in professional sound. Serious hardware units, with bands a third of an octave wide, are often used to fix minor problems in otherwise acceptable monitoring systems. But this has to be done subtly, with accurate measuring equipment, and needs a healthy understanding of the room's acoustics. In a monitoring system, more than a few dB adjustment at any frequency can introduce problems.

Analog graphic equalizers got their name because a bank of volume sliders looks something like the graphs we're using. But there's a newer form found in some software. It lets you draw the graph directly, and then equalizes the sound to match. Figure 11.15 shows one of them, from a popular audio program. The problem with these tools is that nothing stops you from drawing impossible equalizers. You can be fooled into thinking what you've drawn is actually being applied to the sound. The figure shows a graphic set up as a filter, with a slope of greater than 96 dB per octave. When I measured the result, it was actually about 12 dB per octave.

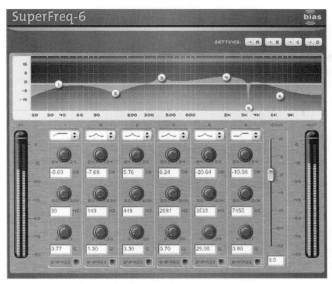

FIGURE 11.16

A parametric equalizer. This one includes a graph. But unlike the previous figure, this one won't let you ask for something impossible.

PARAMETRIC EQUALIZERS

If you want to repair a sound, the best peaking equalizer is one that lets you specify all three parameters: FREQUENCY, Q, and BOOST/CUT. That's why it's called a *parametric equalizer*. The first parametics appeared around 1972, and revolutionized production. Figure 11.16 shows a particularly nice implementation, Bias's Super-Freq.[7] Like many parametrics, it combines multiple peaking sections in the middle of the band with switchable cutoff/shelf/peaking at the ends. Here, section 1 is set as a high-pass and section 6 is a shelf. There are simpler parametrics in most NLEs and audio software, but you can combine multiple instances to get the same effect (as I did with the filters in Figure 11.11).

Parametric equalizers sound exactly the same as any other kind of peaking equalizer, assuming the same circuit or software quality. A parametric's value is the ability to precisely tune multiple sections in real-time. This is particularly helpful for catching specific sounds that you want to remove; you'll learn how later in this chapter.

FREQUENCY-SPACE EDITING

A few programs will draw a spectragram of selected audio, let you select just the part of the image representing noise, and delete or reduce it... in effect,

---

[7]This version has six separate sections; others have up to ten sections. All the versions come as a single package, so you can balance complexity against processor load depending on the specific

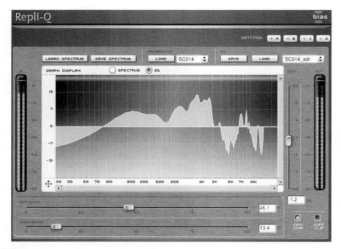

FIGURE 11.17
Using a matching equalizer to make an ADR recording sound closer to production dialog.

fixing the patient by retouching the x-ray. It's really an elegant interface for a precise, time-varying equalizer. It's used mostly as a noise-reduction technique rather than corrective equalization, so we cover it in Chapter 15.

DYNAMICALLY-CONTROLLED EQUALIZERS

It's common practice to control low- or high-frequency noise with equalizers that constantly change either frequency or level depending on how much energy there is at the extremes of the band. This is often used as a film noise reduction technique, also in Chapter 15. Music studios sometimes use similar principles to boost a sound's brightness in tune with its beat.

MATCHING EQUALIZERS

A new category lets you analyze the spectral energy in one audio file—creating a spectragraph like the one in Figure 11.1—and then scan and automatically equalize a second file so its spectragraph matches. If the two files have similar material, this can give them a similar timbre. Figure 11.17 shows this process in Bias' Repli-Q. Here it's displaying the equalization curve it generated to match a piece of ADR to production dialog. The ADR is rolled off on the low end, has its presence boosted around 2 kHz (to match the production mic), and is then dipped around 5 kHz because the studio mic was too bright.

Matching equalizers can be useful, but they're not magic. The sounds you're matching must have similar spectral patterns before any equalization; otherwise, the automatic circuits will try to compensate for the wrong thing. In other words, they're great for matching two takes of the same line by the same actor… but aren't very useful for matching your finished film to a Hollywood blockbuster.

You have to stay conscious of how the software averages both its analysis and the resulting equalizer curve, and be ready to make appropriate adjustments to each. When you first start using these tools, there's a tendency to use too detailed a curve, and apply too much equalization. After you're amazed by what a matching equalizer can do, don't forget to back its settings off.

In all, matching equalizers don't do anything that a skilled engineer using conventional parametrics and good monitors could do… but they're certainly faster, and if you're careful, can be just as good.

Equalizer Quality

There's a lot more to an equalizer than knobs or sliders, and you can't assume that two equalizers with identical settings will perform the same. Depending on its design, an equalizer may contribute noise or distortion, or be hard to tune.

ANALOG EQUALIZERS

While music producers revere the sound of some classic analog equalizers, these are expensive and arguably overkill in the post suite. Cheaper, stand-alone ones, along with the equalizers in analog mixers, can be noisy at their extremes. Their frequencies are usually chosen for music, not media. If you use FireWire and your signal normally stays in the digital domain, there's nothing to be gained—and a lot to be lost—by running through an analog equalizer. If you use analog connections when digitizing footage or sounds, resist the temptation to pre-equalize. It's better to leave the serious equalization to software that lets you save the good settings and undo the bad ones.

A few new systems take samples of the signal processing in classic analog equalizers, and emulate them digitally. Again, this is mostly a music technique used for reasons of taste.

DIGITAL EQUALIZERS

Software-based equalizers can be of varying quality, depending on how well the algorithm was designed and how much they're allowed to load down the CPU. Two critical design choices are the internal gain structure, and how many bits are used in the internal bussing and floating-point math. Both can influence noise, and bad gain staging can also lead to clipping. Third-party plug-ins usually have much better noise and distortion performance than the equalizers supplied with NLEs.

Standalone digital equalizers with AES/EBU connection are often found in sophisticated audio post suites, for real-time processing during a mix. These are DSP-driven boxes, and may have additional processing functions.

TUNING AN EQUALIZER

Forget about specific frequencies. There are no magic numbers that will always improve a sound. It's okay to use your knowledge of different bands to get in the ballpark, but you can't fine-tune an equalizer mathematically. You have to use your ear.

This means you must hear the sound while you're adjusting. A few software equalizers don't let you do this; these are virtually worthless. Better equalizers work in real-time, by changing their sound as soon as you move a knob. Others require a few seconds to render a preview after you've let go of a control. Obviously, the real-time equalizers are more efficient, but the equalizers that need to render are still workable if you're willing to make small incremental changes and have some patience.

 Gotcha

Dude, where's my frequency? One problem with some digital equalizers is the trade-off between resolution and responsiveness. In many designs, the frequency knobs rely on an internal lookup table to speed up operation. Instead of smoothly varying from one frequency to the next, these digital equalizers click over in fractions of an octave. If the fractions are small enough, you can tune them precisely. Otherwise, there's a chance you'll miss a sound that you're trying to fix.

Equalizers that let you enter a numeric frequency don't have this problem. However, knobs or sliders make tuning much faster. Some frequency entry boxes let you increase or decrease their value with the ↑ and ↓ keys, which is certainly a lot faster than typing numbers.

HIGHPASS, LOWPASS

Tuning a cutoff filter is intuitive: Turn the only knob until what you want to lose goes away, without doing too much damage to what you want to keep. If the slope is too gentle for this to happen, apply a parametric instead and find the offending frequency using the steps under parametric below. Then turn off the parametric and enter the frequency you found into multiple, stacked filters.

SHELVING EQUALIZER

Tuning a shelving equalizer takes a little more care since the controls can seem interactive. Because of its gentle slope, a large boost at a high frequency might sound like a smaller boost at a lower one, but it's probably adding more noise. The same happens on the low end. If you want to use more than about 3 dB of boost, check on very good monitors. Or consider using a low Q peak instead.

This problem of extra noise pickup doesn't exist when lowering levels with a shelf.

PARAMETRIC

When using a parametric for subtle, low Q effects, start with a fairly large amount of boost and a medium Q. Find the right frequency. Then lower the Q and adjust the level.

Tuning a parametric to eliminate a constant-frequency noise, like a camera whine, isn't intuitive. The trick is to forget about removing the noise at first; instead, make the noise jump out by boosting it to extremes.

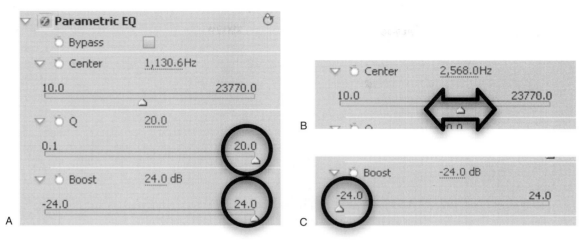

FIGURE 11.18
The steps to eliminate pitched noise with a parametric aren't intuitive. But they work, and the result can be better than using noise reduction software.

1. Set both the Q and boost as high as they'll go (Figure 11.18A).
2. With the clip playing, slowly sweep the frequency until you hear the noise suddenly jump up (Figure 11.18B). Then fine-tune by sweeping even slower in that area: When you've got exactly the right frequency, you'll hear the noise resonate and possibly even distort. Don't worry about the distortion.
3. Don't touch the Q or frequency, but turn the gain or boost/cut as low as it'll go (Figure 11.18C). The noise should be gone, or at least considerably reduced, without much effect on the surrounding sounds.

If the noise doesn't seem to be affected enough, try lowering the Q slightly. If that doesn't help, raise it again. Then apply another section, set to the same parameters as the first to it. This doubles the amount of rejection. If you now notice similar noise at a higher pitch, you're hearing a harmonic. Add another section and start sweeping around frequencies that are twice what you found for the first section.

Hear for yourself

Track 48 lets you hear what these steps can sound like. It consists of a 9-second piece of exterior dialog, repeated five times. The first pass is the original, with a nasty whistle in it. The second pass is step 2. You can hear the equalizer sweep and then find the right frequency, emphasizing the whistle. The third pass is step 3, and the whistle is gone. But now you're aware of a boomy resonance in the space. In the fourth pass, we're sweeping a second section of the parametric to find the boomy resonance. The fifth pass is the

257

result of both sections. It starts with the equalizer turned off, then it turns on, then off and on another time.

Track 49 is an even more extreme example. It's a short clip from an interview recorded on a motorboat, with the mic too far from the subject. An equalizer alone can't save this track—nothing can make it perfect—but it can make the voice more intelligible, as you can hear in the second part of this track.

There's more that can be done to both these clips, but that's for other chapters.

When to Equalize; When Not

In Hollywood, nobody touches equalization until a film gets to the dub stage. That's because this usually is the first place a track is heard on calibrated monitors with good acoustics, and there are proper equalization tools plus someone who knows how to use them. Your project might not be heading for a dub stage, but it still makes sense to put off most decisions until the editing is done. Then you can adjust dialog so it sounds natural and other elements so they work well with it.

On the other hand, Hollywood sound supervisors have the experience to tell whether a piece of raw dialog will be fixable on the dub stage, or needs to be replaced. More inexperienced editors on smaller projects may have to make these decisions, without as much to go on. So it can make sense to apply equalization in the NLE, to help decide if a marginal shot will be usable.

It's a problem. Even smaller projects should put off processing until the mix, yet equalization (or noise reduction) might be necessary to see whether a scene makes it past the initial edit, or to have something to show a client. Just remember: it's very hard to remove incorrect equalization, and impossible to remove bad noise reduction. Best bet may be to use NLE filters that are nondestructive and can be removed before the mix. Even better, keep a *mirror track* that has the same edits but no processing at all; in most software, that's just a question of duplicating a clip or track before you apply the filters. If you equalized properly, you can use the main track in the mix and save time. If not, you've got a clean copy and can start fresh.

EQUALIZER COOKBOOK

A good chef starts with an idea of how to prepare a dish, but will always taste and adjust to the ingredients at hand. Think of these recipes the same way: They're good starting places for most source material, but they're not exact and won't apply to some clips. *Always adjust by ear.*

Most of these recipes assume a parametric equalizer. Values are expressed as frequency, then boost or cut, then Q; for example, *1 kHz/−3 dB/Q = 0.5* means set the FREQUENCY to 1 kHz and the LEVEL to −3 dB, with a Q of 0.5. Vary the frequency around there, until it works best with your material. Then fine-tune the level for the sound you want.

The high- and low-pass filters should be at least 12 dB per octave, and work even better at 18 dB per octave. If yours aren't that sharp, consider stacking a couple of sections.

Working with Voices

- Because the area around 1.75 kHz is the fundamental of most consonants, a 1.75 kHz /+3 dB/Q = 1 boost can subtly improve intelligibility, 1.75 kHz /+6 dB/Q = 0.5 can add strength to some voices.
- An octave above that is the first harmonic of most consonants; 3.5 kHz/ +3 dB/Q = 1 can add clarity, but don't do this if you're using the boosts at 1.75 kHz.
- Male voices can gain a little extra power with 160 Hz/+2 dB/Q = 1.
- Sibilance (spitty /s/ sounds) often happen between 4 and 5 kHz. Sweep around there with +12/Q = 5 until you find them, and then dip as much as possible. This can reduce the sibilance, but if you want to really eliminate it, skip the equalizer and use a *de-esser*, described in Chapter 14.
- Many interior locations are boomy somewhere around 200 to 400 Hz, depending on the room size. A 3 dB/ Q = 2 dip can help, but use maximum boost first to find the exact frequency.
- If dialog sounds dull because of bad mic technique, try 4 kHz/ +6 dB/ Q = 0.25. This can be better than using a shelf, since it doesn't emphasize high-frequency hiss.
- Popped /p/ and /b/ sounds can sometimes be fixed by selecting just the pop and applying a sharp highpass around 160 Hz.

Working with Music

- If a melody is interfering with dialog or voice-over, but you don't want the rhythmic elements of the music to get lost, cut a hole in the melody for the consonants. Start around 1.75 kHz/−3 dB/Q = 1 and vary for the most effectiveness.
- Modern pop-style recordings are often very bright, with a lot going on above 10 kHz. If you have to mix them with older recordings, try a shelf 10 kHz/−3 dB. Then add 5 kHz/+3 dB/Q = 0.5 to the older material.

General Fixes

- For low-frequency noise reduction in dialog, try a sharp highpass around 130 Hz (male) to 200 Hz (female).
- For high-frequency noise reduction in dialog or music, try a sharp, low-pass around 8 kHz.
- What we call 60 cycle hum can have harmonics all over the band. Start with a sharp, highpass at 130 Hz, and then add at least four or five

259

parametric sections tuned to harmonics by ear. Or use a comb filter, described in Chapter 13.

- If these fixes leave the track sounding too dull, add $+3\,dB/\,Q = 1$ at around 1.5 times the highpass frequency.

Special Effects

- For telephones, use sharp high-pass at 400 Hz, followed by a sharp low-pass at 3.5 kHz. Then add some compression (Chapter 12).
- For a radio speaker use a high-pass at 300 to 500 Hz, and then a low-pass at 5 to 6 kHz. Vary these depending on the quality you're trying to simulate.
- A thin voice, reminiscent of old-time radio's *The Shadow* but used in a lot of current production, can be done with a high-pass at 800 Hz and a low-pass at 10 kHz.
- Put voices in the next room with a low shelf around 500 Hz/-24 dB, a resonant peak around 1.3 kHz/$+12$ dB/$\,Q = 5$, and a high shelf at 2 kHz/ -24 dB. Make sure the peak isn't clipping in your equalizer. Then add reverb (Chapter 14).
- Make outdoor sounds more distant by reducing the highs and emphasizing the lows: low shelf 500 Hz/$+12$ dB, high shelf 1.5 kHz/-12 dB. Then lower the volume.
- To dehumanize a voice for sound effects, start notching out vowel formants with a sharp parametric. Depending on the vowel, you'll find them around 400 Hz, 800 Hz, 1.2 kHz, 1.6 kHz, 2 kHz, 2.4 kHz, 2.8 kHz, 3.2 kHz, 3.6 kHz, and 4 kHz.

CHAPTER 12
Dynamics Control

REMEMBER THIS:

- Good automatic level processors are a lot more subtle and sophisticated than the AGC in a camera. They can be a powerful tool for adding punch and controlling some kinds of noise.
- You can also use them to make elements fit together better in a mix, or even change the character of sound effects and musical instruments.
- While there are lots of dynamics processors with different purposes, all have similar controls. Understand the controls in one, and you'll be able to work all the others.

A *compressor* works like an automatic volume control. It uses the envelope of a signal to control the signal's level, keeping the output volume relatively constant even when the input changes.

For most of the history of film and TV sound, compressors—and their close cousins, *limiters*—were used sparingly. Distortion-free compressors were hard to build, so their use was restricted to times where they would help avoid even worse distortion.[1] But in the late 1960s, relatively clean units started to appear on the market, and soon they were considered essential tools—first in music production, then to increase loudness at radio and TV transmitters, and finally in postproduction.

The most obvious use for a compressor is smoothing out unwanted jumps in volume. But compressors are also useful for creatively shaping a soundtrack:

- They can add punch and power to a voice.
- They can keep elements from competing during a mix.

---

[1]To overcome noise, optical soundtracks and analog TV boost highs as much as 17 dB. The projector or receiver has a matching loss, cutting the noise while restoring the original timbre. Unfortunately, all that boosting means that loud, high-frequency sounds are apt to distort.

- They can change the character of sound effects (or destroy the character of music).
- They can compensate for predictable problems in the playback system.

With a slight circuit or software change, a compressor becomes an *expander*, emphasizing volume changes by making soft parts of the original signal even softer, and turning up the ones that were already loud. Expanders (and their cousins, *gates*) can reduce or eliminate some kinds of noise, change the character of sound effects and musical instruments, and add impact to percussive sound effects.

CHARACTERISTICS AND CONTROLS

Figure 12.1 shows what goes on inside a very simple compressor.

The input, on the left of the drawing, is about one syllable's worth of dialog. The tiny waves are the frequencies of the voice itself. The overall volume, small at first and then louder, is the envelope—what a meter would show when you play this sound.

The envelope detector generates a voltage, which tracks the volume. The voltage is then inverted: Where the signal was loud, the voltage is low; where the signal was soft, the voltage is high.[2]

This inverted voltage is fed to a volume-control circuit. Where the original signal was soft, the control voltage is high and keeps the volume control fully on. Where the signal was loud, the control voltage is low and the volume is reduced. The result is a constant-level signal at the output.

This is a brain-dead compressor, appropriate for a two-way radio but not a soundtrack. A lot of the emotional impact of a film depends on the dynamics of each sound, and how they relate to other sounds. This compressor would destroy those dynamics. But by adding just a few additional functions, we can build smarter compressors that do useful things for a track.

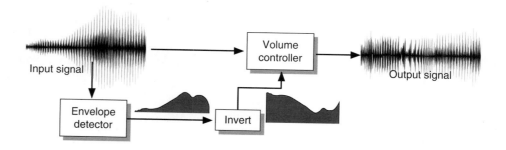

FIGURE 12.1
A very basic compressor.

---

[2]There's another compressor design that looks at the envelope of the output instead of the input. For our purposes, the effect is the same.

Gotcha

Classic compressors. It was a real challenge to control volume in early analog compressors. Tubes would add a thunking noise as they aged, and had to be constantly tweaked. Transistors offered more options, but each option had its own distortion and a characteristic sound.

Music engineers took advantage of the differences between compressor designs, using specific ones for various instruments and musical styles. Some classic 60s- and 70s-era compressors still sell for thousands of dollars. So do newly manufactured analog clones. A few companies attempt to emulate these classics in software.

If you're making movies, save your money. There's no advantage to using analog (or analog sounding) compressors in audio post. Digital algorithms can have a lot less distortion.

Compressor Controls

Better compressors let you adjust almost every aspect of their performance. Using these controls properly can make the difference between a professional sounding track and one that feels squashed and fatigues the ears.

RATIO

The inverter in Figure 12.1 multiplied the envelope by −1, turning every decibel of additional loudness into a decibel of more softness. But there's nothing magic about this number. If we multiplied by −0.5, for example, less of the envelope would be reflected. More of the original dynamics would be retained, and the compression would be more subtle. On the other hand, if we multiplied by −4, small volume changes in the input would result in big changes in the control. A very loud signal might be turned down so much that it becomes the softest part of the track.

Real-world compressors have to consider the response of a particular envelope detector, volume controller, and other factors, so you can't predict how a compressor will perform based only on the multiplier. Instead, compressors have a **RATIO** knob. It controls how many decibels the output will change, for each decibel of change in the input. A ratio of 2:1 means that if the input gets 2 dB louder, the output goes up 1 dB. A ratio of 10:1 means that a 10 dB change in the input results in only 1 dB change in the output. Some compressors have ratios as high as 100:1, and a few click to ∞:1. These ultra-high ratios are useful only for special effects. Ratios can go the other way as well. A 1:2 ratio means that a 1 dB change at the input produces a 2 dB change at the output, and the compressor is really acting like an expander (discussed later in this chapter).

Figure 12.2 shows another way to think about this. Assume that bar graphs A, B, C, and D are tones of different volumes. A 2:1 ratio cuts each in half—reducing the volume difference. A 4:1 ratio makes the difference even less. At 8:1, the tones are almost the same volume.

263

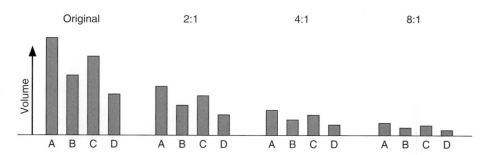

FIGURE 12.2
When you turn up the ratio, the difference between one tone and the next gets smaller.

⚠️ **Gotcha**

Irrational ratios. If you set the ratio to 1:1, a 1 dB change in the input results in a 1 dB change in the output. There's no compression at all! *A ratio of 1:1 means you've turned the compressor off.* Despite this, many software compressors have 1:1 as their default.

If you're using a compression plug-in and don't notice any difference in the sound, make sure the ratio control is set to a more useful number.

PEAK VERSUS RMS

The envelope detector in Figure 12.1 is responding to the loudest waves, and you can see that the envelope follows their *peak level*. But you can also see that only a few waves reach that level. Even at the loudest parts of the signal, most of the waves are much softer. This signal doesn't seem as loud to our ears as the envelope detector would suggest. An *RMS* detector averages levels over the short term, creating an envelope that's closer to the actual sound.

In general, peak-level detectors give a compressor better control over the signal, at the risk of more audible compression effects. RMS detectors may let some of the loudest waves get past a compressor, but the overall sound is smoother and more natural. A few compressors let you choose which mode the detector uses. It's common practice to have an RMS-detecting compressor followed by a peak-detecting *limiter* (described later in this chapter).

STEREO LINK

If you compress each channel of a stereo signal separately, voices and instruments can appear to dance around between left and right. Consider the case of a loud gunshot on the extreme left of an exterior scene. It would cause the left-channel compressor to lower the level. But the background ambience—birds and traffic—should be evenly distributed between both channels. When the compressor lowers everything on the left, this leaves comparatively more ambience coming from the right. Suddenly all the birds and traffic will swing toward the right side. Then, when the left-channel compressor recovers, they go back to their proper places. It can sound very strange.

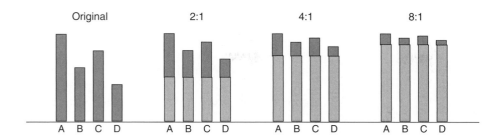

FIGURE 12.3
Makeup gain (light gray) keeps the signal usable, even at high compression ratios.

The best way to deal with this is to use a single level detector, fed with a mix of both inputs, and feeding the level controllers for each output. The image stays stable. (Some compressors use two detectors, but average their results together and sent it to both controllers. The effect is the same.)

Hardware-based stereo compressors usually have a LINK or STEREO switch on their front panels, to let you choose whether the channels should work independently as two mono compressors or in tandem as a single stereo one. Software-based ones often skip this switch, and choose whether to combine the detection based on whether a file is mono or stereo. This works fine for normal clips, but can be a problem if you're working with split dialog that has a boom on one channel and a lav on the other: if something hits the boom mic, the resulting noise turns the lav down as well... precisely at the moment you want to use the lav for replacement. If you're up against this, split the tracks and compress them separately.

By the same token, many NLEs make you put the left and right channels of stereo music on two different tracks. If you compress each separately, the image might dance around. Better here to combine or link the channels in an audio program and compress them there.

MAKEUP GAIN

You probably noticed a problem in Figure 12.2: High ratios made the graphs so small that the ones on the right are virtually useless. That happens in the real world as well. As a compressor applies more volume reduction because of high ratios, the output can get very low.

So all compressors have a way to add amplification to make up for this loss. Technically, it's usually an offset added to the control signal. But it works like an extra amplifier after the volume controller. Figure 12.3 shows it graphically. The dark gray bars are the signals from Figure 12.2. The light gray bars are the makeup gain, which stays the same for each ratio no matter how loud the input was. As the ratio goes up, we apply more gain to keep the output up.

Some compressors call this function OUTPUT GAIN or simply GAIN. Others don't even let the user control it; they change the gain automatically as you change the other settings. This isn't a problem.

FIGURE 12.4
Signals above the
threshold (dashed
line) are compressed.
Those below it,
aren't.

THRESHOLD

Often, you want to compress only part of a signal. Louder sounds need to be controlled so they don't distort or overwhelm a mix. But softer ones may be fine as they are. We need a way to tell the compressor when to kick in—when things are loud enough to worry about—so it can ignore anything softer.

The dashed line in Figure 12.4 represents the THRESHOLD CONTROL, part of the envelope detector. It's designed so that signals below its level don't produce an envelope at all. Volumes A and C are louder than the threshold and get compressed. You can see that A and C's levels are fairly close together after compression. Volumes B and D are below the threshold; they don't generate an envelope or get compressed. They're still affected by makeup gain, but their relative volumes aren't changed. B and D are both much softer than A and C, and D is still softer than B.

In case you've gotten lost in all those initials, think of it this way: with a threshold control you can make everything louder, but only the loudest signals will have their dynamics changed.

Threshold controls are usually calibrated from 0 dBFS down to −40 dBFS or more. But there are no right settings—even if you know exactly how much compression you want, the proper threshold depends on how loud the original signal is. Good compressors give you a way to tell how much compression is going on, so you can set them properly.

> ⚠️ **Gotcha**
>
> **Threshold of insanity.** If you set the threshold at the top of its range, nothing will be compressed. The compressor thinks *every* signal is too soft to bother with. Some programs make this the default.
>
> Again, if a compressor doesn't seem to be doing anything, make sure you've set an appropriate threshold.

GAIN REDUCTION METER

If we monitor the control voltage, we can actually see what the compressor is doing. Adding a meter there lets us know how much the volume will be reduced. When the meter is fully up, the control voltage is high, and there's very little compression. As louder sounds go over the threshold, the voltage goes down and so does the volume control circuit. If there's a high ratio, the meter will swing a lot between loud and soft sounds. If there's a low ratio, the meter may hardly move. Figure 12.5 shows where a meter would be applied.

Good compressors have a GAIN REDUCTION METER calibrated to show how many decibels they'll reduce the signal. It's an important function, particularly when you're first learning to use a compressor. Subtle amounts of compression, only −3 dB or −4 dB on peaks, can be extremely effective. Yet their subtlety makes them hard to hear: you can't tell whether the sound is being technically manipulated or whether the original performance had a little more control.

Even experienced mixers keep one eye on the gain reduction meter while they're adjusting a compressor, and will often glance at it during the mix. Since compression is so dependent on the nature of the incoming sound, engineers often prefer to describe a compressor's settings in terms of how gain reduction and the ratio, rather than a specific threshold setting. That's how I'll describe them in the cookbook section of this chapter, as well.

KNEE

Below the threshold, there's no compression—a ratio of 1:1. Above the threshold, the compressor uses the ratio you've set. But what happens exactly at the threshold? A sudden switch from zero compression to full ratio can be helpful for certain effects. If you've also chosen a high ratio, it can absolutely hold the level to a maximum setting. A gentle transition is more subtle and adds strength to a sound without calling attention to itself.

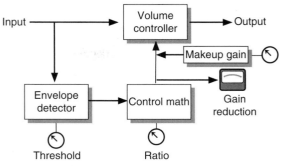

FIGURE 12.5
A compressor with some additional controls and a gain reduction meter.

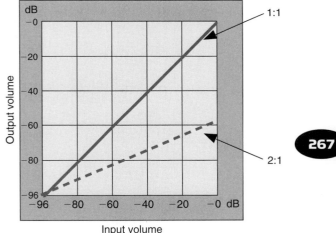

FIGURE 12.6
A very basic compressor graph, showing two different ratios.

Some compressors have a KNEE switch or control to adjust the transition. There is no standard calibration, but generally a SOFT knee will let compression start gradually, going from a ratio of 1:1 to whatever you've set, over a range as wide as 10 dB around the threshold. A HARD knee will kick in compression at exactly the threshold.

Compressor Graph

Engineers have another way of looking at what a compressor's doing, one that can be handy for visually oriented filmmakers. If we draw a graph with input volume along the horizontal and output volume the vertical, we can then plot the action of the compressor as a line.[3] Figure 12.6 shows how it would look.

---

[3] It's very similar to the *curves* function in Photoshop.

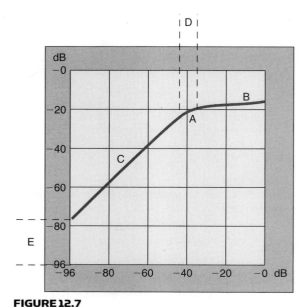

FIGURE 12.7
A graph showing a real-world compressor in use. The text explains what the letters mean, but at a glance you can get an overall idea of what this compressor will do.

The two edges are calibrated in dBFS, from −96 (softest possible sound in a 16 bit system) to 0 (loudest sound in any digital system). The solid gray line represents a ratio of 1:1. If you track along the bottom to an input of −40 dBFS, follow up the gray line and then across to the left, you'll see the output is also −40 dBFS.

The dashed line represents a 2:1 compressor. An input of −40 dB crosses this line at −68 dBFS[4] output. If you don't want to mess with numbers on a graph, just look at the angle of the dashed line. It's 22 degrees, indicating fairly gentle compression.

The beauty of this kind of graph is that you can also add the other compressor characteristics we've discussed. When you do, you can understand a lot about what a particular bunch of settings will do to a sound. Figure 12.7 shows a practical compressor. Point A is the threshold, where compression first kicks in. For inputs above this level, the ratio is about 10:1 (shown at B). Below this level, it's 1:1 (C). But compression starts gradually, with a fairly soft knee D. A signal of any level is affected by the makeup gain, which lifts the whole graph by E.

So at a glance, you can see that signals above −40 dBFS will be heavily compressed (upper right), and the entire clip will be boosted so its levels hover around −20 dBFS (left side of graph). Graphs like this are used to understand the most complicated dynamics control. Dolby even provides one to explain their *dialnorm* concept (page 279).

COMPRESSOR REACTION TIME

It's possible to build a compressor which responds instantly.[5] Such a device lowers the output as soon as the input exceeds the threshold, and restores it the moment that the input goes back. It sounds awful.

The problem—as discussed in Chapter 1—is that both low-frequency waves and quickly changing envelopes look the same to a compressor. Volume changes faster than 1/20 second are usually considered waves. Slower ones are usually envelopes. But any rapidly repeating pattern is probably a wave.

---

[4] −40 dB input is 56 dB louder than the threshold of −96 dB. That volume change is cut by the 2:1 ratio, becoming 28 dB (half of 56 dB). At 28 dB above the threshold, you have −68 dB. But this footnote is just for the curious reader. You don't need math to interpret a compressor's graph. You can tell just as much by looking at the angle and position of the line.
[5] See Lookahead Compression, on page 274.

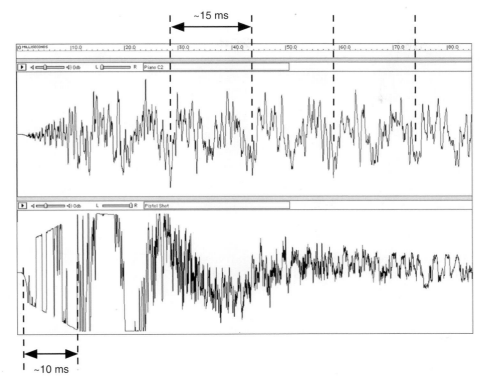

FIGURE 12.8
The repeating fundamental of a moderately low piano note (top) is slower than the initial envelop of a pistol shot (bottom).

269

In the range between roughly 1/20 and 1/100 second, there's no precise way to be sure a voltage change is wave or envelope. The envelope of a pistol shot takes about 10 milliseconds to go from zero to full volume. A moderately low musical note (C2 on a piano, two octaves below middle C) has a fundamental frequency of 65 Hz, meaning each cycle is about 15 ms. You can see this conflict in Figure 12.8.

A compressor fast enough to control the pistol would attempt to adjust the piano's waveform in time with its fundamental, distorting the sound. These timing issues aren't just academic: some deep-voiced trailer announcers have serious vocal energy below 100 Hz, and the wrong compression makes their voices muddy.

So good compressors let you adjust how quickly they respond to a new loud sound, and how long they keep the volume reduced after a sound subsides. Both settings are important. Using them creatively can even change the nature of a sound.

Attack Time

ATTACK affects how long it takes the compressor to respond when a sound first exceeds the threshold. A fast attack (some compressors respond in a fraction

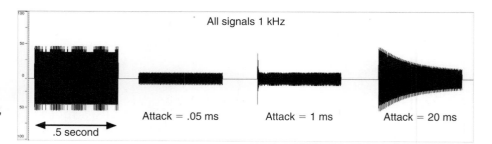

FIGURE 12.9
A signal run through the same compressor, with three different attack times.

of a millisecond) can control sharp transients. But it may also cause distortion. A slow attack is less apt to distort, but will prevent the compressor from reacting to fast sounds. It can be a useful effect sometimes; the last section of this chapter includes some examples.

Figure 12.9 demonstrates various attack times. The first envelope is the original signal, a 1 kHz sine wave at −6 dBFS, lasting half second. The other three envelopes show what happens after the signal is passed through a compressor with a threshold of −20 dBFS and a ratio of 10:1. For the second envelope, the compressor had an attack time of 0.05 ms. You can see that the compressor completely controlled this signal. The third has an attack time of 1 ms, long enough to let exactly one cycle sneak through at full volume before the level is controlled. On the fourth, you can see the compressor gradually kick in during the 20 ms after the signal starts.

But while Figure 12.9 is accurate, it doesn't tell the whole story. Listen to the first part of Track 50. You can hear how the fast attack time caused significant distortion. This was because the timing is just a small fraction of the test signal's frequency, so the compressor is trying to reshape every wave of the signal.

The second part of Track 50 used an attack time of 1 ms. On the graphic, this let one cycle of the signal pass through without compression. But listen to it on the CD: Because 1 ms is too fast for human ears to perceive as a volume change, it has the same volume as the second envelope… only without the distortion. The fourth envelope used an attack time of 20 ms. You can hear how this creates a pinging quality, while the compressor catches up with the signal's level.

 Hear for yourself

Track 50 lets you hear the envelopes in Figure 12.9 and the attack time's effect on the signal.

None of the numbers in the preceding paragraph are golden; they're just intended to help you understand how an attack control affects the envelope.

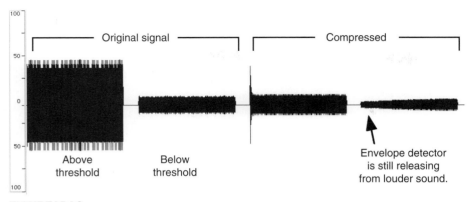

FIGURE 12.10
An input signal with two tones—one loud and one soft—on the left. The result of compression is on the right. The second tone is softer than the threshold and shouldn't be compressed at all. But you can see how the slow release time means the compressor will still be recovering from the first tone, so the second is definitely affected.

Depending on the compressor, attack times can range between a fraction of a second to about one second. Choosing the right timing depends on the signal involved and how other controls are set. Always tune a compressor by ear.

Release Time

All things eventually come to an end, and that includes loud parts of a signal. How a compressor responds after the signal returns to a level lower than the threshold is set by the RELEASE. A moderately slow release can fight the distortion effects of too fast an attack, by keeping the envelope detector from tracking individual waves. In the first part of the previous example, we used a release time shorter than a single cycle. If we had raised the release time to about 10 ms—a few cycles of the 1-kHz test signal—there wouldn't have been distortion.

On the other hand, you don't want too slow a response, or else loud sounds will "punch a hole" in the track. Figure 12.10 shows this graphically. The first two envelopes are a 1-kHz tone at −6 dBFS, then at −20 dBFS. The second two are identical but run through the compressor used in the previous example. The release time is 500 ms. The compressor successfully controls the −6 dBFS tone, but it doesn't recover in time to properly handle the softer one. It adds a rising envelope that wasn't there originally.

This has real-world implications. Imagine an exterior scene: we hear traffic and birds, but they're not compressed because they're lower than the threshold. Then there's a loud gunshot, followed by a softer scream. If the release time is too slow, the volume controller keeps things down after the shot is over, and then slowly recover. The scream will also be turned lower, more than is justified by its actual volume. And we wouldn't hear the traffic and birds for a moment until the volume controller returned to its normal level. Part 2 of Track 50 lets you hear the train wreck[6] I'm talking about.

Hear for yourself

Part 2 of Track 50 consists of the gunshot, scream, and outdoor tone described above, first compressed with a slow release time, and then with a faster one.

Most compressors let you choose a release time between a few milliseconds and a couple of seconds. Some vary the release time, depending on how much gain reduction was applied, and are calibrated in decibels per second.

Gated compression

If you're applying a lot of compression to location audio, noise can be a problem during pauses. While characters are speaking, their voices make the compressor push the track's volume down, which also lowers the noise. But when they pause, the volume returns to normal, making the noise louder than it was during dialog.

One solution is to use a *gated compressor*. It has a second THRESHOLD control. As soon as the input level falls below the gate's threshold, gain reduction is frozen at its current level. If you're using a moderately slow release, there'll still be significant reduction and noise will be lowered. A few gated compressors add a GATE RELEASE time and TARGET setting in negative decibels. If the signal stays below the gate's threshold, gain reduction slowly settles toward the target value.

Don't confuse a compressor's gate with a *noise gate*, described later in this chapter. A compressor's gate is a sophisticated control on high-end processors. A noise gate is a simple level-triggered switch, used for noise reduction and special effects.

Types of Dynamics Processors

Dynamics processors evolved to solve different problems. Most NLEs let you choose among a few; a good audio program or collection of plug-ins has many more. This kind of processing is so useful that a dub stage or audio post suite will often have several hardware-based units as well as software ones.

Despite the variety, dynamics processors fall into specific categories based on their design.

COMPRESSOR

A compressor is the basic device described previously. It's generally used to smooth out levels in voice-overs and the overall mix, with an attack time of a

---

[6]It's a figure of speech. But a recording of an actual train wreck would suffer similar problems.

few dozen milliseconds, a release between a half-second and a second, a ratio under 10:1, and a threshold that makes the gain reduction bounce around −6 dB. More aggressive settings may be appropriate for broadcast.

Current pop music styles use a lot of compression on individual tracks and then on the overall mix as well, but that's a subject for another book... and considerable discussion at engineering conferences.

LIMITER

A limiter's architecture is similar to a compressor's, but it's intended to protect the signal from exceeding a preset limit. It's used to prevent digital clipping or analog overloads. For this reason, attack times are typically extremely fast and ratios are high. Release timing is chosen as the best compromise between distortion and avoiding holes in the audio after a loud signal. Sophisticated limiters vary their release time based on the material.

Since digital limiters are often used with thresholds close to 0 dBFS, good ones are designed with internal protection from overloads: The input is reduced by a fixed amount, processing occurs at a higher bit depth to avoid noise, then the output is boosted and dithered to match the input spec. This is transparent to the user, but indicates why limiting may use a different algorithm (and more CPU resources) than compression.

Limiters are usually the last stage in a processing chain. It's common practice to use a compressor to make a track seem louder, then follow it with a limiter for protection.

273

DE-ESSER

Voice tracks sometimes have problems with excessive sibilance because of bad mic technique, unusual vocal conditions, or being passed through some analog media. The effect is that /s/ sounds, which have the most high frequencies of any phoneme, become emphasized or distorted.[7] An equalizer could reduce those troublesome highs, but that would make the rest of the track sound dull. The best solution is an intelligent equalizer that turns itself on whenever it hears an /s/, and stays out of the way at other times.

One way to provide this intelligence is to combine a compressor with a high-pass and low-pass filter, set to a frequency just below the sibilance. Figure 12.11 shows how. High frequency signals, including /s/ sounds, are split off and sent to a compressor with a high threshold, fast attack, and no makeup gain. Low-frequency signals, including most of a voice's energy, are combined with the compressor's output. A high but average-volume sound doesn't reach the threshold, so it passes through unchanged; when it's combined with the lows, the full

---

[7]Other friction consonants can also present these problems, but that's rarer and usually the result of faulty equipment.

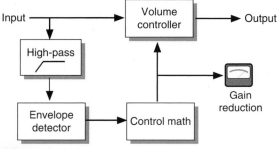

FIGURE 12.11
One form of a de-esser splits the signal in half, and compresses only the highs. It works like an intelligent equalizer.

FIGURE 12.12
A different form of de-esser reduces the entire signal, but only when there's sibilance. It works like an intelligent compressor.

274

spectrum is restored. But loud high-frequency sounds get reduced by the compressor. For just those moments that sibilance is present, the spectrum is tilted away from the highs. Since the /s/ sound had too much high-frequency energy in the first place, the spectrum still sounds normal.

That split-band processing works for dialog-only signals because /s/ sounds are the highest pitches in a voice. But if the voice is mixed with music or broadband sound effects, overall timbres get affected by its action. Fortunately, with a simple circuit change, we can turn the intelligent equalizer into an intelligent compressor. It lowers the entire signal when /s/ sounds are present, reducing sibilance but preserving timbre.

In Figure 12.12, the high-pass filter is moved to the input of the envelope detector. As in the split de-esser, only loud high-frequency sounds will reach the threshold. But the input to the volume controller *isn't* filtered. Once a /s/ triggers the action, the entire spectrum has its volume lowered.

A dynamics processor's envelope detector and control circuit or software is considered its *side chain*, and Figure 12.12 works by filtering the side chain so that only specific frequencies cause an effect. Side chain processing can be very helpful in noise reduction. Even though noise reduction is mostly a combination of dynamics processing and equalization, the subject is so important it gets Chapter 17 to itself.

LOOKAHEAD OR FEED-FORWARD COMPRESSION

There's a limit to how fast a normal compressor's attack time can be. A certain number of processor cycles are required to detect loudness, perform the necessary math, and trigger the volume controller. But by treating the side chain separately from the main signal path, we can create a compressor with instantaneous response. In fact, we can even make a compressor that can read the future: it starts fading *before* a loud sound occurs.

Figure 12.13 shows a compressor with a *delay* in the main signal path but not the side chain. Delays are discussed fully in Chapter 14; for now, just consider it as a device whose output is exactly the same as the input—but some number of milliseconds later. Loud sounds are detected by the side chain in real time, telling the vol-

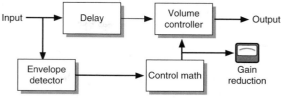

FIGURE 12.13
A lookahead compressor can fade a sound down before it occurs.

ume controller to apply gain reduction. But since the main path is delayed, this reduction occurs before the loud sound gets to the controller. If you use a short delay and fast attack time, the level will be turned down just in time to catch the front of a loud sound. If you use longer delay and attack times, the volume can be turned down slowly and subtly before a sudden, loud sound occurs, making a gunshot or thunder clap seem louder because it stands out more from the background.

A delay of a millisecond or two can be sufficient for some look-ahead processing, and this tiny fraction of a frame won't affect lipsync. If you're using a much longer delay, of course, you'll want to slide the source clip to compensate: Make it one video frame earlier for each 33 milliseconds of delay, or one film frame (if that's how your system is calibrated) for each 42 milliseconds. Some software-based lookahead compressors take an alternative approach: they read the clip's data a little bit ahead of the timeline, so the output stays in sync.

MULTI-BAND COMPRESSOR

Remember disco? That music of the mid-70s was the first style to include a constant, thumping bass. It was great for dancing, but hard to transmit at a radio station. The bass notes were often the loudest thing in the song. They'd trigger the station's compressors, lowering the overall volume. This wasn't a problem at the studio where good monitors would let you hear the bass. But listeners with small radios wouldn't hear the bass notes, only how they affected the overall volume. The result was a song that rhythmically changed loudness for no apparent reason.

The solution was to split the signal into multiple bands, compress each separately, and combine the results—a kind of jumbo extension of the de-esser in Figure 12.11. Bass notes could be controlled without interfering with the midrange, and a loud midrange wouldn't stop the highs from sparkling. This multi-band compression changed the spectral balance of the music, letting radio stations create and jealously guard recipes for their own special sound.

The radio station multi-bands were complex, expensive boxes that also included other processes to maximize a station's volume. But about a decade ago, smaller hardware-based units started appearing in production studios. There are now a few available for the desktop producer. Figure 12.14 shows the Bias Squeez-5 plug-in. Most of the controls are what you'd expect on a normal compressor, multiplied by five—one set for each band. There are also master controls to scale all four bands.

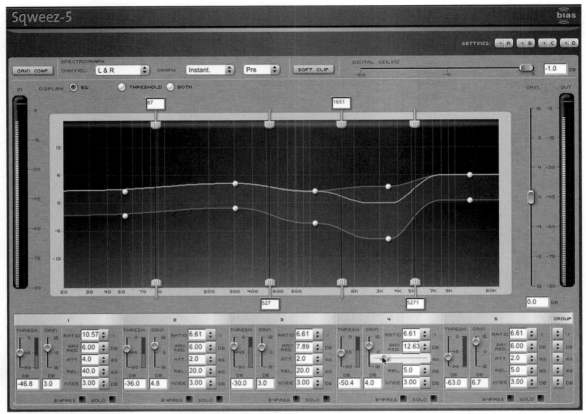

FIGURE 12.14
A five-band dynamics processor, Bias Squeez-5.

Multi-band processing is used by just about every radio, TV, and major Web broadcaster now. It's also part of the secret behind those in-your-face movie trailer and commercial voices. When combined with a low-distortion signal chain, multi-band can be the most important tool for creating consistent, strong mixes that don't sound overly processed. When I'm working on a TV show, I usually use one multi-band for the voice-over, another with more gentle settings for on-camera dialog, and a third one on the overall voice/music/effects mix.

NOISE GATE

A compressor works by inverting the envelope and then using it to control volume. But if you replace the inverter with a simple switch that turns on when the input exceeds the threshold, it becomes a *gate*. Loud signals pass through unchanged, and quieter ones are cut off. It's the audio equivalent of a luminance key. If the threshold is set just slightly louder than background noise, the gate will open for dialog but close during pauses, turning off the noise. That's why this device is called a noise gate. Gates are also useful for other things,

276

including controlling multiple mics in a quiet environment[8] and processing sound effects. Some poorly designed devices even include a noise gate to hide their own circuit noises.

 Gotcha

A gate isn't an eraser. Noise gates don't remove noise. Instead, they count on listeners being distracted by the louder sound that opened the gate. If that sound is loud enough and in the same frequency band as the noise, *masking* takes place and the noise is hidden. (Masking is used by other forms of noise reduction, and is one of the principles behind mp3.)

Unfortunately, most signal-and-noise combinations don't result in masking. We're likely to hear the background switching on and off. This can be more distracting than leaving the noise alone.

A few extra functions can make a gate's action more subtle:

- A gate's ATTACK and RELEASE controls work like the ones on a compressor. You can adjust them to smoothly fade background noise in and out.
- Some gates have adjustable bypass controls, often labeled FLOOR or RANGE and calibrated in decibels. When the gate closes, it lowers the sound by the range amount. Reducing background noise by 10 dB can sound more natural than switching to absolute silence.
- Some gates put an equalizer in the side chain. You can tune it to a voice so the gate opens only dialog, and stays closed for sounds in other bands like wind noise or camera whine.
- Most hardware gates, and a few software versions, provide external access to the side chain. This *external key* input lets you trigger one sound with another—useful in music production and special effects—or delay the main signal, creating a look-ahead gate that doesn't cut off soft initial sounds like /h/.

A few gates include other functions, including a HOLD control to keep them from reopening until a preset time has elapsed or separate open and close THRESHOLDS. These are rarely needed in audio post.

EXPANDER

An even more subtle cousin of the noise gate is the *expander*. As the name implies, it does the opposite of a compressor. Sounds below the threshold have

277

---

[8]Automated mixers, typically used when miking panel discussions, include a noise gate on each input. When people aren't speaking, their mics shut off and overall system noise is lowered.

their dynamic range increased: very soft noises are lowered and moderate background ambiences are raised in comparison. Above the threshold, the sound isn't changed.

Expanders can be better at reducing noise than gates because their action is smoother. They let soft sounds mask even softer noise, and—unless you set them to extremes—never cut sounds off entirely.

What I've described is also known as a *downward expander*, since its action takes place below the threshold. *Upward expanders* are useful for special effects because they increase dynamic range above the threshold, making loud sounds even louder but not affecting moderate sounds. In theory, an upward expander could be used to cancel out the effects of too much compression or automatic level control in a track, but getting the settings right would be virtually impossible.

COMPANDING

On the other hand, a compressor and upward expander can be designed at the same time, to have absolutely complementary actions. A signal could be compressed before it's sent through some medium, and then be expanded after it arrives. The result would sound like the original.

This *companding* is the basis for analog system noise reduction schemes like Dolby and dbx. Companding lets you send a signal with wide dynamic range, like a digital master, through an inherently noisy channel like cassette tape or optical film sound. Betacam SP video—still the professional standard for analog—also uses companding on its main audio tracks. But there's no need to use these schemes with digital recording.

 Gotcha

Surplus compander = noise reducer. Professional Dolby A—the format that used to be standard for music—has four bands of companding. Some film mixers discovered that by carefully controlling the input level to their Dolby decoders, they could use the decoders as multi-band expanders. The result would clean up noisy, but non-Dolby, tracks. Because the audio is split into multiple bands, there's more of a chance that masking occurs than with single-band expanders. These analog decoders have survived on some dub stages. But there are better digital noise reducers available today at much lower prices.

A form of companding is also used in the popular mp3 and AAC digital file compression algorithms. Audio is broken into short chunks, then the volume of each chunk is boosted to work in the algorithm's best range. The amount of boost is noted for each chunk, and on playback the volume is set back to original levels. But there's a lot more to these algorithms, described in Chapter 18.

Dynamics and Digital Broadcasting

Years ago, there were three broadcast networks. They either produced all programs or controlled the production standards. You could switch among channels and be fairly sure the volume would remain consistent among them.

Then advertisers discovered that compression and equalization could make their spots seem louder than surrounding programs. TV stations started adding similar equipment to make their programs seem louder than the competition, and at the same time partially counteract what the advertisers were doing. Today there can be more than a hundred different channels—with totally different standards—on a single cable system. Loudness is all over the place. Many people watch TV with one finger on their remote's volume control, or set their satellite or cable box to compress every signal (at the same time, destroying program dynamics and increasing noise). It's a mess.

Dolby Laboratories has taken the lead in combating this, and their standards have become part of the specification for U.S. digital TV broadcasting. It's good idea in theory.[9] The Dolby system has two primary components affecting perceived volume: *dialnorm* and *dynamic range control*.

DIALNORM

Dialnorm, also known as *dialog normalization* and sometimes just *dialog level*, is a number between -1 and -31 that gets encoded with a program's metadata[10] when it's created. This number is chosen by the producer or station, based on a measurement of the entire show's levels. It tells the receiver how many decibels to reduce the overall volume, if you want to hear the show properly. Of course producers can play games with this number, but since it's based on a technical measurement and the station is the final arbiter, it could eventually result in consistent loudness.

The problem is there are a lot of producers, a lot of stations, and for now this is a very new technology. Most programming doesn't have a dialnorm number embedded, so stations tend to set their encoders to a rough average and leave them there. Embedding is still difficult for producers—Dolby's hardware encoders are expensive, and the very few software encoders (also expensive) don't seem to come with instructions for properly determining an appropriate value.

Dialnorm is a good idea, and eventually some form of it may be used in almost all television. For now you can probably ignore it. Or check the Web for more current information.

---

[9]It'll be hard to tell whether it actually works until the majority of program sources and viewers' sets match that spec. For now, at least one major network has come out against the system.

[10]A scheme for embedding program information along with the digital audio. It can include technical specs, text descriptions of the program, copyright notice, and other useful things.

Dynamic Range Control

Another piece of Dolby metadata, dynamic range control or DRC, controls a compressor in the receiver. It adjusts the volume range around the level determined by dialnorm. Producers choose a DRC profile from the six standard ones for drama, music, or speech. This profile is then modified by the receiver for different viewing conditions or user preferences. The result is an overall dynamic range that's supposed to be right for the viewer while still respecting the producer's intention.

Again, it's a good idea… but it's also very new. There just aren't that many receivers or program streams taking advantage of DRC. How it's actually used in the field, and what you should do about it when mixing a show, belongs in the next edition of this book. Or maybe the one after it.

DYNAMICS COOKBOOK

The best settings for a compressor or expander depend on how loudly the source material was recorded, how dynamic the performance was, and even some design choices within the software. So take these recipes with a grain of salt. Use them more as suggestions for how a process could work, and listen to how they worked in the before-and-after examples on the CD.

 Hear for yourself

Tracks 51 through 58 are before-and-after examples for this section. They're described with the individual recipes.

Working with Voices

PRODUCTION AUDIO

Track 51, part 1, is a well-recorded lav track from a documentary. The male speaker has uneven dynamics which could make him difficult to mix with music, or cause problems with limited-range media like TV and Web audio.

- Part 2 of that track shows the result of moderate compression. The ratio was 4:1, and the threshold was set for about −6 dB gain reduction on peaks; in this example, it's about −13 dBFS. The attack was about 1 millisecond, but a 300 ms release prevented the fast attack from causing distortion. There is reasonably low background noise in the original, but the compression makes the background comparatively louder.
- Part 3 of that track uses downward expansion to control the background noise. Compression is turned off for this example. The threshold is chosen to be just below his softest words, in this case around −40 dBFS. Attack is about 1.5 ms, release 50 ms, and a −10 dB floor prevents noise from totally disappearing—that would sound unnatural.

- Part 4 uses the compression followed by the expansion. This version makes our subject seem stronger, makes the location cleaner, and will be easier to mix. But the differences are subtle. After you listen, go back to part 1 and compare.

Track 52, part 1, is a poorly recorded documentary track. The shooter used a camera mic (almost always a bad idea). Since the subject is far from the mic, noise is relatively louder. The similar distances from mic to subject and mic to reflective surfaces emphasizes the room's echo. The first step in cleaning it should be to use an equalizer to dip the room's resonant frequencies and notch out the noise, and to add some low-frequency energy back to the voice. But we'll skip that step for this chapter and concentrate on dynamics.

- Part 2 of Track 52 shows how a downward expander can partially hide room echoes as well as reduce apparent noise. Again, the threshold should be just below the softest words; in this case it's about -33 dBFS. The floor is increased to -25 dBFS from the previous settings. Since that makes the expander work over a wider range, there's a chance the background noises will click if they turn on or off quickly. So the attack and release time are doubled, to about 3 ms and 100 ms, respectively.

Listen carefully to part 2. The room problems are reduced during pauses, but they're still present when the subject is speaking. If a track has moderate echoes, this technique can make the echoes less annoying. But if there are extreme echoes, they'll still interfere with intelligibility during the words, even if you cut the echoes off entirely during the pauses.

While these examples use documentary audio, the voices in narrative films or broadcast can be treated the same way. Be aware that theatrical dialog usually has less radical processing: it's intended to be shown in a quiet auditorium using a wide-range monitor system, with an audience concentrating on the show, so there's less worry about softer words being lost. Some theatrical dialog is mixed with only a little limiting for protection: Set a threshold around -2 dBFS, a ratio of at least 20:1, an attack in the single-millisecond range, a release of a few dozen milliseconds, and a hard knee. If the processor has a look-ahead feature, use it.

VOICE-OVER

Announcers and narrators are usually recorded in quiet, low-echo environments. They also frequently have better control over their dynamics than interview subjects do, but compression can still smooth things out and add strength to their voices.

Track 53, part 1, is a newscast-style documentary voice-over. While the announcer has a fairly even level, she tends to stress words with volume as well as pitch.

- Part 2 fixes the stressing tendency with a compressor. The threshold is set around −12 dBFS, enough for 4- or 5-dB reduction on peaks. Ratio is 10:1, attack is about a millisecond, and—since her voice isn't particularly deep—release is around 10 ms. A male voice would require twice as long a release time.
- Part 3 shows extreme compression. It destroys most of the dynamics of her voice, but can be useful for special effects (add appropriate filters and it can be a radio or telephone for diegetic sounds) or to help intelligibility in poor playback situations. The ratio is 20:1, and the threshold moved to −35 dB—low enough that there's about −24 dB reduction for most of the words in this example. Attack is 2 ms, release is 35 ms. Although we want a fast response, these longer times are necessary because there's so much more gain reduction than in the previous settings.
- Part 4 shows the effect of a de-esser on her voice. The signal was split at about 4.5 kHz, with a Q around 0.5. Low frequencies were passed unchanged, so there's very little apparent compression on her voice. High frequencies were processed with a ratio of 8:1 and about −6 dB reduction on sibilants—in this case, a threshold of −28 dB. Attack was 1 ms, release was 5 ms; since we're dealing with highs only, there's no worry of distortion because of too fast a response time.

MULTI-BAND

If you've got a multi-band processor available, you can get more subtle control, for stronger tracks without obvious compression. Start with crossover frequencies at 200 Hz and 2 kHz for a male voice, 300 Hz and 2 kHz for a female. Attack and release times should be around 1.5 ms and 1.4 seconds respectively, on the low band, 0.7 ms and 1 second on the midband, and 0.7 ms and 750 ms on the high band. Use a ratio of 2:1, but a threshold that results in as much as −10 dB reduction on peaks.

If the multi-band also includes expansion, you can clean up soft room noises and echoes at the same time. Use a 1:4 ratio, a −18 dB floor, 0.3 ms attack and 300 ms release, and set the threshold sufficient for the expander to act only between words. Even with the fast attack time, look ahead helps avoid clipped words and makes threshold setting less critical.

MUSIC

Generally, compressing preproduced music isn't the most successful way to keep it from fighting a voice. The piece was compressed when it was mixed, and further processing will hurt the dynamics that make it interesting.[11]

If music and voice are competing so you can't mix the music as loud as you'd like, compress the voice. Then use some of the equalization techniques in the

---

[11]Compressing original music is another subject, much too big for this book. Look for a copy of David Moulton's *Total Recording*.

previous chapter. If it still competes, chances are the rhythms are conflicting. Sometimes, sliding voice or music half a dozen frames is all that's necessary to fix it. Otherwise, try editing the music differently or choose a different piece.

But some pieces of music—particularly acoustic and traditional rock—may be too dynamic for your mix, and some compression will be necessary.

- Part 1 of Track 54 is the waltz from chapter 9, compressed to remove some of its schmaltzier expression. The ratio was 8:1, and a threshold of -18 dBFS on this piece gave between -6 and -12 dB reduction on peaks. The attack was 2 ms, and the release about half a second.
- Part 2 is the rock song from that chapter, compressed to smooth out levels in the intro and to take the drums down a bit. Ratio was 10:1, and threshold was -20 dBFS; this resulted in about -12 dB reduction during the intro, and -24 dB on the drum hits. An attack time of 2 ms preserved the front edge of the drums (it could be as slow as 4 ms) and a release time of about 90 ms kept the drums from punching holes in the melody.

SOUND EFFECTS

Compressors and expanders or gates are helpful for changing the nature of sound effects, either to achieve heightened realism or to create nonrealistic designed sounds.

Track 55 shows how this can work with a recording of a mortar, a type of cannon.[12] Part 1 is the original recording. We're standing fairly close to the mortar, and then we hear a distant echo.

- Part 2 is the mortar, compressed. While the firing sound is the same, it seems to last longer because the initial reverb is increased. The distant echo is boosted to the point that it sounds like the explosion of the mortar hitting its target. The ratio is 6:1 and the threshold is -40 dBFS, enough to cause about 25 dB reduction on the initial firing. The attack is 30 ms, slow enough to retain some crunch; the release is 12 ms so the firing doesn't cause a hole.
- Part 3 is the mortar, downward expanded to keep only the firing sound. Without any echo, it seems more like a drum than a weapon. A fairly high threshold, -6 dBFS in this case, assures that most of the sound will be lost. The floor is a low 48 dB. A very fast attack, 0.01 ms (with look ahead), keeps the initial attack. The release is about 50 ms. You can also hear a tiny hit about 3/4 second after the firing, where the initial echo exceeded the threshold. If this expander had a retrigger time limit, we could have lengthened that setting to avoid the hit. But it's easy to just take out the sound with an edit.

283

---

[12]Like the effects in Chapter 10, these original recordings are © The Hollywood Edge, and used by permission.

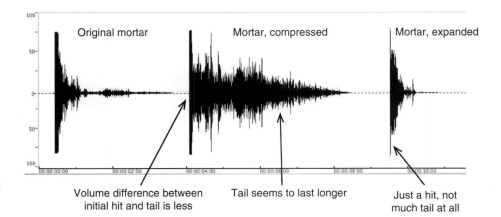

FIGURE 12.15
How compression or expansion affects the sound effect in Track 55.

The same principle can also work on background sounds. Track 56 is an interior ambience from a railroad car. With a little dynamics control, you can change its nature to make it easier to mix. Part 1 is the original sound. There are distinct mechanical noises around :05, :07, and :12.

- Part 2 uses a compressor to smooth over those noises. They're still there, but won't distract from dialog now. The ratio was 6:1, and threshold was −8 dBFS, enough to compress about −6 dB at each noise but only have about −1 dB reduction the rest of the time. Attack was 5 ms, and release was 12 ms. These are timings that could cause distortion on low frequencies, but the noises are midrange.
- Part 3 takes a different approach to improving how a sound will fit in a mix. A downward expander with a fairly high threshold suppresses most of the train's background, emphasizing occasional noises. This lets you mix the effect hotter in a scene with music, or—if you do a little editing to avoid conflicts—with dialog. Threshold was −10 dBFS, floor was −40 dB, attack and release were both 10 ms.

Track 57 shows how dynamics control can change the nature of footsteps.

- Part 1 is a man's footsteps—leather shoes on a pine floor.
- Part 2 uses a noise gate to turn those steps into high heels. Threshold is −8 dBFS, attack is a very fast 0.01 ms (with look ahead), release is 100 ms. A little echo would help the illusion.
- Part 3 was recorded by walking on gritty concrete, wearing running shoes.
- Part 4 uses a compressor to make the concrete a lot dirtier. A threshold of −35 dB (it's a soft effect) and ratio of 12:1 results in about −6 dB reduction on each step. An attack of 10 ms lets the initial hit through, and a release of 300 ms lets the gain return toward the end of the step to let us hear extra grit as the sole of the shoe pushes the concrete. A faster release, around 100 ms, could make things even dirtier.

Track 58 is an old radio effect that shows how a slow attack time can change the nature of a crash. Part 1 is a cymbal being hit with a stick. Part 2 is the same recording, only now it sounds like the instrument is being rolled with a brush. A compressor extends the original sound by making its envelope more rectangular: ratio is 12:1 and threshold is −30 dBFS (almost −36 dB reduction on the hit); it has a 0.01 ms attack and 300 ms release. Then a gate is set to trigger on the hit (−4 dBFS threshold), but the attack is a full second. This fades up on the cymbal sound instead of letting the hit through. Even though the cymbal is a musical instrument, the gate turns it into an effect. A similar process could be used on any other extended sound when you want to remove the initial hit.

Overall Mix Processing

If all your elements are properly equalized and compressed where necessary, very little overall dynamics processing is necessary for a theatrical mix. On the other hand, mixes for more restricted media like broadcast or Web often profit from a 2.5:1 ratio and −3 dB gain reduction, with a 30 ms attack and about a half-second release. This is gentle enough to keep the dynamics of the mix intact, while bringing midlevel sounds closer to the maximum. If a project is aimed at laptop computers, a 6:1 ratio and −12 dB reduction with those timings can be appropriate.

My favorite process for most TV commercial mixes—which should be loud, but never sound compressed—is to use a sharp, high-pass filter at 75 Hz followed by a 3-band compressor. The crossover frequencies are set at 200 Hz and 3.5 kHz. Ratio is 4:1 for the bass and 2.5:1 for the mids and highs, with a threshold sufficient for about −6 dB gain reduction during loud passages. Since it's rare that more than one band has that much reduction at any one time, things don't sound squashed. Attack is 30 ms for the lows and 20 ms for the mids and highs; release is 750 ms for the lows and 350 ms for the mids and highs.

It's a good idea to apply limiting to any mix. The threshold is determined by the medium, and can range from −1 dBFS for computer media to −10 dBFS for professional videotape formats. The attack should be as fast as possible, with a release around 30 ms. This is a safety valve, and very little of the mix should ever reach the threshold—if the limiter triggers more than once every half-minute or so, lower the input level. Since there's so little activity except for rare peaks, don't worry about the fast response times causing low-frequency distortion.

CHAPTER 13

Time-Domain Effects

REMEMBER THIS:

- A precisely timed delay can drastically reduce dimmer buzz and other power-line noises—but at a slight cost.
- A delay with varying timing, common in music production, can also be useful for soundtrack design.
- Artificial reverb can be an impressive effect, a cheesy one, or a natural part of realistic dialog—once you understand how it's made, and how to control it.

The equalizers and compressors described in previous chapters are primarily corrective devices. Most of the time they're used to subtly enhance a sound rather than call attention to themselves. But time-domain effects—long and short delays, and reverberation—are often in your face. You know they're there.

Reverberation is, of course, a natural part of life and art. The ancient Greeks knew how it affected intelligibility in their theaters, and how it affected emotions in their temples. Classical composers wrote differently for small spaces and giant cathedrals largely because of acoustics. Dr. Barry Blesser, who invented the first practical digital studio reverb 30 years ago, recently wrote a book about the effects of reverberant sound on ancient and modern society.[1]

But reverb as a production technique didn't exist until movies learned to talk. Producers noticed that the close miking necessary in early films was unrealistically free from reverb. It didn't appear to match the camera angle. So they built large, hard-walled rooms on the lot, fed the dialog to a speaker in those rooms, and picked up the echoes with another mic.[2] These *echo chambers* were used for

---

[1]*Spaces Speak,* Barry Blesser and Linda Salter (MIT Press 2007). It's heavy reading, but fascinating.
[2]In another example of Hollywood redefining physics, producers of early talkies decided that exterior scenes had to have more reverb than interiors. Why? Because everybody *knows* there are echoes outdoors. So in some old movies, when characters start talking outdoors, they sound like they're in a gymnasium.

special effects in radio as well. But while Hollywood studios could afford to devote rooms to reverb, radio stations couldn't. Substitute echoes often were improvised: according to radio lore, when Orson Welles created his famous *War of the Worlds* broadcast, he had some sounds miked in a nearby tile bathroom just for the reverb.

By mid-century, the primary replacement for an acoustic echo chamber was suspended springs or thin metal plates, coupled to a speaker on one end and a pickup on the other. Vibrations bouncing between the sides of the device acted like sound reverberating in a closed space. If a long delay was also needed to simulate the time it takes sound to travel in a large space, it was done by forcing sound through a very long hose,[3] or recording and playing back on a short loop of magnetic tape.

Digital reverb was invented in 1959, but only as a lab curiosity. A one-minute piece of audio could take a full day to process. It was another dozen years before practical all-electronic delays were available. It wasn't until the mid-70s that the first digital studio reverb was born: Dr. Blesser's EMT 250—a box the size of a small file cabinet, with spaceship-like levers on top.

Today, a variety of excellent sounding low-cost delays and reverbs are available as software plug-ins and DSP-driven hardware. The newest ones will even analyze a test signal played in a concert hall or shooting stage, and then duplicate that room's characteristic reverb. But even the simpler delays and processor-efficient simulations that came with your NLE can be useful:

- While boom mic operators are careful to pick up a mix of the room's natural echoes along with dialog, artificial reverb is necessary to make lavs or ADR sound right.
- Reverb can be used to spread sounds out in implied physical space—even on a mono track—giving you more ways to keep sounds from competing in a mix.
- Delays can be used as a filter to almost completely eliminate some kinds of noise.
- Both reverb and delay can be used as special effects, ranging from subtle enhancements that make a sound seem to be moving, to outright science-fiction or underwater effects.

 Gotcha

You're on your own? This chapter doesn't have a cookbook section at its end. There are too many different ways that time-based effects can be built. Instead, there are sample recipes with the description of each effect. Start with these. Then go nuts with other settings.

---

[3]The speed of sound is roughly 1 foot per millisecond in air. It's the same whether those feet are across a football stadium or in a coiled garden hose with a speaker at one end and a microphone at the other.

REVERB VS. ECHO VS. DELAY

These aren't the same thing.

Reverberation is the collection of thousands of random reflections that real-world spaces contribute to a sound, or it's a simulation that includes specific kinds of individual and modified repeats. As you can guess, good reverb software is very complex.

Echo is a series of evenly spaced repeats that get softer and softer. It doesn't sound like natural reverb. On the other hand, it's very simple to create and might not require specialized software at all.

Delay is a simple, single repeat of a sound. With some tweaks and additional functions, it can be an incredibly useful effect.

THE SHORT DELAYS

A single repeat of a sound, within about 20 ms from the original, may not get heard as an echo at all. Instead, it blends with the original and changes it in interesting ways. By constantly changing the delay time, mixing with other delays, and routing some of its output back to the input, we can create a family of fascinating effects.

Comb Filter

Imagine a sine wave at a fixed frequency. If you mix it with a delayed version of itself, precisely one-half cycle later, the delayed version will be positive while the original is negative. It will cancel itself out. Figure 13.1 shows how this could happen when a 1 kHz wave is mixed with a version ½-millisecond later. On the top is the original signal; in the middle is the delayed version; the sum of the two is on the bottom. Except for that first half cycle, the result is silence.

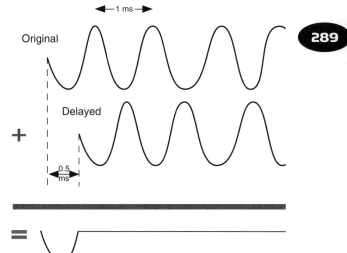

The interesting thing about this effect is that it works for any regular signal, even ones that are rich with harmonics. The delay effectively creates a series of nulls and boosts, extending across the audio band. Figure 13.2 is a spectrogram of *pink noise*, a random air-rushing sound that has equal energy in each octave and is frequently used as a test signal. On the left side of the figure is the original noise. On the right, I've mixed in a 5-ms delayed version of the noise. The dark lines are the frequencies that have been completely filtered out.

FIGURE 13.1
If you mix a constant-frequency wave with one that's delayed exactly one half cycle, the result is mostly silence.

These lines appear to get closer as the frequency increases, but that's only because this spectrogram has a logarithmic scale. If you match the lines to the numbers, you'll see that they're every 200 Hz (starting with 100 Hz). If the

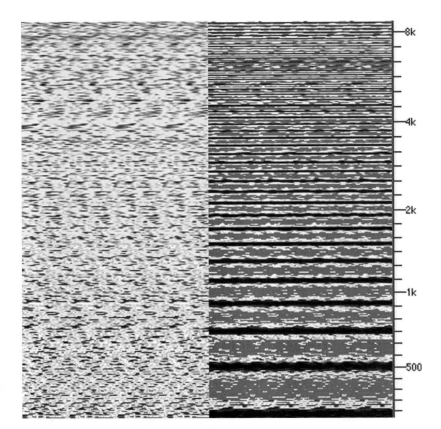

FIGURE 13.2
Pink noise on the left; the same noise combined with a 5-ms delayed version of itself on the right.

290

frequency scale were linear, they'd be as evenly spaced as the teeth of a barber's comb—and that's how this filter got its name.[4]

The location of a comb filter's notches can be predicted with grade-school math. The first notch is at a frequency equal to one-half of the delay in seconds. For our five millisecond example, that's $\frac{1}{0.010}$ (one millisecond = 0.001 second, in case you'd forgotten), or 100 Hz. Every subsequent notch is spaced twice that frequency higher. Twice 100 Hz is 200 Hz, so the next notches are at Hz, 500 Hz, 700 Hz, 900 Hz, and so on.

HUM ELIMINATION USING A COMB

Unlike a traditional equalizer, a comb filter can be sharp without doing damage at other frequencies. This can make it useful for getting rid of constant-frequency harmonically rich signals, such as power-line or dimmer buzz

[4]Not as an abbreviation for "combination filter," as I've heard some people insist. What could it be a combination *of*?

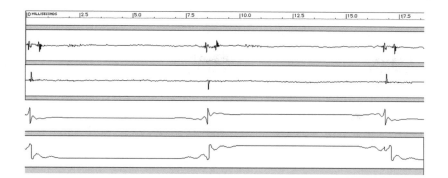

FIGURE 13.3
Power line buzzes can look like these waves. Since they're based on the line frequency, they'll always repeat every 16.66 ms, with a subpattern halfway between.

(Figure 13.3). These annoying noises have lots of upper harmonics from the 60 Hz line frequency,[5] but a notch every 120 Hz will nail them. You could create those notches by mixing the signal with a delay of 8.333 ms. The first notch would be at 240 Hz. There often aren't any components at lower frequencies; but if there were, you could get rid of them with a parametric equalizer.

The problem is a comb's notches are so narrow that absolute precision is necessary. Most desktop software won't let you specify a delay to the thousandth of a millisecond. On top of that, there can be tiny variations in the camera's or NLE's sample rate; these could change the buzz frequency. So it's unlikely you could turn a delay plug-in into an effective comb. But there's an easy workaround: open the noisy clip in multi-track audio software, make a copy of it on a second track, zoom in to a section that's mostly buzz, and slide the copy about 25 ms[6], so you see an inverted version of the pattern of the original. Keep sliding until the pattern and its inverse are perfectly lined up against each other. Mix the two together.

The process isn't perfect (which is why it's always better to eliminate buzzes before you shoot). That 25 ms delay is long enough to hear as an echo, and it adds a metallic hollowness to the track. You can reduce the hollowness, if you're willing to put back a little buzz, by lowering the delayed track −3 dB before you mix.

291

 Hear for yourself

Track 59 is an interview track with considerable dimmer buzz—it's actually the clip shown at the top of Figure 13.3—before and after applying the comb, and then with the comb lowered −3 dB.

---

[5]In the United States. If your local power is at some other frequency, make the appropriate adjustments.
[6]16.6 ms for the basic wave, then another 8.3 ms for another half-wave.

Flanger

Imagine a comb filter where you could constantly vary the delay. The notches would keep moving, imparting a *swooshing* to the audio. In fact, you've heard this effect countless times in pop music and science-fiction films (and you can hear a reprise on part 3 of Track 60).

The effect predates digital delays by close to 20 years. It was originally accomplished by using two tape decks. These had a playback head right after the record head (video people would call it a *confidence monitor*). Since those heads can't be in the same space, there was a delay between them: 60 ms to 400 ms, depending on how far apart the heads were and how fast the tape was moving.

A musical signal would be sent to both recorders, and their outputs would be mixed together. Then an engineer would drag a few fingers on the outer flange of one of the tape reels. The more pressure, the more that recorder would slow down, making its delay longer. The other recorder would still be at normal speed, so the two outputs would combine into a comb filter. By varying the pressure, the engineer could make the comb slide up and down the band. It added a moving tonality to the sound without changing its pitch. We called the technique *flanging*.

Figure 13.4 shows a modern flange effect. The solid lines are audio paths; the dashed ones are the control. Essentially, the original signal is mixed with a delayed version of itself. One knob lets you set the basic DELAY time, usually in a range around 0.5–100 ms. The MODULATION SPEED controls a *low-frequency oscillator (LFO)* in a range from about one-tenth Hertz to a few Hertz. This slow wave modifies the basic delay time in a range set by the MODULATION DEPTH control, usually calibrated in Hertz or percent. For example: if the basic delay

292

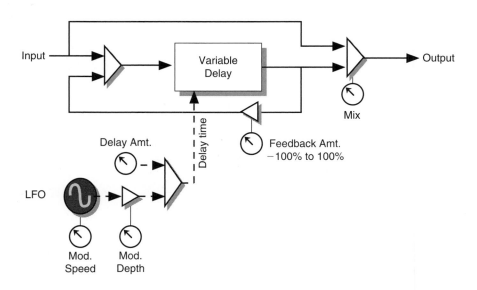

FIGURE 13.4
A flange effect.

were 10 ms, the modulation speed were 1 Hz, and the depth were 4 ms, the actual delay time would change once per second from 6 ms to 14 ms and back.

A MIX control sets the proportion of original signal to delayed, so you can change the depth of the notches. It's usually calibrated from 0 (no delay) through 100 percent (all delay with no original). A FEEDBACK control lets some of the delayed signal recirculate through the delay, which intensifies the effect. It's often calibrated from −100 percent through zero to +100 percent, because negative feedback (that is, with the waveform inverted) can sound different from positive feedback.

Not every flanger has all these features, but good ones have most of them. A few add a switch to control the LFO waveform, which can have a profound effect.

Here are some recipes to give you an idea of what a flanger can do. All of them can be heard on Track 60. Part 1 of that track is unprocessed voice and music samples for reference.

- To add vibrato to a voice (Track 60, part 2), set the DELAY to 2 ms, the SPEED to 6.5 Hz, the DEPTH to 5 percent, and the MIX to 100 percent.
- For classic *wooshing* on music or effects (part 3), use a lot of feedback. Set DELAY to 0 ms, SPEED to 0.15 Hz, DEPTH to 10 percent, MIX to 50 percent, and FEEDBACK to 90 percent. Try it with FEEDBACK at −90 percent as well.
- A more subtle woosh, with no feedback, can add motion to real-world sounds. Part 4 of the track is a steady helicopter exterior, with no processing. But with some flanging (part 5), you can make the helicopter move. Settings were 0 ms DELAY, 0.1 Hz SPEED, 10 percent DEPTH, 50 percent MIX, and no FEEDBACK. I've done similar effects on national car spots.
- To put voices underwater (part 6), use a 4 ms DELAY, 1.5 Hz SPEED, 15 percent DEPTH, 100 percent MIX, and no FEEDBACK. If your flanger lets you select a triangle waveform, use it. A small amount of reverb can heighten this effect.

While these are the settings I used for the CD examples, subtle changes in any of them may produce a sound more compatible with your source material.

 Hear for yourself

Track 60 demonstrates flanging effects on voice, music, and sound effects.

Chorus

Imagine a telescoping trough that lets you change its length, while you're sending a steady stream of ball bearings into it. Okay, that might be difficult to

293

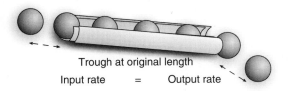

FIGURE 13.5
A trough, with ball bearings running through it.

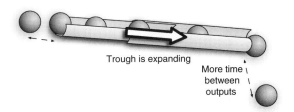

FIGURE 13.6
If you start expanding the trough's length (top), the output slows down compared to the input.

imagine. So I drew one in Figure 13.5. There's a delay before the first ball comes out, because that ball has to travel the length of the trough. Then balls start coming out at the same rate as they went in.

But if you start extending the trough (Figure 13.6), the output slows down compared to the input rate! That's because each ball has to travel a little bit farther than the one before it. When the trough settles at its new length, the output resumes its normal rate.

Replace the ball bearings with individual samples, and the trough with digital memory: you've got a variable delay. When you increase the length of the delay, output samples slow down and the pitch lowers. If you decrease the length, each sample travels a shorter path than the one before, and the pitch goes up. That's how the vibrato effect above works. With the MIX control set to 100 percent, there isn't any comb filtering, but the LFO constantly changing the DELAY length makes the voice warble in pitch.

Take a bunch of flangers, eliminate the feedback loops, and make tiny variations in their LFO frequencies, and you can simulate the tiny pitch variations that happen when a group of people sing the same note. You could turn one voice into many. That's why it's called a *chorus* effect. Figure 13.7 shows one way of building a chorus effect (there are others, but they all sound pretty much the same). Each LFO runs at a slightly different speed, partly determined by the master SPEED control. A RANGE control, usually 1 to 100 percent, sets how much speed variation there'll be. If it's set to a low value, the LFOs all run at about the same speed; at a high value, they can be very different.

 Gotcha

It doesn't sound like any choir to me. Chorus is a fairly simple process and too unchanging to be absolutely realistic. If you want to make one person sound like a real crowd, you also have to include random and subtle changes in the pitch and timing of each voice relative to the others. It takes a lot of computing. We'll describe such an effect in Chapter 14.

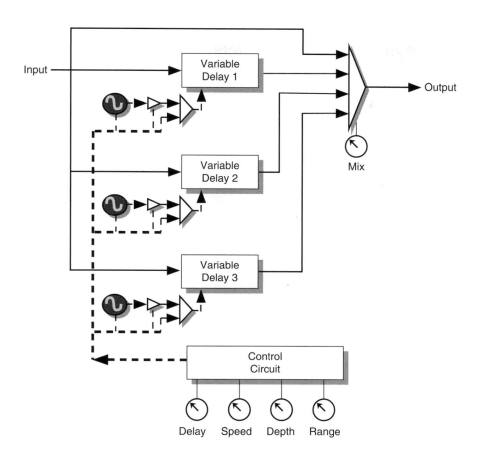

FIGURE 13.7
One way of building a chorus effect.

 Gotcha

Pitch shift? Then turn me into Darth Vader... Sorry, Luke. A chorus-based pitch shift that could smoothly knock your voice down and keep it there would require a constantly growing delay. Your computer would run out of memory.

There are ways around this, but that's for the next chapter.

Here are a few chorus recipes:

- Track 61, part 1 shows a basic chorus effect on speech. You can hear the original voice in the middle with two phantom voices, at slightly different pitches, on the sides. Part 2 is the same process as a mono effect. It sounds something like an echo, but there's still that pitch variation. Part 3 shows the process on music; chorusing is often used to thicken a vocal soloist. The settings were 10 ms DELAY, 0.16 Hz RATE, 10 percent DEPTH, 70 percent RANGE, and 45 percent MIX.

- Part 4 could work as the introduction to a dream sequence. It uses more delay and a faster LFO to spread the phantom voices' pitch and timing unrealistically. Set to 100 ms DELAY, 3.5 Hz RATE, 8 percent DEPTH, 15 percent RANGE, and 25 percent MIX. Or start with 0 percent MIX and gradually raise it as the character falls asleep.
- While chorus is usually used for music production or special vocal processing, I've found it can be wonderful on steady sound effects. It makes them bigger, without the distancing or blurring that reverb can cause. Listen to part 5 of Track 61. The first sound is the unflanged helicopter used earlier in this chapter. The second is the same effect with a chorus. Instead of being next to the chopper, the blades now surround us! Use a 2.5 ms DELAY, 2 Hz RATE, 25 percent DEPTH, 20 percent RANGE, and 50 percent MIX.

Hear for yourself

Track 61 demonstrates various chorus effects.

LONG DELAYS

There are actually two differences between the effects discussed above, and longer *delays* (also known as *digital delay lines* or *DDLs*). One difference is obviously length: The effects in the previous section range from 0–100 ms, and DDLs usually run 10 ms to more than half a second. The other difference is architecture. A long delay line may or may not have an LFO for modulation, but it should include a high shelf equalizer in the feedback loop. The shelf is usually calibrated between about −36 dB and 0 dB loss. This is to simulate real-world losses of highs in air because of friction. Figure 13.8 shows the configuration of most delay lines.

It's the feedback loop that makes delays useful in post (without it, you could accomplish the same thing by simply copying a clip later on a different track). Feedback lets you keep recycling a sound for multiple repeats. This effect is used a lot in music production, with delays chosen to match the song's

FIGURE 13.8
A delay line. Unlike the previous effects, there's often no LFO. But there usually is a shelf equalizer to simulate real-world losses when sound travels a long distance in air.

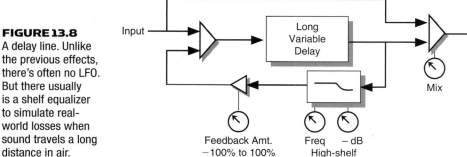

rhythm. Some very long delays are even used for live improvisational music: The performer plays a few bars or a chord progression into a DDL, sets it to keep repeating forever, and then jams against it.

The FEEDBACK control is calibrated from −100 percent to +100 percent. Negative numbers invert the polarity of the audio, which can change the overall effect when the delayed version is mixed with the input.

- Track 62 part 1 plays our two musical examples through a rhythmic repeat. The delay is about 500 ms (this value works fine for the first song in the montage, but is obviously wrong for the second). Other settings were −50 percent feedback, 85 percent mix, and the filter was −3.5 dB at 15 kHz to prevent hiss buildup.

Delays are useful for creating reverberation for outdoor environments, where there are often a few distinct echoes from large buildings or geologic features, rather than the many closely spaced reflections you'd hear in an enclosed space. Start with a rough guess as to how far that reflecting surface would be in feet, and dial that number into the delay in milliseconds. If there's also supposed to be a surface behind you, add a little feedback.

- With a lot of feedback and very short times, delays can act as resonant combs. This adds a metallic edge to a voice, much like C3PO's in *Star Wars*. Listen to part 2 of Track 62, and then create the effect yourself with a 10 ms DELAY, 75 percent FEEDBACK, 90 percent MIX, and no equalization.
- A properly tuned delay can emulate some of the low-budget attempts at artificial reverb, such as tape-based echo. It was a favorite trick at radio stations in the 60s and 70s, and required a tape deck with separate record and playback heads. A little of the delayed playback would be mixed with the signal being fed to the deck, causing a repeating echo that got softer over time. The sound would also get duller, as high frequencies were lost in the usually misadjusted tape deck. Part 3 of Track 65 shows this effect with a moderately high tape speed; it uses a 95 percent MIX, 90 ms DELAY, 35 percent FEEDBACK, and −13 dB LOSS at 10 kHz. Part 4 is at a slower tape speed; the DELAY is changed to 180 ms and the EQUALIZATION to −24 dB at 6 kHz.

Of course, that tape echo doesn't sound like the live reverberation in a concert hall or even the simulation in a good software plug-in. That's because reverb is a complicated process.

REVERBERATION

You're in a concert hall, perhaps 50 feet from the middle of the stage. A percussionist on the middle of the stage strikes a wood block. We'll round off the speed of sound to keep things simple, and assume it travels 1000 feet per second[7] (or 1 foot per millisecond). So 50 ms later, you hear the *tock*.

297

---

[7]That's about 10 percent slower than the real speed of sound. To hear that difference in the real world, you'd need a *gigantic* concert hall.

But that's not all you hear:

- **The sound spreads from the wood block in all directions.** Concert halls usually have reflective walls surrounding the stage area, so the music is focused towards the audience. Perhaps the *tock* hits the rear wall of the stage, 20 feet behind the player, and then bounces back to you. You hear this softer sound 90 ms after it's played, or 50 ms after you hear the first *tock* (20 ms to the rear wall, then 70 ms from the rear wall to you). The sound also hits the sides of the stage and bounces to you. Maybe it goes a little farther—it's a wide stage—and you hear an even softer *tock* at 115 ms. Unless you're sitting exactly on the hall's centerline, you'll be closer to one stage wall than the other. Echoes from the more distant one arrive a little later.
- **Sounds don't stop at your ear.** They continue into the room, where they bounce off surfaces behind you. By now there are so many different-length paths involved, that the reflections arrive too closely together to tell them apart. They merge into a single, long sound. If the concert hall was well designed the merged sound is warm and pleasing, flattering the wood block.
- **Soon, air friction and human bodies in the hall will absorb the sound's energy** to the point where you can't hear it any more. That flattering reverberation dies out. But air friction, human bodies, and wall treatments absorb sound differently depending on frequency. So the reverb dies out unevenly, changing timbre as it does.

The 50 ms it takes the first direct sound to reach you isn't considered part of the sound. While it can be important for video, if there's a tight shot of the wood block and you want lipsync (stick-sync?), it's not an effect we hear.

But the time between the direct sound and the first reflection—40 ms in this case—gives our ears a hint of the size of the room. It's called the *initial delay* or *predelay*,[8] and reverb software should give you control over it.

The spacing and volume of *early reflections* (first 150 ms or so) tells us more about the size of the room, and where we are in it. The timbre of the reflections, relative to the direct sound, gives us an idea of the nature of the room's wall surfaces. Better artificial reverbs let you manipulate all of these factors.

The combined reflections that occur later, merging into a continuous sound, are considered the *reverberation* proper. It's often identified as *late reverb* to avoid confusion. The envelope of this reverb and its timbre are what makes a concert hall sound different from a gymnasium or cathedral. Any reverb program should let you control the decay, usually known as REVERB TIME. Most programs allow some equalization of the late reverb, to simulate different kinds of wall treatments. A few programs give you control over the initial attack, and some even

---

[8]The name makes sense if you consider that before digital reverberators existed, initial delay was created by patching a tape-based delay ahead of a spring or plate reverb.

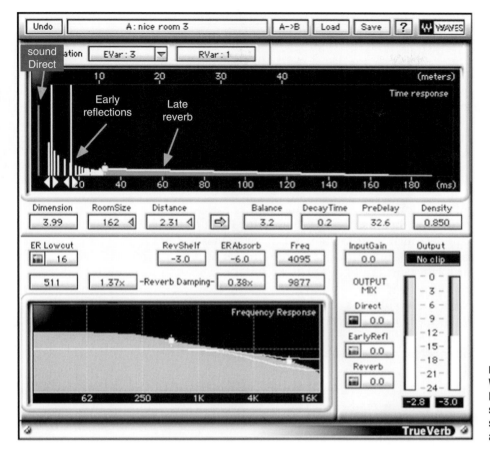

FIGURE 13.9
With some plug-ins, like Wave's TrueVerb shown here, you can see where reflections and reverb will occur.

split the reverb into different bands so the envelope can be different for highs and lows.

Conventional Reverbs

Waves' TrueVerb does a particularly nice job of visualizing the different parts of reverberation. In the top of Figure 13.9, you can see the single direct sound, a group of discrete early reflections, and the smoother late reverb. (This particular setup simulates a large but somewhat absorbent room.) On the bottom are equalizer controls for both the early reflections and late reverb.

One other control is critical: the MIX, or how much reverb you hear relative to the direct sound. It's usually calibrated 0 to 100 percent, but some software gives you separate controls to adjust levels of direct sound, early reflections, and late reverb in decibels. Unfortunately, there's no consistent way to predict where any of these mix settings should be—they depend both on how the software was designed, and how that particular setup has been tuned. You'll have to train your ears by paying attention to echoes in the real world: In most spaces, echoes are not as loud as you'd imagine. Do this ear-calibration live, while you're in various rooms. Don't do it by listening to dialog tracks you've already shot.

Unless you're simulating an unusually echoey space or other special effect, reverb levels should be just at the edge of consciousness. You should notice that the reverb is missing when you turn it off, but otherwise you shouldn't be aware of its presence unless you're actively listening for it. Short reverbs can be a little louder than long ones. Close-ups should have less reverb than long shots, since we're closer to the subject. But the shift should be subtle: don't change the reverb with each camera cut. A character's dialog should have consistent reverb throughout a scene, unless they're moving a large distance.

In standalone audio mixers and sophisticated multi-track software, reverb is usually patched into an *effects bus*. Each input channel has a separate knob to set how much of its signal will be sent to that bus, and it also has a switch to determine if this SEND stays proportional to the channel's fader level or if it stays constant. The bus goes to the input of a reverb processor; the processor's output is then added to the mix through a separate RETURN knob. If you're using a setup like this, any MIX control within the processor itself should be at 100 percent: early reflections and late reverb, but no direct signal.

Sampling or Convolution Reverbs

While reverb simulations have gotten very good, modern desktop computers are powerful enough for a different approach. Convolution reverbs (the name comes from the mathematical process involved) use recordings of actual reverberations in real spaces, analyze how the room is responding, and then apply a matching reverb to your signal. At the touch of a button, your studio-recorded ADR or Foley can be put into a fairly convincing living room, car interior, or wherever the actor is supposed to be.

While it's possible to record your own reverb samples, it's not practical on a film set. So commercial convolution reverbs come with large libraries of *impulse responses* recorded in spaces ranging from cathedrals to car interiors. They also come with tuning controls, letting you fine-tune the size and feel of a room. Figure 13.10 shows the most popular convolution plug-in for film mixes, Audio Ease's Altiverb, with a few of its postproduction impulse responses. The photo on the right of the panel is the actual space they recorded; the two speaker icons on the bottom let you position a sound source within the selected space.

REVERB AND DISTANCING

In real-world interiors, echoes increase as you get farther from a sound source (something you probably learned, to your dismay, if you ever shot dialog with a camera-mounted mic). We usually stand farther away from large noisy objects than we do from small ones, so there's a tendency to associate amount of reverb with size.

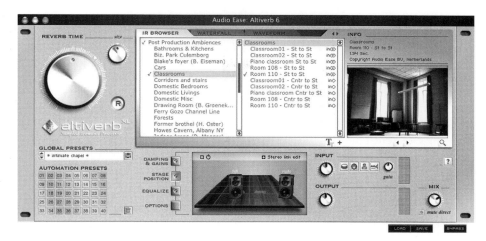

FIGURE 13.10
Altiverb uses recordings of actual reverb in selected spaces, duplicating it on your track.

Most of the time, this works. If a scene is set on a factory floor and you want to imply a large machine, feel free to give it a lot of reverb. But don't confuse reverb and size: One's related to distance and room construction, and the other is usually reflected in volume and timbre. I've had advertising producers insist I put large, long echoes on their up-close and personal voice-overs to make them "bigger." All that really does is destroy the intimacy by moving the announcer farther away.

My personal preference is to avoid reverb any time someone is talking to us from limbo or in front of a drape. That includes voice-overs, of course. It also includes on-camera spokespeople and demonstrators, and interviews where we're not aware of the questioner or surroundings. This keeps their voices in the same room as we viewers, just as their nondescript background doesn't suggest a specific locale. But if we can see where they are—if the scene has walls, furniture, or other fixtures—we should hear that room's echoes as well.

REVERB SETTINGS

Most reverb software comes with factory presets, but these are almost always designed for music mixing and emulate large, flattering spaces. They're much too big and wet[9] for the primary use of reverb in video: matching ADR, foley, or dry lav tracks to what we're seeing on the screen. So you'll have to develop your own settings.

Before you grab knobs and start tweaking, think about the space you're trying to simulate. Decide how far the sound source is from the walls, and where we're listening from (usually presumed to be the camera position). Turn feet into milliseconds, and you'll have a good idea of when the early reflections should start.

---

[9]Recording engineers use this adjective to describe a signal with lots of reverb; "dry" means a signal without any reverb.

Consider the round trip distance that sound has to travel as a clue to how the reflections are spaced. Then ask yourself what's in the room to absorb sound; this tells you about the late reverb's timbre and how long it should last.

Track 63, part 1, has two voices close-miked in a dead studio. Part 2 is subtly different: A tight reverb is simulating a large but absorbent room (perhaps a blue-jean store, since clothes soak up a lot of echo), with the actors close to camera. You might have to switch between these two examples a few times to hear the difference, but it's there and can make the voices more realistic.

- For the large and absorbent room in part 2, EARLY REFLECTIONS started at 40 ms and clustered between the 40 ms and about 100 ms. The LATE REVERB grew quickly, was wide band, and had a 0.3 second DECAY. For what it's worth, on this software, the MIX was set to 40 percent.
- Part 3 is a smaller, but more reverberant room. EARLY REFLECTIONS are between 16 ms and 40 ms. The LATE REVERB also grows quickly and has about a 0.7 second DECAY, though the highs decay a little faster. Since this is a longer reverb, the MIX was somewhat less: using the same software as part 2, it was at 25 percent.

Hear for yourself

Track 63 demonstrates the reverb settings in this Chapter.

Larger spaces—theaters, stadiums, cathedrals, and the like—have radically different reverb characteristics from the previously mentioned spaces. But reverb software already comes with plenty of presets for these larger spaces, because those presets are used in music. Find one you like, tweak at random until you like the sound, and make sure the reverb hasn't hurt intelligibility.

Gotcha

Dude, where's my tail? Many NLEs apply effects to a clip. That works in most cases, but not if you're adding reverb that should continue after a clip's out-point. The late reverb can't make it to the timeline, since the clip stops before it does.

As a workaround, export the clip as an audio file. Using an audio program, add some silence to its end. Then re-import to the timeline.

Some multi-track audio software lets you apply this extra tail automatically, whenever you add delay-based effects to a clip.

Music Reverbs and Special Effects

Music and large sound effects can sound good with longer and louder reverb than you'd apply to a voice, so factory presets are fine for those sounds. Articulation isn't an issue, and these sounds are usually flattered by warm, long, late reflections.

Unless you're producing original music for your project, chances are the score already has appropriate reverb in the mix. Adding more will just muddy things up. But there are a couple of cases where a bit of controlled reverb is useful on a preproduced music track:

- A medium-length late reverb can smooth over music edits,[10] by letting instruments decay across the cut. Part 4 of Track 63 has this reverb. You probably won't even notice it when the music's playing, but you can hear it in two places where the music stops abruptly. EARLY REFLECTIONS are within the first 50 ms, then the LATE REVERB builds up very quickly and has a 3.3 second DECAY. The MIX was 35 percent.
- Source music should be run through a reverb set to match the dialog's sound. This overall wash, on top of the reverb applied to individual instruments when the music was mixed, will help place the sound in the room.
- If you have to fade out of a sustained note at the end of a song because the original is held too long for the video, running through a concert-hall preset after the fade can help. It won't sound like the instruments' natural decay, but can add a nice tail that *almost* suggests the musicians stopped playing. Try to sneak the reverb in gently, a few notes before the end.

Heavily equalized reverbs, or ones where the decay times are radically different for high and low frequencies, can suggest unusual spaces without having to be so loud that they affect intelligibility.

- Part 5 is voices inside a large steel tank. There are no early reflections, and late reverb starts with a medium-fast attack a few milliseconds after the direct sound. But while high frequencies decay in about two seconds, lows take about 10 seconds to decay.

You can add predelay to suggest immense spaces, even if your software doesn't have controls for the early reflections. The bottom half of Figure 13.11 shows some settings from Premiere's reverb, an oversimplified reverb that doesn't even generate early reflections. So I put a multitap delay *ahead* of it in the filters list. The result is a reasonably good railroad station announcement, part 6 of Track 63. Add a high-pass filter around 500 Hz to simulate losses in the PA system, and it's near perfect (part 7 of Track 63).

303

---

[10]This reverb won't help music edits that are basically *wrong*. You still have to respect the beat and chords (Chapter 9).

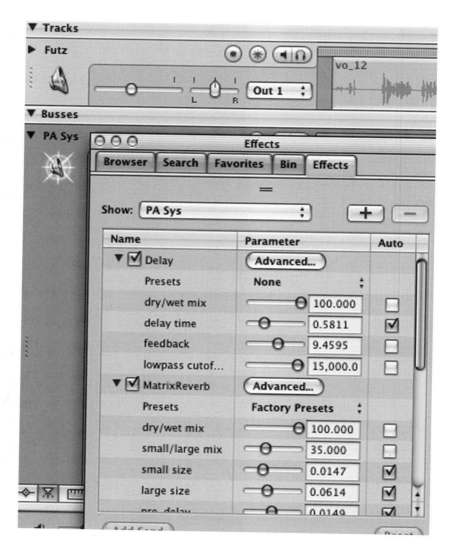

FIGURE 13.11
Stacking a delay
ahead of a reverb, to
make a giant room or
stadium.

One popular fantasy effect is the precognitive reverb, which builds up *before* the direct sound:

1. Take an audio clip and add a few seconds of silence to the head.
2. Use a backwards or reverse function in an audio program, or set the clip speed to −100 percent in a NLE.
3. Apply a reverb. In the CD example, the EARLY REFLECTIONS were within the first 40 ms. The LATE REVERB lasted three seconds, and it was damped with a −3 dB loss at 3 kHz. But since this isn't a natural effect we're creating, other settings can work just as well.
4. Render the reverb, creating a new file that sounds echoey even without a reverb plug-in assigned to it.

5. Repeat step 2. It will now sound like part 8 of Track 63.

6. You can assign the same reverb to the processed track, for a reverb that builds up to the direct sound and then decays after it. The result is part 9 of Track 63.

The reverb settings for this example were EARLY REFLECTIONS within about 40 ms, a LATE REVERB time of about three seconds, and about −3 dB LOSS at 3 kHz.

UNINTENTIONAL TIME-DOMAIN ISSUES

Sometimes, delays are the natural result of other audio processes and can't be avoided. But if you don't know to expect them, they can cause problems. If they're big delays the picture will look out of sync. If they're tiny ones—too small to even perceive as a delay—they might still ruin the sound or affect a performance.

Latency

One unfortunate side effect of the digital revolution is that *things take time*. Back in analog days, electronic signals flowed across studio wiring at a small fraction of the speed of light. But even that's still pretty darned fast. Considering that there were rarely more than a few dozen feet of wire and components to travel through, we could consider it instantaneous.

Bits move just as fast as analog signals on a wire, but computing equipment takes time to think about them. Even though chips may operate in the giga-hertz range, they've got a lot of math to deal with. This *latency* can add a couple of milliseconds for an audio sample to move from one end of a process to the other. Conversions between analog and digital can take even longer, though still usually less than a dozen milliseconds.

What's a few milliseconds among friends? Well, if the output of a process gets mixed with its input, you have a comb filter. It can change the timbre of a sound.

- If a track starts sounding hollow—almost as if it were being miked from too far, in a hard-walled room—suspect that inputs and digital outputs are being mixed somewhere. Having the wrong faders up on an external mixer is often the culprit.

- If talents' headphones are being fed by a digital output while they per-form, the signal has been delayed twice: once at the analog to digital conversion, and again when it's converted back to analog for the phones. What they hear through their phones will mix with the live acoustic sound of their voice in the room, causing hollowness or a disturbing echo in their heads. Many USB and FireWire input converters have a low-latency headphone output that bypasses most of the digital processing. Feed the talents' phones with that, even if you're monitoring the full digi-tal path yourself.

External Processor Delay

Good multi-track audio software knows how long each plug-in processor takes. During playback, it compensates by reading data for the tracks that are being processed a little bit ahead of data for the unprocessed tracks.

NLEs seldom have this capability. Since a plug-in's latency is rarely more than a few milliseconds, it won't affect lipsync and isn't a problem. But if you're processing just one channel of a stereo pair, the latency will be enough to affect stereo imaging and mono compatibility.

- Always process stereo and multi-channel signals symmetrically, with the same plug-ins on each channel of a specific element.[11] If one channel doesn't need processing, set its plug-in's controls to neutral.

Most software can't compensate for the delay through external hardware effects, such as a rack-mount voice processor you've patched into a dialog track. Latency in most external units isn't enough for this to be a problem, but a few—such as compressors with long lookahead times—can delay things a third of a frame or more. If they seem to be affecting lipsync, slide that track a little earlier on the timeline.

Unexpected Delays

Digital video requires a lot of processing, and that can slow things down enough to knock a picture out of sync.

HD cameras have to scan pixels in an imaging chip, and reassemble the data in DSP chips. Depending on the camera's settings, this can take almost two frames! If audio isn't delayed to match, the sound will be recorded on tape ahead of the picture. If you suspect this is a problem, test your camera by recording a slate or hand clap; then examinine its sync in an NLE. After you learn exactly how long a camera takes for a particular shooting mode, you can slide tracks to compensate.

LCD monitors also have to process and scan, and a large screen can introduce a frame or more of video delay. But you can't compensate by sliding the track to match, since this would introduce unpredictable sync errors on other monitors, and make it difficult to place effects when still-framed. A few multi-track audio programs let you dial in *dynamic offsets*: these change depending on the viewing speed to compensate.

The real-time data compressors used for live recordings via ISDN and Internet have a few frames delay under ideal circumstances, and can introduce a few seconds' worth at times. This is a problem if you're recording sync-critical ADR at a distance. There are ways to compensate at the session, but it takes thoughtful engineering.

---

[11]For example, process the left and right channels of a stereo music pair symmetrically. This doesn't mean you have to process dialog or other elements the same way, since they weren't paired to begin with.

CHAPTER 14

Time and Pitch Manipulation

REMEMBER THIS:

- You can change the timing of an audio clip, speeding it up or slowing it down to fit a shot, without changing the pitch.
- Or you can change the pitch without affecting the tempo, retuning music and noises, creating cartoon and science-fiction effects, or altering the character of a voice.
- Humans have two independent factors determining the pitches of their voices. For successful voice-changing, you have to respect both.
- These processes always cause some distortion. If you want good results, understanding how they work will help you choose the best options.

Back in analog days, you'd sometimes hear a radio station run a recording at the wrong speed. If it was too fast, the sounds would be jammed together and come out in a little chipmunk voice.[1] If it was too slow, everything would be deep and s-t-r-e-t-c-h-e-d o-u-t. These effects became a comic cliché.

For most of the history of recorded sound, time and pitch have been inextricably linked. You couldn't change one without affecting the other. (In the late 1960s, there was a device that used a variable-speed tape recorder with rotary spinning heads to accomplish this. It was expensive and mechanically cumbersome, and didn't catch on.)

But in the early 70s, digital devices appeared that could change a sound's pitch in real time. The quality was low, and the devices were originally used to raise the pitch of slowed-down tapes for speech research. By the late 70s, they'd made it into recording studios—still with low quality, but useful as a special effect. In the 80s, you could buy a pitch compensator capable of almost a 10

---

[1]In fact, that's how David Seville created the Chipmunks—Simon, Theodore, and *Alvin!*—in his 1958 hit record and about thirty years of songs and TV cartoons that followed. He recorded his own voice, singing very slowly, and played the tape back at double speed. I haven't seen the 2007 Chipmunks movie and can't tell you whether it used the same technique.

percent shift with acceptable bandwidth and only a few artifacts. The box cost as much as a small car, but was considered essential in commercial production houses. That's because it could jam 33 seconds of copy into a 30-second spot.

Today, very high quality hardware-based pitch changers with three- and four-octave ranges are standard in most music and audio post studios. They're used to fix out-of-tune singers, create virtual choirs, and—of course—to jam more words into a commercial. They can cost as much as several thousand dollars. But reasonable-sounding time and pitch changers are built into almost every audio program, free, and excellent ones are available as plug-ins. Most can change pitch as much as an octave in either direction without audible glitches, many can compress time as much as 25 percent without losing intelligibility, and a few can slow speech down 25 percent without sounding strange. This is a case where cheaper may be better. Because software-based pitch changers don't have to work in real time and have the option of looking ahead into the file, they can use more sophisticated algorithms than the hardware ones.

SPEED-BASED EFFECTS

Despite the ability of today's systems to change time or pitch independently, doing it the old-fashioned way—changing both together—is sometimes more desirable. It's faster and has fewer side effects to hurt sound quality.

Sample-Rate Speed Changes

Believe it or not, you can run a digital recording at the wrong speed and get exactly the same effect that happened with those analog phono records. Some professional CD and DAT players let you do this by changing their internal sample rate. If you play a 44.1 kHz CD at 40 kHz, samples will play about 10 percent slower than they were recorded. The disc will take that much longer to play and be that much lower in pitch. If you play it at 48 kHz, the reverse will happen and the disc will play faster and at a higher pitch. You can do this with files as well, if you manually change the sample rate in the file's header; when a program tries to play the file, it'll use the rate you set. Some audio programs let you do this easily.[2] This speed manipulation is virtually instantaneous, since only a few bytes of the file are changed.

Neither of these techniques affect audio quality. There can be other problems, however:

- In the case of those CD and DAT player vari-speeds, the sample rate on their digital outputs is changed. Some inputs might not accept the new nonstandard rate, making a digital dub impossible.

---

[2]Windows users can change the sample rate in the Properties pane within SoundForge and other programs. Mac users will want Tom Erbe's *SoundHack* (www.soundhack.com), essential shareware for anybody doing creative audio on Macs.

- Many digital inputs lock their internal clocks to the signal. This can be just as bad. If you speed a CD up to 50 kHz s/r to raise its pitch, and digitally dub it a file, the signal might force the file recorder to run at 50 kHz as well. When you play the file back on standard software it'll slow back down and cancel the effect completely.

If you don't have hardware capable of sample rate conversion and want to input a vari-speeded CD or other digital stream, the best option might be to do an analog transfer, redigitizing at a standard rate. This can result in a slight loss of quality, depending on the equipment; whether it's actually noticeable depends on the application.

Things are only a little different in the software world. Some platforms have problems with arbitrary rates, or won't play them at all. Most multi-track programs can't mix audio files that are at different rates, so they either stop playback or re-render the files and cancel any pitch change. On the other hand, many NLEs have a speed change function as a video effect. These often work on audio clips as well.

 Gotcha

Where's the pitch? One of my clients reported unwanted pitch changes on his high-end NLE, when encoding a video project for the Web. We traced the problem down to a bug in how his NLE passed information to a separate data-compression software. Running the compression software manually, rather than calling it from the NLE, fixed the problem.

309

Speed Changes Using Audio Processing

Changing the speed without changing the sample rate can introduce distortion, but most audio programs do this at a high enough intermediate sample rate that the sound is virtually perfect.

Some programs disguise their speed change function or bury it in other processes. Sound-Forge offers a *pitch bender* instead. This is usually used to apply a speed change that varies over time, and it follows a graph you draw. (Figure 14.1 shows a typical pitch bend curve; part 1 of Track 64 plays its effect.) If you want to apply a constant speed change in SoundForge, drag the control points to make a single horizontal line. Peak, a popular editor for the Mac, doesn't call it a pitch bender or a speed control; instead, there's a selection of duration and pitch processors.

Both these programs have a Preserve Duration check box. Turn it off to accomplish the kind of speed change we're discussing in this section (Figure 14.2). Not only does this keep pitch and time linked together, it's also faster and often sounds better. There's a lot of extra processing necessary to preserve duration, and it can introduce artifacts.

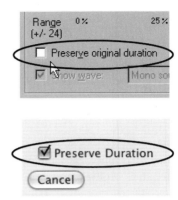

FIGURE 14.1
A typical pitch bender.

FIGURE 14.2
If you want an old-fashioned speed change, turn off the Preserve Duration option.

310

Hear for yourself

Track 64 has the tutorial examples for this chapter.

Gotcha

Aliasing can be your friend. Some audio software does a sloppy job of sample rate conversion when slowing things down, because it doesn't change aliasing filters. This happens in a few older programs, and some modern plug-ins designed to generate distortion. It adds high frequencies that weren't in the original. It can be a useful design effect, creating false harmonics to make sound effects brighter. (It also works on music tracks, but the harmonics aren't at all musically pleasing.)

MAKING CENTS OF SPEED CHANGES

Most audio software is intended for music production. Even though you can use a bender or pitch shift to control speed, the dialog box is probably calibrated in musical values, *semitones* or *cents*. (There are two semitones to a whole step, such as from the musical note C to the note D, and one hundred cents in a semitone.) Each semitone has a frequency ratio of 1.05946:1 to the note below it. An octave—a frequency ratio of 1:2—contains 1,200 cents. Since we hear pitch logarithmically, cents don't have a constant difference in Hertz. The actual formula to convert speed changes to cents is:

$$\text{cents} = 1200 \log_2 (\text{speed}_1 / \text{speed}_2)$$

Don't like logs? Just remember it's about 165 cents for a 10 percent change, or 17 cents for a 1 percent change.

PULLDOWN

Film usually runs at 24 frames per second; NTSC video is at about 29.97 frames per second. Chapter 6 covers the implications of this in a section on timecode. Briefly, if you're editing traditionally shot film as video in a NLE, it's often necessary to apply a speed correction of −0.1 percent when transferring location audio to the editing system. If you don't, sync can drift 1.8 frames for each minute of a continuous take.

Professional timecode recorders have a switch to do this automatically. It changes the sample rate so quality isn't lost in the process. The pitch change that results is too small to be heard by even the most golden-eared listener. For best results, transfer digitally through an input that does sample-rate conversion back to standard file rates. An alternative is to capture the sound normally, then change its speed in an audio program. If your software lets you apply a pitch correction of −1.75[3] cent, things should sync perfectly. If the program accepts only whole cents, −2 cent will keep things within one frame for about five minutes.

But don't automatically reach for that compensation switch. It depends on how the original footage was shot and recorded, and there are lots of options now. The production team and post have to agree on the recipe to maintain sync.

CHANGING PITCH AND TIME INDEPENDENTLY

Most audio editors come with a pitch shifter that can preserve duration while changing the pitch, or a tempo changer that changes duration without affecting frequencies. Depending on the quality of the software, this can sound good or may introduce periodic glitches. The problem lies in how intelligently the algorithm handles overlaps.

---

[3]Actually, −1.728 cent. But −1.75 cent is probably more accurate than the crystals in your location equipment, so don't worry about the error.

> ⚠️ **Gotcha**
>
> **It's not really pitch "shifting."** Shifting all pitches by the same number of Hertz—say, raising everything 300 Hz—is possible, but sounds awful (listen to part 2 of Track 64).[4] We expect frequencies to change in proportion to their pitch, not by a fixed amount.
>
> What pitch "shifting" actually does is *multiply* pitches, changing everything by the same ratio. Raising a 1 kHz tone to 1,300 Hz means multiplying by a factor of 1.3. That same factor would raise a 5 kHz tone to 6,500 Hz: As we demonstrated in Chapter 1, it sounds like the same degree of change. These multipliers are always called *shifters* by the people who make them, so that's the term we'll use.

PITCH SHIFTERS

FIGURE 14.3
Basic pitch shift:
a sawtooth wave
lengthens a delay,
lowering the pitch.
But note the glitches.

Remember chorus effects from the last chapter, with delay lines constantly changing their length? In the chorus, an LFO telescopes a delay from short to long and back again. While the delay is being lengthened, any signal going through the delay has its pitch lowered. While it's being shortened, the pitch goes up.

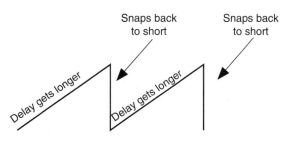

Original wave

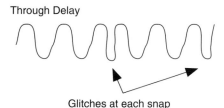

Through Delay

Glitches at each snap

Snaps back to short

Snaps back to short

Delay gets longer

Delay gets longer

How a Pitch Shifter Works

Imagine the LFO had a sawtooth waveform, ramping steadily from minimum voltage to maximum and then snapping back to zero. As the sawtooth's voltage grew, it would lengthen the delay. Any signal going through the delay would have its pitch lowered while the delay was growing. If the sawtooth ran in the other direction, from high down to low and snapping back up again, it would raise the pitch.

This is exactly the same phenomenon as the *Doppler effect*. When a train whistle is coming toward you rapidly, the distance sound has to travel keeps getting shorter. That's why the whistle's pitch appears to rise.[5] When the train passes you and starts moving away, the time it takes soundwaves to reach you starts getting longer, lowering the pitch.

Figure 14.3 shows how a delay can change pitch. A high-frequency wave (on the top) is run through

---

[4]The demo was done using a heterodyne process, since normal pitch routines won't create this sound.

[5]The pitch that reaches your ears actually does rise. But the whistle hasn't changed.

a delay that's modulated by the sawtooth in the middle. While the sawtooth is ramping up, the delay grows and the output pitch is lowered (on the bottom).

There's only one problem with this type of pitch changing: it sounds pretty bad. The problem isn't the pitch shift, which (assuming a well-designed LFO and delay) should be perfect. The problem is the snap: every time the delay jumps suddenly, samples in the delay's memory get thrown away. The result is a sudden jump in the waveform—the glitches on the bottom of Figure 14.3. You can hear it in part 3 of Track 64. The situation is similar if you're raising pitch with an LFO that ramps from maximum to zero. Each time the LFO jumps back to maximum, samples have to be repeated (part 4).

One solution is to have two parallel delays, with two separate LFOs at the same speed. The second LFO runs one-half cycle later than the first. When delay A is snapping back, delay B is in the middle of its pitch change. A third LFO (also at the same speed) controls a cross-fade from the output of one delay to the other (see Figure 14.4). If the cross-fade is properly timed, we're always listening to a delay that's got room to change. The result is a smooth pitch change—except once per cycle of the third LFO. In the middle of the cross-fade, we'll hear both delays mixed together. Because it's impossible for the two outputs to be identical, part of the sound will double. Part 5 of the CD Track 64 demonstrates this problem. I emphasized it by choosing a particularly slow LFO speed.

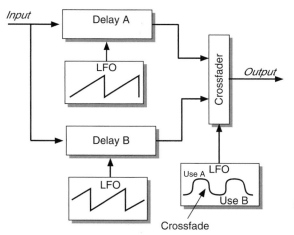

FIGURE 14.4
A "deglitched" pitch changer. All three LFOs are at the same speed, but Delay B's LFO is growing smoothly while Delay A's is snapping back. A third LFO is timed to smoothly cross-fade between the two delays.

The cross-fades in commercial pitch shifters aren't this obvious. They use different cross-fade LFO waveforms and other tricks to hide problems. A few also use extra memory: when a cross-fade is imminent, the pitch shifters compare the two delays and put off the fade until there's a good match.

I've described a simple pitch shifter that works in real time on a continuous audio stream. Others have refinements in how they approach the fade between delays. They may also use a slightly different architecture, with a single memory buffer and three pointers: one pointer writes audio data into RAM addresses, and the other two read that data at a different rate. But the operation is conceptually the same. Part 6 of Track 64 demonstrates a pretty good pitch shifter.[6]

PITCH SHIFTER USES

Obviously, the ability to change pitch without affecting timing can be a cool special effect, particularly in fantasy and science-fiction pieces. The cookbook

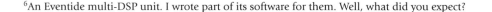

[6]An Eventide multi-DSP unit. I wrote part of its software for them. Well, what did you expect?

section at the end of this chapter describes some ways to use this effect, including a few effects you wouldn't think were based on pitch shift.

But pitch shift is also useful as a corrective device. Special shifters are available that analyze singers' voices, spot when they're off-key, and nudge them back. These often have sophisticated controls to preserve some of the natural slides and vibrato that good pop singers produce, and may have the ability to turn one voice into a choir.

Some songs change key in the middle, ending a whole step (200 cents) higher than they started. If you edit the head and tail together, the change can be jarring. I've found that even the basic shifters found in most audio software can compensate for this by dropping down a whole step, without damaging sound quality.

SHIFTER LIMITATIONS

Large pitch shifts can have problems, even if the software does the job without glitches. Changing the key of most musical instruments by more than a few notes doesn't sound like the performer played in a different register; it just sounds wrong. That's because acoustic instruments have fixed resonances determined by their size and shape. When the performer plays different notes, these resonances—called *formants*—stay at the same frequency. But when you pitch shift digitally, the resonances change as much as the fundamental and the instrument's timbre doesn't sound natural.

This is particularly a problem with human voices. Vowels are created by taking a buzzing from the vocal folds and filtering it through resonant cavities formed by the shape of the tongue, mouth, and sinuses. This creates *vocal formants*: harmonics of the buzzing. As you speak, you continuously change the mixture of these formants by moving your tongue around inside your mouth. Because your head itself doesn't change size, the resonant frequencies don't change very much.

This is so important that I'll give you another way to look at the same thing. Most people can sing *ahh* on two notes, with the second one an octave higher than the first. That means their voice's buzz jumps to twice its original frequency. Since the vocal cavities can't change by that factor, different harmonics of the buzz get emphasized. If the harmonic frequencies were actually multiplied by that octave factor, it would sound like the singer's head suddenly grew or shrank.[7]

Think about this in terms of spoken words as well. Female voices are characteristically at least an octave higher than male ones. With normal variations— some men have lower voices; some women have higher ones; some languages

---

[7]That's one reason why a boy soprano has a different sound than a fully grown woman, even when singing the same note in the same style. The boy's head is smaller.

are spoken in a higher pitch than others—there have got to be at least three and a half octaves of range among adult voices. The frequency of a resonant cavity (including those in your head) is directly proportional to its size. If the difference was reflected in formant frequencies, it would mean some adults' heads are three and a half times larger than some others! You can add your own jokes here.

The point is: The difference between James Earl Jones, me, and the highest soprano occurs at a low frequency, the fundamental of voice's buzz. It's mostly from differences in the size of the vocal folds and how much tension is applied to those folds. To shift a voice realistically, you have to change the fundamental while keeping upper harmonics relatively stable. It can be done.

FORMANT-CORRECTED PITCH SHIFTERS

The simplest way to shift a voice without destroying its timbre is to split it into two bands with filters, one for the fundamental and another for the vowel formants. The bands are processed separately. This is the approach taken in most software.

But there are a few problems with this approach. Unless you're speaking in a monotone, the fundamental frequency changes a lot while you speak. The filters have to be constantly adjusted to sort out the harmonics correctly. This means the software has to detect the lowest frequency, which can take time to do accurately. Also, when the two bands are combined, the harmonics won't have the same phase relationship to the fundamental as they did originally; this can be audible. Any overlap in the bands can cause a flangey smearing, but if the filters are too sharp, they'll add their own phase distortion. Any noise or broadband music in the signal will also be processed and can sound very strange.

A slightly more complicated method involves measuring the lowest frequency, then analyzing whole waves based on the fundamental. The higher frequency harmonics in each wave are captured, then overlaid on a pitch-shifted version of the fundamental. This scheme can also introduce nonspeech strangenesses, but is often fine for background voices.

Both of these methods require accurate frequency detection. To save processing power, many plug-ins ask you to set a frequency range; the smaller the range, the faster the detector can respond. Male dialog should be set for a range between 60 to 275 Hz, and female dialog between 100 to 400 Hz, though of course there are exceptions in both sexes.

A different process constantly analyzes the pitch and volume of each of the harmonics as well. Then it generates electronic filters that match those the mouth was making at the time. It applies these filters to a pitch-shifted re-creation of the fundamental buzz. In effect, it creates an electronic model of a specific human's throat and head, and then speaks through it. This has the additional advantage of other vocal characteristics being introduced. Part 7 of Track 64

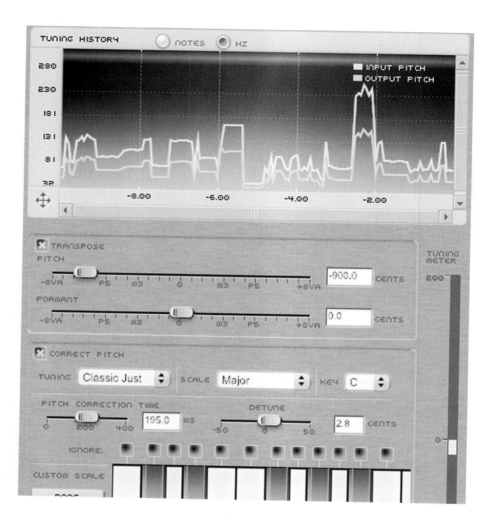

FIGURE 14.5
A formant-corrected pitch shifter, part of Bias' PitchCraft.

demonstrates a piece of gender-bending in TC-Helicon's *Voice Modeler*, a plug-in that requires their PowerCore DSP platform. It's sold for manipulating singers, but has some usefulness in dialog processing and sound design as well. Figure 14.6 shows the settings I used in that example.

Time Changers

Changing the duration of a piece of audio without affecting its pitch is fairly similar to pitch shifting, but you don't have to worry about formants. That's because the final result has the same timbre as its original. Most software gives you options for setting the time factor; you can enter either a percentage or a new duration for selected audio. A few programs let you select a target area on a timeline and visually squeeze or stretch the source material to fit; when you let go of the mouse, the programs apply the proper timing change.

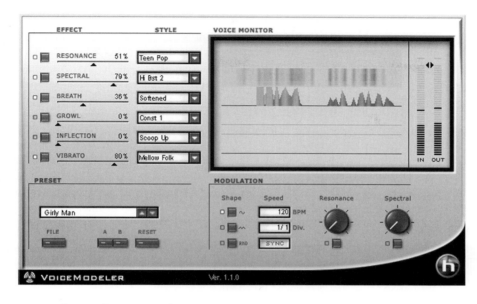

FIGURE 14.6
Gender-bending in
VoiceModeler.

Most software does time-changing as a two-step process: it will vari-speed the
selection to the desired duration, and then do a conventional pitch-shift pass
to put the frequencies back where they belong. The software does it quickly—
some programs appear to do it in real-time—but the pitfalls are the same as
with pitch shifting by itself.

PITCH-SHIFTING WISDOM

Whether you use single-band, formant-corrected, or speed change depends on
what you've got to work with, and what you're trying to accomplish.

- If the goal is high quality, you don't need more than a tiny amount of shift,
  and timing isn't critical: use a speed change. It'll have the least distortion.
  Male voices can usually be lowered 200 cents or raised 100 cents this way.
  The range for female voices is reversed: these can be raised 200 cents or
  lowered 100 cents. This is a good way to change inflection in a VO.
- If you're staying within those ranges but timing is critical (as it would be
  with lipsync), use a conventional pitch shifter. The timbral change will
  probably be less noticeable than the artifacts from most formant-corrected
  shifters. Do this also if you're processing small chunks of a noisy track; a
  speed variation will change the noise's character.
- If you need to change the character of a few background voices to build
  up a crowd, use any of the formant-corrected shifters. But have some non-
  shifted voices louder in the mix, to cover the artifacts.
- If you want to change the character of a foreground voice without calling
  attention to the processing, use a modeling shifter.
- If you're doing other-worldly or cartoon voices, or hiding identity in an
  interview (obvious processing is a benefit here), broadband pitch shifting
  will be fine.

317

- If you're slowing things down, the pitch-shift pass will have to repeat some parts of the waveform. The more radical the change, the more this becomes noticeable.
- If you're speeding things up, the pitch-shift pass has to delete some parts of the waveform. This is usually less noticeable, but can be a serious problem if short phonemes get completely lost.

You can minimize these problems if the software lets you choose the *window size*—how much of the sound it works on at one time. Choose the smallest possible window for speech, 10 to 15 ms or so. Use slightly longer times for solo musical lines and the longest times for music with a lot of instruments. Some software disguises this as a mode control, and lets you select for voice or various kinds of music.

You can also minimize the problems by reducing the amount of speed change. If possible, edit close to the desired length first. Change the length of pauses in a voice-over or during a cutaway, or delete or repeat a bar of music. Skillful editing will always sound better than extreme time-processing.

Part 8 of Track 64 demonstrates a reasonably good speed changer at 75 percent of the original timing, and at 125 percent. When you get beyond that range, some artifacts can become audible. The best way to avoid these is to review the processed file. Then make a different processed copy of the original, using a slightly longer or shorter selection, or with a slightly different percentage. The glitches will fall in different places: edit between the two versions until you've got a perfect one.

ALTERNATIVE TIME SHIFTERS

A few professional products[8] make tiny edits automatically to change timing, and then apply as little pitch shift and speed change as possible. These products will look for individual repeating waves and delete or duplicate them as necessary. Because these changes always happen at zero crossings and no cross-fading is necessary, they don't affect sound quality at all.

How successfully they are depends on the instantaneous nature of the dialog, how radical a change is necessary, and how big a piece they're allowed to work on. If you let them explore a longer time window, the chance of finding good edit points increases—but too long a window can start to distort the patterns of speech because one word may end up with more edits than another. The software may give you just a couple of settings, one that tries to preserve the rhythm as much as possible, and one that compromises rhythm to avoid cross-fades.

The *phase vocoder* takes another approach. It continuously analyzes the spectral composition of the source audio, breaking it into small pieces and performing

---

[8]VocALign (Chapter 7) uses this method to match ADR to guide tracks.

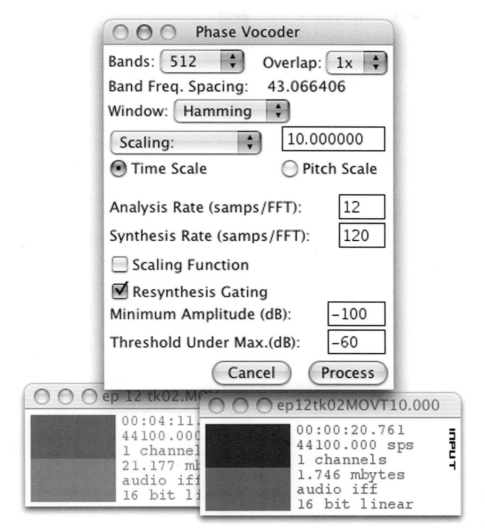

FIGURE 14.7
A phase vocoder
in the shareware
SoundHack.

319

a *Fourier analysis*[9] on each. The pieces run through multiple, sharp filters—as many as a few thousand—and the output at each frequency is mapped. This data is then used to create completely new versions of the sound, timescaled as appropriate. Phase vocoding is processor intensive, but can have a much wider, glitch-free range than other time manipulation methods, often by a factor of 10 or more (Figure 14.7).

---

[9]A process named for mathematician Jean Baptiste Fourier, who invented it about 200 years ago. He proved that any regular wave—no matter how complex or non-musical—can be broken down into a fundamental sine wave and harmonics of varying amplitude and phase. We used to have to compute these harmonics using slide rules and legal pads. It was painful. Digital technology made *Fast Fourier Transforms (FFT)* possible, and they're used in a lot of audio processes.

The success of phase vocoding depends on how the time slices—called windows—are timed and cross-faded, and how closely the filters are spaced. Good software will let you choose from several alternatives for the number of filters and the *window shape*, which affects the cross-fades. If there are more filters, they'll cover narrower frequency bands each and have higher Qs. Window timing depends on filter sharpness, because higher-Q filters need more input samples to be effective. Counterintuitively, more filters aren't necessarily more accurate. Sharper filters not only slow down the windowing, blurring or phasing the sound at cross-fades; they also add their own distortion. Try different combinations on different source files until you're happy.

 Gotcha

Specialized time processors aren't just for dialog. We've described these advanced algorithms in terms of speech because they're seldom found in general-purpose (i.e., music oriented) audio programs. That's partly because it takes a very knowledgeable programmer to create them and partially because they're harder to use.

But their principles work just as well for music and sound effects. If you're lucky enough to have them available, try them. You'll probably be pleased with the results.

TIME AND PITCH COOKBOOK

If you're trying to correct a pitch or speed problem, or fitting dialog into a precise time, the recipe will depend on your specific project. Follow the guidelines in the first part of this chapter for using the particular processor.

But often, time and pitch manipulations are used as a special effect rather than a problem solver. This section provides recipes for a few of the things you can do, but feel free to experiment. There are no firm rules for special effects; play around with the settings until you find a sound that satisfies your creativity.

 Hear for yourself

Track 65 demonstrates most of the effects described in the time and pitch cookbook.

Vari-speed Effects

The lowly vari-speed, simplest of processes, is a powerful tool for creative sound effects work. Most sounds can turn into something completely different when their speed is radically shifted:

- Part 1 of Track 65 is a recording of some boiling water, first at normal speed then manipulated. At half-speed, it starts to sound mechanical.

At 20 percent of normal, it's almost completely metallic, suggesting you're standing between two cars on a moving train.

- Part 2 is a mortar fire, completely recognizable at normal speed. At 20 percent, it's a magnum blowing somebody away. But at 300 percent, it could be a single bowling pin being hit.
- Part 3 is an explosion, pretty big by itself. But the second half of part 3 is the same explosion mixed with a version of itself at 50 percent for depth and a version at 200 percent for brightness—much bigger. You can also spread these variations around the stereo field.
- Part 4 shows how vari-speed can add a unique kind of flanging. First we hear a single helicopter effect. Then it's mixed with a copy of itself, offset one frame later with a very slight 106 percent speed increase. Different small speed changes and tiny offsets would have given different effects.

Pitch-bend Effects

Figure 14.8 shows a pitch-bend pattern for the Doppler effect discussed earlier. Note the calibration on the left of the graph; the actual change is only a couple of semitones. Part 5 lets you hear a before-and-after. I also applied a gain envelop similar to the pitch shift. Real-world Doppler effects are usually also coupled with some echo and high-frequency losses that increase with distance.

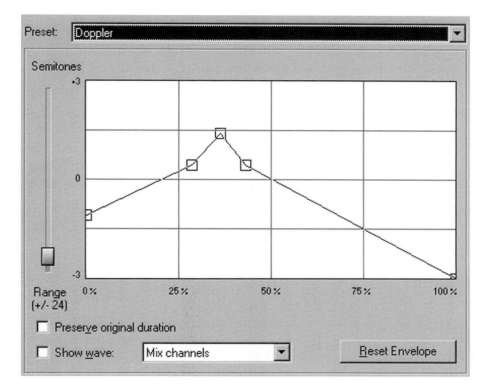

FIGURE 14.8
A basic Doppler shift is easy with a pitch bender.

Try applying pitch bending to a repeating mechanical sound, such as a motor. You'll be able to make it speed up or slow down on command. Pitch bending can also be applied to steady tones to create a variety of sirens, lasers, and other electronic effects.

Pitch-shift Effects

Pitch shifting is seldom as useful on sound effects as it is on music or voices. I suspect that's because there's less to distract us from the periodic artifacts. On the other hand, it's got more vocal uses than you might expect.

These samples are on voices recorded in a quiet announce booth. Voices with small amounts of background noise or reverb can often be processed in a wide-band shifter, though the apparent noise may increase. Noisy tracks are seldom usable in a formant-corrected shifter.

WIDEBAND PITCH SHIFTING

A lot can be done by mixing a voice with a pitch-shifted copy of itself:

- Part 6 of Track 65 shows how a tiny pitch shift—on the order of 0.15 per-cent higher, or maybe two cents—isn't heard as a doubled voice. Instead, the subtle timing changes that the algorithm introduces gives a lightly flanged character, almost suggesting a distant voice blowing on the wind.
- Part 7 uses a much bigger shift—a whole step (200 cents). Now we hear it as two people speaking in unison.
- Three isn't quite a crowd, as you can hear in part 8. The unchanged voice is in the center, and two shifted versions are panned about 20 percent, left and right, one up a half step and one down a half step. One of the shifted tracks is delayed by one frame because three people could never achieve perfect unison. Voice doubling, approximately 6 percent or 200 cents down, becomes two people in unison.
- Part 9 could be a small crowd. It uses eight different shifts, ranging between about 70 to 300 cents, panned across the field. An LFO continuously changes the delay of each shifted output, between 50 and 200 ms. The orig-inal voice is centered and one frame earlier than the shifted voices, to pro-vide an anchor.
- You can take this to the extreme. Start with the processing of part 9, but add a copy of each shifted signal, delayed one frame, and panned elsewhere in the stereo field. A little bit of reverb puts a room around the whole thing. Part 10 shows this effect with the shifted versions added gradually. It starts with a single voice hawking widgets, and smoothly grows to an entire con-gregation reciting the Acme slogan.

We started this chapter with a footnote reference to David Seville's Chipmunks. Let's hear from the little guys, using three pitch shifts (500 cents, 900 cents, 1 octave). Part 11 brings the Chipmunks in, one at a time for each voice. As you can hear, it's more effective on higher voices.

A fascinating class of effects can be created by hooking up a delayed feedback around a real-time pitch shifter. Part 12 gives you a glimpse of this, as an echo that starts on a single word and then spirals up to infinity: 400 cents SHIFT, 75 percent FEEDBACK, and a DELAY timed to the word. Part 13 changes a few settings for a completely different sound, an otherworldly (and possibly underworldly) reverb that would be ideal for a demon's evil laughter: −20 cents SHIFT, 80 ms DELAY, and about 90 percent FEEDBACK.

Formant-Corrected Pitch Shifting

For foreground voices, small shifts—less than 500 cents—seem to work best, and shifts up usually sound better than shifts down. Bear in mind that with few exceptions, these processes don't try to change anything other than pitch. If you want to use them to create new characters or recognizable shouting voices in a crowd, record new lines with a slightly different accent, more or less breathiness, or some other changed vocal characteristic. Then apply just enough pitch shift so the voice itself isn't recognizable. (I deliberately didn't do these things in the gender-bending example, part 7 of Track 64, so you could hear the effect of radical shifts on voice tracks you were already familiar with.)

Despite this, the imperfections of larger shifts can be largely hidden by unshifted foreground voices. Shifts as much as an octave may be acceptable.

Time Manipulation Effects

Every program has different limitations of how far you can go with time compression and expansion. It depends on the quality of the algorithm, and also on how fast and how clean the original recording is.

Normal announcer reads can usually be shrunk at least 15 percent and retain intelligibility. Faster settings may be useful for disclaimers at the end of radio spots, but this rarely sounds real. Stretches of up to 25 percent may be usable. In either case, listen to the result, and make sure nothing important has been lost or doubled. It's frequently necessary to do two processing passes and edit together the best from each.

One favorite trick of mine is to stretch individual phrases or the client's name in a voice-over, to give it more emphasis. When edited smoothly into the original, the viewer isn't aware of the manipulation—just that the reading is slightly more expressive. In part 15 of Track 65, you can hear our Acme announcement. But "earned our place," has been lengthened 20 percent and "top" has been lengthened 25 percent.

CHAPTER 15

Noise Reduction

IT'S NOT REALLY NOISE REDUCTION

Today's sophisticated software does an amazing job of distinguishing mostly random noises from speech. Then it does a bunch of sneaky things to make the noises less objectionable.

But make no mistake; if random noise occurs at the same time as dialog, in the same frequency band, you can't get rid of it. At least, not with today's technology.[1] Sorry. No amount of marketing hype, wishful thinking, or impressive prepackaged demos at trade shows will change that fact.

This isn't to say you can't improve most noisy tracks. You can certainly lower noise levels when they don't compete with dialog. The noise may return when there is dialog, but hopefully the words themselves will distract viewers. If noise isn't too serious and the dialog is otherwise well-recorded, this strategy can be remarkably successful.

That's what this chapter is about. It should properly be called "noise smoke-and-mirrors," but I don't want to confuse casual readers.

---

[1] I can see a future device that would use speech recognition and a highly evolved version of the vocal modeling we used in Chapter 14, to synthesize tiny chunks of dialog when noise obscures the original. But we're not there yet.

> **Gotcha**
>
> **Isn't all noise random?** I'm using random here to mean indeterminate frequency, such as electronic hisses, traffic, generator noise, and mumbling production assistants.
>
> Non-random noise, in a technical sense, has absolutely steady frequencies. This includes pure tones and even constant, harmonically rich sounds like dimmer buzz or ground-loop hum. If it's not too loud compared to dialog, this kind of noise may be completely removable.

THE REALITY OF NOISE REMOVAL

A graphic analogy can help you understand why random noise never really goes away.

Let's assume the photo (Figure 15.1) is the visual equivalent of well-recorded dialog. Constant random noise, such as the hiss from recording at a bad level, would be equivalent to the dirty gray pattern laid over it in Figure 15.2. This noise is too random to remove with an equalizer or filter, since such a filter would also affect the dialog.

But noise-reduction software, properly tuned, *can* tell the difference between a desirable object and its background. It lowers the volume when dialog stops. The graphic equivalent to this would be partially erasing the noise surrounding the recorder, as in Figure 15.3. The picture does look cleaner. But as you can see, the noise *over* the recorder hasn't changed at all. We've also lost a lot of shadow variation in the background, because of the erasure.

The audio noise gate—for decades, this was about the only tool we had—works exactly like the graphic one in the figures. It's off when there's no dialog, and it turns on when it hears sound above a preset threshold. Usually there's a FLOOR control to let a small amount of background through at all times. That's equivalent to the way we only partially erased the shadows in Figure 15.3.

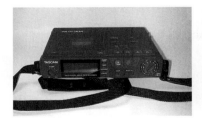

FIGURE 15.1
We'll use this clean photo as an analogy for well-recorded dialog...

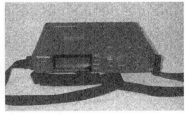

FIGURE 15.2
...and this dirty one for noisy dialog.

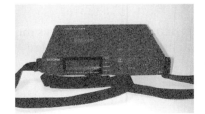

FIGURE 15.3
Noise reduction can make the overall picture look better, but the dirt is still there.

Gotcha

Is noise reduction just for dialog? What about music and effects? Most current pop music is too broadband for noise reduction software to do an effective job. Other forms of complex music that have some dynamics and spectral movement may benefit from noise reduction, depending on the recording. But the algorithms can also destroy some musical details, so use them carefully.

Field-recorded sound effects often benefit from noise reduction. This is particularly true of staccato and moderately soft effects such as footsteps, or loud effects with long reverb tails such as gunshots.

We talk about dialog in this chapter because that's where noise reduction is usually applied. The principles are the same no matter what you're trying to clean up.

Today's noise reduction software is a lot more sophisticated. Systems use hundreds of upward expanders tuned to narrow bands across the spectrum. Noise is allowed through only when that band has dialog going on as well. At the same time, noise in other bands is attenuated. Thanks to a quirk in how human hearing works, this can trick the ear into thinking the noise is completely gone. It's still there; we just don't hear it.

MASKING

Our ears are not particularly precise sensors. While each ear has close to 30,000 nerves on the basilar membrane and while these nerves are tuned to respond to different pitches, there isn't just one nerve for each possible frequency in Hertz.[2] Neural information gets combined in various ways before it reaches the brain.

When we hear a tone at a particular frequency, a group of nerves centered around its pitch fire. How many nerves go off depends on the volume of the tone as well as other factors. A loud sound triggers more nerves. These combined nerves are interpreted as a single pitch at a certain volume. But because that loud sound involved a bunch of nerves, softer sounds at nearby frequencies often can't get through—the nerves or neural pathways that would respond to them are busy doing other things.

This phenomenon has been known for years, and has been measured across very large populations. It affects the threshold of hearing (Chapter 1). The heavy gray line in Figure 15.4 represents that threshold. The decibels are calibrated relative to the frequency where most people's ears are the most sensitive, around 3.5 kHz. You could consider 0 dB on this chart to be true 0 dB SPL—the nominal threshold of hearing—or any other convenient level, depending on the individual.

---

[2]How could there be? The development of human ears predates the scientific concept of Hertz by a million years or so.

The important thing isn't how the vertical axis is calibrated; it's what happens between the center of the band and the extremes. At 3.5 kHz, the short, dark gray bar is louder than the threshold, and it gets heard. But at 50 Hz or 15 kHz, most people won't detect a sound until it gets 40 dB louder. Even though the light gray bars are taller and much louder than the dark one, these light grey ones represent sounds that would get lost.

Unfortunately, that heavy gray line isn't fixed. When something sufficiently loud comes along (dark gray bar in Figure 15.5), it drags the threshold with it. A 250-Hz sound, 25 dB above the threshold, ties up so much neural activity that a simultaneous 200-Hz sound that's 10 dB softer (light gray bar) disappears. The actual amount of masking varies with the frequency, volume, and overall timbre of both sounds, but it's always there to some degree.

A similar effect occurs over time, because it takes a moment for the brain to recognize sounds, and because nerves have to recover chemically after being fired. While this effect also varies, Figure 15.6 shows a typical *temporal* masking. In this example soft sounds, between a dozen milliseconds before to up to 50 ms after, are masked by a louder one.

So if we can arrange to have noise only at times and frequencies where it'll be masked by dialog, the noise will effectively go away. An oscilloscope would still see the noise, but we'd never hear it.

Masking, by the way, is also the secret behind perceptual encoders like mp3 and AAC. When used properly, these algorithms can shrink an audio file's size drastically with no apparent audible

FIGURE 15.4
A typical threshold of hearing curve. Sounds below the gray line aren't heard by most people.

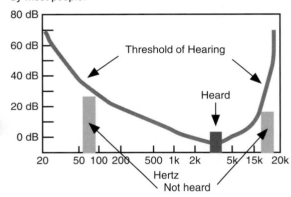

328

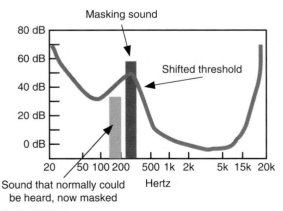

FIGURE 15.5
Frequency-based masking. The louder sound raises the threshold around it, so the softer one isn't heard.

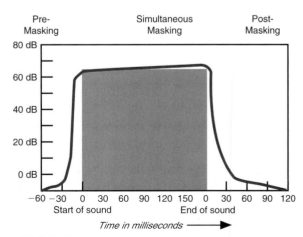

FIGURE 15.6
Temporal masking. You can't hear sounds that occur a short time before or after a loud one at a similar frequency.

effect,[3] or shrink it even more with minor losses in quality. More about this in Chapter 18.

Masking is also the reason why it's important not to have elements of a track compete in spectrum or in time. (That's in Chapter 5… see how it all comes together?) In general, the closer two sounds are in frequency or the greater their volume difference, the more the softer sound will get masked. Masking usually starts when sounds at similar frequencies are within about 10 dB. Low-frequency sounds often mask a wider range than high-frequency ones of the same volume.

A FEW OTHER NOISE REDUCTION FACTS

There are plenty of myths and misconceptions about the process of noise reduction. If you understand what's really going on, you can get better results.

Noise Reduction Without a Noise Reducer

Noise reduction software often offers to do the whole job for you automatically, at the click of a mouse. This does more damage, in most cases, than using other techniques manually first. If you've been following the examples on this book's CD, you've already heard some fairly effective noise reduction that relies on other kinds of processors.

- Get rid of whistles using the equalization techniques in Chapter 11 and demonstrated on Track 51.
- Tracks 54 and 55 show how downward expansion can improve moderately noisy interview tracks (Chapter 12).
- Track 62 virtually eliminates dimmer buzz using a comb filter (Chapter 13).

And of course, the ultimate noise reduction for extremely bad dialog recordings is ADR (Chapter 7). These tools are often the first defense, and should be considered before whipping out general-purpose noise reduction software.

Editing can also be used for noise reduction: replace the noisy part with something else. That's one of the principal uses for room tone, though noise-reduction editing can be as subtle as replacing a few waves that click with copies of adjacent waves. It can even involve changing individual samples by drawing over clicks or other transient sounds with a pencil tool. A few plug-ins can do these things automatically, though they need precise tuning to sound good.

NULLING NOISE?

Folks who know a little acoustic theory sometimes ask, "Why can't I create or capture a sample of the noise, invert the polarity, and use that to cancel the

329

---

[3]Some people swear they can always hear *any* encoding. But auditory studies show this probably isn't true. mp3 has gotten a bad rep, primarily because of awful files on the Web, poorly designed encoders, and people who don't know how to use it properly.

noise out?" The idea behind this is basically correct: The comb filter, for example, works by delaying symmetrical noise exactly one-half cycle. This lines up the negative side of the wave against the positive, *nulling* out the noise. But that's a special case, relying on the consistency of the noise itself.

For the sample-and-invert technique to work on most real-world noise, the noise would have to be absolutely consistent in its waveform and volume, and the sample would have to be exactly in sync. If there is the tiniest error in timing or if the noise changes the slightest bit after you take the sample, you'd be making the noise louder instead of removing it.

Most noise reduction software relies on taking a sample of the noise, but it's not inverting that sample—or even recording its waveform. Instead, it takes a spectral fingerprint of the noise, similar to what you'd see on a spectragraph. It uses that information to control other processes. Nulling isn't involved.

Dolby Noise Reduction

The Dolby process revolutionized analog recording, and is still used in many studios. But it only reduces noise part of the time—just enough to make noisy transmission channels seem quieter.

Dolby A—the original format—worked by breaking the audio into four bands. Each band was then compressed, raising the volume of its soft sounds and decreasing the dynamic range. The four signals were combined and recorded on tape at a high volume. On playback, the signal was again split into bands. Each was downward expanded, restoring the dynamic range and—during average or soft passages—lowering any hiss contributed by the recording medium. This combination of compression during record and expansion during playback is called *companding*.

During loud passages, no compression or expansion took place. The hiss remained at its usual level, but it was soft enough to be masked by the loud signal. The reason Dolby A used four bands was to help the masking; if there were only one band, a loud bass note would reduce the expansion, and we'd hear the unmasked hiss in the mids and highs. It's still used today by music producers who consider analog an important step in creating a unique sound.

Consumer Dolby (*B* and *C*), popular in analog cassette decks, also split the signal. But it passed the low frequencies unchanged and only companded the highs. That's because hiss is more of a problem at high frequencies with these tape formats. Both versions of consumer Dolby required careful calibration so the compressor and expander would precisely match. If calibration slipped (as it frequently did in consumer decks), the timbre would be changed. A competing scheme, *dbx*, used a single band with a different companding model that didn't need calibration.

This kind of noise reduction was called *double-ended* because it required encoding before recording, and decoding after playback. It was specifically designed to reduce noises introduced between those stages. Neither system did anything for electronic noise from the mic or preamp, or that may have been picked up acoustically.[4] Both Dolby and dbx have since moved on to other things: the Dolby digital systems used in movies and HD television don't rely on companding, and dbx now builds preamps and other studio gear.

The very earliest digital audio equipment sometimes used double-ended processing as well. But that was decades ago. It isn't necessary today. Instead, film and video often rely on *single-ended* processing.

SINGLE-ENDED PROCESSING

The term refers to noise reduction of an already recorded signal, and it can be helpful for noise picked up by microphones as well as noise added by faulty or misused equipment. Unlike double-ended systems, single-ended processes have to be told what to keep and what to bury. You do this manually when you adjust equalization, dynamics control, or comb filters for noise reduction. Noise reduction plug-ins also have to be tuned to the noise. If the noise is close to the desired signal, in volume or spectrum, this can be very difficult.

Two Rules

Noise reduction works best when there isn't too much noise to begin with. As noise gets louder, noise reduction becomes less successful. The best way to control noise, always, is to not record it.

If you are doing some processing to reduce noise, make sure you keep a clean copy of the clip as well. It's easy to be seduced by these tools when listening on small monitors, and then regret how much you processed when you hear it on better speakers. If you're bringing the tracks to another studio for the mix, take along a *mirror* track that has all the edits but none of the processing. Many re-recording mixers insist on this before they'll start a job.

331

Dynamic Filtering

This is an old analog technique that works just as well in the digital domain. It's effective against hiss and other random noises that are predominantly high frequency. These noises could also be stopped with a sharp low-pass filter, but that could cut important parts of the dialog and leave things sounding dull and lifeless. Instead, a variable filter is used. Its cutoff frequency is constantly being adjusted by an envelope detector, which is preceded by a fixed high-pass filter. This control arrangement is identical to the de-esser discussed in Chapter 12. Figure 15.7 shows the layout.

---

[4]Dolby A's four-band decoder could also be applied to an unencoded noisy signal and, with careful adjustment, act as a single-ended noise reducer. This use was popular for a while on film mixing stages. We've got much better tools now.

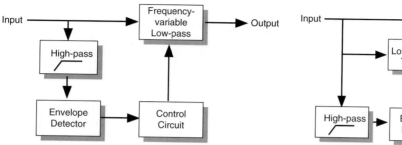

FIGURE 15.7
A dynamic filter. When it hears things happening in the
high frequencies, it raises the filter frequency.

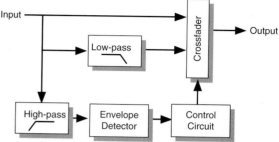

FIGURE 15.8
A different way of building a dynamic filter. This one
avoids timbral shifts.

When there is very little energy in the high frequencies—in dialog pauses, for example, or during a vowel sound in the word *smooth*—the envelope detector has very little output. This swings the filter frequency down to a few kilohertz and reduces the hiss. But as high-end energy increases, the filter frequency rises. During those times there's something to mask the hiss. For relatively narrow-band sounds like dialog, you're not aware of a timbre shift—just less noise.

An alternative architecture (Figure 15.8) helps avoid timbral problems on wide-band sounds like music. Instead of a variable filter, it has a fixed-frequency low pass, sometimes as low as 1 kHz. A cross-fader, controlled by the envelope detector, varies the output between the filtered signal and the unprocessed input. When there isn't much high-frequency energy, the output is only what made it through the filter. But as highs start to appear, more of the unfiltered input is mixed in. When the highs are loud, none of the filtered signal is used at all. This setup isn't as effective as the variable filter, but can sound smoother.

Dynamic filters are often built with only one control, a MORE knob to set the sensitivity of the envelope detector. Start with no noise reduction at all; then, while you play the source material, advance the knob until noise is removed but you're not aware of dullness or a swishing sound. These filters are often followed by a downward expander, sometimes in the same unit, with its own SENSITIVITY control. Time constants are usually preset to be very fast.

Dynamic filtering is effective and often implemented in analog systems. A similar algorithm can be found in some multifunction, DSP-based digital processors, and is available in well-equipped post suites. For hiss-based noise, dynamic filtering is often the least intrusive solution. But you won't see this process in most plug-ins. That's because today's computers are capable of a more powerful solution, *multichannel masking*.

Multichannel Masking

Imagine a bank of hundreds of downward expanders, each preceded by a narrow bandpass filter. Each one would look at a small slice of dialog frequencies,

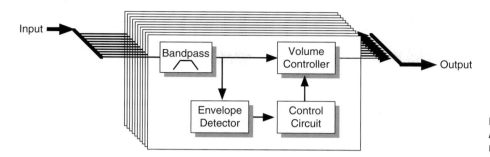

FIGURE 15.9
A multiband noise
reducer, simplified.

sometimes smaller than a single formant. When there's voice energy in a particular narrowband, the expander would pass it through. Any noise in that band would be masked by the voice. When things are silent in that band, its overall level would be reduced, lowering the noise, even though the voice may be speaking (and masking noise) in other bands. Figure 15.9 shows a simplified version; actual multiband noise reducers often have as many as 512 bands.

AVOIDING MULTIBAND ARTIFACTS

While this approach can yield very effective, almost amazing noise reduction, it can also cause problems. With pure tones or very narrow band signals, you can hear flanging artifacts in the noise: if a single expander opens while its neighbors remain closed, this affects the timbre around it. Some plug-ins have a way to avoid this, adjustable with a CORRELATION or OVERLAP control that partially links the bands' actions. Time constants are also important. If the RELEASE time is too fast, you'll hear a chirping artifact as bands respond to transient sounds. If it's too long, noise can remain after the masking sound is gone. Both ATTACK and RELEASE have to consider the frequency of the band as well to avoid distortion, so some programs provide separate timing controls for each end of the band, or a TILT control that does a similar thing.

The most important way to keep a noise reducer sounding good is to manually trim the THRESHOLD and REDUCTION (aka FLOOR or RATIO) of individual expanders, after the software has taken its automatic sample. Preview and listen for the artifacts. When you hear one, guess its band and slightly lower the band's threshold or reduction factor until the artifact goes away. (If you haven't guessed accurately, you can always restore the settings and try a different band. It gets much easier with practice.) Figure 15.10 shows how you'd do this in Digidesign's DINR; other software has similar interfaces.

The point of this fine-tuning is to avoid anything that sounds artificial or metallic. It's almost always better to let a little noise through, than to call attention to the processing. Some people recommend a simpler approach to the same goal: set the plug-in to its minimum, process, process again, and keep processing until you hear artifacts; then undo the last processing. My way is faster.

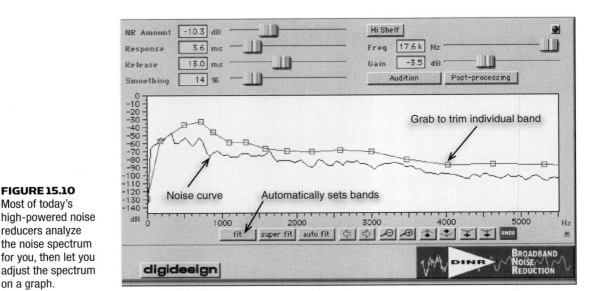

FIGURE 15.10
Most of today's high-powered noise reducers analyze the noise spectrum for you, then let you adjust the spectrum on a graph.

Frequency-space Editing

There's an old joke that if an x-ray shows you need surgery, but you can't afford the doctor, you can pay someone to touch-up the x-ray instead. It might not be good medical advice, but a similar process works for removing some kinds of noise.

Consider the spectragram, a three dimensional graph showing a sound's constantly changing timbre: time is displayed on the horizontal, frequency on the vertical, and volume by the color. Figure 15.11 shows the one in Adobe *Soundbooth* multi-track editor, with the fairly typical exterior dialog recording that's part 1 of Track 66. The wavy pattern and activity around 300 Hz are the vowels; the activity around 1.5 kHz consonants, and the random activity across the whole band is traffic. At 13.6 seconds, we hear a car horn, and that's clearly shown by the burst at 1 kHz.

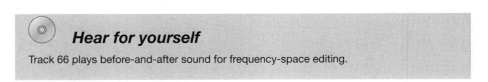

Hear for yourself

Track 66 plays before-and-after sound for frequency-space editing.

The neat thing about Soundbooth and a couple of other programs is that you can select just the horn's burst, graphically, and retouch it! There's an *auto-heal* command that attempts to replace those waves with an average of the surrounding ones. Adobe's version can work on only half a second at a time, and the healing isn't tunable; but conceptually and from a processing point-of-view, it's kind of amazing: listen to part 2. A more powerful implementation appears in iZotope *RX* (Figure 15.12), a plug-in or standalone noise reduction package that also includes multiband expansion and other functions.

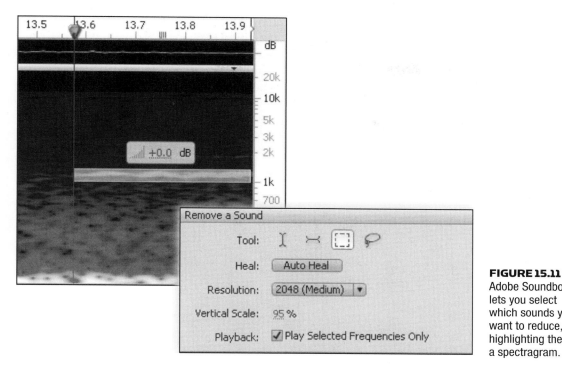

FIGURE 15.11
Adobe Soundbooth lets you select which sounds you want to reduce, by highlighting them on a spectragram.

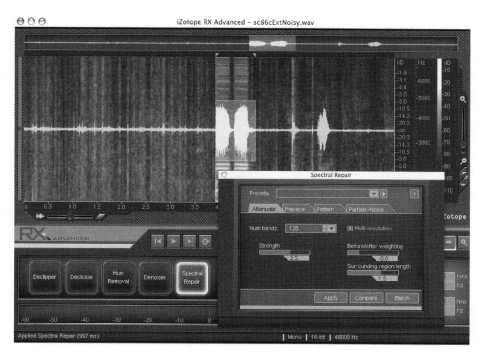

FIGURE 15.12
The Spectral Repair pane in iZoetope RX.

This process—sometimes called *wavelet editing*—is fairly new and has inherent limitations. It can't cope with wideband noises that interfere with non-repeating sounds, such as a car crash during dialog. When confronted by a constant tone, like camera whine, it turns into an equalizer; using a parametric (Chapter 12) is faster and easier. And there are much better ways to fix hiss and other steady random noises. But when I wrote the first edition of this book, the only professional wavelet editor (Cedar *Retouch*) required a dedicated tower running special host software. Now you can do it on ordinary desktops (both Soundbooth and RX are available for Windows or Mac).

Adaptive Filters

It's a movie cliché that before two spies have an important conversation, they turn on radios and start the shower going. All that extra noise is supposed to defeat hidden microphones. But a powerful noise-reduction technique, *adaptive filtering*, can actually sort music and random noise from speech. It's used to clean up airplane black box recordings, make wiretaps more understandable in court cases, and—yes—catch spies.

Adaptive filtering relies on statistical models to predict speech. It's grown out of the same research that originally made it possible to carry intelligible conversations over the tiny radio power of a cell phone. There are two basic forms of this filter, one that uses a sample of the noise you want to get rid of, and one that guesses what the noise is, based on what it knows about speech.

Unfortunately, adaptive filters haven't yet reached the sophistication where they can smoothly clean up a voice without leaving flangey, metallic artifacts. This isn't a problem in forensics, where the technology's benefits outweigh this disadvantage. But it makes adaptive filters unsuitable for video and film tracks, and they're seldom found in the post suite.

Declicking

Back before compact discs, sound recordings were released on vinyl discs with an analog groove on each side: the *phonograph record*. The tiny sides of the groove moved in and out in an exact analogy of the sound waves it represented. The disk would spin, and a needle riding in the groove would wiggle with the groove's undulations. That wiggle was picked up by a device that worked similarly to a microphone, which created a voltage that reflected the original sound wave. (When I was younger, I never thought I'd have to explain that process in a book.[5]) The groove walls were delicate, and vinyl isn't particularly strong. Anything that disturbed the groove could cause a spike in the audio, which repeated each time the disk came full circle. By the time a much-loved record had been played a few hundred times, it could include an unwanted rhythm section of ticks and pops.

---

[5]A year ago, I worked on a film with a scene where a young woman restarts an old record for an elderly friend. The 20-year-old actress had no idea how to operate a phonograph, and had to be shown—step by step—by the director.

Ironically, now that we have click-free recordings, we've also got plug-ins to remove clicks on older recordings. Lower-end click removers usually have a single sensitivity or threshold control; play the source file and slide the control until clicks are controlled but you don't hear too much distortion where they used to be. Better ones, such as the one in Figure 15.12, give you additional settings. Shape or frequency range tells the click detector what to look for. The clicks in old 78 RPM recordings were often bassier than the crackles in 33 RPM; optimize this setting so the detector doesn't get confused by transients in the sound. A low noise level setting tells the algorithm to completely ignore parts of the track that don't have any clicks, avoiding any chance for artifacts in those sections.

NOISE REDUCTION EXAMPLES

 Gotcha

There's more in the arsenal. If you jumped to this section to solve a particular problem instead of reading what came before, you may be missing some major noise-reduction techniques.

Check Chapters 11 to 13 to learn about noise reduction using equalizers, expanders, and delays. In many cases, these can remove noise with fewer artifacts than dedicated noise-reduction software.

I can't provide a cookbook for this chapter, since every noisy recording has its own unique problems. Instead, I'm providing a few examples of real field recordings, showing the basic steps to clean them and playing the results. Use these as a benchmark for your own efforts.

Moderate Interior Noise

Part 1 of Track 67 is the original track of an interior interview. There's some room rumble and HVAC hum. There are lots of noise reduction packages now for this, and they all have similar procedures. These screenshots are from Bias' *SoundSoapPro*. If your software has additional controls that you can't figure out, check the manual or help screen.

1. Isolate a short slice of noise during a pause in dialog. With some software, you have to select it on a waveform before launching the plug-in; with others, you just have to remember where it is. Look for a place that doesn't include breathing or other noises that don't occur during the rest of the track. Make sure you haven't included any of the subject's voice. In this example, I found about 20 frames around 12 seconds from the start.
2. Open the plug-in, play the noise, and press the SPECTRUM, ANALYZE, or LEARN button. The software quickly analyzes the noise you selected, creating a graph of level versus frequency (as in Figure 15.13). If you

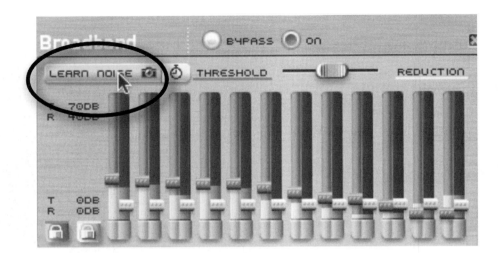

FIGURE 15.13
Learning the noise's
spectrum.

selected just a slice of the clip in Step 1, close the plug-in—it'll remember what it learned—and select the whole clip. Then launch the plug-in again.

3. The display will now show two different bar or line graphs. One controls the threshold of each band; one is for the amount of noise reduction in that band. Play or preview the clip to see if you like the reduction. Chances are, it'll either be too processed and have artifacts (often sounding like things are underwater), or not be processed enough. Grab the noise reduction graph—in most software you can move the whole thing at once, or just select individual points—and raise or lower the whole thing to taste (Figure 15.14). If you're satisfied, process and you're done.

4. You might find that the right amount of processing in some bands is too much for others. In some cases, background sounds might be controlled at the extreme ends of the band, but you can hear them "breathing" along with the dialog in the middle of the band. In others, softer parts of the dialog might be dropping out along with noise. Select appropriate bands in the graph, lower their threshold if they're cutting into dialog, or lower their amount of reduction if you can hear breathing (Figure 15.15). If there's a steady noise in a specific part of the spectrum, you can raise the threshold or reduction to counter it.

5. If you hear chirping as the software works, adjust the timing controls. In general, the ATTACK should be fairly fast unless there's distortion on the low end. The RELEASE will be a compromise between cleanliness and chirping.

6. One final trick is to turn on the NOISE ONLY or PREVIEW NOISE function. This shows you what the software will attempt to remove, without the distraction of dialog to mask it. Make sure you're not taking out anything important; if you are, go back and adjust the other parameters. Remember to set this function back to normal before processing.

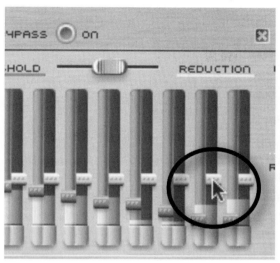

FIGURE 15.14
Adjusting the amount of reduction.

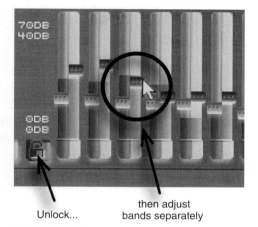

Unlock...   then adjust
                   bands separately

FIGURE 15.15
Adjusting individual bands' threshold
or reduction.

Part 2 of Track 67 lets you hear the final result.

 Hear for yourself

Track 67 plays before-and-after versions of the interior interview.

MODERATE EXTERIOR NOISE WITH WHINE

If the noise has any constant-pitch elements, pre-equalization will always make noise reduction work better. Part 1 of Track 68 is an exterior interview with fairly loud traffic and a machine whine. The whine competes with, and is almost as loud as, the subject's voice; standard noise reduction techniques won't be able to do much.

 Hear for yourself

Track 68 is the whiny exterior before processing, using just a noise reducer, and using a parametric equalizer before the noise reducer.

Part 2 plays the interview after being processed, but with no separate equalization. It's an improvement, but there's still noise. Worse, the expander makes the whine pulsate in step with the voice.

In part 3, the unprocessed interview is run through a parametric first, tuned to eliminate the whine (using the sweeping technique in Chapter 11). Then it's processed through a noise reducer. The whine isn't part of the noise print any more, so the spectrum doesn't have big jumps. This means that expanders are less likely to interact with a flangey sound, and I can lower the floor. Listen to all three tracks. The two-step process sounds a lot better.

CLICK AND CRACKLE REDUCTION

Part 1 of Track 69 is a badly damaged 78 RPM phonograph recording, originally recorded in 1933—probably a lot worse than anything you're likely to encounter. But as you can hear in Part 2, even this can be improved.

Other software may also offer a pop or crackle remover, internally set to look for different kinds of problems. While these plug-ins are primarily sold for people who want to digitize their old vinyl record collections, they're also useful in modern film and video production. With a little tweaking, they can help counteract wireless mic problems or the ticking of an unsynchronized digital signal. With a lot of tweaking, they can change the character of sound effects and some percussion instruments.

Hear for yourself

Track 69 is before-and-after for a historic recording. But the technique can also fix some modern problems (see text).

CHAPTER 16
Other Effects

REMEMBER THIS:

- There are lots of ways to turn a mono sound into simulated stereo, but only one works really well. Fortunately, it's easy and doesn't require an expensive plug-in.
- Similar techniques lets you change the width of a stereo image, or even eliminate the vocalist from many pop recordings.
- Manipulating a sound's harmonic pattern can produce amazing results. You can give it human vocal characteristics, or fool people into thinking there's more bass than their speakers can actually carry.
- Equalization, compression, and other basic effects are important—but the real power comes when you use them together.

It's a lot of fun being a sound designer. Among other things, I get to design new processes to solve problems or create new sounds. Other designers and I share these techniques at industry meetings, and then the techniques become part of the standard repertory—at least among the sound-designing crowd.

Unfortunately, this stuff doesn't fall into standard categories like equalizers or compressors, and there are no textbook algorithms for them, so they seldom appear in NLEs and audio editors. When they do, they're often poorly implemented. If you want to use these effects, you have to get third-party plug-ins or hook up multiple processors yourself. Believe me, it's worth the effort.

In this chapter, we'll cover:

- Turning monaural sounds into something very close to stereo.
- Suppressing or completely eliminating the soloist in some music recordings.
- Making existing stereo recordings seem wider.
- Adding intelligible vocal characteristics to sound effects and music (how about a doorbell that rings *hello*?).
- Processing tricks to make small speakers sound better, without muddying the sound on good monitors.

■ Simulating some everyday sound textures, such as long-distance telephone conversations.

Explanations of these effects and cookbook demonstrations are throughout this chapter. Ideally, they'll inspire you to create your own combinations.

STEREO SIMULATION

Stereo creates a soundstage along a horizontal line between the two speakers (and sometimes beyond). Any individual source in the track, such as one instrument in an orchestra or a single car horn in a cityscape, can come from any point along this line—even though there are only two speakers. Our mind creates intermediate locations by interpreting a sound's subtle volume and timing differences as it comes from the two speakers.[1] When we listen to a well-recorded stereo track, it appears to come from a myriad of locations.

But if a track is recorded in mono, or a stereo mix is converted to a mono file, those volume and timing differences are lost. All the elements that make up the sound—instruments in an orchestra or falling debris in an explosion—are lumped together in one place. Play the track through two stereo speakers at the same volume, and it appears to come from only one point, halfway between the speakers. Add a tiny delay to just one speaker or change its volume, and the sound moves somewhere else—but it still comes from a single point.

That single-point mono sound often can't compete in a finished stereo track, let alone a theatrical surround one. Ambiences, large sound effects, and scoring that's been recorded in mono doesn't sound wide enough next to stereo sounds; if you try mixing them on theatrical tracks they can compete with dialog in the center channel. While we can't recover the original positions of each element in a mono clip, there are a variety of ways to make it seem wider. Most ways can be used in theatrical, kiosk, or other situations where you control the listening environment. But only one is truly mono compatible—an important consideration for broadcast and Web tracks—so we'll discuss it first.

Stereo Simulation with Comb Filters

This nifty trick creates a wide image that is completely compatible with mono listening. Furthermore, it's one of the few techniques that actually spreads the original sound across the soundstage. The placement is based on frequency rather than the original source's location, so it's not true stereo. But it can sure be big.

---

[1]Most pop music recordings are a sort of semistereo, where volume differences alone are used to distribute instruments across the soundstage. The timing differences you'd hear in an orchestral recording—or even a good recording of a background ambience—are missing. This can actually be to your advantage, as you'll learn later in this chapter.

This stereo simulation relies on two processing techniques. One is the comb filter, described in Chapter 13. It combines a signal with a slightly delayed version of itself to cut regularly spaced notches in the spectral distribution of a sound.

PHASE OR POLARITY INVERSION

The other technique is *polarity reversal*. If you flip the polarity of a signal, voltages that were positive are now negative and vice versa. It's as if the compressions and rarefactions in the original sound were reversed. This flipping is often called *phase reversal* or *inversion*.[2] It's easily done in hardware by changing the connection to an op amp or reversing the wires in a balanced connection. In software, all you have to do is multiply every value by -1: this is a single-click command in most audio software.

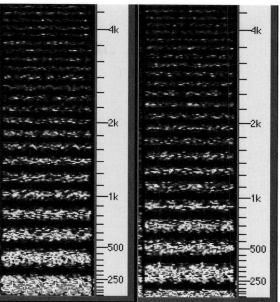

In Chapter 13, we made a comb filter by mixing a signal with a delayed version of itself. If we had inverted the delayed version before mixing, it would also create a comb—but the peaks would be at frequencies where the first comb had notches. You can see this effect on pink noise in a spectragram (Figure 16.1). On the left is noise mixed with a 5 ms delay. It has the expected notches at 300 Hz, 500 Hz, and on up. On the right is the noise mixed with the same delay, but inverted. While it's got as many notches, these are halfway between the ones on the left: 400 Hz, 600 Hz, and so on.

FIGURE 16.1
Pink noise through two comb filters based on a 5 ms delay. The notches are complementary because the delay's phase was inverted.

If you mix both of these comb-filtered signals together, each delay precisely cancels the other. You get the original, unfiltered pink noise back. This is just simple math:

$$\frac{\begin{array}{l}\text{pink noise} + \text{delay} \\ + \text{ pink noise} - \text{delay}\end{array}}{= \text{pink noise}}$$

THE SIMULATOR

You can take advantage of this cancellation to make a mono-compatible stereo simulator.

1. Run a mono signal through a single delay, around 6 milliseconds.
2. Mix the delay's output with the original and call it the *left* channel.

---

[2]Actually, phase has nothing to do with it because there's no delay involved. But the effect is exactly the same as a 180 degree phase shift at all frequencies, and *phase inversion* is the way most audio engineers and software refer to the process, so that's what we'll call it here.

"Left" out

Input ——▶ Short delay

−1

"Right" out

FIGURE 16.2
A basic stereo simulator using one delay, a phase inverter, and two mixers.

3. Mix an inverted version of the delay's output with the original and call it the *right* channel. You're done.

Figure 16.2 shows the schematic. Frequencies are distributed to the left or right depending on where they fall on the comb. A mono viewer hears the two channels equally, canceling the comb and leaving nothing but the original mono signal.

Because most natural sounds are rich in harmonics, it's likely that part of their waves will go to the left, part to the right, and part in between. The result with most sounds: a full and wide stereo-like soundstage. You can hear its effect on pink noise in part 1 of Track 70; first the unprocessed noise, then through the 5 ms complementary combs.

> ⊚ **Hear for yourself**
>
> Track 70 includes examples of various kinds of stereo simulation and other phase-based tricks.

Combs from a fixed 5 ms delay can cause problems with some source material, so a good simulator lets you vary the DELAY between a couple of milliseconds and about a dozen milliseconds. The DEPTH of the combs can be made adjustable by putting a volume control on the output of the delay; this lets you adjust the amount of stereo so things don't get too wide.

SIMULATOR IMPROVEMENTS

There's one slight problem with this stereo simulator. If one channel gets lost, the low frequency notches can make things sound thin. This would also affect people sitting much closer to one speaker than the other. You can resolve this by adding a *crossover*, which splits the signal into two bands at a preset frequency. The lows go directly to both outputs; the mids and highs are fed to the complementary combs. Since bass notes aren't very directional, the effect still sounds like stereo.

You could build a crossover with matched high-pass and low-pass filters, but it's easier and more accurate to use a single high-pass filter and some more phase inversion. The same math applies: if you invert the high-pass filter's output and mix it with its input, the highs are cancelled and only the lows are left. If you combine the unprocessed bass with the two combed mid and high signals—the way a mono listener would—the high-pass filter is cancelled and any phase distortion or other problems it may have caused go away. Figure 16.3 shows the

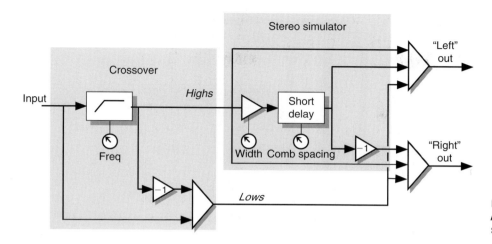

FIGURE 16.3
A complete stereo simulator.

completed stereo simulator, with an additional control to set the CROSSOVER frequency.

While this kind of stereo simulation is available in standalone analog and digital hardware, I've never seen it fully implemented in desktop software. So I did a version myself, which you're welcome to download from my Web site. Go to www.dplay.com/gotcha: you'll find StereoSim, a preset file for SFXMachine, and StereoSim.AU, a plug-in that uses the open-source SonicBirth framework for Mac (sonicbirth.sourceforge.net). Or download Stereoizer from my site. It's a tiny Windows app contributed by DV magazine reader Timothy J. Weber, after I wrote a column about stereo. It uses a similar algorithm and seems to work pretty well. Figure 16.4 shows two versions and their controls.

If you're using the presets I wrote, you'll need either SFX Machine or SonicBirth installed. Open your mono track and convert it to 2 tracks, using a Mono to Stereo function or by manually adding a second track. Then apply this preset, preview and play with the settings until you like the sound, and process. Timothy J. Weber's *Stereoizer* is a standalone app that doesn't require any other editor or plug-in. It doesn't have a preview function, but runs quickly so you can try multiple passes until you get the results you like. Depending on the original source material and how you set the controls, either method creates stereo-like files with a full and rich sound.

Part 2 of Track 70 lets you hear an example of this processing using voice and music examples. You'll notice a couple of things.

- The voices are somewhat wider, but they no longer seem as focused. That's why dialog is rarely run through a stereo simulator. On the other hand, this effect can be a nice sound design trick for dream sequences and other altered points of view.
- The synthesized music is spread only a small amount. That's because its simple "instruments" don't have many harmonics.

345

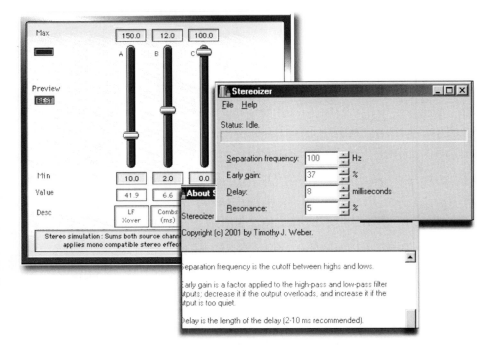

FIGURE 16.4
You can download stereo simulators from my Website. They're free. The one on the left requires the third-party SFXMachine, a low cost plug-in, as host.

- The orchestral music is spread a lot. Acoustic instruments are generally rich in harmonics, and each instrument's can fall in a different range. Note how the high brass seems to wander slightly from midleft to center, as it plays different notes.
- The pop vocal stays relatively centered, compared to the strings backing her up, because the string choir is harmonically richer.
- The rock band changes width on each beat, in time with the highly processed lead guitar. Guitar fuzz boxes, an essential component of rock and roll, distort the signal to add more harmonics.

Compare these with the original stereo recordings on Track 39.

Other Stereo Simulation Techniques

PAN AND REVERB

The most common way to add location to mono sources mix is to pan them, placing each at a specific point in the stereo or surround field and then adding reverberation. This approximates what happens when performers are spread out on a stage, and is perfectly appropriate when mixing individual instrumental tracks into a piece of stereo music. Multitrack audio programs, which are music-centric to begin with, usually have this facility built in. You can do something similar (though with generally poorer-quality reverb) by using a clip's pan line and assigning it a reverb in a NLE.

Unfortunately, the technique isn't as effective on mono recordings of full musi-cal ensembles. That's because if the original mix is panned to just one point, it sounds like all the musicians are jammed together in one spot on the stage. It's also of dubious usefulness on sound effects. Nearby explosions, crowds, and traffic loops *are* big, not a point source with an indoor reverb. Decide for your-self. Part 3 of Track 70 lets you hear this effect with mixed music and sound effects.

The reverb doesn't go away for mono listeners, either, and might be too much on their sets. You can make a reverb effect that disappears in mono, if you have a versatile multitrack audio program or a hardware mixer. Pan the original sig-nal where you want it and also send it to a reverb. Mix both channels of the reverb's wet or 100 percent output, with none of the original signal, and pan to just one side. Then route the reverb's output through a phase inverter and pan it to the other side. For a mono listener, the two reverb signals will cancel each other out, leaving just the dry original. Interestingly, listeners with Dolby ana-log surround will hear the dry signal in the front of the room, and the reverb coming from the rear. This can be effective.

DELAYS

A more appropriate alternative for crowds and other backgrounds is to use a long delay—on the order of half a minute or so. Pan the original mono track midway between the center and the left speaker. Make a copy of the track, off-set by at least thirty seconds, and pan it to a similar spot on the other side. Unless there's a memorable shout or other identifiable element in the source audio, nobody will notice the repeat. Play with the pans until the background is as wide or narrow as you want. If you keep things very wide, the background will be easier to mix with mono dialog because none of it will be in the center. Part 4 of Track 70 demonstrates the technique with a mono crowd loop.

BINAURAL SIMULATION

If you've got very good control over what the listener will hear (this usually requires headphones or a kiosk setting), you can make sounds three-dimensional. They appear to come from front or back, as well as left or right. The trick takes advantage of *Head-Related Transfer Functions (HRTF)*, a measure of how our outer ears and the shape of our head adds subtle delays and filtering to a sound depend-ing on its source direction. Because these subtleties get influenced by room acous-tics, they don't work well in normal listening situations. *Binaural* refers to *two ears*, and that's pretty much where your speakers have to be.

HRTF manipulation is too complex to do with normal delays and equalizers. But there are low-cost plug-ins that'll do the job for you. Figure 16.5 shows Wave Art's *WaveSurround*, which handles stereo or mono and includes rever-beration in its processing. SFXMachine's *ReSpatializer* can process and pan sur-round signals, and includes an auto-rotate function.

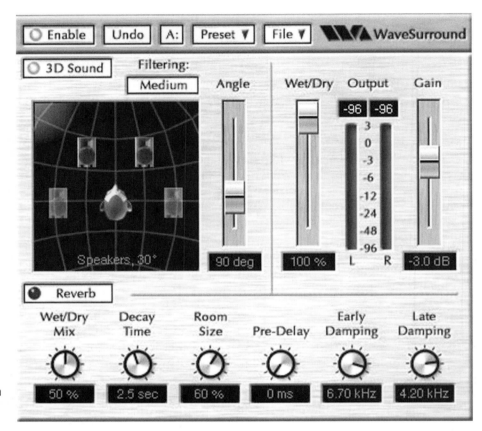

FIGURE 16.5
WaveSurround can simulate three-dimensional effects in some stereo listening situations.

THE WORST WAY TO SIMULATE STEREO

A few benighted audio applications and some older, low cost keyboards generate stereo by sending a mono signal to one channel, with a phase inverted version of it going to the other. This does make the sound wider—and as you might guess, also makes it completely disappear for mono listeners.

Or it might not disappear. Some TV stations use *phase chasers* which assume this condition only happens because of operator error, and automatically compensate by inverting one channel. These boxes look at the entire mix, so depending on how loud the inverted element is, might or might not flip things. If they do, the element remains but everything else disappears in mono. Things get even weirder for viewers with Dolby Surround: elements or possibly the entire track will end up *behind* the viewer, and in mono.

Other Phase-inversion Tricks

You can use the cancellation effect to reduce or completely eliminate the soloist in a lot of pop music, or to control the width of a conventional stereo recording. If you pay attention to what you're doing, there won't be any problems for mono viewers.

VOCAL ELIMINATION

When mixing a multitrack master of a song down to stereo, the lead vocal is often panned to the center of the soundstage. This means the vocal is equal on both the left and right channels. If you phase invert one channel and then mix the two channels together, the voice cancels itself out. That's the basis of the vocal elimination technique, which has been around almost as long as multi-track recording.

Vocal elimination destroys any instruments that have been recorded in mono and panned to the center, not just the vocalist. That usually includes the bass and kick drum—important elements in a music mix. With half the mix inverted, some other production effects can disappear. And since you've mixed the channels together, it's now in mono.

Sophisticated solo eliminators partially solve these problem with two techniques. First, both incoming channels have crossovers set just below the lowest fundamental in the singer's voice. The low frequencies are sent, with no cancellation, directly to left and right outputs. The highs are phase inverted on one channel only and then mixed to cancel anything in the center. Sometimes, there's a variable bypass to control the degree of rejection. The mono output of the mixer is finally routed through a stereo simulator. Figure 16.6 puts it all together.

This technique is often used in radio stations to produce song parodies. It can also be helpful in a mix to lower the melody line in preproduced music, so dialog or voice-over can show through. Or you might just enjoy turning pop music into karaoke versions for parties. Part 5 of Track 70 applies this effect to our two vocal samples. First you'll hear the unprocessed music, then with partial solo removal, then with maximum solo removal.

 Gotcha

No guarantees. The solo elimination technique has its limitations. You can't use it to reduce a centered soloist in acoustic recordings (including most jazz and classical music, and live pop performances) because room acoustics and multiple mics introduce differences between the channels. It usually won't work on soloists who have been double tracked or had other studio tricks done to their tracks. It doesn't eliminate stereo reverberation that might be applied to a mono soloist. In that case, you'll hear the solo go away, but it'll leave a ghostly image of the solo's reverb.

Still, when it works, it's amazing.

BAND ELIMINATION?

Audio novices sometimes ask if solo elimination can also be used to *isolate* a solo line. Their logic is, "Well, the original is band-with-soloist, and the processed version is band-without. If we invert the band-without and mix it with itself, the band will cancel and leave just the soloist."

Crossover

Left Input

Left Highs

−1

Amount

Left Lows

−1

Right Input

Crossover

Right Highs

Freq

−1

Right Lows

Stereo simulator

Short delay

Width   Comb spacing

1

"Left" out

"Right" out

FIGURE 16.6
A sophisticated vocal eliminator.

Unfortunately, this doesn't work. Since the solo-removed version has half the band's polarity reversed, the result isn't what you'd expect. Check the math:

Solo zapping:

$$\frac{\begin{array}{r} \text{Left} \\ -\text{ Right} \end{array}}{=\text{L} - \text{R (no soloist)}}$$

Band zapping?

Mono mix	*or*	L + R	*or*	L + R
−Solo zapped		−(L − R)		+(−L + R)
???		???		2R

> ⚠️ **Gotcha**
>
> ***What's left?*** We've been talking about inverting the right channel, instead of the left one, only for convenience. If you invert the left instead, everything still works the same way. However, the sound may be subtly different. This gets into the realm of absolute phase, which the golden-ear crowd argues about. I don't think it makes much difference in a film or video track.

WIDTH CONTROL

As the previous math shows, solo elimination creates an L – R signal. At the same time, we can mix left and right together to create an L + R signal. Having these two signals at the same time can be handy.

- L + R is equivalent to mono, with every part of the sound coming from one place. This is actually what analog stereo FM and TV broadcast as their main channel, and it's all that mono receivers are capable of picking up.
- L – R is sometimes known as *difference* and contains only those sounds that aren't common to both channels. Analog stations broadcast this signal at a higher frequency for stereo sets.
- L + R is also sometimes known as *mid*: it's what a mic facing directly into the middle of the soundstage would hear.
- L – R is sometimes known as *side*: it's what a figure-eight mic, placed close to the mid mic but facing towards the left, would hear.

M/S TECHNIQUE

Midside miking (*m/s*) is a popular technique for recording acoustic music and is occasionally used in Europe for documentary dialog. Many field mixers and some recording consoles have built-in decoder circuits to turn m/s into standard left/right stereo. It's a simple circuit. Mix the mid and side signals together equally, and R cancels to give you just the left channel. Invert the side signal and mix with the mid, and L cancels leaving just the right.

M/S has the advantage of being inherently mono compatible. Once decoded, combining the left and right channels cancels the figure-eight mic completely. Other stereo miking techniques can have phase problems when combined to mono, if sounds have had to travel different distances getting to each mic.

It also lets you vary the width of the image by raising or lowering the volume of just the side channel. This gives you greater control than just panning the signals closer together because you can make the signal wider than it was originally. It's so handy, it's often used as a separate effect on normally recorded stereo signals. A *shuffler* converts the signal to m/s using the technique at the top of this page, has a volume control in the side signal, and then converts things back to left/right. Figure 16.7 shows such an arrangement.

Modulation

Another kind of processing controls the spectral balance of a signal, either modulating it to match the balance of a different signal, or generating harmonics that weren't in the original. The former can be useful in sound design; the latter in improving what the viewer hears.

MODULATION: THE VOCODER

Vowels and voiced consonants are made by buzzing the vocal folds and then filtering the buzz through resonating cavities in the mouth and sinuses.

351

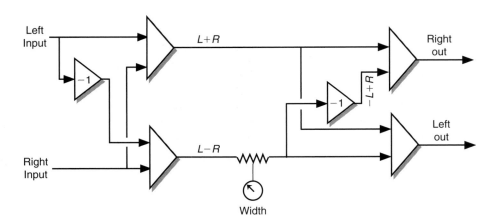

FIGURE 16.7
A stereo width control, or shuffler, turns left/right into mid/side and back.

This creates the vocal formants. Unvoiced consonants are made by applying similar mouth filters to hissing air forced through a small area. This idea of a human voice as a generator and filters was radical in the late-1930s, when it was proposed by Homer Dudley of Bell Labs. His goal was to break speech into standard components—buzzes, hisses, and formant levels—which could be analyzed at one end of a telephone wire and re-created at the other. The signal flowing over the wire would be a lot simpler than a voice, saving money for the phone company. To prove his thesis, Dudley invented the *vocoder*, which really could recreate speech from very simple data. Unfortunately it also turned the voice into a depersonalized monotone, and the phone company had to find other ways to save money.[3]

People started playing with vocoders outside the lab. If you replace the buzz with orchestral chords and vocode a voice, the orchestra seems to sing the words you're saying. In fact, any sound can be used as the *carrier*, so long as it's got enough energy at the formant frequencies. You don't even need a voiced/unvoiced detector if the vocoder has sufficient bands.

When you think about it, a vocoder's construction is very much like the multiband noise reducer in the previous chapter. The only significant difference is that each band has *two* filters, one for the input (known as the *modulator*) and one for the carrier. Figure 16.8 shows a typical construction.

Vocoders are popular in music production, so there are a number of free and low cost versions available. That's good, since they're also valuable in film and video sound design:

■ If you run dialog through a vocoder and use a single, harmonically rich tone as the carrier, the results can sound robotic. That's because normal inflection is replaced by the fundamental of the carrier tone.

---

[3]Today, the monotone effect is solved with computerized pitch recognition. Vocoders are now used in many low bitrate voice compression schemes, including digital cell phones.

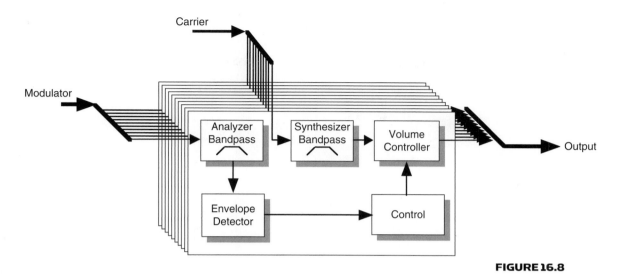

Carrier

Modulator

| Analyzer Bandpass | Synthesizer Bandpass | Volume Controller |

Output

Envelope Detector

Control

FIGURE 16.8
A vocoder is similar to a multiband noise reducer.

- If you use a synthesizer playing chords as the carrier, you'll get an electro music effect (Part 1 of Track 71).
- You can also use sound effects as the carrier. Howling wind, for example, can create a ghostlike effect.

Part 2 of Track 71 shows one application for the vocoder in sound effects processing. First you hear my voice, slowly enunciating a sports cheer. It's followed by some crowd roar from a hockey game. Then I join the two in a vocoder, using the crowd as carrier; the result seems to be the entire crowd shouting my cheer. This solo version sounds slightly artificial, but a little equalization and sweetening with recognizable shouts would make it usable in a mix.

Harmonic Exciters

There's a style of architectural painting that makes a flat wall look like it's got doors, windows, balconies, and other features. Artists call it *trompe l'oeil*, French for "mislead the eye." One class of audio effect achieves a sort of *trompe l'orielle*, fooling the ear into hearing sounds that aren't there.

BASS EXTENSION

We're so used to harmonics that when we hear any tones in the right relationship, we assume they're harmonics of *something*—even if there's no fundamental. You can use this phenomenon to make a small speaker sound like it's handling more bass than it really is.

Waves' *MaxxBass* plug-in is one of a couple of bass harmonic generators available. It takes parts of the signal below a preset frequency, generates an artificial harmonic exactly an octave above, and mixes it back in. If you choose a frequency at the lower edge of a system's capability, this harmonic can imply a fundamental that's actually been cut off.

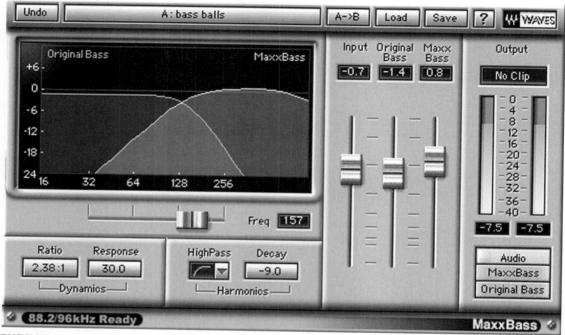

FIGURE 16.9
MaxxBass widens the perceived frequency range by adding harmonics to the bass.

MaxxBass's user interface show how this effect works. In Figure 16.9, I've chosen a cutoff FREQUENCY of about 160 Hz. The dark gray area on the left of the graphic display represents bass energy in the input that the processor will work on. It's not removed by the process, so good speakers can still reproduce it. But it's also fed to the harmonic synthesizer. The light gray area on the right of the graphic shows where the harmonics would fall, an octave above the original. The software also lets you compress the harmonics' volume, to help them be heard.

Part 1 of Track 72 consists of the voice/music demo, twice. The first pass has no processing. The second is through MaxxBass, using the settings shown. While there's a slight difference between these two passes, it's subtle. This is what a listener with a full range system would hear. Part 2 is the same as Part 1, run through a sharp high pass at 175 Hz to simulate a poor loudspeaker. You won't hear much difference between its two halves in the female voices or the brass; they don't have much low-end energy to begin with. But in the second half, with MaxxBass turned on, the male speaking voice seems a little fuller. And the synthesized music and pop songs now have a pulsing bass that's totally lacking from the unprocessed version.

Harmonic extension is better than equalization for improving perceived bass. Merely boosting the lows would make the track sound muddy on a good system and wouldn't be much help at all through a small speaker. The process is most appropriate for kiosks, laptops, telephone transmission, and other situations where you know exactly what'll be lost by the system. It's of very little use in a wide range theatrical mix, since the fundamentals are already carried.

HIGH-FREQUENCY ENHANCEMENT

A related process can be used to improve existing recordings that lack highs. In this case, some of the upper frequencies, a half-octave or so below where the recording falls off, are run through a harmonic generator. A small amount of the generator's output, an octave higher, is mixed with the original signal. This doesn't exactly replace high frequencies that were lost to a bad recording process; those are gone forever. But because many rich sounds have harmonics similar to the ones being generated, it can fool the ear into thinking the original highs are still there. Part 3 of Track 72 demonstrates how it works. First we hear our voice/music demo rolled off at 4 kHz, to simulate a bad recording. Then we process the rolled-off version through an enhancer. Voices aren't badly harmed by the filtering; the extra harmonics in the processed version sound almost out of place. On the other hand, the music is definitely helped by enhancement.

High-frequency enhancement should be used carefully to avoid hitting the Nyquist Limit and causing aliasing distortion. But it can add a little sparkle to an otherwise dull recording. (By the way, it's not the same as high-frequency equalization. If we'd attempted to fix the dull first half of Part 3 by applying a boost above 4 kHz, all we'd accomplish is an increase in the noise level.)

High-frequency enhancement can also be a useful step in hiss reduction. Apply a sharp low-pass filter at 10 kHz to remove some of the hiss. Then use enhancement to restore harmonics that the filter destroyed. If you then want to apply multiband noise reduction, the noise reduction can be less aggressive and produce fewer artifacts.

355

CREATING NEW EFFECTS BY COMBINING OLD ONES

Almost every program lets you apply effects in series, with the output of one processor being the input for another. In many NLEs, you can stack multiple audio filters on a clip. In multitrack audio programs you can usually insert more than one effect on a track. And SonicBirth, mentioned earlier in this chapter, lets you go wild if you're willing to do a little programming. This is a place to get creative—and have fun—with processing. You can design sounds that go far beyond what a plug-in's programmers ever expected. Think of the following recipes as dessert.

A few tips for chaining effects:

- Tune the first effect close to where you want it, before you assign the next one in the chain. Then tune the second, and work your way up. If your effects have bypass buttons, use them to check the sound of individual processors.
- Think about what order you'll be applying the effects. In general, apply equalizers and filters before dynamics controllers; that way, compressors won't react to the level of sounds that are subsequently filtered. Reverbs and

delay effects can be either before or after a dynamics controller, depending on whether you want to affect the original sound or the processed one.

- Make sure each effect's output is at a good volume. If the plug-ins have their own meters, use them. If not, test the output volume of an effect before you add the next. It's very easy for things to get too loud or soft inside the chain. This will add distortion or noise, even if the last effect in the chain restores the original volume.
- Chaining can take a lot of processing power. If you hear stuttering or other problems while in preview mode, use the bypass buttons to turn off all but the first effect. Render it, remove that effect, and turn on the next. Keep rendering and shortening the chain until it plays smoothly.

As an example, we'll combine some effects to create three sound textures that have been lost in the digital world: a movie's optical soundtrack, an old AM radio, and an analog long-distance connection. The challenge in all of these is to make a sound that's true to the original, and yet painted with a broad enough brush that the effect is immediately recognizable through a TV's small speaker.

SOME NOTES ON THE INGREDIENTS

As with any recipe, it helps to get familiar with the individual ingredients first.

Filters and Equalizers

Filters are the most important tool for simulating old media, but they must be true cutoff filters—ones that can reject sounds beyond a preset frequency. Ordinary graphic or parametric equalizers are too gentle to do the job. Effects filters should have at least 12 dB per octave rejection. You'll need both a low-cut and a high-cut to do most effects right; if you have only one good filter, use it for the lows and apply a standard shelving equalizer to the highs.

But don't throw away your parametric equalizer. Early analog media could be very resonant. Almost any old-time effect can benefit from a sharp peak or two, usually around 500 Hz to 1.5 kHz.

Dynamics Processing and Deliberate Distortion

Most analog signal chains used a lot of compression so loud sounds wouldn't produce distortion. Set yours for a fairly low threshold, high ratio, and fast attack and decay. This will add distortion to low frequencies, so be prepared to back off slightly.

Some distortion was inevitable in early analog systems, particularly those aimed at the consumer. Unfortunately, it isn't the kind a badly tuned compressor makes. But you can simulate it on your desktop by hacking the digital signal so it runs out of bits. (It's not exactly the same, but close enough for these purposes.) You can do this with some distortion plug-ins. If you don't have one, just amplify an existing sound as much as your software will let you, and render the louder version. Then lower the amplified file by about 3 dB, so it doesn't crackle on playback. The audio envelopes should have turned into a rectangle. You might have to do two or three passes before this happens.

Delay

If a phonograph or tape player wasn't properly engineered—every mechanical bearing perfectly rounded—you'd hear tiny speed variations (*flutter*) as things turned. You can duplicate this effect with a modulatable delay effect, found in some delay plug-ins and most flangers or choruses. As the delay time changes, it affects the sound the same way an out-of-round bearing did.

Noises

Movie projector shutters, phonograph groove noise, and telephone crosstalk can be mixed in from other sources to make the effect more authentic. If the noise isn't already mangled, mix it with your main signal and apply the filters and distortion effects to both at the same time.

MOVIES

A lot of projects need to turn modern digital film and video into old-fashioned cinema—anything from a torn, dirty classroom film to a Hollywood classic. On the video side, the usual formula is to lower the chroma, add some scratches and dirt, and make a few tiny jump cuts. It's not a true film look, but a parody that emphasizes film's visual limitations to broaden the gag. Optical recording, used for virtually every soundtrack until a couple of decades ago, had plenty of audio limitations you can parody.

357

I'll take time with this first recipe to show the thinking that goes into a convincing effect. The key is to think about how the old-fashioned channel actually operated, rather than just what it sounded like. The bulleted paragraphs are the "thinking" part. The paragraphs below them explain how to accomplish each part of the sound.

 Gotcha

This side of parodies. The steps in this section are designed to simulate old, mistreated film. It's not the same as trying to make a track sound like a modern theatrical feature.

If you want to mimic the sounds of today's blockbusters, record all your elements properly. Then apply the non-parody techniques that fill the rest of this book. Believe me; the folks in Hollywood don't do anything we haven't talked about here.

What makes the characteristic sound of a film?

- The projector has to hold the film perfectly still at the lens, 24 times a second, so individual frames can be projected. A few inches away, the film has move smoothly at the sound head to create a continuous track. These two motions are isolated by a shock-absorbing loop of film. But the isolation was never perfect, and some of that 24 frame-per-second flutter would always sneak in.

- In badly maintained projectors, the mass of the film reels can influence the speed. If the mass isn't perfectly balanced—as can happen when the reels aren't perfectly maintained either—the speed keeps changing as the reel moves. This introduces a *wow*[4] or slow rhythmic pitch change, at a frequency related to the reel's rotation.

Frequency modulate the signal with a 24-Hz sine wave (flutter) combined with about a 0.2 Hz sine wave (wow from a 1200 foot reel of 16 mm film). The easiest way is to mix two oscillators and apply the result to the MODULATION INPUT of a delay at around 40 ms. As the delay changes, it forces the pitch up and down. This delay also knocks the track one film frame out of sync, which may add to the humor of the effect. If you don't like it, set the delay to exactly 33 ms and slip the entire track one frame earlier to compensate.

As an alternative, you can use two flangers in series, one with a 24 Hz modulation and the other set for 0.2 Hz.

- Film projectors also had a characteristic hum. The lamp that poured light through the optical soundtrack needed a pure DC voltage, but this could be hard to maintain in an older projector. Some of the power line's AC would sneak in.

Add a 120 Hz sawtooth, at low levels, for this hum.

- The photocell that read the light coming through the optical track had its own random hiss.

Add a tiny amount of white noise.

- Optical sound was not a wide-range medium. Both highs and lows were lost in the process. Bad projector maintenance could destroy the highs even more.

Band pass everything between 250 Hz and 7.5 kHz. The lower filter should be fairly sharp. The upper one depends on what you're trying to simulate. Well-maintained movie theaters running 35mm tracks could start to fall off around 12 kHz, but a sharp 7.5-kHz filter will make sure the effect is immediately recognizable to an modern audience. Classroom projectors ran at a slower speed, were not high fidelity to start with, and lost treble when they got out of alignment: you could use a filter that starts a gentle roll off around 2.5 kHz.

- It isn't really part of the reproduced sound, but the clicking noise from a projector's gate is part of the cliché.

Get one from a sound effects library. Or make it yourself with a 12 Hz square wave, high-pass filtered very sharply at 5.5 kHz. Modulate the frequency slightly with the 0.2 Hz sine wave you're using for wow, and it's surprisingly realistic.

---

[4]Yes, *flutter* and *wow* are accepted technical terms. You don't hear the terms (or the effects) much these days, since they were a result of mechanical imperfections in analog systems.

For the ultimate illusion, use a pitch bender to ramp both speed and pitch up from zero to normal over about 3 seconds when the clip starts, and back down to zero as it's ending. Classroom projector motors had to fight a lot of mass and always got off to a slow start.

Don't forget to add a click, and delete a few frames of sound, each time you have a jump cut in the picture. If you want to be accurate, the audio jump should be a second after the picture jump; that's just about how long it took the splice to get from lens to sound head in a 16 mm projector.

- Giant movie palaces had a sound of their own. A 75-foot-deep auditorium had a distinct echo from the rear wall, about 2.5 frames after dialog left the speakers. Every theater was slightly different, and the echo depended on where you were sitting.

Use a reverb with a short, diffuse characteristic. Set the time before the first reflection to about 100 ms, and bunch the other early reflections together. If your software doesn't let you control the initial time, use a delay line ahead of the reverb.

Part 1 of Track 73 lets you hear this effect the way I implemented it on a powerful DSP-based hardware processor. Or download my algorithms for SFX Machine or SonicBirth from my Website. As you can see from Figure 16.10, it has almost all of the features above. (I didn't bother with the reverb.)

359

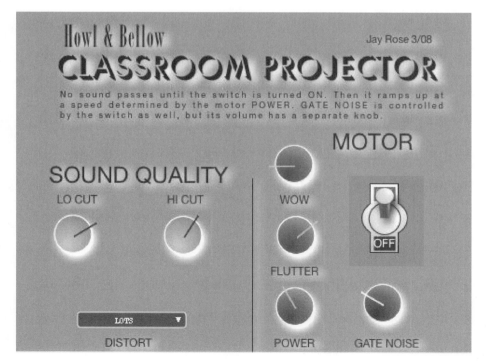

FIGURE 16.10
A free SonicBirth AU plug-in to mimic a classroom projector.

RADIOS

Broadcast radio's quality changed as the years went by, but a low cutoff somewhere between 120 and 500 Hz, and high cutoff around 4 to 8 kHz, is a good place to start. Use lots of compression and a little distortion. Mix in some square wave or sawtooth at 120 Hz; the harmonics simulate AM radio's power-line interference.

Police and CB radios had much more distortion, a bandwidth as narrow as 400 Hz to 2.5 kHz, and hiss. For an even better simulation, cut the hiss off whenever the voice pauses. Two-way radios did this automatically.

Older AM and shortwave radios had a squeal as you tuned them. You can simulate it with a sine wave sweeping from 8 kHz down, reaching its lowest frequency as you center on the desired station. Single-sideband shortwave—a common form of transmission—would shift the voice frequencies up and down slowly. You can simulate this with a delay line heavily modulated with a sine wave around 0.3 Hz (but to do it right, you need a heterodyne frequency shifter, seldom found in desktop software).

PHONOGRAPH

The distortion and band limiting for phonograph was similar to radios, but most players also had a wow repeating at the speed of the turntable: modulate a delay at 1.3 Hz for 78 RPM records, 0.75 Hz for 45s, and 0.55 Hz for 33s. If the record was warped, this modulation could be very deep. Add occasional ticks in the same rhythm, plus continuous groove noise.

TELEPHONE

Local analog calls are easy to simulate. A low cutoff around 380 Hz and a high one at 3 kHz are a little more extreme than modern phones, but work nicely in production. Add compression and distortion before you filter. Local calls also had some hiss, but that's rarely necessary in the mix. Digital calls (on a cell phone or VOIP) are more complicated because of the compression algorithms, but you don't have to simulate that: just run the voice track through a similar codec.

Old-fashioned long distance calls had a few additional wrinkles. A lot of your voice would be reflected back from the other end of the call. Telephone calls move at nearly the speed of light, but over cross-country distances, it would create a noticeable echo. A 6,000 mile round trip takes about 1/30 second—just like the acoustic slap you get from the back wall of a medium-sized room. Mix in a small amount of the original signal, delayed between 20 and 120 ms, to simulate a variety of distances and line conditions.

In those predigital days, long distance also suffered from cross talk as other conversations leaked into your call. Match the sound by adding another track of different voices, with a low-cut around 500 Hz, mixed about 30 dB below the main track. If you flip the second track so it plays backwards, the cross talk will sound foreign and not be as distracting.

Part 2 of Track 73 lets you hear a full-bore old-fashioned long distance simulator. The cross talk is actually the main voice, delayed, pitch shifted, broken into chunks, and reversed. This lets me apply the effect in real time, without needing a separate track for cross talk.

PREPACKAGED MANGLING

Old analog processes are often available as presets in commercial plug-ins. Most of these are approximations, since it takes a lot of processing power to get these sounds right. But ultimately, filmmaking is about story telling. So if one of those presets does the job for you (and doesn't call attention to itself, or "take you out of the film") I won't complain.

On the other hand, my way—thinking about and then building and tuning your own effect—is a lot more fun. There are some tools to make this kind of sound design easier. Audio Ease's $450 *Speakerphone* software combines a lot of the necessary processors with sampled impulse responses, using a convolution engine similar to their Altiverb (Chapter 13). It's both tunable and comes with a large library of presets, and is powerful enough for just about any film or video chore.

Eventide's DSP4000B+ series ($3500 and up) are serious hardware for people who need fully realized effects in real-time, with as many as eight simultaneous channels. They ship with about 100 simulation algorithms[5] plus a flexible high-level DSP language so you can build your own on the spot. I keep one in my studio and reach for it when I can't get "just the right effect" anywhere else. It was also the best way to create most of the specialized tutorial tracks for other chapters in this book.

---

[5]Disclaimer: I wrote them. But I don't get royalties on them.

CHAPTER 17

The Mix

363

Actually, just about everything in the past six chapters relates to mixing. Equalization, compression, and other processing generally aren't applied until the mix. That's the first time you can hear how a processed sound relates to other elements in a track. It also may be the first time you can hear the project as a whole, rather than as individual elements or sequences, and feel how it flows from beginning to end.

If you edit and mix in different places, this might even be the first time you hear the track on good monitors. It's foolish to make processing decisions without them. If you're mixing at an audio post facility, their processors will probably also be a lot better than what's in your NLE. It makes sense to wait until you've got access to them. There are usually only two times when you might want to apply processing before the final mix:

- Clips that are candidates for noise reduction should be tested before you start editing, to make sure you'll be able to get them clean enough to use. But apply the absolute minimum you can get away with. And make sure you've got unprocessed copies available.
- It may be necessary to do a little tweaking when creating a temporary mix for client approval or test screenings. It's usually best to remove this processing and start fresh at the final mix.

This chapter deals with the non-processing aspects of a mix: the techniques involved, and how to keep sounds in a proper relationship with each other.

> **Gotcha**
>
> **Why not mix while editing?** On the face of it, this should save time. As you assemble picture you can apply audio filters and adjust the volume of each track. When you finish editing the last scene, the project is already mixed. This, of course, requires that your NLE has audio monitors you can trust.
>
> But unless a project is very simple—one or two talking heads, a voiceover, and maybe music at the head and tail—mixing in pieces can lead to an inconsistent track that's hard to listen to. It's nearly impossible to produce a smooth sound when each mix decision is separated by long periods of editing.

WHAT A MIX NEEDS

Obviously, you can't start without picture and individual tracks, software that's capable of mixing, and probably some processing plug-ins. But a few other things—operating methods as well as hardware or software—can make the difference between a polished, professional track and one that shouts "amateur."

Know the Elements

It helps to know what sounds are on the timeline and how they relate to the story. It's one thing to see a clip marked "car start," but to mix it properly, you need to know *how* it starts. Is there a long turnover that gets ridden under other sounds, or does the engine catch immediately? Does the engine then idle, or is it put in gear immediately and the car drives away? You also need to know what's supposed to happen to the sound: Does it cross-fade to a tracking car, drive off, or cut to another scene?

You should know where tweaks are necessary in production dialog and where ADR or other effects will need processing. You should have an idea of how music should segue from one track to another and where it should be faded.

Most importantly, you should understand how the track has been designed. Dialog usually dominates, but there are places where sound effects or music may rise above dialog levels. In one scene, music might exist simply to punctuate sound effects; in another, effects may be barely audible under the score. It depends on what you're trying to convey from moment to moment.

If you edited the project and are doing the mix yourself, you're probably on top of all this already. If you're taking the project to a mix studio or dub stage, it's your responsibility to have an intimate knowledge of the track. The re-recording mixer can't know the film like you do.

Know the Audience

Corporate video clients are often surprised when I ask them how a piece will be shown—not what tape format will be used, but where the audience will be sitting. If that surprises you as well, go back and read the first section of Chapter 5.

It's a reasonable question for your own narrative film projects as well. Is your primary goal theatrical and festival? Is it broadcast? Home or office DVD? Is it Web and needs to survive a laptop's speakers but still sound good on headphones? It would be nice to think "all of the above," but that luxury may be beyond your means in terms of source quality, mixing facility, and mixer's experience.

Organize the Tracks

Nothing is harder to mix than jumbled tracks. It's tempting to drop sounds on the first available track while you're building a project, and may save time during the edit. But if a single track has dialog, spot effects, and music at different times, it'll slow down the mix. Keeping similar elements on the same track also means you can save time by applying effects globally instead of on individual clips.

Have a consistent track layout for each kind of project. It's fairly standard to put dialog on the top tracks, sound effects under them, and scoring on the bottom. How many tracks are devoted to each depends on the project. A narrative film will have at least three or four dialog tracks in two sets that alternate with the scenes; many projects have a lot more. A documentary TV show will almost always put narration on its own track, and then devote two or more for alternating interview dialog. Production sound effects and Foley are given their own tracks. Plot-critical hard effects are treated separately from backgrounds. An original score gets its own track of course, but a library score might need two or three tracks for crossfades and overlays. Music that will be treated as source—radios, PA systems, and so on—should be on its own *futz*[1] track for special processing.

The track layout also depends on your software. Some audio programs let you choose whether a track is mono, stereo, or surround. Others require individual tracks for each channel of a stereo or surround element, but let you control and route them from a single fader. Make your setup choices based on how the sound will be heard in the mix, not how a specific clip was recorded. You may want to put mono clips on a stereo track, so you can insert stereo effects. Most Foley tracks should be mono, even if they use stereo recordings, so they can be routed and processed with dialog.

Many NLEs restrict you to mono tracks only. If you're mixing in the NLE, you won't have many setup options. But if you've imported to an audio program for the mix, it's worth spending a few minutes moving elements around.

---

[1] Technical term, meaning "mess up the audio quality so it sounds real-world."

TAKE A BREAK

In Hollywood, editing and mixing might be days apart, and are almost always done in separate studios by different people. It's a good idea to take a similar approach, even if you're doing everything yourself on a single computer.

Editing and mixing are different. One has to be analytical, dealing with discrete units of time. The other is organic, concerned with how elements interact and flow. Even if you're schizophrenic enough to bounce between the two functions quickly, it's hard to keep a sense of perspective about the track while you're also editing clips. If you've just perfected sound effects for a scene, it's likely you'll make them too loud if you immediately start mixing.

Of course you could mix as soon as you've finished elaborate editing. But that almost always means you'll want to come back and remix a few days later, after you've put things in perspective.

Monitor Properly

Mix at a consistent level, on the best speakers you can get.[2] Both of these factors are critical.

If you don't mix on good speakers, you can't make good equalization decisions. In most cases, you can't even make good level decisions: poor speakers don't give you an accurate balance between voice and music. You can't even predict how they'll distort the balance. Some emphasize voice; others make music seem louder than dialog.

Without good speakers, you can miss problems. Subtle clicks and hums might be invisible when you mix, but obvious when your project is shown in a theater or even on a good home system.

MIX WITH CONSISTENT MONITOR LEVELS

The relationship between the volume coming out of your speakers and the level on a track should always be the same. In other words, don't mess with the monitor volume control.

This is critical because we hear timbre and dynamics differently as sound levels change. There's a natural temptation to raise the monitor level as a session wears on and your ears get tired. Resist it. You'll be able to hear the mix more accurately if you take a short break instead.

Don't crank the monitors to hear soft sequences, either. The audience doesn't have that opportunity, so they'll hear a completely different perspective.

---

[2]If you're not building a new facility, you may have skipped Chapter 2 (acoustics and monitoring). If so, go back and read about monitors, particularly the sections on choosing a monitor. Also read about the perils of real-world speakers, and about metering. Your mixes will be better for it.

Professional monitoring setups are usually calibrated so that -20 dBFS pink noise, coming from any single speaker, results in 85 dB SPL at the mix position. That's for a full-size mixing theater. Smaller rooms are often calibrated to 82 dB SPL instead, to reflect the realities of nearfield mixing. You might not need that kind of level precision,[3] but it's still important to have a standard when you mix. Find a position on the volume control that reflects a typical viewing level for your audience, mark it with tape or grease pencil, and *leave it there*. Learn what your monitors sound like when they play a good mix at the chosen volume.

 Gotcha

How loud? Beginners often ask how loud the dialog should be on their NLE's master meter. There's no good answer.

One consideration is the delivery medium. Broadcast contracts often specify "tone and average level -20 dBFS; absolute maximum -10 dBFS." Theatrical mixes sometimes have a similar dialog level (it's really up to the director), and their peaks can go as high as 0 dBFS. Home DVDs are usually somewhere in between.

But those are average readings for tone, and instantaneous ones for peaks. How loud any given dialog or music *sounds* is subjective. It depends on the average power of its waveform, questions of distortion and timbre, and context.

367

WHAT ABOUT SMALLER SPEAKERS?

It's always a good idea to check mixes on a small, TV-like speaker if your mix is headed for that medium. (It's not a good idea to mix on one, for reasons explained in Chapter 5.) If you consistently check on small speakers and pay attention to how the balance is different from your main monitors, you'll soon learn what kind of mixes work best on both sets of speakers. Auratone 5-C Sound Cubes are the standard for small speakers in broadcast post rooms. They cost about $350 a pair, considerably more than comparably small units from a hi-fi dealer. The reason they cost so much doesn't have to do with accuracy—no speaker that size can sound great—but that they're consistent. Every nearfield 5-C sounds like every other, no matter what studio you're in. They're also relatively free from distortion, rattles, and other problems. If you're doing professional audio post for multiple clients, they're a necessity. If you're mixing your own projects on a desktop, they're overkill.

But that's just for checking. The mix decisions themselves should be done on much better speakers, in a room with good acoustics.

---

[3]But don't worry about not being able to afford it: you can get a sound level meter at chain electronics stores for about $45.

HOW ABOUT HEADPHONES?

Mixing on headphones is useful if—and *only* if—you're sure viewers will be wearing them. Otherwise they give you a distorted picture of the sound field and dynamics, and trick you into making subordinate elements much too soft.

Mix with Your Ears and Eyes

The ears should know what a good mix sounds like in the room where you're mixing, and the eyes should be glancing at a good loudness meter[4] as a continuous reality check.

Many professionals also keep a *spectrum analyzer* handy. This is a row of vertical volume meters, each filtered to respond only to the energy in a narrow band. Watching the entire row gives you a graph of volume vs. frequency. Some software does spectrum analysis on an entire file at once; that's not the same thing as having a real-time analyzer available while you mix or listen, and neither is as useful as a three-dimensional spectrogram like the ones in Chapter 11.

But any of them can be helpful, if you first learn by playing some good mixes through them. If the sequence is dialog driven, most of the energy will be below 3 kHz and very little will be above 10 kHz. If it's orchestral music, you might see heavy activity up to about 6 kHz. Only a few pop music styles have significant energy above 10 kHz. (Pop music is often mastered with an every-frequency-loud-all-the-time philosophy, so it stands out on radio and in clubs.)

Don't equalize your mixes to look exactly like someone else's on the spectrum analyzer. Your source material isn't the same, and tweaking it to fit some other source's spectral balance will make it sound bad. Instead, use the analyzer to make sure the average spectral balance is appropriate for the medium, to verify what you're hearing, and as a quick diagnostic for problem tracks—particularly at the extremes of the range. It's also handy to know, if you've got a head cold, when the lack of highs is in your head and not on the track.

These days I rely on a couple of software-based analyzers along with my Dorrough. Bias' *Reveal* (Figure 17.1) is a $150 plug-in that'll run in most Windows or Mac programs while you're mixing. It includes a couple of different spectrum displays and both peak and RMS (average audio power of a waveform) metering. Metric Halo's *SpectraFoo* is a $400 Mac standalone that analyzes signals being generated in other programs or playing from a file. It's got a few more tools and is more tunable for specific measurements. You can also learn things from the free version of Roger Nichols Digital Inspector (www.rndigital.org).

---

[4]Either use the Dorrough in Figure 2.14 or similar hardware meters, or a software suite like the ones described below.

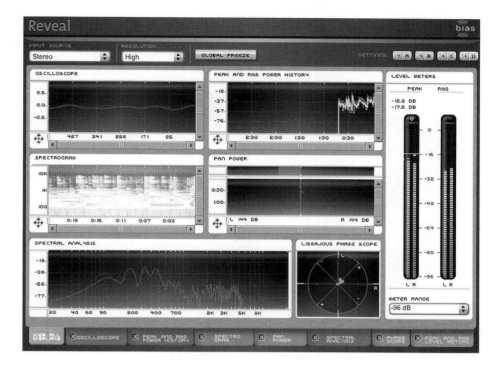

FIGURE 17.1
Reveal is a visual nightmare in this black-and-white capture. But on your computer's color screen—if you understand what you're looking at—it says a lot.

 Gotcha

Beware the master. When you mix tracks together, their volumes can add up to be more than 0 dBFS. But no digital system can faithfully reproduce signals above zero, so that could result in distortion. You can usually avoid this by keeping an eye on the master level meter.

But the meter only reads volume after the signal has gone through the master fader. If that fader has been pulled partially down, the meter may show an acceptable level—even if the internal volume is clipping and distorted![5]

If you're mixing in a digital system, leave the master at 0 dB so you can trust the meter. Turn the master down only when you want to perform a smooth fade on an overall scene.

A similar thing happens in analog mixers, though a different kind of distortion can be introduced. Depending on the manufacturer, there'll be a 0, dot, or U marking the proper position for the master.

---

[5]Some well-designed programs assign extra bits for internal headroom to protect against this. They actually convert signals to a higher bit depth, lower levels as they mix, and then boost the overall level and restore the original bit depth at the output.

HAVE LOCKED PICTURE

It's relatively easy to go into finished video and remove a couple of problem frames or fine-tune the length a little bit. Often, all you have to do is re-render a small section and print the whole thing back to tape or DVD.

It's next to impossible to add or subtract a couple of frames from a finished soundtrack, unless the section is strictly dialog and you find an appropriate pause. You often have to remix an entire sequence from the start of that element to the end.

So it's wasted effort to mix a track before the picture is thoroughly finished and *locked*. Occasionally, you'll need to mix while still waiting for an artist to complete animations or graphic sequences. This may be acceptable if you know exactly how many frames the missing sequence will take, and you have the timeline with a "missing clip" message or other *slug* of the same length. If the new picture needs audio sweetening, you'll have to go back and add it. While this can be time-consuming, it's not as drastic as having to change a scene's length.

Unfortunately, "locked" can be a slippery concept on bigger projects. Movies need to be mixed before they can be screened, and they get changed a lot after the test screenings. Directors often want to keep tweaking almost until the moment the audience buys tickets, even though producers know this adds to the cost. If the changes are minor the simplest solution is to import a fresh OMF, lock its tracks, compare it to the existing tracks, and delete or add time across the whole project as needed.[6] Then you can go to each of those edits and adjust them as needed. You'll probably have to re-edit some music, but other elements' cuts can often be hidden with a little creative nudging. If there are a lot of changes, look for software that handles *change logs* generated by the NLE.

Mixing Elsewhere

You may have access to good mixing software and monitoring away from your NLE and want to use it for the mix. Or you might want to take a project to a professional who specializes in film and video sweetening. In either case, the challenge is getting edited video and individual audio tracks out of a NLE and into another system. It doesn't have to be difficult, or require special software.

You'll need to provide tracks for the mix, of course. The best way is with one of the interchange systems described in Chapter 4.

You'll also need to provide picture to mix against. This can be on videotape, DVD, or as a file. Sync can be an issue with consumer media, even DVDs. Files and professional tape media are usually self-syncing after you've established a start mark, if everybody has done their jobs right. Check with the facility before

---

[6]Most software lets you protect the new OMF tracks so they don't get affected when you edit across the timeline.

you make copies for them. There are lots of different and incompatible video formats. Even if a format is compatible, some codec settings might obscure important picture details that an effects editor or mixer will need to see. It never hurts to do a test.

Put matching two-pops and countdown leader or flashframes at the head *and tail* of the picture and of all the audio tracks. They don't absolutely guarantee sync, particularly if you're using consumer media, but can be a valuable diagnostic when things don't work perfectly. Having timecode supered on the picture (known as a *burn-in*) can be handy. But it can also get in the way. Check with the facility: many generate their own burn-in as needed.

Gotcha

Don't trust; verify. While facilities that do a lot of broadcast or film work have interchange standards that preserve quality and sync, music studios and desktop editing systems often don't. Before you move your project to another facility for mixing, talk to the technicians who'll be doing the work. Make sure they and you understand exactly what the process will be.

TRACK CHART

If someone else is mixing your film, they'll want to know what's coming up on various tracks. A simple chart (Figure 17.2) used to be a necessity for this. It's not needed if you're using a clip transfer system like OMF, since the clip names get carried from the NLE to the mixer's screen.

BRING EVERYTHING

Hard drives are cheap; blank DVDs are even cheaper. Make sure you have available copies of everything: tracks, source elements, multi-track project files, original sound rolls and logs… everything. They might just sit in the trunk of your car while you're mixing, but it's always better to have backups nearby, instead of waiting for someone back at the office to find an element and ship it to you.

Putting Things in Perspective

In an analog mixing console, each channel goes through some processing and has its volume adjusted by a volume fader and pan-pot. The audio is then fed to a pair of electrical busses, where it's combined with other channels to create a single stereo pair. Software does just about the same thing with internal math.

Don't think of your mix that way. Forget faders, pan-pots, and busses for a moment. The *human* act of mixing gives each sound a place in an imaginary two-dimensional sound field. The field is roughly a rectangle, parallel to the floor,

371

Creative Media Group
Homeowner's Advantage: "Flying Through" Intro Video
5830 TRT 8:14

M:S.F	VO	OC 1	OC 2 / ADR	FX 1	FX2 /Alt Foley	Foley	Ambience	Music
0.01				Woosh				Intro
0.19	Anncr intro							—
5.22	—	Wow!					Street	—
5.25	—						—	—
9.18	—			Woosh			V	—
17.17	V							—
17.23					Cymbal			V
18.07							Store	
20.01							—	
20.18		Marge					—	
32.13		—	walla	Crash!			—	
34.16		—			"Cleanup aisle 2"	<-need proc	—	
37.12		—				mop	—	
51.28		—		cart			—	
59.21		—			cash reg		—	
1:06.17		—	clerk				—	
1:11.05		V				coins	—	Stab
1:16.12							V	—
1:19.05				woosh	Cymbal			V
1:21.12			Philip					
1:37.12			—	woosh				
1:53.19			V		Cymbal			
2:12.05								Music under
2:14.21	Anncr			Woosh				—
2:25.05	—							—

FIGURE 17.2
A track chart helps if you're not using a system that preserves individual clip names and waveforms.

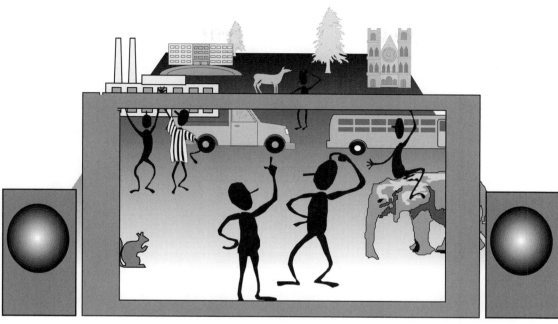

FIGURE 17.3
A stereo film mix creates a horizontal plane, starting on a line between the speakers and extending behind the screen to infinity. You can put elements anywhere on that plane.

at the height of the screen. It's bounded on the front by a line between the two stereo speakers, and on the sides by the speakers themselves. The rear is behind the screen, away from us, almost at infinity. Figure 17.3 shows how it can be visualized.

Stereo theatrical mixes typically drive three speakers: one each for left and right, and one for dialog in the center. But the concept of a horizontal plane between the edges of the screen is still valid. It also holds if you're working in theatrical 5.1 surround, except the front boundary doesn't exist. You sit in the middle of the horizontal field, which stretches behind you as well as behind the screen. Some surround formats, such as the 6.1 used in IMAX, add a sense of vertical as well.

Different media have limitations, as discussed in Chapter 5. If you're mixing for broadcast television, home video, or classroom use, the horizontal plane still exists. But you can't use it as complexly as you would for theatrical film. Usually, no more than three distinct distances from the screen, or *layers*, are appropriate: close, middle, and farther away. Figure 17.4 visualizes this simpler plane.

For mono listeners, everything is on a single line, starting at the center of the screen[7] and running behind the screen to infinity. There may be a sense of spaciousness imparted by the natural reverb of the viewing room, but every element still stays on that one line. See Figure 17.5.

---

[7]Assuming a home viewer's screen is properly located. It often isn't.

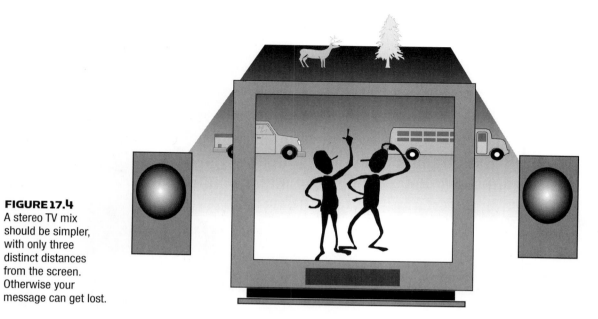

FIGURE 17.4
A stereo TV mix should be simpler, with only three distinct distances from the screen. Otherwise your message can get lost.

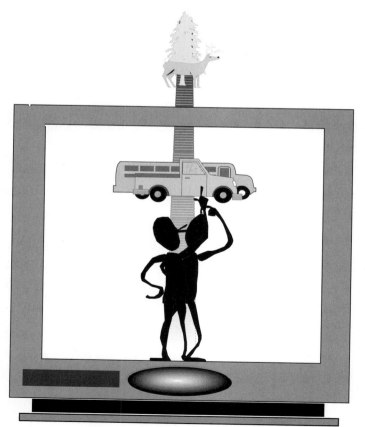

FIGURE 17.5
A mono listener hears everything squeezed into a single line.

NOBODY LISTENS IN MONO, MAN!

Want to bet? While you and your friends may have elegant stereo or surround setups, simple economics dictates that much of the home audience will hear things in mono.

- Low-cost TVs often don't have stereo capability. They may have two speaker grills in front—it makes them look more impressive—but lack the circuits to drive them properly. This is a bottom-line cost decision: the few extra chips needed for stereo could make a 10 percent difference in the manufacturer's profit.
- Low-cost VHS and DVD decks may be stereo... but only if you hook up through their RCA jacks. The antenna connection, which many people use, is almost always mono. It's a bottom-line thing as well.
- Smaller cable systems have been known to run stereo satellite channels through mono downlinks rather than stereo ones. Care to guess why?

Unless you're mixing exclusively for theatrical use, kiosks, or other situations where you can control the playback, mono is very much alive.

Tools for Placing Sounds

The idea of sound field as horizontal plane isn't just a theory for film schools. When we hear real-world sounds, we're very conscious of location. We compare specific loudness, reverberation, and (to a lesser extent) timbre with what we'd expect for similar sounds. That gives us a sense of how far away the source is. We compare differences in volume and timing as the sound reaches each ear, and know what direction it's coming from. Those two factors, distance and direction, tell us where the sound is originating.

DIRECTION

The primary tool for setting direction is the pan pot. It might appear in software as a knob, a horizontal slider, or as a secondary rubber band in a timeline. You can place it in any position between left and right, and the sound will come from a matching location between the two speakers.

Panning only makes sense for mono signals. Multi-track audio software and some NLEs treat every signal as mono. When you import a stereo file, it goes on two different tracks which can be panned separately. Usually, you'll pan one to the extreme left and the other to the extreme right, but other arrangements might be appropriate. Even if elephant rider on the right of Figure 17.3 had been recorded in stereo, you'd still want to keep him on the right side of the screen. But you could give his animal some width by panning one channel to the *center* and the other to the right.

In the real world, timing is also a component of direction. A sound coming from the right will reach our right ear sooner than it reaches our left one. The sub-millisecond it takes a sound to cross the width of our head helps paint a more accurate picture of the world around us. But this is usually ignored when mixing mono sources into a stereo or surround track.

Precedence Effect

A similarly short delay can sometimes fool the ear about the direction a sound is coming from. If we hear the same sound panned to two different points in the sound field, but one is delayed by a millisecond or so, we'll believe that it's coming from only the earlier location—even if the later sound is almost as loud. This *precedence* or *Haas effect* is noticed most on sounds with sharp attacks, such as gunshots or piano notes.

If you're mixing a theatrical track, you can use the precedence effect when a loud sound has to match a visual on the side of the screen. Just panning to that side wouldn't be fair to viewers on the other side of the house, who wouldn't hear it as loud. Add a delayed version on the opposite side. Everybody will hear it loud, but the source will stay with the picture. Don't do this if the track is destined for TV, though: When the channels are combined to mono, the delay will turn into a comb filter.

Visual Anchoring

Our aural sense of direction can get overwhelmed by an image, particularly immersive images like a movie screen. Imagine a race car zooming across from left to right and then off the screen. At the same time, we hear its sound Doppler pan from left to right and then fade out. Most people will swear the sound continued to move to the right, beyond the sound field—even though there's no speaker there to reproduce it. The visual is enough to steer our perception.

On the other hand, if a film is projected on a widescreen, there has to be at least an attempt to match a sound's panning with the on-screen source. Most people start to feel uncomfortable if an important sound is coming from a direction more than 15° away from where they see its apparent source. Dialog, which by convention always comes from the center, is an exception.

This match between visual and acoustic direction isn't as important in television, both because of how people watch and the need for mono compatibility. Documentaries and other non-narrative projects—even those destined for a big screen—frequently ignore specific sound placement as a convention of the medium.

Sound Effects and Surround

In most films, the action takes place in front of us, on a stage roughly defined by the screen. If we see something making noise, the noise should come from the front as well. Off-screen noisemakers or occasional character voices can come from the side or behind us, but a sudden change of direction will call attention to itself; it can pull viewers out of the movie. The jarring effect may be creatively useful; some directors think of it as "ear candy" or almost an in-joke for the film crowd. But there are only a few cases when it'll seem like a real part of the characters' world.

One case is when the sound is supposed to shock us. If we're suddenly dis-oriented—where did that sound come from?—it adds to the shock. This can be useful for gunshots or explosions; just be careful to keep the direction anchored to a logical place. (If we see the explosion on the screen, we should hear its initial or loudest sound as coming from the front. Then smaller crashes and debris, as well as the reverb, can come from all around us.)

The disorientation can also be useful with more subtle sounds. In one film I worked on, the first shot after the titles is a flattened, discolored image of the main character's face. A few seconds later we realize he's asleep on an airplane, with his face pressed against a window: we're seeing him through the glass. Then we move inside, a flight attendant wakes him, and the story begins. That first image doesn't shout "Hey, he's on an airplane!" The director wanted to keep it ambiguous, since the character was coming out of a deep sleep. So I cre-ated a synthesized airplane interior that sounded almost real, but not quite. Its elements slowly panned in a circle around the theater, fading up from the main title music. You didn't know where you were supposed to be. As he woke up, the sound became more real and more localized to the front. By the first line of dialog it was an authentic airplane interior, in a conventional left/right spread.

It may be tempting to build surround ambiences for real-world large scenes, putting footsteps all around us in a train station or animal calls from every direction in a forest. If the sound is convincing, the scene can work. But only by itself: the transition from normal placement to surround, and then back to normal for the next scene, will be jarring. If you're going to use surround for real-world ambiences, be prepared to treat the whole movie that way.

If you're mixing for home viewing, be aware that surround will be unpredict-able. Some viewers will hear discrete wide-range channels properly spread around the room. Most won't. Other factors, such as room shape or decor, usually trump speaker placement. If not, people use tiny satellite speakers that don't sound natural. Analog hookups and conventional TV are even worse: decoders in the playback system steer different sounds to different places, but seldom where they were at the dub stage.

You can use this to your advantage by adding surround and delay processing to sudden loud stereo effects. Stereo viewers will hear it big, and analog surround viewers will hear it even bigger, even though you can't define exactly where it'll seem to come from. There's an example of this on a gunshot sound, later in this chapter.

DISTANCE

The principal tools for establishing a sound's distance are the volume control and reverb.[8] Don't forget there's much less reverb outdoors, and it's almost

---

[8]Timbre can also imply distance, since high frequencies can be lost to air friction. But this doesn't happen until very large distances are involved.

always less complex than indoor reverb. That's because there are fewer surfaces to bounce sound around.

Volume as Distance

The effect of a volume control is obvious: All other things being equal, louder sounds seem closer. Of course, things are seldom equal. Volumes are adjusted during recording, to preserve technical quality. So you can't simply use the fader position as a distance gauge.

In most scenes, dialog is the most important element. Set its volume first, based on the nominal level for the medium. Once dialog is set, imagine how loud each other sound should be, compared to the voice, at the distance you want to simulate. Then move its fader to match. This procedure becomes intuitive after very little practice.

Reverb as Distance: Dialog

Reverb takes a little more thought. That's partly because most people aren't conscious of how much reverberation surrounds us, until they walk into a nearly anechoic space like a good voice-over studio. (Even then, the usual reaction is "How quiet," not "How echo-free.")

Actors should sound like they look, at least in terms of their distance from the camera. A close-up should have very little reverb. A long shot will have more reverb, particularly indoors. The actor's volume should also change with distance. But these volume changes are more subtle in a film than in the real world: Dialog has to stay intelligible.

Don't change reverb or volume with each new camera angle in a scene. We don't hear anything equivalent in the real world, so it's disorienting. Find a perspective that works for most of the scene and stick with it.

The type of reverb depends on the space. Most reverb presets in software are designed for music recording, and simulate much larger spaces than appropriate for a film. Chances are, you'll have to work up your own settings using the tips in Chapter 13.

The amount of reverb depends on both how dialog was recorded and the visual distance. That's because some of the location's natural reverb is picked up by the mic:

- Production dialog shot with a properly used boom will have a small amount of echo, just enough to suggest the room. It's usually not necessary to add more, unless a character is far away from us or the presumed setting is much more echoey than the location was. Remember that any level compression on the track or overall mix makes the echo seem bigger.
- Production dialog shot with properly rigged lavs is usually too dry. While there'll be a tiny amount of reverb, it's never enough to match the camera angle. Add a little more in the mix. Documentary interviews shot with lavs will also be dry, but it's accepted in that context.

- ADR, when properly recorded, is dry as a bone. When combining it with production dialog, follow these steps:

  1. Set the volume of the ADR track to match the dialog track.
  2. Tweak the equalization to make the timbre match. If ADR was recorded with the same kind of mic as production audio and at the same distance, this might not be necessary. Otherwise, you'll almost always need to dip the low frequencies and usually boost the high mids. Then fine-tune the volume.
  3. Add reverb, but not too much. Remember the production mic should have been only a foot or so from the sound source. In most cases, you should just barely notice the reverb when listening to just the ADR track. You shouldn't be aware of it when effects and music are added.

 Gotcha

Wide 'verb, narrow mic. The natural reverb picked up in production tracks is mono,[9] usually centered on the screen. Artificial reverbs in audio programs and hardware have stereo or surround outputs.

- If you're adding reverb to match an ADR insert to production dialog, collapse it to mono. Otherwise the perspective will be wrong. This happens automatically in most NLEs, if you apply the reverb as a filter on a mono source clip.
- If you're adding reverb to increase the apparent size of a room, it can be stereo or surround.

In the language of film, Foley effects belong to the dialog track. Treat them with a similar reverb, including how the reverb is applied in stereo. A little equalization is almost always necessary, too: When small effects are recorded close to a mic, their low end gets boosted. Use a shelf to turn things down. In general, Foley usually should be a little softer than you'd expect; its purpose is to fill a track, not call attention to how good the Foley artist was.

Reverb as Distance: Sound Effects

Hard effects are often recorded fairly dry. If you're adding them to an interior shot, reverb will help. Large hard effects, such as explosions, usually have their own reverb; adding more isn't necessary unless the explosions are very far away. Gunshots come either wet or dry, depending on the whim of the recordist. A gunshot without reverb sounds wrong.

---

[9]Except in those very rare cases where production dialog is shot m/s.

Good ambiences are recorded in stereo or surround and include natural reverb. Adding extra usually makes things sound artificial. If you've added walla or stingers to improve a background, give those elements reverb to match the background recording.

Reverb (and other Tricks): Source Music and on-screen Loudspeakers

Source or diegetic music is supposed to be coming from the film's world, whether it's a radio on a character's desk, or an off-screen band at a party. As such, it should have a fixed place on the sound field. The same thing is true of disc jockeys on a radio, newscasters on a TV, intercoms, and any other electronic voices in the scene.

- Narrow the stereo width of source music. If the source is a loudspeaker, it should usually be mono. If the plot calls for us to admire a character's expensive stereo, it should still be much narrower than the full sound field.
- If there's any excuse, add a lot of room reverb. The sound should be far more echoey than a studio recording would be, because we're listening with three separate reverbs: the one from the "studio recording," the presumed one in the film's scene, and the real one the viewer sits in.
- Apply appropriate equalization. Radios, TVs, and even that expensive stereo should have seriously limited bandwidth, with sharp cutoff filters. Dialog in the scene has to sound more real than the loudspeaker.
- To simulate music or effects and dialog in the same TV or film source track, mix all the source's elements down first. Process this version all at once to make it diegetic.

One technique for making a sound diegetic is *worldizing*. Play it through a cheap speaker, in a real room. Mic the speaker in stereo from a distance. Be aware that mono compatibility will suffer unless you're using m/s miking. The choice whether to worldize or process with plug-ins depends on how big the sound is supposed to be and what tools you have at hand.

Remember, It's a Movie

The idea of the sound field as a flat plane between the speakers applies only to sounds that are supposed to be natural in the characters' world.

SCORING

Underscores don't need a realistic place on the sound field. Music is usually recorded in wide stereo and there's no reason not to leave it that way. If you're using it in surround, the usual convention is to keep the direct sound in front and put the reverb in the rear. If the music has been recorded in surround, it may already be processed that way. Some surround recordings assume we're sitting in the middle of the orchestra with instruments all around us. This can be overwhelming during dialog scenes, as we're constantly torn between actors in front of us, and an orchestra that surrounds. But in emotional scenes where the score predominates, it can be very involving.

Sometimes, it's appropriate to take music out of the center of the screen, to leave that space for dialog. Use the techniques in Chapter 16.

EVERYTHING

As filmmakers, we can play games with reality when it advances the story. Sound effects, ambiences, and scoring can come closer—that is, louder—when they've got something important to say, and recede when other elements are more important. Sudden sounds like crashes or explosions can jump right in front of us, then slowly fall back as their reverb takes over.

Even if you have the luxury of a theatrical track's many layers, you don't have to use them all. Take advantage of the medium's wide dynamic range, instead. Just a soft hint of Foley and one or two voices or other quiet effects at the sides, can be a powerful reminder of where we are.

Equalization and compression can help define individual sources on the soundfield by giving each source a unique timbral fingerprint. This lets you place them closer together without interfering, a necessity when mixing for TV or other limited media. This kind of processing is more important in mono than in stereo, and even less so in surround: When you've got more physical space to deal with, you don't have to use as many aural tricks.

381

HOW TO MIX

You're the only one who can know what your track is supposed to sound like. But there are pro techniques, developed over decades of mixing film and TV, that can help you get there faster and better.

Build from the Top Down

The human voice is the critical element in most films. It has to be heard and sound natural. Get it right before you worry about other elements.

1. Do the dialog premix or any processing to a narrator first. Make those decisions in a vacuum. Turn off every non-voice element, and do what you can to make sure the voices sound natural.

If music or sound effects are turned on while you're adjusting the voice's processing, you're likely to overprocess to help the voice compete. This can make it thin or artificial. Make the voices sound real, and then let everything else work with them.

This is the opposite of how a multi-track music mix is generally done. They start with the bottom: bass and drums. But you're not trying to get people to feel the rhythm. You want them to be absorbed by a human story.

Watch out for a honking around 1–2 kHz on voices, particularly if you've recorded them in a music studio. Many of the popular condenser mics for pop music have a peak in that range.

2. Pan dialog to the center, unless you have a very good reason to put it elsewhere.
3. Leave the voices up and find appropriate volume and panning for the second layer. In a narrative film, this is almost always the sound effects.

If this second layer seems to compete with the voice when it's at the right level, use an equalizer to reduce its energy at speech frequencies. That's usually around 400 Hz and 2 kHz, but you should fine-tune while listening to both this track and dialog.

4. Repeat as necessary for other tracks.

That sets basic levels, panning, and equalization. Now go back to the start of the scene and mix. Be ready to make continuous subtle adjustments as the scene plays. I usually mix with one finger on dialog and another on the second layer, and trim both a few dB in either direction to emphasize individual words or bring out other elements during pauses. Needless to say, this is much easier if your system has a hands-on control surface than if you're mixing with rubber bands or with a mouse.

Starts and Stops

Everybody makes mistakes. Sometimes I'll bring an element in at the wrong volume, or make a segue that doesn't sound smooth, or just decide that one word is coming through a little too loudly or softly.

As soon as I notice that kind of error, I stop. I back up a few seconds and start mixing again. I try to lose as little time as possible, so the flow of the scene stays in my mind. It's almost always best to fix mistakes this way, rather than try to patch corrections in later.

Sometimes, fixing things this way can make a mix disjointed or incoherent. Every transition may be perfect, but there isn't a smooth flow between them. If that happens, try again. The only way to achieve both perfection and smoothness is sometimes to keep practicing on an entire segment. I've found this to be more of an issue with short, intense pieces like commercials. Long-form documentaries and narrative films usually have enough going on that they pull the viewer through complex mix segments, making a slightly disjointed mix seem smoother.

Just about every mixing system lets you save intermediate versions while you try new mixes, or save the project under a new name without having to copy media files. So don't worry about making mistakes, or losing a mix you thought was good. You can always go back.

Gotcha

Stop, even if you never make mistakes. Ears get fatigued, and concentration wanders. Even if things are going perfectly and you don't need to stop, take a break every half-hour or so. It'll be easier to hear subtle details if you do.

Think You're Finished?

If you're creating a mix with rubber bands or an on-screen mixer, you've built each scene from a lot of smaller, disconnected movements. Listen to the whole scene before moving on. Make sure the sound is consistent in terms of levels and timbre. Watch for distortion on peaks.

Whether you mixed with a mouse or an elaborate hardware controller, there still are final steps:

5. Walk away from the mix. Overnight is good, over a weekend is best. At least take a meal break.

6. Come back with your ears fresh. Set up for a proper playback, with the volume calibrated and the room lights dimmed. If at all possible, provide a way to constantly read running time: a burn-in on the screen, or a large timecode or footage counter.

7. Invite the producer, client, or others who have a stake in the film. Novices—business associates or family members—can also be helpful for general audience films. Make sure each has a comfortable chair and some way to take occasional notes. Tell them you'll listen to their comments *after* the film is over.

8. Play the film from start to finish. Don't stop for anything. Have your test viewers make brief notes of minutes-and-seconds locations of anything they want to comment on. Don't tell them *what* or *how* to comment; just that if something seems jarring or strange, they should make a note.

9. Finish the film and ask for the comments. Usually this will be in order of hierarchy: director or client first, then producer, and so on. For each comment go to the noted location, review, see if anything needs changing, and revise the mix as necessary. Then move on to the next comment.[10]

Now the mix is done. There are still technical operations and other kinds of creative review, but that's for the next chapter.

---

[10]This may seem tedious at first, but that's why you start with the most important viewer. By the time you've made a few changes, you'll probably find that the notes are less and less frequent: either the issue was covered by someone else, or a viewer has decided it wasn't really important, or the producer has said "Enough already... It's done!"

NO COOKBOOK, BUT A TASTING

Here are two examples using some of the techniques in this book. They're not intended to show you how to do your own tracks: every film is different. Consider these merely as jumping-off places for your own work, and as a hint about techniques you can also adopt.

Narrative Film, Split Mics

Scotch Hill consists of two interweaved stories, one set in the present with a man who just inherited a house from an elderly uncle, and the woman he unexpectedly finds living there; one six months ago, with the woman as caretaker for the man's uncle. The first flashback scene, a few minutes into the film, is a two-shot in the uncle's bedroom. Uncle is in bed; woman is sitting at the foot of the bed and playing with a Polaroid camera. It was shot with two mics (a fixed boom over the man's head, and a fishpole held over the woman's) and recorded to two separate tracks in the camera.

After director Mike Kuell cut the scene to his satisfaction, it sounded like Part 1 of Track 74 of the CD (listen in stereo if at all possible), and looked like Figure 17.6 on the OMF. Mike was alarmed at how disjointed and echoey it sounded.

The first step was to separate the voices by character and mic (Figure 17.7). The woman's is on the top track, the man's on the middle; a Polaroid shutter sound that got recorded with dialog was moved to a PFX track on the bottom. Then I deleted the parts of each characters' track when they weren't talking. This fixed the echo.

FIGURE 17.6
Woman and Uncle, as originally cut.

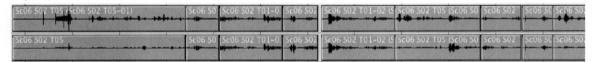

FIGURE 17.7
Tracks split by mic, with the quiet portions deleted.

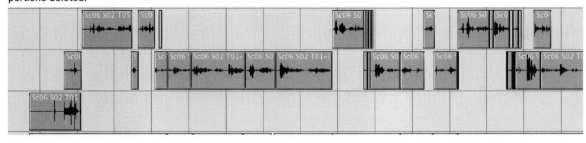

There are fades added to the start and end of each clip, though you might not be able to see them in this zoomed-out screenshot. These prevent abrupt ambience shifts when switching from one mic to another. There's also a section, about halfway through the screenshot, where the top track has a bunch of vertical lines; they indicate very short clips strung together as fill. Figure 17.8 is a zoomed-in version of that section.

That's the section you can hear on the CD where the woman jokes "Are you the only Scottish guy around?" and the uncle laughs. It was important to hear both his laugh and her almost simultaneous intake of breath as a reaction, without the echo of bringing both mics up. Since these are non-verbal sounds, they wouldn't distract from the shift in ambience if we did fast dissolves between the tracks. So those very short clips were added. They're room tone, taken from pauses elsewhere in the take. The woman's track is filled with a little of her mic's room tone while the uncle laughs. Then we dissolve to the intake of breath on her track while the uncle finishes laughing. Then, since her track would have to be boosted to hear the breath, his track is filled with room tone for a moment. This screenshot is zoomed in enough that you can see some of the fades and dissolves: light gray lines at the borders of each clip. A little equalization and leveling, and the result was the dialog premix in Part 2 of Track 74. Note how much cleaner and smoother it sounds, compared to the original edit.

There was one more step. Remember, this scene is a flashback. I wanted it to sound older in some subtle way, the audio equivalent of slightly desaturating the colors or tending toward sepia. The scene's dialog premix, room ambience, and a source music track were routed to a submix just for the flashback. Shelf filters were applied with about $-12\,dB$ starting at $140\,Hz$ and $9\,kHz$, to make the timbre more like an optical recording's. A gentle compressor (about $4\,dB$ on peaks, with a 2:1 ratio) was added for the same reason. Then the stereo soundstage was narrowed to about 25% by panning the channels inward. There isn't much stereo in the scene—just the ambience and a little direction and reverb on the source music—but it was enough to make a difference. You can hear the result in Part 3.

The effect is subtle—the mix doesn't sound bad or futzed by itself—but it makes the current-day scenes a lot more alive by comparison.

385

FIGURE 17.8
A two-voiced section, with fill.

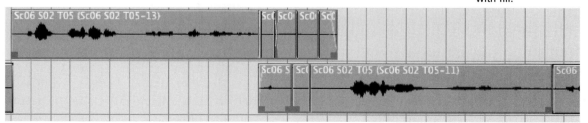

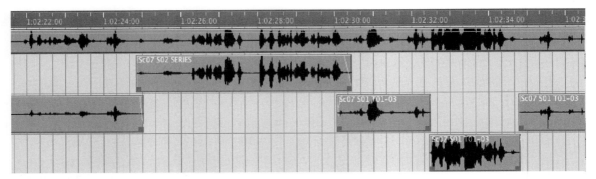

FIGURE 17.9
An earlier scene, showing how a single character's yell is split to a separate track for control.

 Hear for yourself

Tracks 74 and 75 are mixing examples from a low-budget narrative film, Mike Kuell's *Scotch Hill*.

NARRATIVE FILM, BIG DYNAMIC RANGE, SPECIAL EFFECT

Track 75 is from the final mix of a scene before that flashback: The man walks into the house's kitchen, unaware that the woman is there, and looks for a beer in the refrigerator. She appears in a doorway with the uncle's old pistol, and thinking he's a burglar, shoots him in the leg. The scene was filmed in one take with a single mic. The OMF original is the top track in Figure 17.9. The tracks are split by character in the middle two tracks. His sudden yell was too loud to control precisely with a single fader, so it's split out to the bottom track.

Track 75 also includes the gunshot, taken from a separate sound effects source and spotted to a different track. Since it's unexpected and dramatic we decided to give a special stereo treatment: you can hear the *bang* repeat, and then spread wider through a delay. Using the soundstage this way, along with the wider dynamics and frequency range of the dialog and the stereo scoring, highlights the difference between this scene and the flashbacks.

Scotch Hill wasn't a particularly elaborate project, had a minuscule budget, and used far fewer tracks than most feature films. Even so, it's probably worth a glance at how the mixer was set up (Figure 17.10). Track names are on the bottom. The top half gives quick access to effects. Mostly it's showing equalizers, but you can see how the flashback dialog premix (Track 3 on the screenshot) is routed to a separate "flashback" chain; so are the flashback sound effects, though that track (Track 9) is showing an equalizer as well. The dialog futz track (Track 4) goes through an adjustable phone filter. The bottom half of the screenshot, of course, is showing the faders. Even though I mixed this film on a hardware control surface, it was handy having individual track meters next to each fader on the screen.

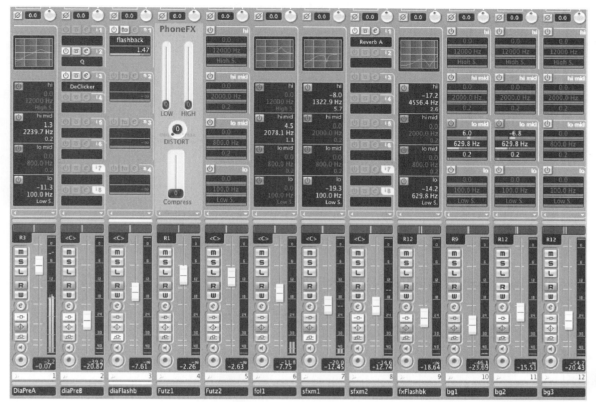

FIGURE 17.10
Part of *Scotch Hill's*
on-screen mixer.

TV REALITY: OUTDOOR WHISPERING

Part 1 of Track 76 is from original footage of an outdoor adventure TV series. Host Bill Urseth turns to camera and very softly describes the situation. He's whispering so he won't alarm a nearby animal. Even though he's wearing a lav, his dialog is barely intelligible and partly buried in noise. Figure 17.11 shows how tiny the waveform was on the OMF.

There was no point splitting this single-character scene onto separate tracks, but some of those original clips definitely needed individual help. Figure 17.12 shows me adding a 6 dB boost to the third clip: just enough to make it more consistent with some louder neighbors. Boosting specific clips also makes the background level jump, but relatively long crossfades (white Xs in the screen-shot) smooth that out.

Now that the scene is smoother, if still soft, we can clean up the whole thing. Most of that is done by a parametric equalizer. There's a low cut at 150 Hz to remove wind rumble, then a 4 dB two-octave-wide boost at 1100 Hz for intelligibility, then the equalizer applies a 12 dB boost to the whole thing. This

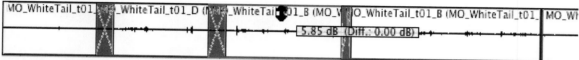

FIGURE 17.11
A lav track from an outdoor show, where the host is whispering.

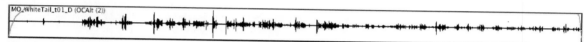

FIGURE 17.12
Boosting the softest clips, and crossfading between them.

FIGURE 17.13
The same scene as Figure 17.12, after some tweaking and processing.

means we've boosted some frequencies on a few clips by $22\,dB$[11]! Of course this also increases both background noise and electronic hiss from the camera, but now the scene is loud enough—and consistent enough—that noise reduction software can be applied. Figure 17.13 shows what the adjusted scene looks like, after this processing. Part 2 of Track 76 is what the rendered scene sounded like.

Hear for yourself

Track 76 is mix examples from an outdoor adventure TV series, Trev Gowdy's *Quest for the One*.

You can hear a little high-end distortion from the noise reduction in Part 2. While it would be intolerable in a theatrical mix, this project was TV. After mixing with a library music score and adding some stereo outdoor background, the result (Part 3) was better. Not perfect, but good enough... and the cleanup didn't take very much time to accomplish, which is a major consideration for a weekly TV show.

---

[11]I wouldn't try this in many programs. Fortunately, the one I use has lots of internal headroom.

CHAPTER 18
After the Mix

> **REMEMBER THIS:**
>
> - A film has to sound good in the real world. Don't be satisfied with just how it sounds in the studio.
> - Audio data compression is essential for Web videos, theatrical films, and most DVDs. Knowing how these processes work will help you get the best results from them.

Your film is done. You've edited dialog to sound completely natural, even though it's assembled from tiny little takes. You've cleaned up noisy source material, created engaging sound effects, found perfect music, and made it even more perfect with editing and processing. You've put everything together in a smooth, compelling mix. You even reviewed and fine-tuned the mix the next day.

Your film may be done. You're not.

- You have to marry the track back with the picture, and may need to provide submixes for distribution. This can be a simple copy-and-paste in your NLE, or it can take an extra day on the dub stage. That depends on how you're delivering the final product.
- You should test the track to make sure it's listenable under real-world viewing conditions. You also should test to make sure it has the desired effect on the audience.
- It's almost certain, these days, that you'll want to put at least part of it on the Web.
- You might also need to convert it to a format for film or DVD release.

This chapter will help with all of these things.

LAYBACK AND PRINT MASTERING

The mix might not exist at all until its automation moves and effects have been rendered. Depending on the complexity of the track and the system being used, this rendering can take anywhere from a few minutes to a bit longer than real-time.

A video mix doesn't do any good until you marry it with the picture. If you've mixed on your own desktop system, it should be a simple matter to import the mixed audio back to the NLE and sync it with picture. Otherwise, there are a couple of good options:

- Have the facility copy the mix to an uncompressed file for your NLE. This will usually be AIFF, .wav, or .bwf. They should keep the two-pop and tail pop for sync; you can delete these before the final NLE output. How they deliver—on optical disc, your hard drive, or Internet—won't affect the quality.
- If you brought your video on a professional tape format, they probably can *layback* the finished track right to your tape (it depends on the format). Depending on the project, this may become the master. It's a good idea to ask for a file also, as backup.
- Or have them dub to a blank tape in the DV format you use. Take it back to your desktop, capture the mix via FireWire, and sync it in your NLE. This is more time-consuming since you have to capture in real time. It may also introduce quality loss, unless the facility dubs DV via a digital input.

A theatrical film mix will have to go through *print mastering*. This is a technical process done on the dub stages, converting the surround mix to the data format used for the release prints or a surround DVD. If the film is carrying a Dolby license,[1] that company will send a technician to make sure these transfers are done properly.

Stems and Mix-minuses

Networks and feature distributors often require separate mixes of dialog, music, and effects for foreign translations. These should be in the same stereo or surround format as the full mix, and may be delivered as separate files, as a multi-track digital audio tape, or as individual tracks on various digital picture masters. Networks might also request a stem of just the voice-over, for translators to use while writing their versions. They might want the whole show with dialog and sound effects but no music to use in promos. Specifics will be in your contract. Producing on spec without a contract? Don't worry—they'll probably have you remix some changes; you can do the stems then. Unless you're mixing on an immense stage with a large traditional console, these *stems* take as long to render as full versions would.

---

[1]You can master a project in Dolby Digital or Surround just by sending the mix through an encoder. Basic encoding software is bundled with some NLEs. But if you want to *advertise* Dolby or use their trademark, the you'll need their license. Contact Dolby for more information. DTS and Sony have similar requirements.

Music and Effects stems for a narrative film are usually prepared with all the fades already in place, as if these tracks were being ducked for dialog. Stems for voice-over translations generally aren't pre-faded, since the translations can take longer than the original narration. Preparing these stems takes a lot longer: essentially, you have to mix a new version of the film.

KEEP LOTS OF COPIES

Ask about the facility's archiving policy. A few facilities leave projects on a hard drive for a day or two as a convenience for client changes. Others archive immediately, and there's a charge if they have to de-archive. Some don't archive unless you request it, or ask you to supply a hard drive for the archive.

Don't assume an archive from one facility will be readable at another. There are a lot of different digital audio mixing systems. Even if two facilities use the same software, they may have different ways of storing inactive projects. Even if the backup formats match, actual mix settings depend on a facility's arsenal of plug-ins and patchbay setup.

Stems and mixed tracks—as opposed to archives—are almost always in standard audio file formats. They should be universally readable.

TESTING THE TRACK

I'm an avid viewer of my own work. I scan cable listings to see when a show I edited or mixed will be aired, and then I try to catch a few minutes of it on as many different TVs as possible. I watch DVDs of films I've worked on, and then watch them again at friends' houses. It's not just ego (though I have plenty of that). It's professional education.

How Does It Sound?

A lot can happen to a track after it leaves your hands. Some of it is electronic—tapes get badly dubbed, signals get data-compressed for servers or satellite, broadcasters and cable channels add processing, and no two TV models have exactly the same sound. On top of that, a track has to survive echoey environments, bad speaker placement, and competition from every possible type of noise.

That's why I listen to mixes in the real world. I'm checking for specific things:

- Is dialog clear, crisp, and natural sounding?
- Are music and critical sound effects loud enough without interfering with dialog?
- If it's narrative, does every scene have a sense of place?
- If it's stereo or surround, is there a sense of spaciousness?
- Overall, how does this mix sound compared to others on the same channel or at the same multiplex?

Over the years, this kind of listening has altered my views about processing—I still use compression, but insist the original material is as distortion-free as possible first. It's convinced me to mix underscores and hard effects a lot louder than I originally thought. It's changed the way I think about reverb, and now I make TV tracks dryer than theatrical ones.

How Does It Act?

The other important test is how it affects other viewers. Are they engaged? Are they motivated or educated? You can often tell from their body language, just as you could when originally reviewing the mix in your studio.

This isn't just the writer's or director's responsibility. Movies are a collaborative effort, and everybody's technical or artistic contribution is important.

DATA COMPRESSION AND STREAMING

While audio data is tiny compared to high-resolution video, each channel of a 48 kHz sample rate, 16-bit signal requires more than 5 megabytes per minute. Much of that bandwidth can be better spent on other things, and so virtually everything you hear on TV or in a movie theater has gone through some kind of data compression. Web audio couldn't exist without it.

Actually, compression may be the wrong word; it implies expansion might be possible. These algorithms work by reducing data, throwing it away forever. When done right, this data tossing is fairly benign. In large audience tests, it was determined that almost nobody can tell the difference between a well-encoded mp3 at 256 kbps (kilobits per second) and the six-times-bigger CD-quality audio file it came from. A lot of what's on FM radio has been reduced to half that data rate before it gets to the transmitter. Dolby Digital theatrical tracks have even more radical reduction, and very few moviegoers complain.

On the other hand, there are plenty of idiots posting badly encoded mp3s on the Web—that's why the format has gotten such a bad reputation. We'll deal with its problems, and how to get around them, later in this chapter. But to understand them, you need to know what's happening inside the encoder.

How They Work

The key to all modern *psychoacoustic* audio data compression is masking, the same phenomenon that powers high-powered noise reduction algorithms. Briefly, a loud signal will hide a softer one at a similar frequency, even if they don't occur at precisely the same time. Chapter 15 explains the process more thoroughly.

To apply masking for data compression, the process first breaks the audio stream into frames, lasting up to a few milliseconds each. The length of each frame depends primarily on the data rate; lower rate files with more compression have longer frames. Each frame is boosted so its loudest wave reaches

0 dBFS, to take advantage of every bit during processing. The amount of boost is noted so the frames can be restored to their original volume on playback.

Then the algorithm measures how much energy the frame has at different frequencies. The number of frequencies is a trade-off: more bands allow tighter masking, but require sharper filters that respond more slowly. The mp3 format uses up to 512 bands while other compression systems have more or less.

- If a particular band is silent during the frame, the process notes it and doesn't waste any more data on it.
- If a band is loud, it *reduces* the number of bits. The loud signal will mask noises at the same frequency.
- If a band is soft, it's processed with more bits, unless there's a masking sound in an adjacent band (and in some algorithms, in the previous or next frame). Then it assumes this band won't be heard.
- The resulting audio is run through a data packer similar to WinZip or Stuffit. Normal audio is too complex to compress well in these systems, but they can handle the simplified masked audio easily.

The common mp3 algorithm uses this scheme. How good it sounds depends on how well the encoder has been written, and on the bitrate chosen. The newer AAC algorithm couples it with a quick look at adjacent frames to see if temporal masking will hide even more details. For a given bitrate, a good AAC will sound better than a good mp3.

ADAPTIVE DELTA

Adaptive Delta Modulation is an early encoding scheme that doesn't rely on masking. Instead, it makes a mathematical assumption. 16-bit audio is capable of more than 65,000 different values from the most negative to the most positive part of a wave. But this process assumes real-world sounds won't jump that far from one sample to the next.

Instead of measuring each sample and storing the value, Adaptive Delta stores the difference between samples. It assigns 4 bits for this, with additional scaling information every few dozen samples so jumps of more than 16 values are possible. This algorithm is found in QuickTime IMA and Microsoft *ADPCM*—the other three letters are for *pulse code modulation*, the technical name for normal digital recording. While ADPCM was simple enough for early desktop computers, it fails on sounds with very fast attacks such as gunshots. These get noisy for the first split second, before the numbers catch up. More importantly, ADPCM is capable of only 4:1 compression—and at ratios like that, masking algorithms can achieve true CD quality. So except for cases where there just isn't enough processing power to encode or play modern formats, it's been largely abandoned.

LOSSLESS ENCODING

Modern computers can cope with the math to predict the total delta between individual samples, no matter how big a jump, with enough processing power to go back and refine their guesses until they're accurate. Depending on the content, this *linear prediction* can shrink a file between 40 and 60 percent. That's because while every waveform is faithfully recorded, high-value bits aren't wasted on tiny changes between samples. When decoded, the original waveform is completely restored. There's no added noise, distortion, or bandwidth problem. This is the engine behind *FLAC (Free Lossless Audio Codec)*, a cross-platform open source implementation, and behind *Apple Lossless*, a codec in QuickTime for Windows and Macintosh. Either of these can be used to save transfer time when sending critical elements via Internet.

Making Data Compression Sound Good

The most critical setting in a data compression system, including mp3 encoders, is the bitrate. Lower bitrates mean longer frames, increasing the chance that the masking sound won't be available for the whole frame. The result is noise and a flangey or chirping sound.

Which bitrate you consider low, and how much noise or distortion is acceptable, depends on the application. But if you do things right, broadcast-quality sound can be achieved at 128 kbps. One of the most important factors is which encoder you use. Even in a standardized format like mp3, there are multiple trade-offs that program designers have to make. Commercial encoders are usually better designed in this respect than freeware. Because they've also paid licensing fees to the Fraunhofer Institut—inventors of the mp3 format—commercial publishers may have had more access to inner workings of the system.

It makes sense to use a high-quality encoder. Other things will help as well.

- If you have to encode at a low bitrate, get rid of high frequencies first. Apply a low-pass filter at 8 kHz to 12 kHz (or use a good sample-rate converter to lower the rate to 22 kHz, which filters sounds above 10 kHz). The moderate dullness this imparts will be less objectionable than low bitrate noises.
- *Do not* try to help the high-frequency filtering by boosting just below the Nyquist Limit (this boost is often available as a Preserve Highs option in a sample rate converter). It wastes precious bits on unimportant sounds, and can increase the chance of flanging or chirping.
- *Do not* use extreme level compression, particularly multiband compression. This makes it harder for the algorithm to tell the difference between important sounds and those that can be lost.
- Speech is harder to encode than music because it changes faster. The most common distortion at low bitrates is a reverberation-like noise tail on the words. It can be lessened by lowering the number of bands in the encoder, which raises the internal filters' response times. Most encoders don't let you control the number of filters, but many let you select an optimization for speech.
- Higher background noise levels also increase problems with encoding. Start with the cleanest recording possible.

OTHER CHOICES DURING ENCODING

Processing the source sound and selecting a good encoder and bitrate is only part of the story. A few other decisions can help you get the most from a compression system.

Stereo or Joint Stereo

Most algorithms expect the left and right channels of a stereo pair to be similar. This is usually true in music. A *joint stereo* mode encodes only major differences between the channels, particularly at high frequencies, freeing up more of the bitrate for better quality. But ambiences and crowd sounds can be very different on the left and right, if the space isn't reverberant and there are lots of spread-out sources. With these sounds, joint stereo pushes things toward the center.

- If this is a problem, choose *true stereo*, an option on many encoders. This halves the bitrate available for other characteristics of your sound, but encodes each channel separately to preserve the stereo image.
- You should also select true stereo when the left and right channels are totally independent, as in a split voice/music track.

Variable Bitrate

This option, also known as *VBR*, can both reduce file sizes and improve the sound. The algorithm specifies a different bitrate for each frame, between limits you set. This avoids wasting bits on pauses or easy-to-encode sounds, making the overall file smaller, while making sure bits will be available when needed.

- VBR works best on simpler or slower-moving sources, including a lot of new age or classical music. It presents little advantage on faster and highly processed sounds, such as most pop styles, because the maximum bitrate must be used for most frames.

MULTIPLE GENERATIONS

Both mp3 and AAC compression are lossy. When you convert a compressed file back to 16-bit linear audio, something will be missing. If you encode it again, the algorithm has a harder time finding details that can be safely deleted. Noise and distortion build up with each subsequent pass.

- Don't encode more times than is necessary. While it may be tempting to save file space with an algorithm like mp3, always keep backup files and intermediate sources in uncompressed versions. Blank discs are cheap; noise or distortion is forever.
- If you must go through multiple encodings, stay with the highest bitrates possible. If the final release format will be at a low bitrate, don't apply it until the last step.
- There is some evidence that multiple generations through the same compressor sound worse than the same number of generations through a variety of algorithms.

RELEASE FORMATS

In many cases, the physical format of a project won't make much difference in how you treat the sound, beyond the issues discussed in Chapter 5. But there are some technical things you should be aware of, mostly dealing with data compression.

Web

Apple's QuickTime and Microsoft's Windows Media are the two most common Web video formats at this point. While free players for both are available for both computer platforms, features usually lag behind in the non-native one. Flash uses mp3 encoding for its audio, with additional information in the file header. Free players are available for most platforms from Adobe. Many mp3 encoders will also create Flash audio content.

Film

Dolby Digital, DTS (Digital Theater Systems), and SDDS (Sony Dynamic Digital Sound) are somewhat similar. All three use some form of data compression. In some cases, the compression is fairly extreme; ratios can be as high as 17:1.

Dolby Digital uses an optical data track in the space between sprocket holes. SDDS runs its data down the edges of the film. DTS puts timecode on the film and runs audio from a separate CD-ROM. While DTS is more work than the other two formats, it provides the highest bitrate and so needs the least compression. All three use a stereo analog optical track on the film for backup.

> **Gotcha**
>
> **What about THX?** THX (named for its inventor, film sound guru Tomlinson Holman) isn't a format at all. It's a set of specifications for equipment and acoustics in theaters, home setups, and mastering labs, and a certification process to see that users and films meet the spec.

DVD

Digital Versatile Disc (almost never referred to by that name) is capable of the three film formats plus noncompressed PCM audio and MPEG encoding. PCM is obviously the highest audio quality, and the format can handle 16-, 20-, or 24-bit resolution at up to 96 kHz sampling on up to eight channels. Extreme sampling is almost never used for multichannel sound because of the high data rates required.

DVDs can also be recorded in standalone decks that take standard computer blanks. These decks now look and cost about the same as home VCRs. The low-cost models aren't capable of multichannel sound. Check the manual and user groups; some combinations of recorder and blank disc won't play reliably in other brands of player.

Standalone Blu-Ray recorders are much harder to find as of this writing, but that's already starting to change. Check the Web for the latest information.

AFTERWORD

I started this book with the assumption you're an intelligent film or video maker who knows what you want your track to sound like, but aren't quite sure how to get there. That's why I've stayed away from creative or aesthetic concerns, except where they're thoroughly wedded to the technical.

But over the years, I've adopted a working philosophy that helps my creative side as well as my engineering. It applies to any filmmaking style and to creating visuals as well as soundtracks. I want to step beyond the technical, and end with this philosophy.

LITTLE THINGS MEAN EVERYTHING

Studs Terkel ends the preface of his book *Working* by interviewing a stonemason. This man loves his job, and stones are his life. When he's at work, he's totally aware of each piece's different grain and shape. He knows the success of his projects depends on respecting the individual stones. If one wasn't placed perfectly, it will bother him years later.

This is a paradox in any creative craft. The more attention you pay to individual elements—for our purposes, every syllable and sound—the more you can appreciate the whole. You see the forest better if you know the trees are healthy. For me, this has meant the most enjoyable projects have been with clients who let me fine-tune the details... or when I had a similar commitment on my own.

This attention to detail also keeps you from being bored. It's only human nature to look at each new assignment in terms of what you've done before, because you want to reuse techniques you've already developed. But even the most mundane project has something different about it. It doesn't matter whether that difference lasts only a few seconds on-screen or drives an entire sequence; solving the new problem is what makes it fun. For me, there's genuine joy in discovering new ways to make sounds work together in time or timbre. For you, it might be a new way to move a camera, reveal a personality, or fool the eye. Figure out what's unique about a project, and you've got something to look forward to.

SPREAD THE JOY

I learned a lesson decades ago. I was given a hard-sell commercial script to produce, and the copy was one cliché after another. The ad agency executive actually apologized, saying every good creative concept had been shot down and those awful lines were from the client. He asked me to do the best I could.

I hired a couple of good actors and presented them with both the script and the story behind it. Big mistake. As hard as we all tried, we couldn't make the readings justify even the poor writing. The actors believed the agency and I didn't care, so despite their professionalism they didn't care either.

What I learned immediately was to look for some aspect of the job you can be positive about. If not the script, then the visuals, or the quality of the product, or even the creative challenge of delivering old lines a new way. It will motivate you and the people around you. One cliché wasn't in that awful script, but should have been: "What's worth doing is worth doing well."

After a few years, I learned another lesson—one that hapless agency executive apparently never discovered. The best way to express it is a saying I developed when teaching a college film sound class. I told students there was a secret key to success in our business, and they should repeat it after me:

- Never give the clients what they ask for.

Of course, everybody in the room would start laughing. Then I told them this was only *half* the rule. They also had to repeat the second part:

- Always give the clients what they want.

If clients knew exactly what to ask for—how to frame a shot, edit a sequence, or mix a track—they could do the job themselves. On the other hand, even the most inept client knows what the message should be, usually better than we do. Our task is to deliver that message in a way that's memorable and engaging.

So while you can ignore the details of outlandish client requests, you still have to figure out what was in their mind when they framed it. Their ideas are only a starting point. Apply your own creativity and production expertise, and you can turn it into something that satisfies all of you.

If a client doesn't like what you suggest, there's probably a reason—even if they can't express it well. Find a way to satisfy their objection, or drop the concept and move onto something else. (Don't expect to win every creative battle. Even if the client rejects all your ideas and insists on doing something you know will be awful, you'll have given it your best effort.)

LEARN BY PLAYING

Almost every mechanical skill from my early career is now obsolete. Clients have absolutely no interest in my ability to cut magnetic film, repair a tubed amplifier, or even edit dialog on a CMX computer keyboard. But these technologies died because more exciting ones replaced them. Cultivate that excitement; if you let yourself get caught up in the thrill of a new technology, learning how to use it gets easier.

Notice that I said *technology* and not *tool*. There are plenty of new production devices introduced every year. Each has its own interface, idiosyncrasies, and power-user tricks. Keeping up with them can be a chore—and an unrewarding one, when next year's hot product makes this year's interface obsolete. But a few times a decade, some part of our industry discovers a radically different way of working. When it happens in your field, you've got the choice of being thrilled or threatened.

Be an early adopter, even if it means taking very modest steps. When it first became possible to edit sound on a desktop computer about twenty years ago, I was thrilled to spend $75 on a little application for my Mac Plus. It was slow and sounded horrible, but it was fun. Trying to accomplish things with this awkward new technology forced me to learn about digital audio—and become a better engineer—than if I'd started with a powerful workstation.

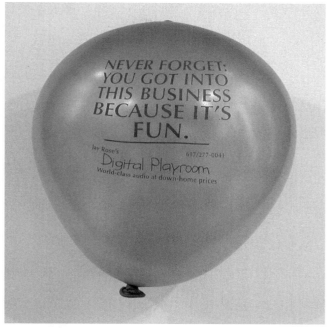

FIGURE 18.1
One year I packed tapes with balloons instead of bubble wrap. Most clients were happy to receive this message.

399

REMEMBER THIS:
- *No matter where the technology goes, ultimately you're selling creativity.*
- *What you learned with your first set of finger paints is still true: creating is fun.*
- *Keep that sense of play while you learn the technology and you'll never be bored.*

CHAPTER 19

Help!

It's possible you bought this book because you're trying to solve an immediate problem. Think of this chapter as Frequently Asked Questions, addressing the most common concerns in postproduction sound. Be aware that many sound problems can't be resolved in a couple of sentences; all I can do with those is tell you where in this book you'll find the answer. A few can't be resolved at all, and I'll suggest workarounds.

Use this chapter to solve the immediate problem. But don't forget to read the rest of the book. It'll teach you the techniques professionals use to improve marginal sounds, and to make well-recorded ones jump out of the speakers. These are the secrets behind a great soundtrack.

PROBLEMS WITH SOUND QUALITY

These questions are about technical issues of distortion or noise in your unmixed tracks. Later sections of this chapter deal with mix and compatibility issues, computer behavior, and lipsync. There are also large sections elsewhere in this book on solving problems with studio wiring (Chapter 3), and with getting signals from your camera or recorder into the computer (Chapter 6).

Tracks Are Too Soft in My NLE

We're talking about too soft to *hear* properly, not that the waveforms are too small to see their tiny details on the timeline. There's usually no reason to see those details—Chapters 8 and 9 show how to edit by ear, which is faster and more accurate. But if you really need to study a waveform, open the clip in its own window.

FIREWIRE, I.LINK, OR IEEE 1394 SETUP

If you transferred from the camera digitally using a FireWire connection, the levels you have were those on the tape. The scene was shot too softly. Next time, check the camera's instructions about setting volume, or check the discussions about production sound in the companion book *Producing Great Sound for Film and Video*.[1]

---

[1] By yours truly. Focal Press, 2008. ISBN 978-0-240-80970.

Your track might still be savable. Open the clip in an audio editing program and apply the *Gain* or *Amplify* command, set to bring the loudest sound in the clip to about −6 dBFS. Or use a *normalize* command, if it lets you apply a similar −6 dBFS or 50 percent setting. Save the result.

■ Read about dBFS in Chapter 1.

Bringing the clip to −6 dBFS, instead of to the maximum 0 dBFS or 100 percent, leaves some room for equalization and other processing. Many NLEs will distort if you attempt to process a file that's too loud. If you're not planning any processing at all, you can make the clip louder, but it's usually best to wait until you're finishing the project.

Since the original footage was shot too softly, there's a strong chance raising its level will also boost hiss and other electronic noises from the camera or recorder. While you can't totally remove hiss, you can make it less objectionable with an expander or noise reduction software.

■ Read about expanders in Chapter 12.
■ Read about noise reduction in Chapter 15.

MIC DISTANCE PROBLEMS

If increasing the clip's volume also increases room noise and echoes, the microphone was too far from the subject. *This seems to be the most common problem with amateur sound*. It's often because a camera-mounted mic was used.

In real-world interior spaces, there's no way a camera mic can do as good a job as a properly placed boom or lav. It doesn't matter what brand or type of mic you use. Distance is the enemy: basic physics dictates that any mic more than a couple of feet from the speaker's mouth won't pick up sound cleanly. Professionals use camera mics only for breaking news, when there's no time to rig up something else, or for in-your-face interviews where both camera and mic are close to the subject. Chapter 7 of this book talks about mic technique for postproduction audio. There's a large section on production miking in *Producing Great Sound*.

You may be able to improve intelligibility with equalization, and reduce apparent echo level with an expander. Unfortunately, you can never make a distant mic sound like it was close.

■ Read about equalization in Chapter 11.
■ Read about expanders in Chapter 12.

ANALOG TRANSFER FROM CAMERA TO NLE

This also applies to analog transfers from a DAT or other digital player, or live mic recordings in your computer.

If you've digitized by connecting the source's analog audio output to a soundcard or converter, any of the previous questions also apply. But there's also a chance that problems were introduced during digitization, and these can be completely fixed. Play some sample footage in your camera using good monitor speakers or headphones. If the camera sounds better than what's in your computer, you should redigitize. Before you do, calibrate your system so you can transfer at a proper level.

If you've already done large amounts of editing, it may be faster to digitize only the audio. Sync the new audio files to what's already in the timeline. If you're just starting the project, it's faster to redigitize sound and picture simultaneously, and then delete the original clips.

Track Sounds Fine, but Waveforms are Too Small in My Editor

This might not be a technical problem at all, but a user-interface issue in your software. Most editing systems are programmed with linear waveform displays. In these displays, a properly recorded production track with dialog around $-20\,\mathrm{dBFS}$[2] will be only about an eighth of the waveform's maximum height. Check the meters before you decide something is too soft.

Some software gives you a way to scale or boost the display, to make editing easier. Check the manual.

Tracks Are Too Loud in My NLE

If audio is so loud that waveforms extend from top to bottom of a clip window, it probably also sounds distorted or has a crackling noise at the loudest spots. If you transferred into the computer via FireWire, the likelihood is the camera audio is also distorted or crackling, and most of these problems can't be fixed. Check the original footage to make sure.

Certain kinds of distortion can be made less offensive with equalization. You may be able to replace individual words with ones from alternate takes or rerecord the dialog in a studio using ADR techniques.

- Read about equalization in Chapter 11.
- Read about dialog editing in Chapter 8.
- Read about ADR in Chapter 7.
- An occasional click from too loud a waveform can be repaired in an audio program, either by applying a *declicking* process or by drawing a smoother waveform with a pencil.

If you transferred through an analog connection and the camera track sounds fine, follow the redigitizing advice in the previous section.

Once this kind of distortion and noise gets onto a track, lowering the volume won't make it go away. But there is a slim possibility the track isn't really

403

[2]Proper level for pro cameras and recorders. Consumer gear often records louder, to compensate for noisier internal circuits.

recorded wrong, but is just too loud for your computer's sound card or monitors. This happens frequently when ripping music CDs into a computer, since pop music is often mastered at the maximum possible level.

- Try lowering the volume on the timeline. If that fixes things, export to an audio program and make the tracks $-2\,dB$ softer.

If individual tracks on the timeline are fine, but things get too loud and distorted when you mix them, read about mixing in Chapter 17.

Sound Is Distorted

Distortion refers to a fuzziness in the sound, making dialog hard to understand. Noise, thin sound, or boominess are different problems addressed in the next section.

In most cases, distortion happens because sound was recorded or digitized too loudly. See the previous section. If sound is distorted but the volume isn't too loud, there are two likely causes. Listen to the original tapes in your camera or recorder, using good speakers or headphones, to find out which one applies.

SOUND IS DISTORTED WHEN YOU PLAY IT IN THE CAMERA/RECORDER

Something went wrong at the shoot. This could be defective equipment, a weak battery in a mic or wireless rig, or levels that were set badly in the camera or a mixer or preamp. These problems are beyond the scope of this book about post. Many are covered in *Producing Great Sound*.

You may be able to improve intelligibility with equalization, or replace the on-camera dialog with studio voices in an ADR session.

- Read about equalization in Chapter 11.
- Read about ADR in Chapter 7.

SOUND IS OKAY WHEN YOU PLAY IT IN THE CAMERA/RECORDER

Either your computer's system-level audio controls are misadjusted, or you've got a problem in how a mixer, preamp, or other equipment has been set up. Fix it and redigitize.

- Read about analog wiring in Chapter 3.
- Read about other necessary adjustments in Chapter 6.

If you've done digital transfers, and sounds that are okay in the camera are distorted in your computer, check the output or sound card calibration. If that's not the problem, make sure there aren't any sample rate or conversion issues. Some NLEs distort when trying to preview non-matching sample rates. Check Chapter 6 for this.

Otherwise there might be a software setup issue, corruption in the computer, or conflict. Check the manufacturers' help sites, reinstall, or ask a local guru to examine your particular system.

Tracks Are Too Noisy

Decide what kind of noise you're hearing, because the cures are different. Noise may be acoustic and environmental, picked up at the shoot. Or it can be electronic, including steady hisses and whines, steady hums and buzzes, occasional beeps, or periodic pops and clicks.

ACOUSTIC NOISES

The best way to eliminate very short noises is to substitute syllables from elsewhere in the scene or an alternate take.

- Read about dialog editing in Chapter 8.

If continuous traffic, air conditioner, or similar noises are softer than dialog, the track can be improved with a combination of equalization, expansion, and noise reduction. This kind of combination is almost always more effective and does less damage than using noise reduction software alone.

- Read about equalization in Chapter 11.
- Read about expansion in Chapter 12.
- Read about noise reduction software in Chapter 15.

If acoustic noise is louder than dialog, the above techniques can also be of help. But they're also likely to leave metallic-sounding artifacts because of the extreme processing involved. If that's a problem, you'll have to do what Hollywood does: Replace the dialog in a studio session.

- Read about ADR in Chapter 7.

Noise reduction is as much about hiding noise as eliminating it, and some noises never really go away. That's why postproduction noise removal isn't as effective as proper mic placement and noise control at the shoot.

Wind Noises

When wind hits a microphone, it can create a low rumbling that overpowers the voice. The rumbling can be removed with a filter. But if the rumble has also overloaded the equipment, it can cause distortion and make that part of the track unusable. The only solution is to edit replacement syllables from alternate takes or rerecord the dialog as ADR.

- Read about filtering in Chapter 11.
- Read about dialog editing in Chapter 8.
- Read about ADR in Chapter 7.

Noise Combined with Echo

The microphone was too far from the subject. The camera's volume control might have been turned up to compensate, but the situation is identical to the one discussed in Section 1 of this chapter.

ELECTRONIC NOISES

Hisses and Whistles

Treat them as you would acoustic noise, mentioned previously. Whistles and other constant-pitched high frequency noises can be controlled with a parametric equalizer.

- Learn how to tune a parametric equalizer in Chapter 11.

Hums and Buzzes

Comb filtering can be surprisingly good at eliminating moderate dimmer noise or ground-loop buzz.

- Read about comb filtering in Chapter 13.

Really strong buzzing from a disconnected ground at the shoot can't be fixed. Use some of the replacement techniques in the previous section.

Lamp ballasts can create an electronic-sounding humming noise that's picked up acoustically by the mic. This is a mic placement (or lighting) issue on the set, and usually can't be reduced with a comb filter.

Occasional Beeps

If there's a beeping in digitally captured tracks that isn't on the camera footage, the problem is most likely either a driver issue or a timecode break.

- Check the manufacturer of your FireWire card and editing software, and Apple's or Microsoft's Web sites, for driver updates that have anything to do with the FireWire or audio capability in your computer.
- If the camera was wound forward between shots and the tape was new, the internal time-code and control tracks may have dropped out between takes. Attempting to capture from this non-recorded area can cause problems, including occasional beeps. Stop the capture and manually wind the tape to the next valid section. Or redigitize the audio with an analog connection.
- Timecode breaks can happen even when you do something as innocuous as reviewing a take. Some NLE manufacturers recommend you prerecord the tape with black, from start to finish, before shooting. That will eliminate the dropped timecode.

Periodic Pops and Clicks

If this kind of noise is in the computer but not on the original footage, there are two likely culprits: either a sample rate issue or dropped frames.

- Read a lot about solving pop and click problems in Chapter 6.

Sample Rate Issues

If popping or clicking occurs in a FireWire transfer, it can be from incompatible sample rates. Digital video uses 32 kHz or 48 kHz sampling. The timeline and capture sample rate should match what was used at the shoot.

- Read about sample rates in Chapter 6.
- Even if the file is good, popping or clicking can occur during NLE playback if there's a sample rate incompatibility. Open the file in an audio program and listen for clicks. If it sounds okay there, use that program to convert the file's sample rate to match the NLE's setting.
- If the footage is at 32 kHz, it may not be possible to capture at that rate, and you may have to use an analog transfer for the audio.

Clicking and popping can also occur when an audio CD, which uses 44.1 kHz sampling, is ripped and the file is put in an NLE timeline running at 48 kHz.

- Open the 44.1 kHz file in an audio program and convert its sample rate. Some programs will let you rip a CD directly to a 48 kHz file.

If popping or clicking occurs when transferring audio over s/pdif or AES/EBU digital wiring, the culprit can be a lack of audio word sync.

- Make sure the recording program and audio input card are set to synchronize from the card's input.
- Read about digital wiring in Chapter 3.

AUDIO IS THIN, BOOMY, OR HOLLOW

These are usually caused by bad mic technique at the shoot, and may not be fixable. But some conditions can be improved.

Thinness

Thin sound—a lack of low frequencies—can be a problem in the original tracks or be due to wiring problems in your setup. It usually can't be fixed with an equalizer because the low frequencies aren't on the track to be equalized. Attempting to boost lows, in this case, just results in noise and distortion.

Check the camera footage. If it's good and you're doing analog transfers, suspect the wiring between camera and computer. If everything coming out of the NLE sounds thin, there's probably a problem between the computer and your monitors.

- Read about postproduction wiring in Chapter 3.

If the footage sounds bad, either the mic was defective or there was a wiring problem between mic and camera. This can also happen when some transformer-equipped XLR adapters are used improperly. It can't be fixed in postproduction, but monitoring on good isolating headphones can help you spot it on the next shoot.

Boominess

A boomy sound is usually caused by low-frequency resonances in the room. It can often be improved by setting a parametric equalizer exactly to the room's resonant frequency, and dipping by about −12 dB.

- Read how to tune a parametric equalizer in Chapter 11.

Hollowness

Hollow sound can be caused by two nearby mics being mixed together.

- If the mics are on separate tracks in your NLE, audition them separately. If they sound good individually, pick just one or edit between them as different characters speak. Read about track splitting and mixing in Chapters 9 and 17.
- If the mics are on a single stereo track in your NLE, use the Take Right or Take Left command to listen to each separately.

If the mics were mixed together at the shoot, it can't be fixed.

Hollowness can also be caused by too great a distance between mic and subject. You can't fix this in postproduction. Read about mic distance in the first section of this chapter, so you'll know how to avoid this problem next time.

DROPPED FRAMES

Processor overload can cause both audio and video frames to be lost, but the video ones are often less noticeable unless there's very fast motion on the screen. Dropped audio frames, on the other hand, cause an easily heard jump in the waveform. The problem can occur during both FireWire and analog captures.

Dropped frames can also cause lipsync problems, but in some footage you might notice the popping before you notice a sync error.

- Avoid processor overload by turning off any nonessential function in the computer and disconnecting it from the network before starting a capture. This includes virus protection and auto-save software, which are notorious for disrupting audio recordings.
- Create a user profile with the simplest possible setup, and log in as this user before digitizing. Be sure you know what you're doing, or consult your local operating system guru, if you're going to mess with system-level settings.
- Real-mode drivers can slow a Windows machine down. If there are any running, they'll show up as "MS-DOS compatibility" in the System Properties dialog. Removing them is a guru-level adjustment.
- Windows TSRs may be running in the background and cause dropped frames. Remove any you don't need.
- Excessive monitor depth makes the CPU work harder. Digital video doesn't need 32 bit color (certainly not when you're doing sound operations). Be aware that some software has display problems if you've reduced the monitor depth.

- Virtual memory affects system performance. Make sure you have enough RAM.
- Defragmenting the hard disk can also help.
- In a marginal system, even real-time monitoring is enough extra work to cause dropped frames. You may have to turn off on-screen and audio monitoring while capturing.

RANDOM STRANGENESSES

If a program is behaving unpredictably, quit it and start again. If that doesn't help, restart your computer. On Macs, use your Disk Utility to check and repair permissions. In extreme cases, it often helps to delete a program's preferences files. This can cause other problems and often requires that you re-enter a serial number and other information, so don't take this step unless you understand what you're doing.

NLE Audio Drops Out When Playing from the Timeline

This can happen if clips with different sample rates are playing together. The NLE can't convert them fast enough.

- Check the sample rate of each clip. Use an audio program to convert any that don't match the project's settings.

Speed or Pitch Has Changed for No Apparent Reason

Some part of your setup is using the wrong sample rate. This can happen at the system level, or it can be an incompatibility between two programs.

- Exit or quit nonessential programs. An audio application may have taken over the computer's sound hardware.
- Restart the computer.
- If your computer is connected to a digital audio sound source via s/pdif or AES/EBU, check the source's sample rate. It may be forcing the computer to the wrong rate.
- Some digital audio cards occasionally have trouble recognizing the connected rate and need to be manually reset in their control panels.

Some NLEs send the wrong information to encoding systems when converting a project for the Web.

- Save the project from the NLE with no audio data compression. Then open it manually in the compression software.

DV or DAT Deck Won't Record Audio

If you're using a digital connection and the deck won't go into record mode, it's probably a sample rate sync issue. This is different from lipsync.

- Make sure the recorder is set to the same sample rate as the project.

409

Professional recorders such as Digital Betacam won't accept a digital audio stream unless it's also locked to the video's blackburst. This is a facility setup issue.

- Read about digital audio wiring in Chapter 3.
- In an emergency, use an analog audio connection. This may compromise the quality.

VHS Dub Has Static, Noise, or Poor Audio

(Yes, those decks are still around. Not every office or employee lounge has converted to DVD.) VHS Hi-Fi depends on accurate tracking of the video heads, and the playback machine might not match the recorder. This can cause the deck to keep switching between Hi-Fi and linear mode, which has more hiss and distortion.

- Adjust the tracking on the playback set.
- A head cleaning cassette might help.
- In an emergency, manually set the deck to Standard, Linear, or Mono audio. It won't sound as good as Hi-Fi, but you won't have noises or dropouts as the deck switches modes.
- Have the deck professionally serviced.

LIPSYNC PROBLEMS

Some audio and video cards have known issues with particular NLEs. Check the manufacturers' Web sites and online forums for the latest information.

- There is a large section about lipsync problems in Chapter 6. If the quick tips here don't help, you may find an answer there.

The key to diagnosing lipsync problems is to analyze how they occur. Is the entire sequence consistently out of sync by the same amount? Does the error continue to grow over time? Or is it variable and sporadic?

Consistent Lipsync Errors

Check your video monitoring setup. Picture can get delayed while passing through a video output card or FireWire converter. Even if audio takes the same path, it might not be delayed by the same amount. Large LCD monitors can delay the picture even more, particularly if you're using DSP functions like noise reduction or zoom.

- Some software lets you set a dynamic offset to compensate for this. Picture is output ahead of sound, but only when you're running at normal speed. When you still frame, the offset goes away since output card and LCD delays quickly catch up with stills.

It can also be incompatibility between camera and the capture setup. Check the audio and video card manufacturers' Web sites for updated drivers. If you're capturing via FireWire, check the FireWire card maker's site as well as Apple's or Microsoft's.

- Try capturing or playing the clip in another application.
- Turn off any audio data compression in the capture settings.

Cumulative Lipsync Errors

If sync gets progressively worse as the film goes on, the cause can be a tiny sample rate issue.

- Make sure the project and capture settings match the footage's sample rate. Some NLEs introduce odd errors if everything doesn't match.

Some cameras cheat and don't output at exactly 48 kHz. This isn't a setup problem; it's the result of cost-sensitive design and can't be fixed. It can cause cumulative errors in FireWire transfers.

- Transfer the audio as analog instead of FireWire. Some NLEs let you select a different audio input while capturing video over FireWire; this will maintain picture quality. Others may require separate passes for audio and video if you want to keep the picture digital. Be aware that audio quality can suffer in an analog transfer; it depends both on your setup and how well you calibrate things. Read Chapters 3 and 6 for advice.
- If that doesn't help, suspect the video frame rate isn't accurate either. (Cost-sensitive design, again.) Redigitizing the picture instead of transferring it over FireWire can help, but the quality will depend on your video input card. If that's an issue, try the next two suggestions.
- Measure how many frames out the end of the film is, and apply a clip speed adjustment to compensate. This may sacrifice quality. If you're changing speed in an audio program, *don't* use pitch correction; it can hurt quality even more.
- If film or HD video was used for the original shoot, its speed could have changed when the picture was converted to standard definition video for editing. Check for pullup or pulldown issues (Chapter 6).
- Use cutaways in the video or tiny edits during audio pauses to correct sync. This doesn't harm the sound or picture quality.

411

Sporadic Lipsync Errors

If sync drifts in and out, or errors seem to happen unpredictably, suspect dropped frames.

- See the previous section regarding dropped frames.

This can also happen because of problems in a particular section of the footage. An analog transfer may help.

EDIT AND MIX PROBLEMS

Problems with Dialog

If the sound quality is generally good but specific words are garbled, they can often be fixed by replacing syllables from elsewhere in the scene or alternate takes. When done right, this doesn't cause noticeable lipsync problems.

- Doing this kind of microsurgery is always more precise, and often faster, by using an audio program instead of an NLE. Read about dialog editing in Chapter 8.

Individual words can also be replaced with studio recordings. This isn't as complex as ADR, but the same mic techniques should be used.

- Read about ADR recording in Chapter 7.

Musical Issues

- Read about music searches, copyright, and related issues in the first half of Chapter 9.
- Read about easy ways to trim music to precisely fit video in the second half of that chapter.
- Read about keeping music from fighting with dialog in Chapters 11, 12, and 17.

Problems with the Mix

MATCHING DIALOG

If a character's voice quality changes during a scene because different camera angles were miked differently, split the dialog onto multiple tracks, one track for each miking situation. Apply equalization and reverberation to make them sound the same.

- Read about track splitting in Chapters 9 and 17.
- Read about equalization in Chapter 12.
- Read about reverberation in Chapter 14.

If all the recordings are good quality, process the shorter clips to match the unadjusted longest clip. If some of the recordings were badly miked or have other problems, you'll have to sacrifice the quality of better clips to match.

DISAPPEARING ELEMENTS

If you could hear a sound when you mixed the project but not when you play the final tape, and the playback system is mono, the most likely cause is a polarity[3] inversion.

---

[3]Often called phase inversion.

If just one element is gone, there's a problem with its clip. Either it was recorded incorrectly, or it was processed through a badly designed stereo simulator.

- Use an audio program to invert the phase of one channel. Or use a Fill Left or Fill Right command on that sound in an NLE.
- Read about stereo simulation in Chapter 16.
- Read about mono compatibility in Chapters 5 and 17.

If dialog or narration is missing but music or sound effects seem to remain, there was probably a problem in the connection between NLE and the recording VTR. This happens most often when a stereo cable is inadvertently plugged into a balanced jack on a mixer or NLE pod.

- Change the connection and dub the tape again. Read about wiring in Chapter 3.

Most stereo VCRs become mono when you connect their antenna output to the antenna jack of a TV. This can cause polarity problems that show up on a client's set but not on your monitors.

- In an emergency, use the RCA audio output jacks on the back of the VCR to feed a stereo signal to an amplifier.

This doesn't fix the basic problem, and the tape won't sound good under many playback conditions. Go back and apply one of the other cures as soon as you get the chance.

413

MUSIC IS TOO LOUD OR SOFT COMPARED TO VOICE

If it sounded right when you mixed it and not when you play it on a different system, it's a monitoring issue. This often happens when you mix or process using the speakers bundled with most NLEs, which are notoriously poor, and then play the tape in a home theater system or auditorium.

Either get new speakers, or take the project to a sound studio, and remix. Headphones—even good ones—aren't a cure unless your viewers will be using them as well. Headphones present a very different impression of a track, and mixes done on them often have effects or music too soft to play well on normal speakers.

- Read about choosing a monitor in Chapter 2.
- Read about taking tracks to a studio in Chapter 17.

MIX, OR INDIVIDUAL ELEMENTS, ALTERNATE BETWEEN TOO SOFT AND TOO LOUD

You need to apply compression.

- Read about compressors in Chapter 13.

MIX DOESN'T SOUND GOOD WHEN ENCODED FOR THE WEB

Data compression processes work best when the source material was mixed with awareness of the processes limitations. This can be totally nonintuitive: things that make a track sound better in the studio can seriously hurt the compressed version. Extreme equalization and level compression are the worst offenders.

■ Read about data compression in Chapter 18. Then remix.

IT JUST DOESN'T SOUND AS GOOD AS WHAT I HEAR AT THE MOVIES

■ Read the rest of this book.

Glossary

Every industry creates its own jargon, mostly to save time when talking about complex subjects. But it can be intimidating to the uninitiated.

Here are some of the audio terms I've thrown around in this book. I've also included a couple of production terms you probably already know, in case sound people are reading this as an introduction to the video world.

AAF: See Interchange Format

ADAT: Alesis Digital Audio Tape, an eight-track format using S-VHS cassettes and named for the company that invented it. ADATs were the first practical, low-cost digital multitracks and became a favorite of scoring composers. A similar but more robust eight-track format, Tascam's DTRS (also known as DA8 or DA88), uses Hi8 cassettes. The DTRS format was adopted by Sony and is the standard in feature production, and when supplying D/M/E stems to a network. Both systems allow multiple decks to be linked for unlimited tracks. ADAT and DTRS are not compatible.

ADPCM: Adaptive delta pulse code modulation, a math-based audio compression system now largely replaced by more efficient perceptual encoding. See Chapter 18.

ADR: Automatic (or automated) dialog replacement, also sometimes known as looping. Production audio can be noisy and, even if recorded on a quiet sound stage, can be inconsistent from shot to shot. ADR systems let actors go into a sound studio, hear short pieces of their own dialog repeated over and over in a constant rhythm, and then recreate the performance—line by line—in sync with picture. See Chapter 7.

AES/EBU: Literally, the Audio Engineering Society and European Broadcasting Union. But the combination of initials almost always refers to one of its standards for interconnecting digital audio devices. See Chapter 3.

AIFF: Audio interchange file format, the standard for Macintosh audio- and video-editing systems. Different from Microsoft's WAV format. Fortunately, most programs are smart enough to open either, and there are plenty of shareware converters for both platforms.

Aliasing: A form of distortion in digital recording that takes the form of annoying whistles accompanying high-frequency sounds. See Chapter 1.

Ambience: Background sounds. Usually a track or two of an environment, such as a factory or traffic noises, played under a scene to set the place. Careful choice of ambiences can eliminate the need for a lot of *Foley*. Acousticians and music recording engineers frequently use this term to refer to a room's characteristic reverberation, a totally different meaning.

ASCAP: American Society of Composers, Arrangers, and Publishers. A performing rights organization, which collects royalties from broadcasters and others who play music for the public, whether it's a live performance or a recording. The money is distributed to the writers and composers of the music through their publishers, not to the performers or record companies.

ATTC: Address track timecode. LTC recorded on a special track of an analog videotape or down the center of an analog audio tape.

Auto-conform: In the dark days of analog video editing, each generation would add noise to the soundtrack. Because a video master could be three or four generations removed from the original, the production audio was often treated only as reference. An automatic conforming system (or hapless audio engineer) would use the original field recordings and an edit list, and rebuild the sound. Modern nonlinear and online systems keep audio as 16-bit digital data, so this step shouldn't be necessary. But in professional productions, audio is frequently digitized into a NLE by an assistant editor, using less-than-perfect equipment. So auto-conforming is frequently required. It's also used in feature productions that work with 24-bit audio for greater dynamic range.

BGs: Another name for *ambience track*, pronounced like the disco group.

BMI: Broadcast Music Incorporated, a performing rights organization. See *ASCAP*.

Boom: Literally, a fiberglass or metal stick used to hold a microphone near an actor, just out of camera range. But the term is also used to refer to the mic as well, or to a soundtrack that was recorded with one.

Bump: To adjust the timing between sound and picture in precise frame or subframe units, while both are running. While this is most often used to fine-tune lipsync and sound effects placement, bumping a piece of music a frame or two can have amazing results.

Burn-in: A videotape with timecode numbers superimposed on the picture.

BWF: Broadcast wave format, an audio interchange format standardized by the European Broadcasting Union. It's similar to Microsoft WAV and can be read by standard audio programs, but software designed for this format also lets you embed sync and other information, or distribute multi-channel files.

CD-quality: Properly speaking, a digital audio signal or device capable of 20 Hz–20 kHz bandwidth within a decibel, with very low distortion and a 96 dB dynamic range. Many manufacturers use the term improperly to imply a quality that isn't justified by the system's analog components, or to describe any processing they think sounds good. Unless you can verify specifications, the phrase is meaningless.

Click track: An electronic metronome played into headphones, or a track on a tape with that signal, so that musicians can perform to precise timing.

Codec: Coder and decoder processes that turn audio or video into a format that can be transmitted or stored more efficiently (such as mp3) and then restored. The term is sometimes used to refer to the data format itself.

Cue sheet: A document listing music used in a TV production, including information about the composer and publishing company. These are given to the TV station so it can report the usage to a performing rights society (see *ASCAP*). See Chapter 9.

D/M/E: Dialog, music, and effects stems. Separate tracks carrying only one kind of sound, used for foreign translations. More flexible than an M&E mix.

DA8, DA88, DTRS: See *ADAT*.

DAW: Digital audio workstation. A computer system designed specifically for editing and mixing sound, often in sync with picture. While the term was originally reserved for high-powered and expensive systems with dedicated computers and hands-on controllers, now just about every software publisher calls its multitrack audio software a DAW.

dBFS: Decibels referenced to *full scale*, the largest signal that can be expressed in a digital system. See Chapter 3 for discussion of this and the following three decibel standards.

dBm: Decibels referenced to 1 milliwatt across 600 Ω. Some manufacturers use this term when they really mean dBu, but 600 Ω hasn't been part of most equipment specifications for more than a decade.

dBu: Decibels referenced to 0.775 volts. That's the voltage which one dBm, properly terminated, produces.

dBV: Decibels referenced to 1 volt.

Decibel: Also dB. A precise, and often misunderstood, measurement of the ratio between two acoustic or audio signals. See Chapter 1 for an explanation of all these *dB* terms.

Dipole speakers: Speakers that radiate out of their front and back simultaneously. Sometimes used for surround channels.

Distortion: Anything that changes the output of an audio system so it no longer reflects the input signal. Noise and changes in frequency response can be forms of distortion, though the term is usually reserved for unintentional, gross changes in the waveform.

Dither: Specially shaped random noise added to a digital signal to improve its quality at low levels. See Chapter 1.

DM&E: Dialog, music, and effects; three *stems* commonly provided with a mix for foreign-language dubbing.

Dolby Digital: A *codec* used in film and DVD sound. See Chapter 18.

Dropframe: A way of counting timecode so that frame numbers stay, on average, in sync with real-world time. No actual frames are dropped in the process. See Chapter 6.

DTS: A *codec* used in film and DVD sound.

Dynamic range: The range between the loudest signal a system can carry without distortion and its low-level noise that would obscure any softer signals, expressed in decibels. In a purely digital signal, each bit is worth about 6 dB dynamic range. But when you start involving analog circuits, dynamic range gets harder to pin down. Low-level noise is contributed by the electronics itself and distortion increases as the volume increases beyond a nominal value.

EDL: Edit Decision List, a database file describing all the edits in a production. Used for interchange among NLE and DAW systems. Frequently in human-readable form.

Foley: Generating sound effects by duplicating the actors' on-screen movements in a sound studio. A team of good Foley artists can watch a scene once, gather armloads of props, and then create everything from footsteps to fist fights in perfect sync. *Digital Foley* refers to the process of recording the sounds without picture and then matching them in an audio workstation. See Chapter 10.

Full-scale: See *dBFS*.

Haas effect: Also known as *precedence effect*. Part of our hearing that assumes a sound is coming from the direction from which we first hear it. Because of this, it's also a way of fooling the ear into thinking a sound comes from one specific place, when it may be coming from two or more. Used in film mixing, but may not be suitable for broadcast (see Chapter 17).

Hard effect: Also known as *spot effect*. Sounds that are impractical to Foley (such as telephone bells, explosions, and light sabers) and usually important to the story. These are often drawn from large CD or hard drive effects libraries, but may be created for the project. In feature film production, the term often refers to *any* sound effects that are in sync with picture.

High fidelity: An ambiguous term. It often refers to somewhere near a 20 Hz to 20 kHz frequency range with less than 2 dB variation between sounds of different frequencies, and a dynamic range of at least 60 dB with less than 0.3 percent distortion—but the bar keeps getting raised as technology improves. Has nothing to do with whether a system is analog or digital.

Hitting a post: Audio people use this term to refer to the cues within a long sound effect or music track. It's not enough to make a sound begin and end in sync with the picture; you also have to make sure that internal elements match the on-screen actions. A good sound editor will make lots of tiny edits and use other tricks to hit as many posts as possible.

House sync: In large facilities, a single video signal (usually an all-black picture in color TV format) is distributed to just about every audio and video device. House sync is not the same as timecode. See Chapter 3.

Interchange Format: A standard method of passing audio elements and editing instructions between audio and video editing software. Usually a file or directories of files on a hard drive or DVD-ROM. OMF and AAF are the most popular forms. Although the formats are standardized, there can be problems between different manufacturers' implementations.

ISDN: Integrated services digital network. A way of combining standard telephone wiring with special equipment, to create 128 kilobit per second dial-up connections as needed. In the world of audio, the term usually refers to realtime transfers and remote recording sessions using ISDN and specialized codecs. While ISDN is much more reliable for real-time connections than high-speed Internet, it's also somewhat slower and much more expensive. The newest audio codecs have ways to trade speed for reliability, for *almost* real-time operation.

419

Lav: Short for lavaliere, a small microphone originally worn on a necklace (hence the name). Lavs are mounted on actors or interview subjects, often concealed in their clothing or hair, for close-up miking. Lavs are frequently used with wireless transmitters to give the actor freedom of movement, but will sound better if wired directly to the recorder. The term is also used to refer to a soundtrack that has been recorded with a lav.

Layback: Copying a finished mix from an audio workstation or separate audio tape back to a videotape master.

Layup: Transferring production sound from edited videotape to an audio medium for further manipulation. Networked nonlinear editing systems can make both layback and layup unnecessary.

Lipsync: One technical goal of a soundtrack, in which sounds occur at the precise moment we see what's causing them. An example would be actors' voices matched to their mouth movements.

LTC: Longitudinal timecode, a biphase digital stream in the audio range, sounding something like a fax machine signal. When it's recorded on an analog audio track it's called longitudinal, since it runs parallel to the tape. LTC also refers to the audio signal itself, so the wire that plugs into a timecode input is often referred to as carrying LTC no matter how the data originated.

M&E: Music and effects, a sub mix of a production's soundtrack with no dialog to make foreign translations easier.

Masking: A phenomenon where sounds at one frequency make it difficult or impossible to hear other simultaneous (or, in the case of temporal masking, closely occurring) sounds at a nearby frequency. It's the basis behind a lot of noise reduction and every system of perceptual encoding. See Chapter 15.

MIDI: Musical Instrument Digital Interface, a common language and electrical standard for describing events such as the turning on or off of a note.

Mid-side (M/S, *also written as* mid/side, M-S, *or* MS): Stereo microphone technique with excellent control of width and mono compatibility.

Mono: Short for monaural, literally "one ear." An audio signal with no directional information, frequently recorded with a single mic. In most systems, mono signals are automatically placed in the center of a stereo field. Dialog is almost always recorded and mixed in mono.

MOS: Scenes that are videotaped or filmed without any audio, usually because the camera setup or location makes sound impractical. The expectation is that a track will be created using foley and other effects.

Mp3: *MPEG* II layer 3, the most common file format and data reduction scheme for delivering audio over the Internet. See Chapter 18.

MPEG: Moving Pictures Expert Group, a standard-setting body primarily concerned with applying perceptual encoding to sound and video.

Music library: A collection of music intended for use by film and television producers, written in specific styles but not for a specific project. You can license the music for use in a particular production, usually for considerably less than original music of the same quality would cost. See Chapter 9.

Needle-drop music: A scheme for buying library music where you pay very little for the discs—sometimes they're free—but report each use and pay a licensing fee when you do. Needle-drop libraries often offer an annual blanket covering every project a producer does, a bargain for busy filmmakers. Also sometimes known as laser-drop music.

NLE: Nonlinear editor. Software, often with dedicated video input and processing cards, for cutting picture and sound. Today's NLEs are capable of a wide range of special visual effects and some audio processing. A few also include automated tools for mixing sound.

Noise, pink: Electronic noise that averages an equal level of signal in each octave. It reflects how we hear better than *white noise* does, and is used for acoustic testing.

Noise, white: Random electronic noise that averages an equal level of signal at any frequency. This is the kind of noise commonly generated by analog circuits.

Nyquist: A mathematical proof that digital sample rates must be more than twice as high as the highest frequency a system will be called on to carry. The Nyquist Limit is that highest frequency. See Chapter 1.

Octave: the musical interval of 12 semitones, or a frequency ratio of 2:1.

Offset: The difference in timecode between any two tapes, elements, or time-lines. Video editors typically start their programs at 1:00:00:00 (one hour; no minutes, seconds, or frames) to allow for color bars and slates. If an audio operator decides to start that same program at 00:01:00:00, the sound would have a -59 minute offset. Some digital audio processors introduce delays to handle the sound more intelligently, so small offsets are sometimes necessary.

OMF: See *Interchange Format*.

Pan: To move a mono audio signal across the stereo field, or place it in a specific left/right or front/back position.

Perceptual encoding: An audio data compression scheme that relies on the masking phenomenon. Also known as psychoacoustic encoding. See Chapter 18.

Phantom image: A location where sound seems to be coming from in a stereo or surround setup, even though there's no speaker there. A good mix can have a lot of these, depending on which medium the project will be shown in. See Chapter 17.

Production audio: Sounds recorded in the field while the picture is being shot, usually dialog. It may be recorded directly on the videotape, or as *double-system*.

Production effects (PFX): Footsteps or prop noises captured by the dialog microphone during shooting. These are often isolated and used in the final mix.

Public domain music: Legally, a composition that has fallen out of copyright, usually because of its age. But that refers only to the notes on paper. Recordings, even of public domain pieces, are almost always protected by other copyrights. Not to be confused with *royalty-free music*.

R-DAT: Exactly the same as a standard or timecode DAT tape. When R-DAT was first invented, some digital audio systems used stationary heads (like an analog audio tape deck) and others used rotating heads (like a helical-scan video deck).

Royalty-free music: A scheme for buying library music where you pay a premium for the discs but then can use the music as many times as you wish without extra fees. Also known as buyout music. See Chapter 9.

s/pdif: A standard for interconnecting stereo digital audio devices, similar to AES/EBU but using a lower-cost wiring scheme and carrying information that's appropriate for consumer audio. See Chapter 3.

421

SDDS: Sony Dynamic Digital Sound, a *codec* used in film and DVD sound.

Sibilance: A speech sound with considerable high-frequency energy, which can often distort in a system. A de-esser can control it. See Chapter 12.

Slate: A board with handwritten scene and take information, photographed at the beginning of a scene. Often has a hinged, wooden stick that can be slapped against it, so that sound and picture can be precisely matched. Modern ones display timecode as well. The term also refers to a human voice calling out scene and take information, to identify sound recordings.

SMPTE: Usually short for SMPTE timecode, the frame-accurate time data recorded on video and audio tapes to control editing and keep elements together. It stands for the Society of Motion Picture and Television Engineers, who invented the format, and can also be used to refer to the organization itself.

Sound designer: Someone who creates special sounds or sound effect montages for a project and often oversees dialog and music as well. Usually a person with both engineering and musical experience, though there's no reason it can't also be the producer/director/editor.

Spotting: Going through an edited film to find places where music would be appropriate, and deciding what kind of music to use there. See Chapter 9.

Stem: A fully mixed and processed version of a soundtrack, but containing only one category of sound, such as music. See *DM&E*.

Stereo: An audio signal that includes two distinct channels of information, one intended for the left ear and one for the right, to help the listener locate sound sources across an imaginary line in front of them. This is not the same thing as two channels of identical information, which is just a mono signal with redundant data.

Sync license: The right to use a piece of music in a production. See Chapter 9.

THX: A set of specifications for film and DVD speakers, acoustics, and equipment quality, and a program to certify that they've been adhered to. It's not a soundtrack format.

Timbre: A characteristic of a sound wave that has to do with the number and strength of a wave's harmonics (Chapter 1), and often referred to as its *brightness* or *richness*. Timbre is different from volume or pitch, though an untrained ear can easily be tricked into confusing these characteristics.

Timecode: See *SMPTE*.

Toslink: Standard for carrying digital audio between devices as light pulses on an optical fiber. Named for Toshiba, the company that invented it.

Tri-level sync: A form of video sync used in high-definition production.

VITC: Vertical interval timecode. Time data encoded as a series of dots at the top of each video field. Unlike LTC, it can be read when an analog tape is paused. This makes it easier to jog a tape to find a specific action, and then match a sound to it.

Walla: Voices of people in a crowd, recorded at an event or studio or taken from a sound effects CD. On-camera crowds are usually told to mime their conversations to make dialog pickup easier; walla is then added in post. Walla can also be used to simulate an off-camera crowd to make a scene larger.

Wet/dry: Refers to echoes. Most foley, hard effects, and ADR are recorded dry, without any natural reverberation. Appropriate echoes are then added during the mix, to make the sounds appear to belong to the on-screen environment.

Wild: Recorded without synchronization. Sound effects are usually gathered this way and matched up in an editing system. But some things are wild by mistake and have to be carefully resynced.

XLR: The most popular connector type for high-end analog and digital audio, originally known as Cannon's XLR product line. However, the presence of this connector doesn't guarantee any particular electrical standard. See Chapter 3.

Zero level: Literally, a ratio of 1:1 to some specified standard; if expressed in decibels, the ratio 1:1 is 0 dB. In practice, zero level means different things depending on whether you're working in analog or digital, and what the format's standard is. See Chapter 6.

About the CD

This is an audio CD, rather than a CD-ROM, so you can play it on the best speakers you've got.

Everything on this disc is protected by copyright, but you have permission to load its tracks into your computer to practice the tutorials. Any other reproduction, public performance, or derivative work is strictly prohibited.

Individual music cues may be licensed for productions, and full-length versions are available. Copyright information for those cues appear in the text, when a specific cue is first mentioned. Contact DeWolfe Music for licensing information.

The tracks that are voice or music demos have been mastered around –2 dBFS, comparable to commercial CDs. Most of the tone-based tracks have been mastered at –10 dBFS, to play at a lower level on your system. **Follow the volume instruction on Track 8 to protect your ears and speakers**: parts of it are at 0 dBFS, the loudest sound your system can handle.

Instructions and identifications are in my voice, sharply filtered, so they're not mistaken for the material being demonstrated.

TRACK LISTING

1   Frequencies   01:08
     First, some pairs of tones with the same musical relationship... but
     their frequency relationships are very different. Then some specific
     frequencies, with and without voice identification.

2   Harmonics   00:14
     Two notes. The first has no harmonics and sounds like a test tone.
     The second has only two harmonics added... and begins to sound
     like a pipe organ.

425

3   High frequency diagnostic   05:42
This may be the most revealing track on this entire CD. It has a montage of three well-recorded selections: one acoustic jazz, one classical vocal, and one rock. The montage is played seven times, alternating between full fidelity and then through a lab-quality filter that precisely removes all the highs above a specific setting. Each version has the filter's frequency lowered somewhat.

If you can't hear the filter switching in and out on a particular version, it means your system[1] wasn't reproducing that frequency to begin with (hint: listen for the highest percussion). The frequencies are 20 kHz, 17.5 kHz, 15 kHz, 12.5 kHz, 10 kHz, 7.5 kHz, and 5 kHz. Filters were switched on and off in exactly the same place in each example.

4   The envelopes, please   00:17
Volume envelopes of specific sounds, noted in Chapter 1.

5   Low bit depth, low sample rate   00:21
The organ-like tone from Track 2, recorded with 2 kHz sampling and 4 bits' depth, then converted back to CD standard.

6   Frequency sweep   00:20
A continuously-rising pure tone to test speakers. It should sound equally smooth across the band. Harshness or rattles indicate a speaker problem. Extra tones moving in the opposite direction are aliasing distortion from your soundcard or CD player.

7   Speaker polarity check   00:28
This track has 10 seconds of simultaneous low and high frequency narrowband noise on both channels. Then it dips momentarily. When it returns, one of the channels has its phase reversed.

Sit between the speakers and listen through the entire track. If the first half seems to have both bands of noise coming from the same place, and the bass is full and centered, your speakers are correctly wired. If the second half sounds that way, you need to change the wiring as suggested in the chapter. If the second half is very soft— or the sound disappears entirely after 10 seconds— your system is set up for mono, not stereo.

8   Computer output test   01:34
Play this in your computer as a test for its audio output.
First, there's a pure tone swept from 15 kHz to 20 kHz to check for aliasing. Listen for random whistles whose pitch is moving downward. (If you don't hear much for twenty seconds after the first voice announcement, don't worry: It just means that your system isn't carrying those high frequencies.). Then there's acoustic

---

[1]Try it on different stereos, and then on your laptop. In this case, "your system" also includes your ears: everybody's high frequency sensitivity decreases with age, so it's unlikely older listeners (including me) will hear the highest tones on even the best speakers.

music: the guitar should sound natural, with no harshness and no rattles. Finally, three pure tones to test for harmonic distortion at high levels. Follow the track's instructions about setting volume, and the tones should sound the same. If the second set of tones sounds richer or brighter, you're actually hearing distortion that can prevent accurate monitoring or mixing.

When you adjust the volume for the final test, **don't do it in your computer**. Any software or system-level adjustment will invalidate the test. You need to leave the computer alone, and turn down the volume on your external amplifier or on your powered speakers.

9	Lineup tone: 100 Hz, −20 dBFS	00:30

Feel free to copy these lineup tones, and the countdown on Track 14, to use at the heads of your productions. It must be a digital copy from your computer's CD-ROM drive, with no volume adjustment, or else the lineups won't be accurate.

10	Lineup tone: 1 kHz, −20 dBFS	00:30
11	Lineup tone: 10 kHz, −20 dBFS	00:30
12	Lineup tone: 1 kHz, −8 dBFS	00:30
13	Demonstration of scrubbing algorithms	00:57
14	Countdown leader	00:08
15	How to tell stereo from mono	00:31
16	Record level meter calibration	00:27
17	A technical nightmare	01:08

Samples of analog and digital overload distortion, noise caused by too low a level, thin and dull, and aliasing. Recognize these symptoms and you'll be able to diagnose problems in your own system. (For aesthetic reasons, I mastered this track a lot more softly than the others.)

18	Microphone directionality	01:04
19	Material for dialog edit	00:37
20	Edit demonstrations	00:32
21	Using loops to find an edit point	00:27
22	Edits constrained by frame lines	00:11
23	Hearing phonemes in normal speech	00:10
24	Dealing with dialog noise by editing	00:07
25	Editing unvoiced consonants	00:08
26	"Marine Hymn," for your own counting practice	00:28
27	"Marine Hymn," with counts	00:28
28	Typical corporate theme	00:27
29	Music edit with double note	00:21
30	Same edit, fixed by rolling	00:21
31	Mellower corporate theme	00:29
32	Music edit diagnostics	00:50
33	Rock sound-alike	00:30
34	John Williams sound-alike	00:29
35	Editing in threes	00:29

36	Door squeak and close	00:04
37	Looping a rhythmic sound	00:41
38	Using a C-loop	01:14
39–47	Contents of the audio bands	00:26 each
	See text for identification and descriptions.	
48	Tuning a parametric for noises	00:59
49	Equalizing a very noisy track	00:25
50	Envelopes and release time	00:25
51	Compression and expansion on an interview track	00:52
52	Removing noise with an expander	00:28
53	Compressing and de-essing a voice-over	00:55
54	Compression on music	01:02
55	Compression to change sound effects	00:20
56	Compression to help a mix	01:05
57	Compression on Foley	01:04
58	Gating an attack	00:10
59	Comb filtering for noise reduction	00:40
60	Flanging cookbook	01:20
61	Chorus cookbook	01:07
62	Delay cookbook	00:51
63	Reverb cookbook	01:27
64	Pitch bend, shifts, and formant-corrected shifts	01:43
65	Pitch manipulation cookbook	03:05
66	Frequency space noise reduction	00:21
67	Noise reduction: interior interview	00:35
68	Pre-equalization in noise reduction	00:41
69	Click removal	00:37
70	Stereo simulation techniques	01:51
71	Vocoder techniques	00:39
72	Harmonic extension	02:41
73	Multi-effect cookbook	00:25
74	Mixing a 2-shot in a dramatic film	03:19
75	Mixing effects in a dramatic film	01:10
76	Mixing whispers in an outdoor reality show	02:11
77	Hollywood Edge demo	02:15

These people were kind enough to provide the sound effects on this CD, and the text tells where you can get more of the same quality—free—to use in productions. So the least you can do is listen to their sales demo.

PRODUCTION NOTES

Music courtesy of DeWolfe Music Library, 25 West 45th St., New York, NY 10036, 212-382-0220 or 800-221-6713. This is an immense and well-produced library, which I use in a lot of productions. Hear their demos at www.dewolfe-music.com.

Sound effects courtesy of John Moran at The Hollywood Edge, 7080 Hollywood Blvd., Hollywood, CA 90028, 213-603-3252 or 800-292-3755.

Location audio for noise reduction and other demos was supplied by friends in the Boston production community, and is acknowledged in the text. But thanks again.

Most of the studio voices are me and my wife Carla Rose; we've both done voicing for a living. One voice track was contributed by popular PBS announcer Don Wescott. The disc was edited and mastered at my studio using Orban Audicy, Steinberg Nuendo, Bias Peak, and Eventide Orville; monitoring on JBL 4412A speakers.

Index

Index

Index

435

Index

Index

439

441

Index